THE BOOK OF AUDACITY

COLLECTION MANAGEMENT

12/6/11	2	11/29/11

THE BOOK OF AUDACITY

Record, Edit, Mix, and Master with the Free Audio Editor

by Carla Schroder

no starch
press

San Francisco

15 14 13 12 11   1 2 3 4 5 6 7 8 9

ISBN-10: 1-59327-270-7
ISBN-13: 978-1-59327-270-8

Publisher: William Pollock
Production Editor: Serena Yang
Cover and Interior Design: Octopod Studios
Developmental Editor: Tyler Ortman
Technical Reviewer: Alvin Goats
Copyeditor: Kim Wimpsett
Compositor: Serena Yang
Proofreader: Paula L. Fleming
Indexer: Nancy Guenther

For information on book distributors or translations, please contact No Starch Press, Inc. directly:

No Starch Press, Inc.
38 Ringold Street, San Francisco, CA 94103
phone: 415.863.9900; fax: 415.863.9950; info@nostarch.com; www.nostarch.com

Library of Congress Cataloging-in-Publication Data
Schroder, Carla.
 The book of Audacity : record, edit, mix, and master with the free audio editor / by Carla Schroder.
     p. cm.
 Includes bibliographical references.
 ISBN-13: 978-1-59327-270-8
 ISBN-10: 1-59327-270-7
 1. Audacity (Computer file) 2. Digital audio editors. I. Title.
 ML74.4.A84S37 2010
 781.3'4536-dc22

7 8 1 . 3 4 5 6   2010037594

Thank you, TJ! It just keeps getting better!

BRIEF CONTENTS

CONTENTS IN DETAIL

9
MULTITRACK RECORDING
165

10
MAKING YOUR OWN RINGTONES
195

11
AUDACITY PLUG-INS FOR SPECIAL EFFECTS
207

12
FIX-ITS AND CLEANUPS

233

13
CONFIGURING LINUX FOR BEST AUDIO QUALITY

257

14
CONFIGURING WINDOWS FOR BEST AUDIO QUALITY   291

15
CUSTOMIZING AUDACITY   303

A
AUDIO HARDWARE   317

B
GLOSSARY   323

C
SEVEN MYTHS OF DIGITAL AUDIO   333

REFERENCES AND RESOURCES   337

INDEX   344

ACKNOWLEDGMENTS

Any book is the result of the labors of many people, and this book is no exception. The Book of Audacity has benefited from the hard work and talents of:

- Tyler Ortman
- Alvin Goats
- Serena Yang
- Travis Peterson
- Megan Dunchak
- Riley Hoffman
- Bill Pollock
- The Audacity developer team
- All of the wonderful Linux and Free/Open Source developers who made it possible for me to write this book on my Linux system using Kile, LaTeX, Kmail, GFTP, Gimp, Digikam, Dolphin, Kate, Firefox, Gnome, LXDE, KDE, XFCE, Audacity, KSnapshot, Hydrogen, FFADO,

Shutter, Brasero, K3b, Totem, K9Copy, VLC, Amarok, Kaffeine, Image-Magick, JACK, ALSA, PulseAudio, Phonon, Ubuntu Studio, 64 Studio, Arch Linux, Fedora and Planet CCRMA, and Debian Linux. (And lots more! Linux rocks! Thank you!)

Thanks everyone!

INTRODUCTION

Audacity is an open source, free-of-cost, cross-platform audio recorder, editor, and mixer for Linux, Windows, and Mac OS X. It comes packaged in easy-to-use installers for Mac OS X and all versions of Windows, and Linux users will find it in the software repositories of their favorite Linux distributions. Visit *http://audacity.sourceforge.net/* for downloads, documentation, and mailing lists.

In this book, we'll be using Audacity 1.3.12 (and newer) on Ubuntu Studio and Microsoft Windows XP, Vista, and Windows 7. The stable 2.0 release will appear soon and should look very much like what you see in this book because the 1.3.*xx* series is the run-up to 2.*x*. This book is based on the very latest releases as they came out, so it is as current as any book can be. The 1.3.*xx* Audacity releases are considerably advanced from the old 1.2.*x* series. Every new release is full of wonderful improvements and bug fixes, so if you're still using those old 1.2.*x* versions, you should consider upgrading.

Ubuntu Studio is Ubuntu with a huge set of multimedia applications. It is 100 percent Ubuntu-compatible, and it uses the standard Ubuntu software repositories. You can download Ubuntu Studio or simply add the Ubuntu Studio packages and artwork to any Ubuntu installation. There are several excellent multimedia Linux distributions, which you can read about in Chapter 13. You can use any Linux version you like; a few important system modifications you may need to make are covered in Chapter 13.

Windows requires some modifications too, which you'll find in Chapter 14. Since Windows XP continues to hang on and refuses to enter retirement, you'll find information for Windows XP, Vista, and Windows 7.

What Can Audacity Do?

Audacity is fast and easy to use. What can you do with it? A whole lot:

- Work with a wide number of different audio file formats and encodings, including WAV, AIFF, MP3, FLAC, AU, OKI, MAT4/5, Ogg Vorbis, WMA, M4A, and AC3.
- Record live audio.
- Convert legacy analog media to digital.
- Make movie soundtracks.
- Perform unlimited multichannel recording.
- Edit and mix multiple tracks.
- Overdub.
- Use special effects of all kinds: wah-wah, change pitch and tempo, bass boost, echo, reverse, phaser, and more.
- Add graceful fades, both in and out.
- Normalize volume levels.
- Fix defects such as hiss, static, pops, and hum.
- Perform frequency analysis.
- Write your own plug-ins for special effects.
- Cut, copy, splice, and mix sounds together.

Audacity can open and edit audio files faster than most other audio applications and has nearly unlimited undo and redo.

So, what can't you do with Audacity? Audacity does not support the RealAudio format, and it does not support MIDI. While it is wonderful for making mono and stereo recordings, it is not quite as good at making multichannel surround sound recordings.

What This Book Covers

In this book, we'll use Audacity in a number of (I hope) fun and useful audio projects. In Chapter 1, we'll plug a microphone into a computer and learn the basics of recording, editing, playback, and Audacity controls. We'll also learn some important digital audio terminology and concepts. If you are new to digital audio production or new to Audacity, you should go through this chapter first.

In Chapter 2, we'll go into detail on audio gear, how to select it, how to connect it, and how not to spend too much money. The world of audio gear is vast and confusing, but this chapter sorts it all out for you.

If you're like me and have a hoard of treasured vinyl LPs, 45s, or vintage 78s that you want both to enjoy and preserve, read Chapter 3 to learn how to copy them to your computer. From there, you can transfer them to CDs or export to MP3 or any other digital audio format you want. You can do the same with any kind of legacy media.

Audacity is a great program for recording live shows or for editing recordings of live shows made with portable recorders. Chapter 4 shows you how to clean up and optimize your recordings for compact disc or DVD-Audio.

Chapter 5 goes into more detail on making audio CDs and compilation CDs. You'll learn how to normalize different volume levels, break long files into separate tracks, transition smoothly between tracks, and edit track metadata.

In Chapter 6, we learn how to author super high-fidelity DVD-Audio discs. DVD-Audio is a special audio standard for DVDs; it is not the same as the audio formats used on movie DVDs. With DVD-Audio, you can author very high-fidelity DVDs or load several CDs' worth of music onto a single DVD.

Podcasts are all the rage, and Chapter 7 tells you how to make podcasts that sound good and are bandwidth-efficient, and it covers the basics of Internet streaming audio.

Chapter 8 goes into detail on making the highest-quality audio recordings for distribution and tailoring your releases for different types of distribution, such as Internet radio, downloadable formats, and CD. It also offers some guidance on finding distributors and other business basics.

Audacity handles multitrack recording capably, so Chapter 9 shows you how to record multiple tracks, mix, dub, edit, and mixdown to your final mono, stereo, or multichannel surround release. You can play or sing along to an existing track, record as many tracks at once as your recording interface supports and your computer can handle, and mix separate recording sessions together.

Don't pay for ringtones—study Chapter 10 to learn how to make your own easily. Ringtones need to be not too big and not too small, and they can be any snippet of music or sounds or even your own voice. Learn some tips for tailoring your ringtones to sound better on the tiny lo-fi speakers of your phone.

You can go nuts playing with special effects in Audacity—strange noises, sound effects, echo, wah-wah, bass boost, tremolo, and so on. Chapter 11 introduces you to a number of them, tells you where to get more, and shows how to learn to write your own.

In movies and television, ace crime techs take shredded audio remnants and create detailed, high-quality, beautiful recordings as they natter about their magic algorithms. It's all hooey. But you can do a lot to clean up recordings afflicted with pops, hiss, and other defects, and Chapter 12 tells how.

Chapter 13 details how to select a Linux distribution for audio production, how to configure it for best performance, and how to troubleshoot and fix common problems.

Chapter 14 covers the important tweaks Windows users need to make for quality audio recording.

Audacity is easy to use, but it has a number of options that may not make sense to anyone who isn't already an audio engineer, so Chapter 15 goes in-depth into customization and configuration.

Appendix A is your hardware reference; you'll find examples of audio hardware in several price ranges that work on both Linux and Windows.

Appendix B is a glossary of audio terminology written for real people; that is, people who are not physicists or audio engineers and who appreciate clear explanations in plain English.

Appendix C debunks popular but silly audio myths and saves you from some common—and expensive—mistakes.

NOTE   *Audacity is also available as a source tarball. What do you do with a source tarball? It contains Audacity's source code in a compressed archive. You can install Audacity from source code if you want and customize the compile-time options, examine the code, modify it, or even modify and redistribute it. If you're feeling adventurous and want to help debug daily builds, you can grab the newest Audacity version from Concurrent Versions System (CVS) and give it a test-drive.*

Audacity vs. Ardour

Another popular audio recording application for Linux (and Mac OS X) is Ardour, which calls itself a digital audio workstation. Ardour aims to meet the needs of professionals and competes with the likes of ProTools, Nuendo, Pyramix, and other expensive commercial audio applications. It has a more sophisticated mixer than Audacity and some nice audio-for-video tools. It has advanced dubbing abilities, synchronizes with MIDI sequencers, and supports control surfaces, which are hardware devices for controlling your software mixers. It has more automation, as well as a number of useful real-time features such as changing plug-ins on the fly and moving samples to different tracks or timelines while they are playing.

Which one is better? That depends on what you want to do. Both are 100 percent free software because they are licensed under the GPL, both are excellent, and both are getting better all the time. For complex multitrack mixing or precise video soundtrack synchronization, go with Ardour. For recording long tracks such as live shows, converting LPs and tapes to digital formats, cleaning up files marred by hiss or hum or other defects, making podcasts, making simple video soundtracks, and recording in the field, Audacity is an excellent, quality application with a short learning curve and a lot of useful and advanced features.

1

AUDACITY FROM START TO FINISH

Let's fire up Audacity and make a recording. We'll begin with a quick-start tutorial and make a simple recording to demonstrate basic usage. Then we'll cover the fundamental Audacity functions in detail from start to finish: recording, performing common editing tasks, saving your work, and exporting to various audio file formats and quality levels.

We'll deal with fancy audio hardware later; for now, all you need is any Linux or Windows computer with an ordinary sound card and either a microphone with a 1/8″ mini-plug or a USB microphone or headset. Any microphone will do for this initial test, even a little cheapo computer microphone. I recommend an external microphone because built-in computer mics sound pretty bad and are positioned inconveniently. Of course, if you have something better and know how to hook it up, by all means use it.

USB devices need to be plugged in before you open Audacity. If you change a USB device while Audacity is open, you'll have to close and reopen Audacity for it to detect the change.

Audacity Quick-Start

Okay then, enough fiddling around (unless you're going to play a fiddle)! Let's make a quick recording, because that is more fun than sitting around reading about it. Figure 1-1 shows what a new Audacity window looks like before you make a recording on a Windows PC.

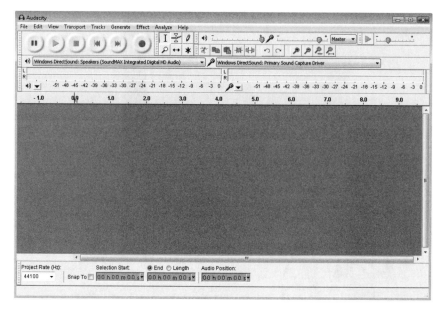

Figure 1-1: A new, blank Audacity window on a Windows PC

Figure 1-2 shows a new Audacity window on an Ubuntu Linux PC. As you can see, Audacity is nearly identical on both platforms. The only significant difference is the recording and playback device chooser. The audio subsystems on Linux and Windows are very different, so the device choosers present different options.

Select **Edit** > **Preferences** > **Devices** to set up your default recording and playback devices. These can be overridden easily from the main Audacity window using the Device toolbar. Figure 1-3 shows a Plantronics USB headset selected on a Windows PC. (Chapter 15 goes into detail about configuring and customizing Audacity.)

USB devices always announce themselves by name, so you don't have to guess. For example, on both Linux and Windows, the recording device selector will say "Plantronics Headset." If you plug a microphone directly into an internal sound card, you will need to know the name of your sound card's driver. On Windows systems, don't select MME, which is the antiquated, generic Windows audio interface. You want to select the modern Windows audio subsystem, which in the **Edit** > **Preferences** > **Devices** dialog

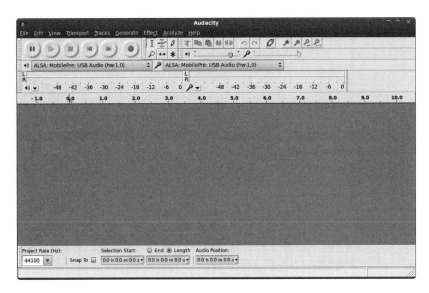

Figure 1-2: A new, blank Audacity window on an Ubuntu Linux PC

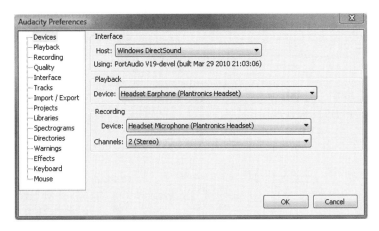

Figure 1-3: Select **Edit** > **Preferences** > **Devices** to set your default
recording and playback devices.

appears as "Windows DirectSound" in the Host line. Figure 1-4 shows what
the selections should look like on a laptop with an onboard SoundMAX audio chipset.

On Linux, you'll have even more choices. "ALSA:default" on the Device
lines will work for an internal sound card (unless you have changed the default sound device for your Linux system; see Chapter 13 to learn all about
Linux audio). Pick the device name for a USB device. When you're finished,
click **OK** to close the Preferences dialog.

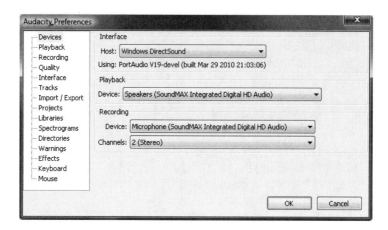

Figure 1-4: Selecting your default recording and playback devices on Windows Vista.

NOTE *Doing digital audio production on a PC means you'll have to get very involved with your sound card drivers and in configuring your PC for good quality and performance. Visit Chapters 13 and 14 to learn how to tune your system for audio production and how to manage various operating system quirks for controlling volume levels, balance, and input and output devices.*

Before you start recording, save and name your new Audacity project by selecting **File > Save Project As**. It is a good habit to do this right away for every new recording.

In the next section, we'll learn all about all the tool buttons. For now, hover your cursor over the toolbars and buttons to learn their names.

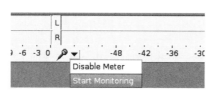

Figure 1-5: Input Level Meter

Now let's test recording levels before we actually start recording. Go to the Input Level Meter, shown in Figure 1-5. Click **Start Monitoring** and start making noise. Unlike analog recording, with digital audio you don't need to push your recording levels right up to the redline. Try recording to a peak of −6 or −9 dB.

You can use the Mixer toolbar to control recording and playback volume, sort of. It isn't really a mixer but a recording and playback volume control. This is the little toolbar with the speaker and microphone icons and volume sliders for each. It does not control volume on all internal sound cards, because some low-end sound cards do not have drivers that support volume control. It may not control volume levels on USB devices either, again depending on what their drivers support. If this is the case, in Windows go to the Sound module in the Control Panel to control volume levels. Linux users should use alsamixer. (Remember,

Chapters 13 and 14 will help with these.) Or you can just make louder or quieter noises.

The Input Level Meter uses two different shades of red: bright red bars for displaying the average volume and dark red bars to show the peak volume levels. The little vertical blue lines mark the highest volume levels attained during the session, and the little vertical red lines mark the peak volume levels of the last three seconds. On the right edge of the recording monitor are clipping indicators that will turn red when your recording level is too loud. They're pretty small and stay lit after your recording levels drop, which limits their usefulness. However, you do need to pay attention to clipping, which occurs when input levels are too high. Anything over 0 dB creates clipping, and clipping causes distortion.

Now let's record some sounds. Click the red **Record** button and keep making noise. You'll see something like Figure 1-6. When you're finished, click the **Stop** or **Pause** button. With the Stop button, a new track starts the next time you click **Record**; the Pause button lets you pick up where you left off on the same track. If you stop when you meant to pause, don't worry— you can append to an existing track by pressing the SHIFT key and clicking **Record**.

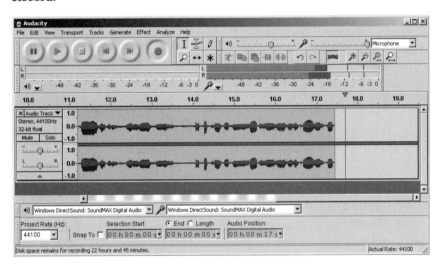

Figure 1-6: At last, a recording session! When you see blue waveforms, you know it's working.

Naturally, when you're done recording, you'll want to hear what you just recorded, and Audacity offers instant gratification. Click the **Play** button. If you don't hear anything, it's because you either selected the wrong playback device or have a volume control set too low. Stop playback before changing the playback device. The cursor changes to a little hand when you hover over the Time Scale, and you can click any point on the Time Scale to start playback again.

In digital audio it is common practice to record to a low peak level, as low as −24 dB. The digital audio decibel scale is measured in negative numbers up to zero. About the smallest change we can perceive is 1 dB, and −60 dB is as good as silence for most people, so a practical range to use is −60 to 0 dB. A +3 dB change doubles the volume, and −3 dB halves it.

A super-low peak such as −24 dB is useful when you're recording something with unpredictable levels, such as a live performance. For other, more controlled circumstances, a good peak level is between −12 dB and −6 dB. Any sound level over 0 dB will result in clipping, which creates distortion. Avoiding distortion is very important in digital audio recording. The signal-to-noise ratio is extremely high, so you don't need to push your recording levels to the maximum just to keep noise at tolerable levels.

A low peak level means that your recording won't be very loud, but that is no problem. You can easily fix this. Select the whole track by clicking the track label (Figure 1-7). Then open **Effect** > **Normalize**. Check both boxes in the Normalize dialog and make the maximum amplitude 0 (Figure 1-8).

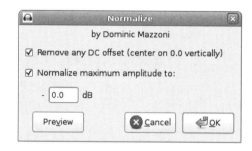

Figure 1-7: How to select a whole track

Figure 1-8: Normalization uniformly raises (or lowers) the volume level of your track.

The final step is to export your new recording to a playable audio file. Audacity uses its own special file format that doesn't work in anything but Audacity, so you have to export to an audio file format that works in playback devices. Select **File** > **Export** to export the project as a WAV file, which should be the default choice (Figure 1-9). Name your export file whatever you want, maybe something creative like *test.wav*. The WAV format is almost universal and will play on nearly any digital playback device or computer software media player.

Now you can play your *test.wav* file on your computer and hear it in all its glory. Windows users can use Windows Media Player, which is installed by default, or choose from a host of third-party programs. Linux users also have any number of media players to choose from: Amarok, Rhythmbox, VLC, Mplayer, and many more.

It is best to use WAV as your default export format because it is a lossless, uncompressed format that provides the highest-quality recordings. WAVs stand up to a lot of editing without deterioration, whereas lossy formats (such as MP3 and Ogg Vorbis) lose information with each edit. You

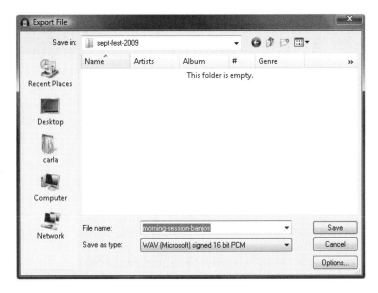

Figure 1-9: Saving your new audio file in WAV format

can always export from WAV to a lower-quality, lossy format, but you can't go from low to high quality.

All righty then, that's the short story. Read on to get the unabridged version.

Audacity in Detail

Keep in mind that Audacity supports nearly unlimited undo, so it is safe to experiment. Undo works even after saves; you lose your undo history only when you close your project file.

When you work on a project, Audacity does not operate directly on your audio files. Instead, it copies them into a temporary file, chops them into a lot of little pieces, and converts these to files with *.au* extensions that play only in Audacity. You can see this by viewing your project directories in any file manager. There is a single *.aup* file for each project; this contains all the metadata Audacity needs to put these little files back together with the correct settings. When you open an Audacity project from your file manager, select the *.aup* file.

Suppose you have a recording of a splendid performance where you outdid yourself and brought tears to all eyes (of joy, not pain) and this recording is in WAV format. When you import this WAV into Audacity, it is copied and converted to Audacity's internal *.au* format. Your original WAV is safe and sound and won't be changed, as long as you don't overwrite it by exporting the project back to the same WAV file.

Converting and splintering your files might sound like an odd thing to do, but operating on many little files is a lot faster than manipulating a few large files. Audio files can consume many megabytes and even gigabytes. Audacity has an automatic crash recovery mechanism, which you will see only if something bad happens; when you reopen Audacity, it will display a recovery message. Unsaved data are kept in a temporary file, so Audacity can usually recover them. Select **Edit > Preferences** to set an autosave interval; mine is at two minutes. And, as with everything we do on computers, good backups are essential. Hard disk space is cheap these days, so don't pinch pennies on storage.

Let's start our detailed tour with a look at Audacity's toolbars. All of the toolbars have handles on their left sides so you can drag them anywhere you want, even outside of the Audacity window. If you hover the cursor over the toolbar handles, the toolbar name pops up. Hover over the buttons to see their names.

Select **View > Toolbars** to control which toolbars are visible.

Figure 1-10 shows the Control toolbar, which has the Pause, Play, Stop, Skip to Start, Skip to End, and Record buttons.

Now let's meet the buttons on the Tools toolbar: Selection, Envelope, Draw, Zoom, Time Shift, and Multi-Tool (Figure 1-11). These affect the cursor functions.

Figure 1-10: Control toolbar

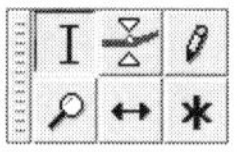

Figure 1-11:
Tools toolbar

Next to the Tools toolbar is the Edit toolbar (Figure 1-12), which contains the Cut, Copy, Paste, Trim, Silence, Redo, Undo, Link Tracks, Zoom, Fit Selection, and Fit Project buttons.

Figure 1-12: Edit toolbar

Table 1-1 lists all the buttons found on the Tools and Edit toolbars with descriptions of what they do.

Table 1-1: The Tools and Edit toolbar buttons

Button	Name	Description
I	Selection	Click to mark a playback starting point. Click and drag to select a portion of a track. Double-click to select a whole track. Click anywhere on the Time Scale to start playback (it changes to a little hand).
⌇	Envelope	Use for fine control of amplitude (volume levels) on a track and for creating fade-ins and fade-outs. Click to create control nodes, and then click and drag nodes to increase or decrease amplitude. Control nodes can be dragged both vertically and horizontally. Drag nodes past the track border to get rid of them.
✎	Draw	Click the Zoom In button until you can see in-dividual audio samples and then use the Draw tool to manipulate them. Use this for very fine-grained smoothing out of clicks and pops.
🔍	Zoom	Left-click to zoom in, right-click to zoom out. Remember the Zoom buttons! You will probably use them a lot: Use Zoom In for precise edits and use Zoom Out to make long tracks manageable. See the View menu for more Zoom commands and keyboard shortcuts.
↔	Time Shift	Synchronize tracks by dragging them backward or forward along the timeline. You can also drag a track or clip into another track, as long there is enough empty space to hold it.
✳	Multi-Tool	This is five tools in one, activated according to mouse position. Get the Selection and Envelope tools by moving the cursor vertically, the Time Shift tool by hovering over the track handles at the beginning or end of the track, and the Zoom tool by moving left into the decibel scale; the zoom view will center over the decibel number you hover over. The Draw tool appears when you zoom in far enough to see individual samples.

Continued on next page.

Table 1-1 (*continued*)

Button	Name	Description
	Cut	This removes the selection and puts it on the clipboard.
	Copy	This copies the selection without removing it and puts it on the clipboard.
	Paste	This inserts the clipboard contents at the cursor position or replaces a selection.
	Trim	This deletes everything but the selection.
	Silence	This replaces the selection with silence.
	Redo	Audacity supports nearly unlimited undos and redos, even after saving your project, so it is safe to experiment. The Redo button reverses an undo action or series of undo actions in sequence. You can't skip back to a selected action; you have to redo all of them in order.
	Undo	This undoes your last action, or any number of actions before that in sequence, even after saving your project. You can't skip back to a selected action; you have to undo all of them in order.
	Link Tracks	This tool has a somewhat misleading name. You might think it's for selecting multiple tracks, but its function is to "link audio and label tracks," which is quite different. Link Tracks is enabled by default when you start a new project, and it keeps your audio and label tracks synchronized when you modify a track. If you don't have a label track, it does nothing. Use it when you make changes that affect the track length, such as deleting part of a track, inserting silence, or changing the tempo. Turn off Link Tracks when you copy and paste entire tracks, because it will mess up your paste. Link Tracks appears in Audacity 1.3.9, will be inactive in the 2.0 series, and is scheduled to reappear in the 2.1 series.

Table 1-1 (*continued*)

Button	Name	Description
	Zoom In	Magnify. You can zoom in far enough to see individual samples. Click the Selection tool cursor on the point you want to magnify, and the zoom will center on that spot.
	Zoom Out	Shrink. You can zoom out far enough to see your whole track at once. As with Zoom In, Zoom Out will center on the point that you clicked with the Selection tool.
	Fit Selection	You can enlarge the selection to fit the window horizontally. This tool is a great time-saver when you need to select a small part of a long track to work on.
	Fit Project	This tool sizes your whole project to fit horizontally in your Audacity window. Select **View** > **Fit Vertically** to fit your entire project into the window.

Figure 1-13 shows the Meter toolbar, which displays the recording and playback levels. When it's squished, the Meter toolbar might not display smaller values on its scale. In that case, grab it by the handle on its left side, move it somewhere with more room, then grab it by the resizing handle on the right side, and finally stretch it out until you can see the whole decibel scale.

Figure 1-13: Meter toolbar

Figure 1-14 shows the Mixer toolbar, which is not really a mixer. Instead, it is supposed to control the input and output volume levels on internal sound cards. However, these functions work only if supported by your sound card driver, so if they don't, blame your sound card maker. (For more information on operating system audio controls, see Chapters 13 and 14.)

Figure 1-14: Mixer toolbar

Figure 1-15: Transcription toolbar

The Transcription toolbar (Figure 1-15) changes the speed of playback. For example, you can use it to slow down when transcribing lyrics or to sound sinister and evil. Or you can speed it up for giggles, like Alvin and the Chipmunks. This toolbar only affects Audacity playback and won't change your project file. (**Effect** > **Change Speed** behaves the same way, except it changes your project file. **Effect** > **Change Pitch** changes the pitch higher or lower without changing playback speed, and **Effect** > **Change Tempo** changes the speed without changing pitch.)

Figure 1-16 shows the Device toolbar, where you can select your recording and playback devices without selecting **Edit** > **Preferences**. If you plug in or remove a USB device, you need to restart Audacity, or it won't see the change.

Figure 1-16: Device toolbar

Finally, the Selection toolbar, shown in Figure 1-17, offers a number of different scales for precise timing and selection of portions of your audio tracks and for setting the correct frame rates for video soundtracks and compact disc audio.

Figure 1-17: Selection toolbar

Managing Audacity Projects

Your first step on a new Audacity project should always be to name it using **File** > **Save As**. Then you can press CTRL-S periodically to save changes or use **File** > **Save**. In addition to the *.aup* file, which is the project's master metadata file, Audacity creates a directory that holds the associated audio files. You can view these in your file manager; there will be many subdirectories full of files with the *.au* extension.

Adding Audio Files: Import vs. Open

Select **File** > **Open** to add an existing audio file to a new, empty project. After that, select **File** > **Import** to add more files. Selecting **File** > **Open** in a nonempty project opens the file in a new window.

Saving Your Work

Audacity projects are optimized for use as fast workspaces and are not suitable for archival storage. There's no snapshot mechanism for preserving your work at different stages, and users have reported losing data when projects become corrupted. I use a belt-and-suspenders approach: I make backups of my Audacity project files, and I also make studio master files in WAV format, because each approach has its advantages and weaknesses. First we'll look at a method for saving Audacity projects at different stages, and then we'll look at how to make studio masters in WAV format.

You can create something akin to project snapshots by creating multiple Audacity projects from your original project. First, make a directory to hold related projects so they don't get mixed up or lost. Then select **File** > **Save Project As** and give the project a name to help you remember what's in it, such as Summer-Festival-1, Summer-Festival-2, or something more descriptive like Summer-Festival-No-Banjos or Summer-Festival-Mondo-Banjos. When you do this, you'll see a dialog like Figure 1-18. The crucial question here is "Copy audio from the following files into your project to make it self-contained?" Say yes by clicking the **Copy All Audio into Project (Safer)** button. This duplicates project files and uses more disk space, but it is the safest option. Sharing files across multiple projects saves disk space, but the headaches aren't worth it because changes in one project affect all projects. Even worse, you lose redundancy, which is your insurance against any one project becoming damaged and unusable.

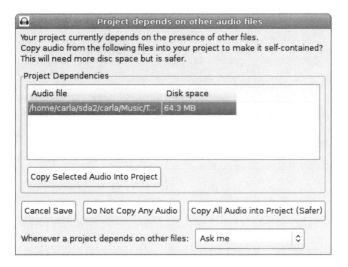

Figure 1-18: Saving a copy of your project under a new project name

You can control this behavior in the **Edit** > **Preferences** > **Projects** dialog: When saving a project that depends on other audio files. This offers three choices: "Always copy all audio into project," "Do not copy any audio," or "Ask user."

To make a high-quality studio master WAV file, export your project by selecting **File** > **Export**. You can do this as many times as you want during your work on a project, creating multiple masters to preserve your work at different stages (or until you run out of disk space!). Then you can import a WAV master whenever you want for further editing, and you can export to any other audio format from your WAV master. This also gives you the option of importing your WAV master into another audio-editing program, which you can't do with Audacity's project files.

The default export quality setting for WAVs is 16-bit integer, which is not the highest quality. Audacity's default recording quality setting (select **Edit** > **Preferences** > **Quality**) is a sampling rate of 44.1 kHz and a bit depth of 32-bit float. (Audacity terminology refers to bit depth as *sample format*, but *bit depth* is the correct term.) You can create a high-quality studio master by exporting to 32-bit float WAV. Follow these steps:

1. Select **File** > **Export**.
2. Select Save as type: Other uncompressed files.
3. Click **Options** and then select Header: WAV (Microsoft) and Encoding: 32 bit float.

You will see a window like the one shown in Figure 1-19.

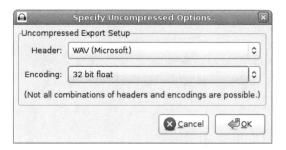

Figure 1-19: Exporting your project to a 32-bit float WAV file

The resulting file is not a playable WAV file, except in Audacity and other audio editors and digital audio workstations that use 32-bit float for editing. However, it is great for studio masters because you can import and edit 32-bit float WAVs with very little loss of quality and export them to other audio formats: 16- and 24-bit WAV, Ogg Vorbis, MP3, FLAC, and so on. WAV supports a maximum of 32 tracks in a single file.

However, this has its drawbacks too. It works fine when you have only a few tracks to manage—my limit is four—because Audacity does not save the track names but instead renames all of them with the WAV filename. Let's say you have a four-track recording and the tracks are named *vocal, piano, violin,* and *vocal2*. Export this project to a single WAV file and name it *testwav.wav.* When you import *testwav.wav* into Audacity, all four tracks are renamed *testwav 1.wav*, *testwav 2.wav*, and so on. It also makes tracks 1 and 2 Right and Left, even if they were originally mono tracks. Figure 1-20 shows the before and after.

You still have all of your individual tracks, but you lose the track names. On multitrack projects, I rely very much on track names to stay organized, so combining them all into a single WAV file doesn't work for me.

For projects that have more than four tracks, I prefer to save each track as a separate WAV file. To do this, select the tracks you want to export and then select **File** > **Export Multiple**. (We will discuss selecting tracks in the next section.) Each track will be saved as a separate file, and the track name will become the filename of the corresponding file. When I do this, I put them in their own project directory so they don't get mixed up with other projects.

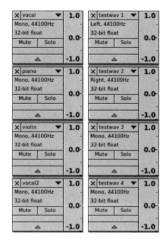

Figure 1-20: Exporting your project to WAV (on the left is the original project before exporting to WAV, and on the right is shown what happens when the WAV is imported back into Audacity)

Selecting Tracks and Segments of Tracks

Now let's learn how to select tracks and parts of tracks. Audacity supports the usual editing functions computer users are used to—copy and paste, delete, select, and so on, but it will drive you crazy if you don't learn how to do them the Audacity way. A nice feature of Audacity is that it supports keyboard shortcuts for nearly all functions, so you can use the mouse or keyboard.

First, make yourself a new recording or import an existing audio file by selecting **File** > **Import** so you have some tracks to experiment with. Be sure the Selection tool is active. If you're using the Multi-Tool, move it up or down until it changes into the Selection tool, which looks like a little I-beam.

Track focus and track selection are two different things. A yellow track border shows which track has focus, but if the Track panel is light colored, then that track has not been selected. Having focus means that the track is ready to accept keyboard commands; the cursor line is active in that track, and you can move it back and forth with the arrow keys.

Figure 1-21 shows two tracks: The bottom track has focus, which is indicated by a yellow border, and the top one is selected, which is indicated by the shaded Track panel. The cursor line extends into both but is active in the bottom track. Having a selected track without focus and an unselected track with focus isn't much use. You can select a starting point for playback in the track with focus and move it back and forth with the arrow keys, but that's about it.

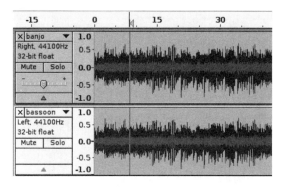

Figure 1-21: The top track is selected but does not have focus, and the bottom track has focus, indicated by a yellow border, but is not selected.

When a track is selected, it becomes the target of any editing operations you perform, such as copying, cutting, or applying effects. These will be applied to the whole track, even if it doesn't have focus. There are two ways to select an entire track: You can double-click anywhere on the waveform, or you can click the track label in the Track panel (see Figure 1-7).

Most times you won't have to pay attention to focus and selection because in the normal course of editing, they'll be where you want them to be. But sometimes things behave oddly, and being aware of this distinction should help you understand what's going on when Audacity seems to be responding mysteriously.

You can also select part of a track. Figure 1-22 shows a track with only a segment, rather than the whole track, selected. Note the difference in shading between the selected and unselected portions.

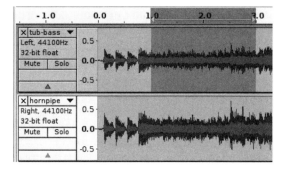

Figure 1-22: A segment of the top track is selected. Some laptop screens are not bright enough for the shading to be readily apparent in the Track panel, so look at the timeline as well.

CTRL-A selects all tracks, and SHIFT-CTRL-A deselects them all. Double-click inside a track to select just that track, or left-click in the track label. SHIFT-click the track label to select and deselect multiple tracks one at a time, as well as nonadjacent tracks. In Figure 1-23, the first and third tracks were selected with SHIFT-clicking.

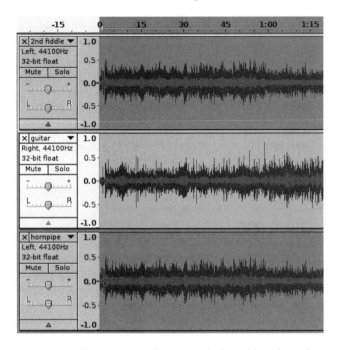

Figure 1-23: Selecting nonadjacent tracks by holding down the SHIFT key and clicking the track labels

To select part of a track, click and drag with the Selection tool. To make your selection bigger or smaller, move the cursor over either boundary of your selection, where it will turn into a horizontal arrow, and then click and drag that boundary (Figure 1-24).

You can navigate between tracks and adjust selections with your keyboard's arrow keys. Pressing the SHIFT and the left-arrow or right-arrow key enlarges a selection; pressing CTRL-SHIFT and the left-arrow or right-arrow key makes it smaller. A slick trick for making a selection across several adjacent tracks is first to make the selection in the top or bottom track and then to press the up-arrow or down-arrow key to repeat the selection in the other tracks.

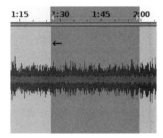

Figure 1-24: Changing the size of a selection by clicking and dragging a boundary

The Skip to Start and Skip to End buttons in your Control toolbar move the cursor to the start or the end of the track. Pressing the SHIFT key while clicking the **Skip to Start** button selects from the cursor position to the beginning of the track, and pressing the SHIFT key while clicking **Skip to End** selects from the cursor position to the end of the track.

You can also use the Selection toolbar to make precise selections based on various track parameters, such as time, samples, and various audio and video frame rates. You can see these parameters by clicking the drop-down menu in any of the three fields on the toolbar (Figure 1-25).

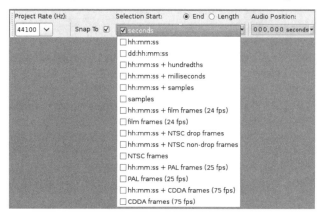

Figure 1-25: The Selection toolbar supports selections based on a number of useful track parameters.

Suppose you want to select a 12-second segment that starts 48 seconds from the beginning of the track. There are several ways to get to the 48-second mark—click with the Selection tool, navigate with the arrow keys, or use the Selection toolbar. Set Selection Start: seconds and enter 48. Select the "End" radio button and enter 60 in the middle box. There is your 12-second segment (Figure 1-26.)

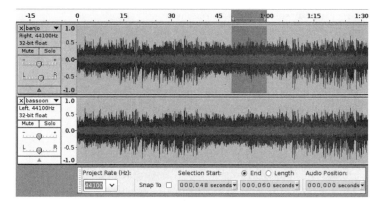

Figure 1-26: Using the Selection toolbar to select a precise section of an audio track

The up-arrow and down-arrow keys also change the numbers, and the right-arrow and left-arrow keys navigate back and forth.

Track Panel

The Track panel puts a number of useful shortcuts at your fingertips (Figure 1-27). The little *X* on the top left deletes the track. The arrow at the bottom collapses and expands the track. You can also grab and drag the

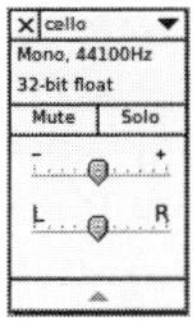

Figure 1-27: The handy Track panel

track borders with the mouse to change their widths. The Gain slider amplifies or reduces the track volume without permanently changing it, which is essential when you're mixing multiple tracks. The Pan slider controls the left-right balance.

By default, Audacity plays all tracks on a project when you click the Play button. Use the Solo button to select one track for playback or the Mute buttons to silence tracks you don't want to hear. This only affects playback in Audacity and does not change your project files.

The Track menu has an interesting grab bag of functions (Figure 1-28). You can use it to create track names— and when you're working with a lot of tracks, you definitely want to name them. It also offers different waveform views; lets you split or join stereo tracks; lets you set mono, right, or left channel; allows you to move tracks up or down; and lets you change the bit depth (which Audacity calls the *sample format*) and sampling rate.

A stereo track is split into two separate mono tracks with Split Stereo Track or Split Stereo to Mono. With Split Stereo Track, one will be Right, and one will be Left. With Split Stereo to Mono, two mono tracks are created. To create a stereo track, place two mono tracks adjacent to each other and then click **Make Stereo Track** in the Track menu of the upper track. Move tracks by clicking and dragging the track label or by selecting **Move TrackUp/Down** in the Track menu.

Figure 1-28: Track menu functions

The vertical scale to the right of the Track panel is your guide to the volume levels of your tracks. The default display is Waveform, and you can change this to Waveform (dB), Spectrum, or Pitch (EAC) with the Track menu. Waveform is a commonly used visual scale for displaying the *amplitude* (the strength or volume of a signal) of your track. The Waveform vertical ruler has a *linear* scale of $+1.0$ to -1.0; anything that goes over these values represents clipping, which means you're getting some distortion. Linear means that all frequencies are given equal weight on the scale. Decibels are logarithmic rather than linear, so this is not a true representation, but it is easy to read.

Waveform (dB) displays amplitude using a *logarithmic* decibel scale. Without diving into the mathematical details, logarithmic means that each 3 dB increment represents a doubling in loudness—hence, a sound measured at 6 dB is twice as loud as a sound measured at 3 dB, and 9 dB is twice as loud as 6 dB. About the smallest increment of change that humans can perceive is 1 dB. (Read more about audio terminology in the glossary.)

There is a special decibel scale for digital audio, the Zero Decibels Full Scale. This represents the digital audio volume range with negative numbers up to a maximum of 0. In Audacity you can control the decibel range displayed in the Waveform (dB) view and on the Meter Toolbar in the **Edit** > **Preferences** > **Interface** dialog. Click the Meter/Waveform dB Range dropdown menu to see your options. The smallest scale is −36 dB to 0, and the widest scale is −145 dB to 0. This only affects the display and does nothing to your audio tracks.

You can use either waveform display to monitor your recording levels; I think the default waveform display is easiest to read. You'll notice the displays use two shades of blue, one lighter and one darker. The light blue represents the RMS, or *root-mean-square*, which translated into ordinary English is the average volume over time. The darker blue represents the peaks, which are the transient extremes.

NOTE *RMS and peak ratings are (mis)used in the marketing of audio gear to make you think you're getting more than you really are. For example, a set of speakers is rated at 50 watts RMS/150 watts peak. Ignore the peak value—RMS tells you how much the speakers can handle continuously. The peak value indicates what the speakers can tolerate in very short (fraction of a second) bursts.*

The Spectrum view represents the energy level (amplitude) of the different frequencies in colors. Red is "hot," or higher amplitude, and blue is "cool," or lower amplitude. If your waveform is mostly blue, it's not very loud, and if it's more red, it's louder. You can easily test this by selecting a track or a segment of a track, selecting **Effect** > **Amplify**, and giving it a negative Amplification value of −30 dB. This should make it mostly blue. Give it a value closer to zero to make it more red.

Pitch (EAC) displays the contours of the pitch of your audio using the enhanced autocorrelation (EAC) algorithm. The EAC algorithm is interesting for doing pitch detection; if you are interested in learning more about this, *enhanced autocorrelation* and *pitch detection* are some good Internet search terms to start with. Audacity's implementation of this is pretty basic, so if this interests you, you'll probably want to find more sophisticated tools.

Cutting Out Unwanted Chunks

You can easily remove parts of tracks that you don't want. Just select a section and then press the DELETE key on your keyboard. If you want to keep only a small part of the track and remove the rest, select **Edit > Trim** or click the **Trim** button on the Edit toolbar. This saves the part of the track that you have selected and deletes everything outside of it.

Sometimes you might need to silence a large section of a track while leaving the track intact. In that case, select the part you want to convert to silence, and then click the **Silence** button or select **Edit > Silence Audio**.

Fade In and Out

When you delete part of a track, you might want to smooth the cut with graceful fades. Fades are integral to audio editing, and Audacity has two ways to create fades. The easiest way is to select a portion of a track and then select **Effect > Fade In** or **Fade Out**. You control the length of the fade, and Audacity does the rest.

The Envelope tool can fine-tune the amplitude levels; it is good for controlling fades and for fine-tuning amplitude anywhere on an audio track, including over relatively long segments. Figure 1-29 shows what this looks like. Click different locations to create control nodes. To get rid of a node, drag it outside the track border.

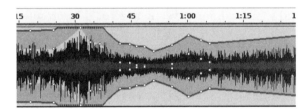

Figure 1-29: The Envelope tool creates graceful fades and gives you fine-grained control of amplitude.

Each node has four handles. The node handles can be moved in any direction. The outside pair behaves a little differently than the inner pair—use the outside handles to create more graceful, gradual curves.

The dotted lines on either side of the 30-second mark show where the borders of the envelope go outside of the track display.

NOTE   *In addition to the Zoom buttons in the Editor toolbar, the View menu has some nice options for manipulating and navigating your tracks such as Fit In Window and Zoom to Selection, and it shows useful keyboard shortcuts such as CTRL-2 for Zoom Normal and SHIFT-CTRL-F for Fit Vertically.*

Making Quiet Recordings Louder

Suppose your recording is too quiet and you want to amp up the volume. No problem! Select the part you want to amplify and then select **Effect** > **Amplify**. Audacity automatically calculates how much amplification can be applied without clipping; that is, without going over 0 dB (Figure 1-30). Don't check the "Allow clipping" box unless you are very sure you want to do so.

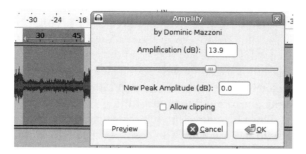

Figure 1-30: Using **Effect** > **Amplify** to raise or lower the volume of your selection

Another way to amplify a too-quiet recording is to select **Effect** > **Normalize**. Check "Remove any DC offset," check "Normalize maximum amplitude to," and set a maximum level up to zero. *DC offset* refers to the mean amplitude; if this is not zero, then normalization won't be applied correctly because the amplitude levels will be unbalanced, and it might create some distortion.

The difference between Amplify and Normalize is seen when they are applied to multiple tracks. Amplify changes the volume on all tracks by an equal amount. If you amplify volume by +9 dB, a track that peaks at −20 dB will be raised to −11 dB, and a track that peaks at −9 dB will be raised to 0 dB. Normalize, on the other hand, adjusts all tracks to the same maximum volume level, so some tracks may be changed more than others.

The default maximum setting for both is zero. It's useful to lower this to −12 dB or so on your studio masters in order to leave a bit of headroom for more tweaking without risking clipping. For example, when you downmix multiple tracks into a single track, the latter will have the combined amplitudes of all those tracks and get louder, maybe a lot louder. Experience will tell you how much headroom you need. Don't normalize to zero until you are making your final exports.

Amplify and Normalize can also be used to lower amplitude. In the Amplify dialog, enter a negative value, like −6. The Normalize dialog uses only negative values and won't allow anything higher than zero.

Timer Record and Sound Activated Recording

Both Timer Record and Sound Activated Recording are in the Transport menu. To use Sound Activated Recording, select **Transport** > **Sound Activation Level** and set the decibel level you want to trigger recording. It may take a bit of trial and error to figure out a level that balances capturing what you want without also capturing lot of sounds you don't want. Then turn on the recording monitor (Meter toolbar) and click the **Play** button. When a loud enough sound is detected, Audacity will automatically create a new track and then use that track for as long as you leave Timer Record activated. Click the **Stop** button any time to stop Sound Activated Recording.

Timer Record is just as easy—just set the start and stop times for recording. You can use this together with Sound Activated Recording to set a start and stop range so that you can go away and leave Audacity running without worrying about it filling your hard drive.

Mixer Board

The Mixer Board is a new feature that first appeared in Audacity 1.3.8 (Figure 1-31).

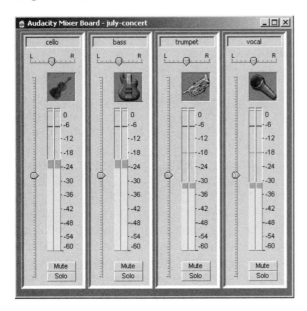

Figure 1-31: The Mixer Board puts Pan and Gain controls front and center.

This is a slick little board with volume units (VU) meters for each track, plus Pan and Gain sliders. It puts your essential mixing controls within easy reach, without having to make your tracks extra wide so that you can access the sliders on the Track panels.

To use the Mixer Board, play your tracks in Audacity and adjust the relative volumes of your tracks with the Gain sliders, which are on the left side of the VU meter, and the left-right balance of each track with the Pan slider. Then make your export. The Pan and Gain sliders do not change your project files—they only affect playback in Audacity and how your exported file will sound. See Chapter 9 to learn more about multitrack mixing.

Track Metadata

You can preserve useful data in your Audacity projects, such as song titles, date, artist name, and genre, with the metadata editor. Before your final export, select **File** > **Open Metadata Editor**. You'll see a window like the one in Figure 1-32. Fill in any of the Artist Name, Album Title, Year, Genre, and Comments fields, and these will be applied to each song track. Audacity will fill in the Track Titles and Track Numbers fields automatically.

Figure 1-32: Using **File** > **Open Metadata Editor** *to store useful information in your Audacity project*

If you select **Edit** > **Preferences** > **Import/Export**, there is a "Show Metadata Editor prior to export step" option. If you check this, the metadata editor will open for each track before it is exported so you can review or edit the metadata.

Final Mixdown

Usually your goal is to mixdown however many tracks you have recorded to a stereo track. However, Audacity also supports multichannel surround sound, which is covered in Chapter 9. Before you export, select **Edit** > **Preferences** > **Import/Export** and select the "Use custom mix" radio button. At export, an Advanced Mixing Option window appears, which is a simple channel mapper. Map your tracks to whichever channels you want. Your tracks can go to the left channel, the right channel, or even multiple channels. Channel 1 is always the left channel when there are two tracks. (See Figure 1-33 for a simple two-track example.) When you are using this tool, you will be glad you named your tracks. Chapter 9 goes into more detail on multitrack mixing and channel mapping.

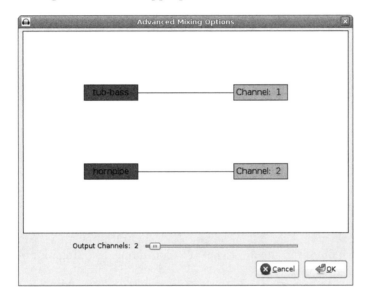

Figure 1-33: Using Audacity's mixer to map your tracks to the correct channels

Audio File Formats and Quality Settings

There are many different audio file formats, and Audacity supports a lot of them. Let's look at WAV, MP3, FLAC, and Ogg Vorbis. These well-supported, popular formats serve different purposes.

Understanding File Formats

WAV files are uncompressed, high-quality pulse-code modulation (PCM) files. They are large. One minute of a CD-quality stereo WAV recording consumes about 10MB of disk space. WAV is the best-supported format and is the quality standard by which other formats are measured.

MP3 (MPEG-1 Audio Layer 3, not MPEG-3) is a popular compressed, lossy encoding format; an MP3 file can be as small as one-tenth the size of a similar WAV file and still sound pretty good. This means you can cram a lot more music into a portable player and have faster downloads and better online streaming. The trade-off is that quality is lost. See Chapters 13 and 14 to learn how to enable MP3 support in Audacity.

Although MP3 is extremely popular, it is encumbered with messy patent problems. A number of different companies in different countries claim they own patents on MP3, and depending on where you live, you may be expected to pay licensing fees if you want to distribute music encoded in MP3. The final patents won't expire until 2017. However, the patent situation is not clear-cut because many independent musicians distribute their music in MP3 format without paying patent royalties, and patents do not apply in all countries outside their countries of origin.

Free Lossless Audio Codec (FLAC) is an excellent open and free format. This lossless, compressed format is equivalent in quality to WAV but with file sizes that are one-third to a half smaller. FLAC is a great format for a PC media server, because you get great quality without eating up as much hard drive space. Online music services distribute their highest-quality downloads in FLAC. You can even use FLAC for your studio masters if you need to conserve storage space. Although the FLAC format does not support 32-bit float, 24-bit FLAC files are still very high quality.

Ogg Vorbis was created as a high-quality, free, and open alternative to MP3. Ogg files range from about the same size as MP3 to about 25 percent larger. Ogg Vorbis is not as widely supported as MP3 and WAV, though its popularity is increasing. Linux, Windows, and Mac all have a number of software music players that support playing both standalone Ogg files and streaming Ogg. The iPod and Zune do not support Ogg (not a big surprise, coming from the two titans of lock-in), but a growing number of other playback devices do.

Chapter 7 goes into detail about different quality levels for Ogg Vorbis and MP3, and Chapter 6 discusses WAV and FLAC.

The next section explains some important fundamental concepts of digital audio and terminology that you'll encounter a lot, so grab a cup of tea, put your feet up, and read on.

Understanding Bit Depth and Sampling Rate

Digital audio production can be summed up as converting analog signals to digital and back again. In other words, you capture sound from an analog microphone or electric musical instrument, run it through an analog-to-digital converter (ADC), and record the digitized bits to a hard drive or solid-state storage. The ADC can be a sound card, a preamp/ADC, a standalone ADC, or some other combination device. Somewhere down the road this digital data will be retrieved and converted to analog form for playback.

Your computer's sound card performs digital-to-analog conversion during playback, and so does an ordinary CD or MP3 player.

Your goal is to convert those analog signals as faithfully as possible. Once they are in digital form, you have a whole world of tools at your disposal to manipulate them in all kinds of creative ways, and you have a multitude of options for playback formats and media.

16/44.1, 24/96, 32-Bit Float

Two common digital audio specifications are referred to as 16/44.1 and 24/96. Sometimes 16/44.1 is shortened to 16/44. These designations specify *bit depth* and *sampling rate*. Bit depth affects dynamic range, signal-to-noise ratio, and fidelity. Sampling rate determines the frequency range.

CD-quality audio is defined as 44.1 kHz, 16-bit, two-channel WAV, and 24/96 is higher-than-CD audio quality, such as digital audio tape (DAT), DVD audio, and studio master recordings. So, we should just go for the highest numbers to get the best quality, right? Well, no—there are a number of factors to consider.

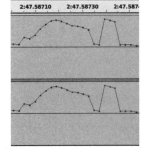

Sampling is done by the analog-to-digital converter; it samples the electric voltage in an analog audio signal at intervals and converts the measurements to digital form. The more times per second this is done, the more accurate the digital representation of the signal. So, a sampling rate of 44.1kHz means 44,100 samples per second per channel. This is Audacity's default. You can see a picture of this by enlarging a section of any Audacity waveform. This will look something like Figure 1-34, where each dot represents a single audio sample.

Figure 1-34: Audacity waveform, enlarged so that the sample points are visible

Each audio sample is represented as a numeric value—in computers, everything is a number. In CD-quality audio, 16 bits is the range of possible values per sample, and 16 bits = 65,536. This is the *bit depth*. Each sample is not 65,536 bits in size but is given a single 16-bit value that is equal to or lesser than 65,535 (0 to 65,535.)

For 24/96 recording, which is often used in professional recording, 24 bits gives 16,777,216 possible values. Larger bit depths mean wider dynamic ranges and finer tonal shadings—and also significantly larger file sizes. One minute of a stereo recording is about 10MB (5MB per channel) at 16/44.1 and is about 34MB at 24/96.

Theoretically, the dynamic range of 16-bit digital audio is 96 dB, for a scale of −96 to 0. For 24-bit audio, it is 144 dB, and for 32-bit audio, it is 192 dB. In the real world, the actual dynamic range is lower because of limitations in electronic hardware: around 90 dB for 16-bit audio and 115 dB for both 24-bit and 32-bit audio.

The value of a wide dynamic range is not that you can shock your listeners with sudden extreme volume changes but in having a very high signal-to-noise ratio, which is also called "having a low noise floor." The more signal and less noise, the better.

As far as adjusting the dynamic range with the listener in mind, a range of 50 dB to 60 dB in a recording is the maximum most listeners will tolerate, and that is under ideal conditions with a good system in a quiet environment. A picky audiophile with good equipment and a quiet listening space will enjoy a symphony that uses every bit of a 60 dB dynamic range. A live symphony concert might encompass an 80 dB range.

Someone listening to music in a noisier environment or on lower-quality audio gear might be more comfortable with a dynamic range of 20 dB or even narrower. Audacity lets you tailor your recordings to any dynamic range you want. (See Chapters 6, 8, and 11 to learn more about dynamic range compression.)

There is a famous theorem in the audio world called the Nyquist-Shannon theorem. It is long and detailed—the part that matters here states that a perfect digital representation of an analog audio signal is possible when the sampling rate is at least twice as high as the highest frequency in the signal. The best human hearing can hear up to 20 kHz to 24 kHz, so a sampling rate of 40 kHz to 48 kHz can (theoretically) reproduce the entire range of human hearing.

Audacity's default recording bit depth is 32-bit float. Many digital audio workstations, including Audacity, operate at 32-bit float internally. It is important to understand that this is 32-bit *float*, not 32-bit integer. In contrast, the 16- and 24-bit depths represent integer values. As usual, the math is complex, and audio geeks will bore you to tears telling you about it if you let them, so here is the oversimplified short story: Integers are whole numbers, and *float* means floating decimal point. This 32-bit float number is a 24-bit mantissa plus an 8-bit exponent. This is significant in terms of audio production—it gives you a dynamic range of about 1500 dB, which means virtually no noise or clipping, and you get a smoother, more accurate response curve across the whole range of your analog-to-digital conversion. (In comparison, the dynamic range of 32-bit integer is 196 dB.)

Recording and editing at 32-bit float is beneficial even with a 16-bit recording interface. If you work to a peak of -24 dB, which is very low and safe to avoid clipping, your available dynamic range will still exceed what any hardware supports, and you'll have plenty of extra bits to throw away without harming quality. That means you'll be able to edit and manipulate your audio files as much as you want and still be able to make high-quality 16-bit and 24-bit exports. The more processing you apply to your recordings, the more you want all that extra headroom.

You will always export to a lower bit depth because there is no such thing as a 32-bit float playback device. Playable formats must be integer data, so your exports will always be to 8-bit, 16-bit, or 24-bit integer. (The word *linear* is often used instead of integer; they're referring to the same thing.)

In practice, many factors will affect the bit depth and sampling rate that you choose: How good is your hearing, how good is your gear, and what are the final format and playback medium going to be? How good are your recording techniques? What sort of recordings are you making—nuanced acoustic instruments and vocals or head-banging rock? Is your computer powerful enough to process larger audio files, and do you have enough storage for them?

You can get some good bargains on 16/44.1 recorders and ADCs because of the "bigger is better" mentality. On the other hand, it doesn't hurt to have the extra bandwidth—you can always reduce quality and size, but (despite what they show you on TV crime shows) you can't recover what wasn't available in the first place. When you're experimenting, my recommendation is to try increasing the bit depth before increasing the sampling rate. If your hearing and audio gear are good, you should be able to hear the difference between 16-bit and 24-bit recordings, though I suspect it will take a side-by-side comparison to make the differences apparent. I record and save my studio masters at 32-bit float/48 kHz WAV and export mainly to CD-quality 16/44.1. Going to higher sampling rates makes no difference that I can hear, and it eats up hard drive space.

Audacity supports recording at 16-bit integer, 24-bit integer, and 32-bit float. For comparison, professionals record and edit at 24-bit, 32-bit, and even 64-bit depths.

NOTE *As we discussed earlier, exporting to 32-bit float WAV is a good option to consider for creating and archiving studio master files. Then you can import your 32-bit float WAV back into Audacity (or any other audio editor that uses 32-bit float), process it, and export to 16- or 24-bit without loss of quality.*

Bitrate, Bit Depth, and File Size

Bit depth is a term with a specific meaning, which we just learned. Another common term is *bitrate*. These two terms mean different things and are often confused with each other. Bitrate is the amount of data per second needed to transmit an audio file and is most commonly expressed as Kbps or Mbps; 16/44.1 stereo is roughly 1.4Mbps, and 24/96 is about 4.6Mbps. You can easily figure this out for yourself:

> bit depth × sampling rate × channels = bitrate (bit/sec)
> 16 × 44,100 × 2 = 1,411,200 bits/sec
> 24 × 96,000 × 2 = 4,608,000 bits/sec

MP3s (and other lossy formats) are described in terms of bitrates rather than bit depth/sampling rates. The MPEG-1 Layer 3 standard specifies a range of bitrates from 32Kbps to 320Kbps. Pretty lo-fi, 128Kbps is a common MP3 bitrate left over from the early days of slower Internet download speeds and players with small storage capacities. Now 192Kbps is pretty common, and a person with good hearing and a decent MP3 player will hear the difference.

Total file size is an important figure to ace recording geeks. Digital audio files are large, and you can eat up a large hard drive in no time during a busy recording session with a lot of takes.

You can calculate the approximate file size with this equation:

bit depth × sampling rate × channels × (60 seconds) / 8 = file size in bytes for a 1-minute recording

One stereo minute at 24/48 kHz is about 17.3MB:

$24 \times 48{,}000 \times 2 \times 60 / 8 = 17{,}280{,}000$ bytes

You must divide by 8 to get bytes because there are 8 bits per byte.

Now What?

At this point, you should have a good grasp of the basics of Audacity. Audacity is easy to learn; the hard part is learning audio concepts and terminology. I'll be talking about those a lot in the rest of this book, translating them into practical terms and showing you how to implement them in Audacity.

2

BUILDING A GOOD DIGITAL SOUND STUDIO ON THE CHEAP

There is a saying in the photography world: The person behind the camera matters more than the camera. The same applies to making great audio recordings—the person behind the gear matters more than the gear. This doesn't mean that the gear doesn't matter, because it does. But merely owning the most expensive, elite audio equipment won't turn you into Tom Dowd or Rick Rubin or Quincy Jones or George Martin or whoever your favorite legendary music producer is. It won't turn average musicians into stars.

When you're shopping for audio gear and getting drawn into the "higher specs and price tags is better!" zone, take a step back and reboot your mind. Take a deep breath, slow down, and concentrate on learning how to get the best out of lower-end equipment. Because today's average digital audio gear is better than the top-of-the-line analog studio gear of yesteryear, with more accuracy, fidelity, wider dynamic range, and less noise, it's a whole lot easier to record, mix, edit, and apply special effects. You won't have to fuss so much with learning how to use your equipment, and you can concentrate more on learning how to make good recordings with artistic and technical fidelity. Then if you find yourself yearning for a better preamp, better microphones, better speakers, or what-have-you, you'll have good reasons, and you'll know and appreciate better quality when you find it.

In this chapter we're going to turn a PC into a digital audio workstation, and we won't break the bank to do it. We'll also look at portable digital recorders, which cram amazing fidelity and storage capacity into tiny devices and are endlessly useful in all kinds of circumstances.

Getting Sound In and Out of the Computer

One of the biggest hurdles with PC-based audio production is figuring out audio gear. There is a huge and bewildering selection of audio components with every imaginable combination of features and price tags. In this chapter I'll discuss the basic elements of a small recording studio. Appendix A goes into more detail on hardware, with examples of different models and brands in different price ranges.

There are several ways to interface audio gear with a computer: a PCI or PCI-E sound card for a desktop computer; a Cardbus or ExpressCard sound card for laptops; USB 1.1, USB 2.0, or FireWire audio interface for any computer. You will need one of these. Which one? For one- or two-track recording, any of them will do. For heavy-duty multitrack recording, USB 1.1 is not a candidate. But it's great for one- and two-track recording, and you'll have a lot of excellent, moderately priced devices to choose from. For serious multitrack recording, you need the faster protocols, especially if you're going to record at high bit depths and sampling rates, so we'll look at their strengths and weaknesses.

The most essential component in digital audio production is the analog-to-digital/digital-to-analog converter. The ADC/DAC is how you get analog audio in and out of your computer. It takes the analog signal from a microphone or instrument and converts it to a digital signal. Then it converts a digital signal to analog for playback. ADC/DACs come in a multitude of forms: The most low-end, cheapskate onboard sound chip has one, and of course so do higher-end audio interfaces. There are all kinds of USB and FireWire recording interfaces that connect microphones and instruments to your computer, and with them you don't need to bother with an internal sound card at all. There are also slick little portable ADC/DACs for connecting turntables, cassette recorders, and stereo hi-fi amplifiers to a computer, as well as USB microphones and turntables with built-in USB ADC/DACs. And for the studio geek with a healthy budget, there are the more expensive rack-mount ADC/DACs.

An Example Studio

Let's start off with a photo of a basic, moderate-quality computer recording studio, which just happens to be mine all mine. Figure 2-1 shows the whole works: The computer is underneath the table. Starting from the left are various headphones; then on the desk is an external USB CD/DVD writer, a four-port powered USB hub, an LCD monitor, a color printer, the all-important hot beverage mug, a turntable, an excellent old Pioneer stereo hi-fi amplifier, a Behringer powered mixer, and a MobilePre USB preamp/analog-to-digital converter. In front are two dynamic microphones. Not shown are a pair of nice JBL speakers mounted up on the wall. You can cram a lot of functionality into a small space.

Figure 2-1: My own little recording empire (the mics don't really sit right there in front of the amp and mixer; that's a pose just for the photo op)

Also not shown is a nice Focusrite Saffire Pro 26 I/O FireWire multi-channel recording interface. Focusrite makes great audio hardware and supports Linux, Mac, and Windows. We'll see more of the Saffire in Chapter 9.

This is how they all fit together:

- Recording: microphones and instruments > Behringer mixer > MobilePre > computer
- Playback: computer > MobilePre > Pioneer stereo amp > speakers

For recording, the Behringer mixer has a pair of RCA recording outputs. These send a stereo signal via an RCA-pair-to-two-1/4″ mono TRS adapter to the two 1/4″ TRS jacks on the MobilePre. The MobilePre connects with a USB cable to the computer. Everything plugged into the Behringer is then captured in Audacity.

NOTE   *The terminology for connectors is a bit mixed up, so I am going to refer to the connectors on cables as* plugs *and the sockets on mixers, preamps, amps, and so forth that they plug into as* jacks. *I will also bow to convention and refer to* male *and* female *connectors even though that has always sounded weird to me.* Male *and* female *at least have the virtue of having precise meanings, unlike a lot of audio terminology.*

For playback, the MobilePre has a 1/8″ stereo output. This connects with a stereo-mini-plug-to-RCA-pair adapter to the Aux input on the Pioneer amp. The MobilePre also has a pair of 1/4″ TRS outputs, so for these I would need 1/4″ TRS-to-RCA adapters. Figure 2-2 shows the plug-ins on the back of the amp. A nice amp like this plus a good ADC/DAC makes a great hub for a conversion studio, because anything that connects to the amp can be recorded on your computer.

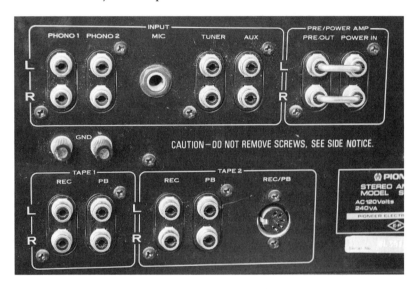

Figure 2-2: This is the back of a treasured old but versatile Pioneer stereo amplifier. It can connect two turntables (it even has proper ground connectors for turntables), two tape decks, a microphone, a tuner, another amp, a preamp, and an Aux connector for a CD player or other input devices.

I could also cut out the Behringer entirely, for example for interviews and podcasts, and use only the MobilePre in combination with any computer.

When I'm copying vinyl LPs to CD, it goes like this:

- Recording: turntable > Pioneer amp > MobilePre > computer
- Playback: computer > MobilePre > Pioneer amp > speakers

The turntable plugs into the phono ports on the amp. The amp connects to the MobilePre from a pair of recording outputs. I could use an RCA-pair-to-two-1/4″ TRS adapter or an RCA-pair-to-stereo-mini-plug, because the MobilePre is flexible when it comes to making connections.

You can digitize any legacy media with this kind of setup, because whatever connects to your hi-fi amp or receiver can be copied into your computer.

Both recording and playback are routed through the MobilePre, so I get to hear the playback on good speakers instead of lo-fi computer speakers. The MobilePre has a headphone port for zero-latency monitoring during recording, which is a nice thing to have. The Behringer mixer (Europower 1280S) isn't really intended to be a studio mixer; it's for powering live shows, which it does most ably, because it is an integrated mixer and 1200-watt amplifier. When I'm recording a live show, I hook up to it with a laptop and the MobilePre. I also have a Zoom H2 portable digital recorder, which I can use in place of the laptop plus MobilePre. The best-quality recordings at live shows come from plugging directly into the mixer board.

NOTE   *The local old-time country band that I like to listen to and record has a rather eccentric sound system. They have a nice PA system, but instead of plugging everyone into the mixer board, only the singers' mics are connected to the mixer. All of the musicians have to bring their own instrument amplifiers. This makes for a cluttered stage, and recording is a nightmare—plugging a recorder into the mixer means the only instruments it hears are whatever the mics pick up. The Zoom H2 has a neat little adapter to mount it on a mic stand so I can position it anywhere, but it's not as good as a proper setup with everything routed through the sound board.*

Let's take a closer look at the MobilePre because it is representative of a lot of USB recording interfaces. The MobilePre supplies 48v phantom power for condenser mics and has XLR and TRS jacks, a 1/8″ stereo input, two 1/4″ mono outputs, and a 1/8″ zero-latency headphone port for monitoring. Both dynamic and condenser mics can plug into the XLR jacks, as long as they have XLR connectors. You could also use an XLR-to-TRS adapter to plug a dynamic mic into one of the 1/4″ inputs. Its built-in ADC supports sampling rates from 8 to 48 kHz at 16 bits, and it draws its power from the USB bus of your computer, so it doesn't need its own power cord. It has physical gain control knobs and a volume control knob for headphones, so you don't need to dink around with software controls. (I'd rather twist a knob than fumble around some weirdo software interface any day.) You should be able to find one for under $150. At 16-bit/48 MHz maximum recording quality, it's becoming obsolete because comparable devices support 24-bit recording. Still, it's a great little device, and because it is USB 1.1 class-compliant, it runs on any computer without special drivers.

Figures 2-3 and 2-4 show the front and back of the MobilePre.

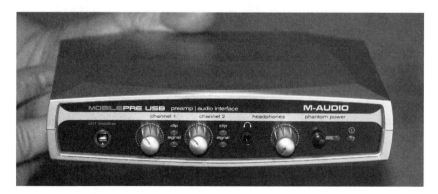

Figure 2-3: M-Audio MobilePre, front. From left to right: Channel 1 1/4″ mono TRS jack, Ch. 1 and 2 gain controls, clip LEDs, headphone port, headphone volume knob, phantom power switch, phantom power LED, and power LED

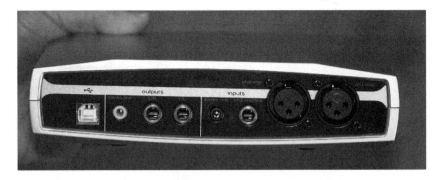

Figure 2-4: M-Audio MobilePre, backside. From left to right: USB jack, stereo line out, 1/4" mono TRS right and left outputs, stereo mic in, Ch. 2 1/4" mono TRS input, Ch. 2 XLR mic jack, Ch. 1 XLR mic jack

Sorting Out Connectors

Where do the terms TRS and XLR come from? TRS is *tip-ring-sleeve*, which is the physical description of a TRS plug. Figure 2-5 is a labeled photo of a stereo and a mono TRS jack.

The origins of XLR are a little more complicated. Cannon Electric was the original manufacturer of the XLR connector, and some old-timers still call it a *cannon plug*. It started out as the "Cannon X" series of connectors. Then later versions added a latch, so there is the *L*, and then the contacts were encased in rubber, for the *R*. Figure 2-6 shows a pair of three-pin XLR plugs.

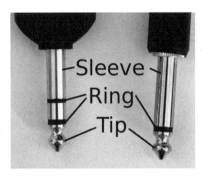

Figure 2-6: Here is a three-pin male XLR plug and a three-pin female XLR plug.

Figure 2-5: One stereo 1/4" TRS plug (left) and one mono (right).

Figure 2-7 shows a collection of plugs and adapters. You can find adapters to make anything fit anything. However, you must be careful—just because something fits doesn't mean it belongs there, so read your product manuals. Stereo TRS plugs have two black bands near the tip, and mono TRS plugs have one.

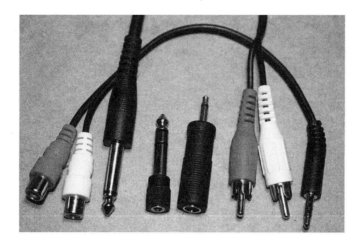

Figure 2-7: Two stereo RCA to 1/8" TRS plug, 1/4" mono TRS to two stereo RCA, 1/8" to 1/4" stereo TRS adapter, 1/4" to 1/8" mono TRS adapter

Figure 2-8 shows the three-pin male XLR connector on a Behringer dynamic mic.

Figure 2-8: Behringer dynamic mic showing off its three-pin male XLR connector

Multichannel Recording, PCI, USB, FireWire

Multichannel recording is done in several different ways. One way is to use a simple two-track recording interface like the MobilePre. It supports up to six inputs at once and routes them into two channels. There are no mixer controls, so this requires some finicking during recording to get a decent balance. A better way to do multichannel recording with a two-channel interface like the Pre is to record two tracks at a time, giving each instrument or performer its own individual track, rather than trying to cram them all through the Pre at once. Then Audacity is your mixer, and you have individual control of each track. Another option for two-channel recording is a good-quality two-channel PCI sound card like the Emu 1616M PCI, which you can find used for under $200. It comes with a breakout box that supports all kinds of plug-ins, 24-bit/192 kHz recording, phantom power, and preamps.

My Behringer 1280S gets pressed into service when I have a larger group over for recording. Any analog mixer will work as long you have an ADC/DAC to plug it into. My setup is a bit of a hack job since the Behringer is not really a studio mixer, but it works and sounds good, and it is an example of how a little ingenuity goes far in the wild world of audio. Like many mixers, the Behringer outputs to two-channel stereo, so I need to get the mix right during recording—I'll have only two channels to work with in Audacity. I could also record one or two tracks at a time with the Behringer and then knit them together in Audacity; there is no rule that says you have to plug in everything at one time. (Though corralling and organizing musicians can be a bit of a cat-herding experience, and sometimes you have to take what you can get.)

Audacity from version 1.3.8 supports recording as many tracks at once as your recording interface supports. Older versions max out at 16. This is where FireWire and the higher-end PCI sound cards shine, because they allow recording many tracks at once. The Focusrite Saffire Pro 40 is an example of a good value in a FireWire recording interface at about $500; this gives you 8 mic preamps, 20 total inputs and 20 outputs, 24/96 recording, blinky LEDs, and phantom power on every mic channel. The M-Audio Delta 1010 is a popular higher-end multichannel PCI sound card that connects to a rack-mount breakout box. It goes for about $600.

A cool new family of devices is USB and FireWire mixers. These give you everything in one device—preamps, phantom power, mixer board, ADC/DAC, and direct plug-in to your computer. There are a lot of nice choices in the $300 to $1,000 range. Behringer's line of Xenyx USB mixers costs between $150 to $600. They use class-compliant USB 1.1, so they plug into any computer with no special drivers needed. The M-Audio NRV10 is a nice little FireWire mixer/preamp that costs about $700.

How to choose which of these to use? USB and FireWire are portable and easy to hook up. PCI Express is the fastest. One lane of PCI-E moves about 250MBps both ways at the same time. That's 250 megabytes, not megabits. Plain old PCI maxes out at 133MBps. Also, unlike PCI-E, PCI uses a shared bus, so more PCI devices means more bandwidth contention. Every PCI-E device has its own dedicated data pipeline, so PCI-E devices don't have to share bandwidth. USB 1.1 is rated at 12Mbps (megabits per second), and USB 2.0 is rated at about 480Mbps, but both figures are highly theoretical, and in real life you're likely to get half that. FireWire is rated at 400Mbps. However, FireWire gives you higher sustained throughput and better performance than USB, a difference that is discussed in more detail in the following section.

A common problem with internal sound cards is picking up noise and electrical interference from hard drives, power supplies, and fans inside your computer case. This usually isn't a problem with the better sound cards like Emu, M-Audio, and RME Hammerfall, but it tends to be more of an issue with consumer-level and gamer sound cards and low-budget onboard sound. If you are getting some noise, the first thing to check is all your connections— make sure everything is hooked up correctly and anything that needs to be grounded is grounded. Sometimes moving a PCI card to a different slot makes a difference. Check your motherboard manual to see if you have shared PCI slots; you don't want to use a shared slot if the other slot is populated.

USB or FireWire?

If you like the convenience of a USB audio interface, you might also consider FireWire devices. How do you choose between FireWire or USB? USB devices usually cost less than FireWire, but the trade-off is you may get poorer performance because of the differences in the two protocols.

All FireWire interfaces have special controller chips, so they do not add any extra load to your computer's CPU. FireWire is a peer protocol, which means FireWire devices negotiate bus conflicts without using host CPU cycles. FireWire gives you two operating modes to choose from: asynchronous or isynchronous. Isynchronous mode means a device can reserve a certain portion of bandwidth all for itself that no other devices can use. So there are no collisions, which translates into high sustained throughput.

If your PC doesn't have a FireWire interface, it's easy to add one. PCI FireWire interfaces cost about $50, and many laptops include a FireWire port. When you're shopping for FireWire audio interfaces, be sure to check for hardware compatibility. As one example, the Presonus FP10 has known conflicts with certain video chipsets, and it has a limited set of FireWire interfaces that it is known to work well with.

The Future of FireWire

"FireWire is doomed!" is a common cry of late. That may be true, though it is going to be with us for some years yet. USB 2.0 supposedly offers the potential to equal FireWire performance, and USB 3.0 supposedly will eclipse it. Audio hardware manufacturers have been slow to release USB 2.0 recording interfaces, though there are now a respectable number of them. A lot of them rely on custom drivers that are not USB 2.0 compliant, so shop carefully lest you buy one that won't run on your computer. USB 3.0 is still a work in progress, and audio hardware manufacturers are not known for moving quickly. If you like FireWire recording devices, by all means buy and use them, and if FireWire ever does become obsolete, you can still use your gear because nobody is going to come and take it away from you.

USB operates only in asynchronous mode. *Asynchronous* means that any device on the same bus can send data whenever it wants to, so sometimes there are collisions, which cause latency. USB is host-dependent and puts a load on the CPU, which can also cause latency. Latency is the enemy of quality audio.

You'll see a lot of USB audio devices that still use USB 1.1. USB 1.1 has two speeds: 1.5Mbps and 12Mbps. The latter is also called *full-speed*. It's unlikely that a USB recording interface will be geared down to 1.5Mbps. The number of channels you can record at once depends on the quality level you want to record at. CD quality, two channels at 16/44.1, has a bitrate of 1,411,200Mbps. Two channels at 24/96 equals a bitrate of 4,608,000Mbps, so it seems you could record four 24/96 channels at once. However, that 12Mbps maximum is theoretical, and your real-world throughput will be half that or less. Most likely you'll be limited to two-channel 24/96 recording at best. Four channels at 16/44.1 or 24/48 are possible if you are careful and have a good, fast multicore PC and have it tuned for audio production. (See "Bitrate, Bit Depth, and File Size" on page 29 to learn about different bitrates.)

USB 2.0 audio devices require careful shopping, because many of them are not USB class-compliant and instead supply their own special drivers. Even Windows users have to do their homework because vendors are slow to release drivers for new Windows releases. Mac support is decent overall, and Linux, Unix, and users on other platforms are at the back of the bus as usual. Some multitrack USB 2.0 devices are getting good reviews. For example, the M-Audio Fast Track Ultra 8R (eight in, eight out) gets high marks and works on Mac, Linux, and Windows.

Microphones

The microphones in Figure 2-9 are middle-of-the-road dynamic mics that cost less than $100 each. The microphone is very important—you won't get good recordings from low-quality microphones. There are two common types of microphones: condenser and dynamic. *Condenser* mics have a wider frequency response, are more sensitive, produce louder output, and have a faster transient response. *Transient response* is any abrupt change, such as a rim shot, a hard-strummed guitar, or a singer hitting some hard consonants (and probably spraying a bit of spit).

Figure 2-9: Audio-Technica stereo condenser mic, Behringer dynamic mic, and wind sock

Condenser mics require power. This is called *phantom power* when it is delivered through the microphone cable, because there isn't a separate power cable. They are more fragile than dynamic mics. Condenser mics live mostly in studios. They are also used onstage in combination with dynamic mics on drum kits; the condenser mics hang overhead to capture cymbals and transients, and dynamic mics are placed next to the drums. Figure 2-9 shows an Audio-Technica stereo condenser mic, a Behringer dynamic mic, and a wind sock. (Experienced singers know to avoid brightly colored wind socks because they look like clown noses.)

Condenser microphones that require phantom power typically use XLR connectors. Dynamic mics use both XLR connectors and TRS plugs. Dynamic mics do not require phantom power, so make sure that the phantom power is turned off before you plug one in to a phantom-powered XLR jack. It shouldn't damage the mic, but it will change how it sounds. It's common to see audio gear with both types of microphone connectors, and newer devices have combination jacks that accept both.

The little Audio-Technica Pro 24 stereo condenser mic in Figure 2-9 is a different kind of condenser mic. It is self-powered by a little mercury battery, it has a built-in cable, and it plugs into any 1/8″ TRS stereo microphone jack, like on laptops, digital recorders, and camcorders.

There are two types of condenser mics: large diaphragm (LDM) and small diaphragm (SDM). Both record sounds evenly and accurately across their entire range, though LDMs have a reputation for creating a "warmer" sound. A large diaphragm mic has a better low-frequency range than a small diaphragm, but a small diaphragm mic of the same type has a better high-frequency response. Low tones are characterized as warmer, and high tones are characterized as cooler and brighter. You're going to hear all kinds of characterizations for sound quality: warm, cold, brittle, soft, hard, bright, dull, and on and on. Trust your own perceptions, and don't worry about what other people tell you you should like.

Dynamic mics have a narrower frequency response and are less accurate than condenser mics. They are rugged, are moisture-resistant, and don't need a power supply, so dynamic mics go on stage and in the field. Dynamic mics generally cover the human vocal range plus a little bit, so this makes them good for singers.

Another type of microphone is worth consideration, and that is the ribbon mic, which is a type of dynamic mic. The guts of ribbon mic are a metal ribbon suspended in a magnetic field. These are expensive but are prized for their clarity, spatial depth, and realism. They revolutionized the audio industries back in the 1930s; ribbon microphones set new standards for realism and accuracy that the condenser mics of the day could not match. Ribbon mics fell out of favor somewhat as condenser and dynamic mics improved. They were expensive, the metal ribbon was fragile, and their output was so low they needed more amplification than other types of microphones. Modern ribbon mics are more affordable and durable and produce louder output than their ancestors, so they're definitely worth trying (Figure 2-10).

Ribbon mics are natively bidirectional, which means they are sensitive to sounds from both the front and the rear of the mic in a figure-eight

Figure 2-10: A modern AEA R84 ribbon mic

pattern. They are effective at blocking sound from the sides. The figure-eight pattern is on the horizontal axis, so you can tip them sideways to get a different effect. A pair of matched ribbon mics placed next to each other at a 90-degree angle is called a *Blumlein pair*, or crossed figure eight. This creates a realistic stereo image. If you don't want to capture sounds from one side, for example the audience side, you'll have to block it somehow or find a ribbon mic with the capture pattern that you want.

Polar Patterns

Important considerations for microphones are *polar patterns*. Polar pattern describes a mic's area of sensitivity, as Figure 2-11 shows. These two-dimensional diagrams don't show that polar patterns are three-dimensional, so keep in mind that they're not flat and horizontal; they encompass areas with height and depth.

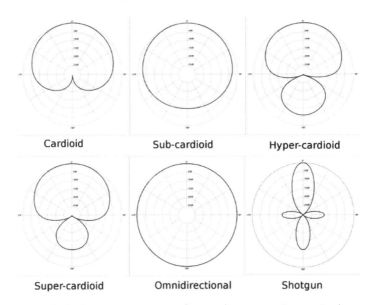

Figure 2-11: Some common microphone polar patterns (Image Credit: Created by Wikipedia user Galak76, released under the GFDL.)

These are the common polar patterns:

Cardioid   Picks up sound from the front and rejects sounds from the rear. Sub-cardioid is rather like omnidirectional, with a smaller range to the rear. Hyper-cardioid and super-cardioid have a narrower range in front, plus small lobes of rear sensitivity. This is common for stage mics and especially for vocalists. Different cardioid mics have different levels of sensitivity. Some have a wide pickup range, so they are good for a performer who moves around a lot, and some have a small area of sensitivity, so they are better at not picking up background noises.

Omnidirectional   Picks up sound equally from all directions in a spherical area. Try arranging your band in a circle with an omnidirectional mic in the middle to get a spacious, natural sound.

Shotgun   The most highly directional of all with a long, narrow front and smaller rear pickup range. These are commonly used with movie cameras of all kinds, from film to digital, professional and consumer, and are favorites of wildlife photographers.

Bidirectional   Picks up sound equally well from front and back; does not pick up sounds from the side. (Not pictured in Figure 2-11.)

Half-omnidirectional, or hemispherical   Picks up about a 180-degree hemispherical area. You can get some nice live recordings with one of these because it has a wide pickup area to the front and does not pick up noises from behind. (Not pictured in Figure 2-11.)

You might be thinking, why not just use shotgun or cardioid mics for everything so you zero in on just what you want to record? Do whatever you want; let your own ears and taste be your guide and select your mics to suit the occasion. Different brands and models of mics have different levels and types of sensitivity. For example, some are forgiving of a singer who moves around a lot, while others do a good capture only up close. Wireless headsets are wonderful for the energetic performer, and wireless mics mean no tripping over cables. Some mics emphasize bass frequencies more as you move closer, like radio DJs that boom forth with exaggerated bass. This is called the *proximity effect*.

The Cowboy Junkies *Trinity Session* album was recorded using a single *ambisonic* microphone that reportedly cost about $9,000. Ambisonics refers to surround-sound recording techniques and equipment that are supposed to produce a realistic, spatially natural sound. An ambisonic mic has multiple capsules to capture sound from different directions, anywhere from four to dozens. It's an interesting niche in audio production; look up *ambisonic* and *SoundField mics* if you are interested in learning more.

Which Microphones for Which Occasions?

There are different microphones for all occasions, such as voice, guitar, drum, and so on. Vocalists can be especially picky, because different mics color their voices differently. You'll find plenty of passionate opinions on this subject. Keep in mind that there are a multitude of factors that affect how good a recording sounds to you: how it's edited, the type of equipment you're listening to, your listening location (home, friend's house, performance hall, outside, vehicle), and your mood and expectations. We've grown up with decades of recorded audio of all types: acetate, vinyl, different types of tape, and now digital. So what sounds "right" is heavily flavored by what we're used to hearing. Some folks still hanker for the sound of tinny '60s AM radio or boomy jukeboxes or quadrophonic eight-tracks. Some believe that vinyl sounds "warmer" than digital and that tube amps sound warmer than solid-state.

I've always wanted to do some blind tests just to see whether the picky audiophiles in my life can really hear a difference. Number one on my blind testing wish list is tube amp versus solid-state, and cold tube amp versus one that has had a 24-hour warm-up, because some of the aforementioned picky audiophiles insist that tube amps need a long warm-up period or they sound "cold."

There are real differences between tube and solid-state. Tube amplifier systems drive a transformer, which in turn drives the speakers. The transformer suppresses a lot of transients like spikes, pops, and clicks, resulting in a cleaner sound. A cold preamp has more noise than a hot preamp. Tubes also have a singular noise source, whereas semiconductor devices have multiple noise sources, increasing the amount of noise you might hear. Still, on good-quality gear it's going to take some mighty fine hearing to detect the difference.

It is nearly impossible to define a "pure" experience, because even live performances are colored by their environments and equipment, ambience, and the way our brains process data. It always surprises me how much worse my favorite local band sounds on the recordings I make of its performances. During the shows, I'm having a great time and thinking they sound wonderful. Then later when I hear the playback, I hear all kinds of flaws: off tempo, out of key, lackluster, you name it. Maybe I'm too picky and too attuned to listening for mistakes on recordings; maybe during the live shows my brain is too busy having fun to notice flaws. Maybe I make lousy recordings.

The moral is sound quality depends on your own ears and experience—what sounds good and right to you is what matters. You can try for the most realistic fidelity or try for the best artistic and creative fidelity. It's all subjective.

Microphone Cables

There are many brands of microphone cables, and you can waste a lot of money on a snooty brand name. Don't spend a mint; there are many reasonably priced, good-quality choices. You may run into some confusion over *balanced* and *unbalanced* cables. In the context of connecting microphones, an unbalanced cable is a coaxial cable that terminates in a tip-sleeve (TS) connector. It has a single conductor wire surrounded by a combination shield and ground. These are effective at blocking external interference but are vulnerable to induced hum and noise and tend to be noisier than balanced cables. A balanced cable terminates in either a three-pin XLR connector or a TRS connector. It has two internal wires, one hot and one cold, surrounded by a shield that is not part of the signal path, so it supplies a cleaner signal. Balanced cables can run for much longer distances than unbalanced cables without picking up excessive noise.

Keep in mind that it is the signal that is balanced or unbalanced, and using a balanced cable will not make an unbalanced signal balanced. However, a TS cable will convert a balanced signal to unbalanced. You need to match your cables to your mics and your preamp, amp, mixer, or whatever you might be plugging into. Condenser mics that depend on phantom power mostly likely use three-pin XLR balanced cables, and dynamic mics use balanced cables with both XLR and TRS connectors. A balanced signal doesn't care what carries it, so you can use XLR-to-TRS adapters as needed, provided that whatever you're plugging into sends the correct signal.

These days this shouldn't be something that you have to spend a lot of time figuring out, since most contemporary audio gear supports balanced mic connections.

Microphone cables are either stiff or flexible, depending on where they're going to be used. Flexible cables are for live performances, and stiff cables usually reside in studios where they are not moved very often.

Don't cross electric lines with any of your audio cables if you can help it, because you may pick up interference. If you have to, cross them at right angles to reduce the overlap.

Smart Miking

Placing your microphones for best results is an art in itself, and the only way to get good at it is to practice a lot. You want to be as close as possible but not so close that you pick up electronic interference or unwanted sounds such as lip smacks and spit from vocalists. Pop filters are helpful for vocalists, and windscreens are essential for outdoor recording.

The "3-to-1 rule" is a simple guide for microphone placement for live performances or in the studio when you have several mics and performers set up at the same time in the same room. When microphones are placed too close together, you may get squeals, dips and peaks, or other forms of unpleasant interference. The 3-to-1 rule means the distance between adjacent mics should be approximately three times the distance between the mic and the sound source. If there are multiple amps present, as with my fave local band where every performer lugs their own amp onstage, these will cause problems too. Sometimes simply turning an amp to face in a different direction will cure feedback problems.

Microphone stands are essential—don't depend on hand-holding. Goosenecks take up less space and are fast to adjust, but over time they wear out. Boom stands last forever but take up more space. Some folks prefer tripod feet, which I always trip over, so I prefer weighted bases. Shock mounts and cages are great for isolating your mics from vibrations and don't cost very much.

Microphone Preamp

Microphone preamps are the second most important devices in your audio chain, after ADC/DACs. As I've already talked about in this chapter, I have an M-Audio MobilePre and a Focusrite Saffire Pro 26. With these I don't need an internal computer sound card or separate preamp, because they have their own built-in microphone preamps. However, even if you prefer to use an internal sound card or have good external recording interfaces, you may still want to use a separate microphone preamp. Let's talk about why the preamp is so important.

A preamp—short for *preamplifier*—amplifies a low-level signal to *line level*. The output from a microphone, a turntable, and many instrument pickups is lower than line level. Line level is a standard analog audio signal voltage that is designed for connecting different audio components. What is this voltage? Well, that's a good question because even though it is billed as a standard voltage, it varies depending on the manufacturer. Most are around 1 to 2 volts. A preamp has a significant effect on audio quality: A low-quality preamp will introduce noise and distortion. A good preamp amplifies the signal cleanly, without introducing defects or color.

NOTE   *Audio terminology gets bent in all kinds of ways—many of the preamps you see for home hi-fi systems are not like microphone preamps because they don't do any amplification but are just switching units where you plug everything in.*

Preamps range from bare-bones models that supply only *gain* (amplification) and phantom power to gaudy delights larded up with all kinds of special effects, dials, and blinky lights. A lot of audio devices come with gobs of special effects because it costs practically nothing to add them, and they make you feel like you're getting something special. If you like lots of special effects, this is a nice bonus; just don't let it distract you from a device's real quality. At the least it is nice to have some physical knobs. Debates over which preamps are best almost take on a religious quality. Professionals might spend thousands of dollars on a single preamp. You're welcome to do this, but in my opinion you're better off starting out with inexpensive gear and investing in perfecting your recording techniques. Then when you're ready to move up to better gear, you'll appreciate the difference and know how to get the most out of it.

Speakers and Headphones

Having both speakers and headphones in your audio chain lets you hear your recordings in different ways. Studio monitor speakers are supposedly dead-flat and accurate and don't add any color of their own. They also tend to be expensive. My own studio speakers are a set of nice JBL three-way speakers. They're not real studio monitors, just nice speakers that I like. Headphones are essential—you need these for monitoring your recordings. Audio interfaces that include built-in zero-latency headphone ports are perfect for monitoring. I seem to collect headphones: I have a nice Plantronics USB headset, which is great for recording podcasts; a set of Sennheiser headphones with an ordinary 1/4″ TRS plug; and wireless Audio-Technica headphones. My studio speakers are powered by a nice old Pioneer SA 7500 stereo amplifier. I've had it repaired twice, and I'm going to keep it going as long as I can. It's rated at 45 watts per channel, which doesn't sound like much, but it powers those watts with some serious amperage. Amps are the real measure of power in an amplifier; that is what makes the difference between a wimpy amp and a good strong clean amp. Wattage doesn't mean all that much—that's just the number salespeople like to focus on.

None of this is super-duper hi-fi, at least not according to fussy audiophile standards, but they're all good components, and they please me.

Your Computer Must Have Muscle and Vast Drawers

Your computer should be a good modern machine with a high-powered CPU and a lot of RAM. My studio PC has an AMD Phenom triple-core CPU with 4GB RAM. Multicore CPUs make a big difference. A single-core CPU should perform fine for two-track recording and simpler recordings like podcasts and interviews. For example, I have an old ThinkPad with an 800 MHz CPU and 256MB RAM running Linux that performs nicely as a field recorder for interviews. For more than two tracks, multicore is the way to go. Don't worry about AMD versus Intel; they're both fine, so use whichever you like best.

You need as much storage as you can afford. CD-quality audio (44.1 kHz, 16-bit WAV) uses around 5MB per track per minute. Don't forget to add up all the tracks you are using and all the retakes. You can buy terabyte hard drives, and by the time you read this, they'll probably be even larger. Another option is to combine the capacity of several hard drives in a RAID (redundant array of inexpensive disks) array. The two RAID levels that are useful for audio production are RAID 0 and RAID 10. RAID 0, also called *striping*, makes two hard disks look like one, so two 500GB drives appear as a single terabyte drive. RAID 0 is very fast but has the same weakness as a single drive—if one drive in the array fails, you'll probably lose all of your data.

RAID 10 (using a good-quality hardware controller) is *mirroring* plus striping, so you get speed and redundancy. Use a good-quality hardware controller; you don't want some cheapie that dumps more load on your CPU but instead one that handles the load itself. It's more expensive of disks than the popular RAID 5, but it's more reliable and a lot faster—you get faster reads and writes and much faster recovery from a failed drive. I wouldn't use RAID 5 or 6 arrays for audio recording; in fact, I don't use them at all anymore because they're too fragile, they're too slow for writes, and they propagate parity errors too readily.

I wouldn't worry about building some super-duper RAID array for recording and editing with Audacity, unless you find yourself burning through terabyte hard drives all the time. I use a single large hard drive on my studio PC and am ruthless with housekeeping and getting rid of unneeded files. I use a nice little four-disk Linux-powered RAID 10 server for backups.

Operating Systems

In this book I will be covering both Linux and Windows. Each one has its strengths and pitfalls. If you're a Windows user, XP is still the most reliable version even though Vista and Windows 7 have been released. You'll get the best hardware and software support and the best performance. Vista presents special problems because of its own high hardware requirements—it may bog down your system to the point that you can't comfortably use it for audio recording, and driver support for many audio devices is immature. Audio hardware manufacturers seem a little more interested in Windows 7, but it is still a hog compared to XP. If you want to upgrade from XP, don't bother with Vista; go straight to Windows 7. If your audio hardware and software work well on XP, then keep them as long as you can.

Linux users have the usual hassles with hardware manufacturers pretending they don't exist no matter how many products they buy, hype, and give free support for. Appendix A will tell you what works well in Linux, and you'll also find links to sites with current information on audio hardware support in Linux. If it's any consolation, a lot of audio hardware vendors don't release very good Windows drivers either. Why? Who knows; it is a mystery that I waste too much time wondering about. Don't they want happy customers?

Latency is the enemy of quality audio, so please refer to Chapters 13 and 14 for tips on tweaking your operating system for best audio performance.

Here are system requirements per the Audacity documentation. Assume the same for Windows 7 as for Vista:

Windows 98, ME   128MB/500 MHz recommended, 64MB/300 MHz minimum

Windows 2000, XP   512MB/1 GHz recommended, 128MB/300 MHz minimum

Windows Vista Home Basic   2GB/1 GHz recommended, 512MB/ 1 GHz minimum

Windows Vista Home Premium/Business/Ultimate   4GB/2 GHz recommended, 1GB/1 GHz minimum

Linux   "Audacity will run best with at least 64MB RAM and a 300 MHz processor," says the Audacity documentation for Linux users. I recommend a minimum 800 MHz CPU and 256MB RAM for podcasts, interviews, and two-track music recording and the most powerful three- or four-core CPU you can afford for multitrack recording and editing.

Portable Recording

There are several good methods for field recording. My two favorites are to fix up a netbook as a portable recording studio or to use a portable digital recorder. Netbooks are so cool; I've been wishing for netbooks ever since I discovered computers. Ordinary laptops work fine too, and you get more powerful CPUs. You have all the same options as you do with a desktop computer—your choice of preamps, mixers, and other audio interfaces, microphones, software—and you can do all of your editing on the spot and even burn CDs. You also have a nice screen and keyboard, instead of the tiny screens and buttons found on portable digital recorders.

Pocket digital recorders work wonderfully well and are fun. These range from tiny keychain fobs that are the audio equivalent of sticky notes to little recorders for good-quality voice dictation to high-quality multichannel recorders. Let's see what goes into a high-quality unit.

There are a large number of them that are priced reasonably, and you can slip one in your pocket and carry it anywhere. Carry extra batteries and some extra storage cards, and you're ready for anything. My personal favorite is the Zoom Handy H2 (Figure 2-12). It runs on two AA batteries and also has an AC adapter. It has four built-in good-quality microphones, so you can record either in two-channel stereo or in four-channel surround. It has no speakers, but it comes with earbuds, and it can also be used as a USB audio interface on a computer. Its 1/8″ line input can be connected directly to the sound board at concerts, and it also accepts an external microphone. It uses SD cards for storage and supports both WAV and MP3 file formats. It costs about $150.

Figure 2-12: The Zoom H2 with an RCA-to-1/8″ stereo plug adapter for connecting to a mixer or any other two-channel stereo RCA recording or line output

Some other popular and excellent portable digital recorders are the Olympus LS10, Marantz PMD 620, Marantz PMD 660, Sony PCM-D50, Yamaha Pocketrak 2G, and Zoom H4. All are under $600, and all have built-in mics. Ideally you'll be able to get your hands on them and give them good test drives before purchase because they share a common weakness—tiny LCD control panels with complicated menus. You'll also want to test noise levels, because some of them are nice and quiet when you use the internal mics but are scratchety with external mics. Most of them accept external mics—some have only 1/8″ mini-jacks, and some accept full-sized XLR or TRS plugs. The ones that have XLR jacks don't always supply phantom power for condenser mics. A nice option is to use a battery-powered condenser mic, and then you don't have to worry about phantom power.

NOTE   *Devices that supply phantom power usually advertise "48v phantom power." But few mics actually use 48 volts. They usually use much less—as little as 8 to 10 volts.*

Some other things to look at are battery life, type, and size of storage cards. Does it have any built-in storage, and what audio file formats does it support? Does it come with useful accessories such as AC adapters, windscreen, earbuds, and stands?

An interesting variation is the M-Audio Micro Track II. This has no built-in mics but is a miniature two-channel recording studio meant to be used with high-quality external mics. It supports both dynamic and condenser mics and supplies a full 48v phantom power for condenser mics.

I prefer to use a USB card reader for transferring files from a portable recorder to my computer. Usually it's faster, and it doesn't run down recorder batteries.

The Secret of Recording Your Own Great Audio

The "secret" behind making good-quality audio recordings isn't much of a secret: The most important factor is blocking out unwanted noises. Our brains are wonderful at ignoring sounds we don't want to pay attention to, but microphones give equal attention to all noises. Blocking unwanted noise is harder than it sounds because our modern world is very noisy: vehicle traffic, airplanes, appliances, televisions and stereos, fluorescent lights, $2,000 powered subwoofers roaming the streets at 120 decibels in $500 cars, construction, and so forth. High-frequency noises are easier to block than low-frequency sounds, as we all know from our futile attempts to escape those four-wheeled powered subwoofers, which pound their way through all barriers.

Computers add their own sounds—it's common to pick up hard drive and fan noise. So before you stock up on fancy recording equipment, job one is preparing your recording studio:

- Use a quiet room with sound-absorbing walls or wall coverings. Old carpet and blankets work as well as spendy acoustic foam.

- Place a good directional microphone close to whatever you are recording and aim it carefully.

- Shield your mic from your PC.

- Adjust your sound levels carefully, neither too low nor too high.

- Mount your microphones in shock cages.

But, you may ask, why go to all that trouble? Why not just fix it later? It's all just software anyway. My dear reader, if it were as easy as silly TV shows and movies portray it, there would be no need for soundproofed music recording studios, and no one would ever holler, "Quiet on the set!" You can mitigate problems somewhat in Audacity, but you get better results making as good a recording as possible and saving the fix-its for problems you can't avoid. It's nothing like crime shows where ace audio techs can clean up any recording, no matter how mangled, to perfect high fidelity. That's beyond fiction and well into fantasy.

Hearing Ranges

People who live in so-called primitive societies, without all of our modern "conveniences," retain keen hearing well into old age. I suppose if they wanted to make audio recordings, they wouldn't have to work so hard at blocking unwanted background noises.

American Indians and Australia's Aborigines are reported to have hearing ranges of 10 Hz to 25 kHz. The average person is on the order of 32 Hz to 18 kHz. The excellent technical reviewer for this book, Alvin Goats, has an extended hearing range of about 22 kHz. It is not as cool as it sounds because most sounds above 18 kHz are noise: fans, power supplies, speaker distortions, and such. He is sometimes accused of being hard of hearing due to all of the extra sounds masking what other people are saying.

Gordon Hempton is a wonderful artist who calls himself the Sound Tracker (*http://www.soundtracker.com/*). Mr. Hempton has made a career out of recording the pure sounds of nature, with no human sounds at all. In 1992 he recorded the chorus of dawn around the globe. In later years he recorded the sounds of the Mississippi river according to the writings of Mark Twain and the sounds of Yosemite National Park according to the writings of John Muir. He uses a Neumann KU-81i Dummy Head (named Fritz) to simulate as closely as possible how we hear sounds. He has a released a number of high-quality CDs so you can hear what a world without noisy people sounds like.

Mr. Hempton began his recording career in the early 1980s. A lot of the locations that he recorded back then are now too noisy to record.

Your PC should be dedicated to the job and not used for anything else, neither gaming nor web surfing nor emailing nor anything, because you want all of your computer's power dedicated to recording. If you don't, you risk generating skips and stutters. Turn off screensavers, all power management, and any antivirus or antimalware software. (Windows users, do I need to say, don't be connected to the Internet after doing this?) Turn off all unnecessary services, scheduled jobs, and everything that is not essential.

Your microphone will pick up noise, vibrations, and interference from a surprising number of sources. If you still have an old cathode ray tube (CRT) monitor, replace it with a modern flat thin-film transistor liquid crystal diode (TFT-LCD) monitor, because CRTs emit radiation and noise. Sometimes they even resonate to certain sounds and create echoes.

You can make an effective sound barrier between mic and computer for cheap by attaching a piece of carpet to a piece of plywood or particle

board. Give it feet so it stands on its own, and you have the equivalent of
an expensive piece of a high-tech sound barrier. Both laptop and desktop
machines should sit on nonresonating surfaces. In a pinch, you can set your
laptop on a coat or a pillow, being careful to not block its cooling vents.

Although many how-tos advise making your studio as acoustically "dead"
as possible, without any echoes or resonance, feel free to experiment. You
might like how some things sound in a space with some hard surfaces. Psychoacoustics come into play in professional recording studios; they don't make
perfect anechoic chambers because those are so flat that they sound unpleasant. There is no sound reflection, nothing that gives depth to sound.
So, professional studios reduce the amount of random noise while preserving some depth to the sound.

Visit Appendix A

Now that you have some ideas on what
you need, please visit Appendix A for a
sampling of good audio gear in all price
ranges. This should help you navigate
the huge and splendid world of audio
hardware.

Layla and Firecracker, the official
studio dogs, wish you well (Figure 2-13).

Figure 2-13: Layla and Firecracker
waiting for their cues

3

TRANSFERRING VINYL LPS (AND OTHER LEGACY MEDIA) TO CD

A great way to preserve and enjoy old recordings is to transfer them from any legacy medium—vinyl LPs, cassette tapes, reel-to-reel tapes, vintage 78s, videocassettes, even eight-track tapes—to CD. Or you can transfer them to a hard drive, solid-state drive, or whatever digital storage medium you prefer.

Transferring phonograph records to CD is in demand, and you might even be able to get a nice sideline going doing this. A lot of people are still hanging on to their record collections but are afraid to enjoy them because LPs are fragile. A lot of great albums have never been released on commercial CDs, or the modern CD remasters are not done well. Some people simply prefer the sound of their old records.

Although you can copy any analog media and convert it to any digital audio format, in this chapter we'll talk mostly about transferring vinyl record albums and singles to CDs. Once you have converted your old analog media to a digital format, Audacity has a number of tools for cleaning up the sound quality. You may not always be able to perform perfect restorations, but you can reduce hiss, clicks, pops, and other defects to quite tolerable levels.

You can also customize dynamic range compression to suit your own needs, which is a nice thing because on modern popular CDs, dynamic range compression is abused to where it spoils the music. Even if they did it well, it might not be right for you, so Audacity lets you do it your way.

Finally, we'll discuss the merits of vinyl versus CD and other media, as well as the ins and out of connecting your various playback devices to your computer. If you need help setting up your hardware, skip ahead to the "Connecting Legacy Devices to Your Computer" on page 67 first.

For those of you with golden ears who are not satisfied with 16/44.1 CDs, the DVD-Audio format supports up to 24/196. That's right, 24 bits at 196,000 samples per second. DVD-Audio supports 5.1 surround sound, and so does Audacity in the 1.3.x releases. If you're not into surround sound, you can cram several CDs worth of music at 16/44.1 onto a DVD. We'll learn about authoring DVD-Audio disks in Chapter 6.

Okay then, let's dive into copying, editing, and then making CDs. Please review Chapter 1 if you need a refresher on the basics of using Audacity.

Preparing Vinyl LPs for Copying

First, clean up your vinyl records as well as you can. Sure, you can do a lot to clean up digital audio files, but it's not like on TV where the ace lab tech makes pristine restorations effortlessly. That's fiction, my dear readers, and we are stuck in the real world. It's better to start with the best-quality recording possible; it's less work, and you get better results.

I have my nice old Discwasher brushes from the olden days, and it's a good thing because the new ones are inferior. Real Discwasher brushes have a directional nap—hold them one way to clean the record, and then reverse your stroke on a clean lint-free cloth to clean the brush. There is an arrow embedded on the handle that points to the leading edge. You can use a real Discwasher brush dry or with a wet cleaning solution. The correct way to wet-clean with Discwasher is to apply the cleaning solution to the leading edge of the brush only, leaving the rest of it dry. You can clean a record on your turntable while it's rotating, but be careful you don't apply so much pressure that you damage the motor. Apply the wet leading edge of the brush for three to four turns, and then roll the brush to bring the dry part in contact with the record for another three to four turns. Give it time to dry completely before playing it, because playing a wet record can damage it. (However, on a record that is already in bad, nothing-to-lose condition, playing it wet might make it sound better. Moisten it carefully with distilled water or Discwasher D4 fluid, and give it a whirl. It won't hurt your stylus.)

A nice thing to have for everyday cleaning is a carbon antistatic brush. These are always used dry and are pretty good at lifting out dust, lint, and other particles that try to make a home on your records. But they're no good for cleaning fingerprints, sticky goo, or other muck that requires a wet cleaner.

There are all kinds of cleaning solutions, microfiber cloths, brushes, and even wet power washers. The debates over the best ways to clean vinyl

> ### The History of Record Production
>
> The earliest recordings were made on rotating wax cylinders with a needle in the middle of a vibrating diaphragm attached to a horn, like an old-fashioned ear trumpet. The horn functioned like a microphone. The needle vibrations cut an uneven groove into the wax. Modern mono recordings were made using the same principle of a vibrating needle cutting into a softer material, except the needle was moved by a magnet.
>
> Stereo came about when someone experimented with the angle of the magnet with respect to the needle and found that it could be controlled precisely enough to cut each side of the groove differently, creating two stereo channels. The technology for producing vinyl records, even with the advent of CDs and digital audio, has continued to improve, and some record labels are still producing high-quality vinyl recordings. With all of these advances, it's still a single needle doing the recording and playback for two channels, which results in a bit of *crosstalk*, so precision tuning of your turntable is required to get the best performance.

records are endless and loud; I shall leave it to you to do your own homework and figure out what you prefer. You can pick up nasty, dirty, nothing-to-lose records to practice on at thrift shops for cheap. Given the variety of claims over what works best, I suspect that vinyl is tougher than we give it credit for.

NOTE *Never use any kind of alcohol on vintage 78 rpm records or any acetate or nonvinyl records because it will damage them. The earliest records were made of wax, and there were many different wax compositions using carnuba, beeswax, and other materials. People who know about these things recommend not using liquid cleaners at all. If you have vintage records, I recommend consulting experts who know how to handle them safely. Solutions containing alcohol are fine for modern vinyl records, and most record cleaners contain alcohol. Whatever cleaner you use, it must be something that leaves no residue.*

You should also invest in a stylus brush and cleaner, because gunk builds up on your stylus. This is less controversial; I use the Stanton SC-4 brush and cleaner, and they do the job just fine. Remember, you cannot be too careful when you're handling your turntable's stylus; handle it as gently as you possibly can by its mounting brace only. Never touch it with your fingers.

Use a stylus gauge to adjust the vertical tracking force of your stylus. High-quality cartridges require a mere 0.5 to 3 grams. Medium-quality styli, and those designed for DJs, go as high as 5 grams. Set the tracking force per the instructions for your particular hardware. Too light and too heavy will both cause too much wear, so you really want it just right.

Depending on your turntable and tonearm, you may also have antiskate, vertical tracking angle, and azimuth adjustments. Your turntable documentation should tell you all about what these are and how to adjust them. The idea is to make correctly aligned contact without causing asymmetrical wear. It is worth spending some time tuning your turntable, and you may be surprised at how much difference tiny adjustments make.

Eight Steps to Converting Records to CDs

First let's list all the steps and then in the next sections go through them in detail. Vintage records require some special handling, which we'll get to in "Copying Vintage 78s" on page 66. If you don't know how to hook up your turntable, visit "Connecting Legacy Devices to Your Computer" on page 67 first. These are the steps to follow:

1. Set Audacity's frame rate to CDDA frames in the Selection toolbar.

2. Set the project rate to 32-bit float/44.1 or 16/44.1.

3. Copy your album into Audacity into one long track.

4. Make any fixes such as removing noise and pops, normalizing, compressing, and deleting unnecessary bits.

5. Enter metadata.

6. Export the Audacity tracks to CD-ready audio files.

7. Use your favorite CD-writing software to copy your songs to a CD.

8. Pop your new CD into a player and enjoy.

The most time-consuming part is fixing defects. This chapter has some tips for common fixes, and Chapter 12 is devoted entirely to fix-its and cleanups.

I like to record singles a little differently than in step 3: I prefer to record each single into its own track, so it looks like Figure 3-1.

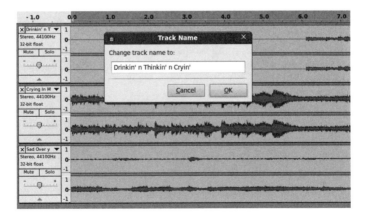

Figure 3-1: Putting each song into a separate Audacity track

Use the Track menu on each track to enter the song titles as the track names. At export, when all the tracks are exported to CD-ready files, each file will take the track name.

The advantage of using individual Audacity tracks per single is it's easier to reorder them, and you can normalize volume levels in one operation. When all the songs are in one track, normalization won't bring the quiet songs up to the same volume as the loud songs. Any variances have to be corrected one song at a time. But when multiple tracks are normalized, all of them are brought up to the same volume level in one step.

Audacity Settings

First, set the correct frame rate for CD audio in the Selection toolbar, as Figure 3-2 shows. This ensures that any splits you make will start and end on a CD frame. Any audio that lands outside of these frames will be lost and possibly create clicking noises. You can choose either hh:mm:ss + CDDA frames (75 fps) or CDDA frames (75 fps). The former shows the time plus CD frames, and the latter displays only CD frames. Check the "Snap To" box to ensure that stops and starts are always on the CD frame boundaries.

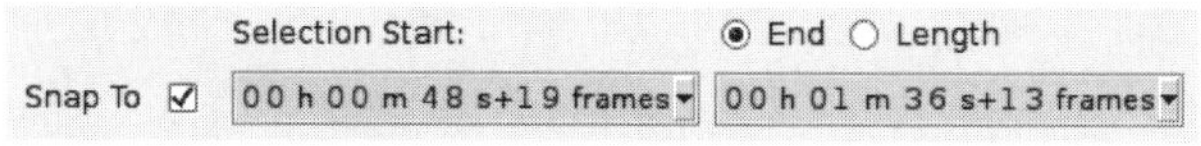

Figure 3-2: Setting the correct frame rate for CD audio

Then set your quality preferences in the **Edit** > **Preferences** > **Quality** dialog to a sample rate of 44,100 Hz and a bit depth of 32-bit float. The Red Book CD Audio standard is 16/44.1, but if you have enough disk space, working in 32-bit float has a number of advantages. It gives you the largest possible dynamic range, which means less noise and a lot of headroom for editing, so you can do a lot of processing with losing quality.

Recording at 16/44.1 works fine if you want to conserve disk space, especially if you're doing straight copying with minimal editing. The more manipulation you do, the better it is to work in 32-bit float.

While you're in the Preferences menu, review these options as well:

- On the Recording tab, uncheck "Overdub: Play other tracks while recording new one" and "Software Playthrough: Listen while recording or monitoring new track."

- On the Import/Export tab, check "Show Metadata Editor prior to export."

- Make sure the number of recording channels is set correctly (Devices tab), which is two-channel stereo. Even old mono LPs use two tracks.

Recording

Then click **File** > **Save Project As** and give your project a name, start your record player, and set your recording levels. You have plenty of headroom, so give yourself some space to avoid clipping. Using a 32-bit float bit depth means you can record to a peak of −24 dB and still have more dynamic range than your hardware can use; I usually record to a peak of −9 dB because a record is not unpredictable like a live show. If it surprises me with a sudden super-loud passage, I can easily re-record it. Click **View** > **Show Clipping**, and Audacity will highlight any clipping with a bright red line.

Then click the **Record** button and start playing your record. There's nothing much to do except kick back and enjoy the music until it's time to flip to side two. Click the **Pause** button to pause recording while you flip the record. Every time you click **Record**, it starts a new track, so use **Pause** to keep going on the same track. If you accidentally hit **Stop** instead, you can append to your existing track with SHIFT-Record.

It is a good idea to record some noise, like at the beginning of the record before the music starts and at the end after the music stops, so you can do some effective noise removal later. A pure noise sample with no music in it is best. Save this in a separate track.

Fixing Defects

First do a rough trim to delete any unwanted sections. Don't cut too closely but leave some extra, and then apply the finishing touches later. Trimming away unwanted sections of your tracks is easy; just select the parts you don't want and press the DELETE key, or click the **Cut** button. Another way to do deletions is to select what you want to keep and then click the **Trim** button. This keeps your selection and deletes the rest.

Deleting part of a track makes it shorter, and sometimes you might not want to do this but rather keep it the same length. Do this by silencing instead of deleting—select the part you want to get rid of and click the **Silence** button. This makes it silent instead of removing it, and your track stays the same length.

The next step is to fix any clipping or scratches. It is common for defects to be in only one channel. This is more characteristic of vinyl because the needle is pushed by the groove, so the side pushing the needle inward gets more wear. Tapes will also wear unevenly because one track is on the "inside" away from the edge of the tape. The track closest to the edge will be affected the most by magnetism, electrical fields, and physical damage from the tape guides.

NOTE   *The definition of* track *is a bit squishy. An audio track is a single mono track or a two-channel stereo track, or it's a single song on a long track with multiple songs.*

To fix a defect in only one channel, use the **Split Stereo Track** command in the Track panel to break your stereo track into two separate tracks. Then you can edit each one separately, and when you're finished, you can use

Make Stereo Track to put them back together. A nice benefit of dividing them is that the undamaged track will mask less-than-perfect repairs in the other track.

Did you know you can insert silence? If you need to pad a track and make it a little longer or you need to insert a silent gap, first click to mark the point where you want to insert some silence. Then click **Generate** > **Silence**, enter how long you it want to be, and click **OK**. The new silent portion will be inserted to the right of your mark. Figure 3-3 shows how to create a two-second silence. Note that it contains a drop-down menu just like the Selection toolbar, with all different types of values to use: seconds, hours/minutes/seconds, different frame rates, and so on.

Figure 3-3: Inserting two seconds of silence

Fade In, Fade Out

Fading in and out is done a lot in recordings. In Figure 3-4 I deleted a long boring stretch of applause and left about a three-second gap, and then I used the Envelope tool to gracefully fade out to silence and then back in. The Envelope tool gives you a great deal of control over fades and volume levels. The little white squares are *control nodes.* Create new nodes by clicking wherever you want them, drag them in any direction to raise or lower volume, and drag them beyond the track borders to get rid of them. Envelope tools are standard in nearly all audio-editing applications.

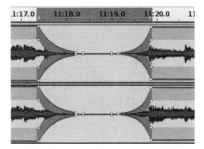

Figure 3-4: Fade to silence, then back to normal using the Envelope tool

Another way to apply fades is with **Effect** > **Fade Out** and **Fade In**. Select the part of your track where you want it to fade, click **Effect** > **Fade Out** or **Fade In**, and it will automatically apply a graceful, uniform fade for you. You control only the length of the fade.

Some CD-writing applications automatically create a two-second gap between audio tracks, so beware. You might not want a gap between songs in a live performance or a gap added to the one that you created in Audacity. Good CD-writing applications let you control this behavior.

Fixing Warps

Audacity won't fix a warped record. A top-quality turntable will track a warped record more accurately than a low-budget turntable. Many how-tos suggest flattening the warp by carefully warming the record to soften it—in an oven, in a sunny window, in a warm vehicle—and then placing it inside a clean paper sleeve and putting it under a heavy weight. I have tried the warm vehicle method because the idea of using an oven scares me, and sometimes it works well if you are careful and finicky about keeping everything clean. Pressing debris into the soft, warm vinyl won't improve it any.

You can use Audacity to mitigate some of the bad sounds created by a warped record, such as clicks, pops, and hiss; see the next section.

Fixing Skips and Pops

You can find any skips or pops caused by scratches or warps pretty easily by looking at the waveform, as Figure 3-5 shows. They appear as abrupt, slender peaks. **Effect** > **Click Removal** is pretty good at removing clicks in batches without removing music. It looks for spikes in the waveform that are typical of the pops caused by scratches, deletes the scratches, and then does a bit of interpolation to reconstruct the waveform. The Select threshold setting determines the sensitivity for deciding when a spike is a scratch. Smaller Select threshold values are more sensitive, and larger values are less sensitive. Too much sensitivity means something you want to keep might be identified as a click and removed, such as some percussion effects.

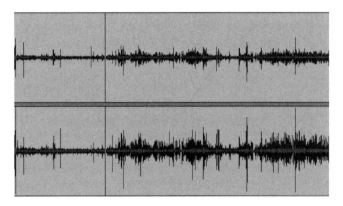

Figure 3-5: The area to the left of the cursor line is between songs and should be relatively flat, but this example is from a record with a lot of little scratches, so you see many sudden, slender peaks instead.

The Max spike width value determines the maximum length of a segment, in milliseconds (ms), that the Click Removal tool will remove. The default is 20 ms, which is longer than most scratches.

Select a small segment of a track that has some scratches on it and try a bit of trial and error, which goes quickly thanks to the Click Removal effect's Preview button. Listen to the preview, and if it doesn't sound right, change the settings and try again. The defaults are pretty good, and once you have the settings tweaked to your satisfaction, go ahead and apply them to the whole track.

NOTE *The default preview length is three seconds. If that is too short, open the **Edit** > **Preferences** > **Playback** > **Length of Preview** dialog and make it longer.*

You may want to repair a click or pop manually, especially if there are only a few of them. It doesn't take long. One way is to select **Effect** > **Amplify** and lower it to −50 dB, which will silence it. Another way is to use the Repair tool, which is more surgical. Zoom in until you can see the individual samples, select a segment to operate on, and click **Effect** > **Repair**. The Repair tool operates on a maximum of 128 samples. Just like the Click Removal tool, it uses interpolation to reduce and smooth out the edges of the repaired segment, so it doesn't leave a gap. (Figure 3-6 shows the before and after.)

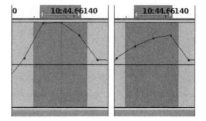

Figure 3-6: Using the Repair tool, before and after, to repair some clipping

NOTE *Remember the Zoom tool—you can magnify your waveform enough to see the individual samples and give yourself plenty of room to make precise edits. To keep your place when you're zooming in and out, click to mark your location on the track, and the Zoom tool will automatically center on your mark.*

Finding and Repairing Clipping

Use **View** > **Show Clipping** to quickly find any clipped segments. Clipping is caused when the volume of your recording goes over 0 dB. Clipping is nasty in digital audio because it causes distortion. An easy way to fix a brief clipped segment is with the Amplify effect. Zoom in and carefully select the clipped segment, and then select **Effect** > **Amplify** to bring it down a notch or two. Use a negative value for the Amplification setting, such as −3.0. One decibel is about the smallest level of change we can perceive, and every 3 decibels doubles or, when reducing amplitude, halves the volume level. So −3 dB is half as loud as 0 dB, and −6 dB is half as loud as −3 dB. Clipped passages over a few seconds long should be rerecorded.

Noise Removal

Vinyl LPs, on even the finest systems, are never completely silent. There is always some sort of background noise: hiss, turntable rumble, tiny scratchy noises from static electricity or pressing defects in the vinyl. Open the **Effect** > **Noise Removal** effect to get rid of this unwanted noise. It's not perfect, and there is always a trade-off between removing noise without causing too much damage to the music. It works best when you have a good noise profile and the noise is distinctly different from what you want to keep.

First you need to build a profile of the noise you want to remove, so select a few seconds of your track that has only noise, such as the very beginning or very end where the stylus is traveling over the record but not over the music. The longer your noise sample, the better, from 5 seconds up to 30 seconds or so. Select your noise sample, and then in the **Effect > Noise Removal** dialog, click the **Get Noise Profile** button. Next, select the segment that you want to apply noise removal to and click **OK.** You can use the Preview button to make sure it's doing it right before hitting OK. Apply Noise Removal as precisely as you can to minimize side effects. Hiss, wow and flutter, hum, and low-level scratchiness are all common defects, and the Noise Removal tool works well if you have a good clean noise sample.

If you don't like the results, press CTRL-Z to undo, change some settings, and try it again. The default noise reduction level is −24 dB, which means segments identified as noise are attenuated by −24 dB. If this removes too much of the recording, reduce this and try it again. A similar tactic that often works well is to go back to your noise sample, reduce its amplitude a few dB, create a new profile, and try again. You don't want to erase the noise completely because this may erase things you want to keep, just lower it to where it's not bothersome.

The Frequency smoothing and Attack/decay time sliders are more aggressive when you move them left and less aggressive on the right sides of the scales. A larger value for frequency smoothing means it treats a wider range of frequencies as the same, so it makes larger changes. *Attack* is how hard a note is hit, and *decay* is how long it takes to fade away. Since there is only one Attack/decay time slider, the attack and decay times will always be the same. Smaller values are more abrupt, and larger values are more gradual.

Another slick trick is to use the Equalization effect (see Chapter 11 to learn more) to reduce hiss or rumble by reducing the amplitude of frequencies below 500 Hz and above 15,000 Hz. Of course, this will also affect any sounds in this range that you want to keep, so it's not always the best solution, but it is one more thing to try. You can try this in any part of the frequency range that contains unwanted noise.

Another way to limit a range of frequencies is to use a *high-pass* or *low-pass* filter. A high-pass filter blocks low frequencies and allows high frequencies to pass, while a low-pass filter blocks high frequencies. You may need to install some plug-ins to get high- and low-pass filters for Audacity; look in your Effects menu to see what is installed on your system. (Chapter 11 tells where to find and how to install plug-ins.)

Customizing Dynamic Range Compression

You may want to tailor the dynamic range of your recording for more comfortable listening in different environments. Because listening to a recording with a wide dynamic range in a noisy environment like a vehicle or at work means it's always too loud or too soft, you can change this with a *dynamic range compressor*. Compressors are used all the time in audio production. I think they're overused, but the neat thing with Audacity is you can adjust it to please yourself. A compressor usually attenuates the louder frequencies, reducing the difference between the soft and loud passages. Some compressors also boost the quieter frequencies. "Compress Dynamic Range" on page 240 tells all about how to apply compression to your recordings.

Normalization

Now that you are finished with repairs, it is time to normalize the volume for the whole album. If you copied everything to a single Audacity track, select the entire track and apply **Effect > Normalize**. This won't affect the dynamic range or change audio quality; all it does is raise the overall volume level. Set your maximum amplitude no higher than 0.0, which is the maximum for digital audio, and make sure that "Remove any DC offset" is checked. DC offset refers to the mean amplitude. If this is not zero, then normalization won't be applied correctly because the amplitude levels will be unbalanced, and it might even create a bit of distortion. When this is finished, you're ready to go on to the next section.

If you put each song into a separate Audacity track, press CTRL-A to select all tracks and then apply normalization. Then skip ahead to "Exporting to CD-Ready Files, Multiple Audacity Tracks" on page 64.

Dividing a Long Track into Individual Songs

If you copied everything into one long track, you can export this to a 16-bit WAV file and then copy it to a CD. But you won't have individual songs; instead, you'll have one long track with no way to skip between songs. So here is how to divide it into individual songs. Start at the very beginning; make sure you are exactly at the beginning of the track by pressing the HOME key. Then press CTRL-B. This will create a new label track under your album track, and the cursor will be inside a little text box. Type the name of the first song into this little box and press ENTER. Then click wherever you want the break to go between the first and second songs, press CTRL-B, and type in the name of the second song. Keep going until all the songs have their name labels (Figure 3-7).

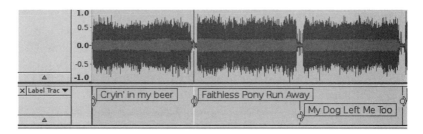

Figure 3-7: Dividing one big track into individual song tracks and labeling them

Exporting to CD-Ready Files, One Long Audacity Track

If you have copied all your songs into one long Audacity track, this is how you export them to individual CD-ready audio files. First open **File** > **Open Metadata Editor** and enter the album title and artist's name, as well as any other information that you want to preserve in the track metadata. Leave the Track Title and Track Number fields blank, because Audacity will fill those in for you.

Next, go to **File** > **Export Multiple** and choose Export Format: WAV (Microsoft) signed 16 bit PCM. You'll see a window like Figure 3-8. I recommend exporting to a separate directory and not mixing your exports with your Audacity project files. Select the "Split files based on: Labels" and "Name files: Using Label/Track Name" radio buttons. Check the "Overwrite existing files" box only if you are sure you want newly exported files to replace old files with the same name. Click **OK**, and you're on your way.

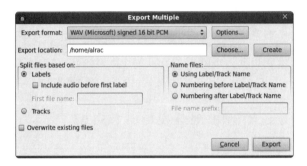

Figure 3-8: Exporting each song into an individual, CD-ready audio file using the label names as the filenames

If you enabled "Show Metadata Editor prior to export" in the **Edit** > **Preferences** > **Import/Export** dialog as I suggested, the Metadata Editor will appear for every song as it exports. It is okay to turn it off if you don't need to review the metadata for every song.

Exporting to CD-Ready Files, Multiple Audacity Tracks

If you copied each song to an individual Audacity track, this is how you export them to individual CD-ready audio files. First open **File** > **Open Metadata Editor** and enter any information common to all the tracks, such as date, genre, or artist's name. Leave the Track Title and Track Number fields blank, because Audacity will fill those in for you.

Next, go to **File** > **Export Multiple** and choose Export Format: WAV (Microsoft) signed 16 bit PCM. You'll see a window like Figure 3-9. I recommend using a separate directory and not mixing your exports with your

Audacity project files. Select the "Split files based on: Labels" and "Name files: Using Label/Track Name" radio buttons. Check the "Overwrite existing files" box only if you are sure you want newly exported files to replace old files with the same name. Click **OK**, and you're on your way. You will end up with each song in a separate file, and the track names you created will become the filenames.

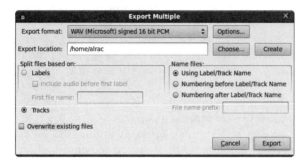

Figure 3-9: Exporting each track into an individual CD-ready audio file, using the track names as the filenames.

Writing Songs to a CD

Now you have a batch of nice individual WAV files, one file per song. Write your songs to a CD with your favorite CD writer application, and you're done. Don't burn at the maximum speed, but throttle down to half speed to make sure you get a good disk. Be sure to select "New Audio Project," or whatever your particular application calls making a music CD, because this creates a CD in the proper Red Book Audio format. Don't make an ordinary data CD because then it won't work in standard CD players, like in your vehicle or hi-fi system. Standard CD players can't play WAV files. (Computer CD players will handle just about anything, because it is all done in software media players.)

Watch the order of your song tracks—your CD-writing application may put your songs in alphabetical order, rather than track order. A quick way to sort them is by date, if your CD-writing software supports this, since the first song exported will always be the oldest and the last one the newest.

If you have an inkjet printer that supports printing on CDs and DVDs, you can get special CD blanks that are made to be printed on. These have either a white or silver side that is designed to hold ink and not smear. Another newfangled printable CD/DVD requires a special thermal printer, which can be purchased for about $100. A third printable disk type is called *LightScribe*, which requires a special CD/DVD writer. These are in the same price range as ordinary CD/DVD writers, about $50.

> **"Do I need to buy a special audio CD?"**
>
> The answer to this commonly asked question is no. All CDs are exactly the same type. Some countries charge a tax on "audio" CDs that supposedly gets paid to musicians to compensate for lost income from illegal copying. (If they actually receive a fair share of this tax, I will eat my favorite vinyl LP.) The other special thing about them is a pressed data flag that is part of the Serial Copy Management System (SCMS) to control copying protected material. The SCMS encoding controls three states: copy allowed (00), copy once (11), and copy prohibited (10). It won't stop you from making copies of an original CD. If the "copy once" flag is set, it might interfere with putting a copy on a CD writer that attaches to your hi-fi system. Computer hardware and media are exempt from the laws that mandate SCMS. I use ordinary nonaudio CD blanks, and they work fine in all CD players.

Copying Vintage 78s

Vintage 78s is shorthand for old monophonic phonograph records made from about the 1890s to the late 1950s. These are also called *short-play* records and *wide-groove* records. There were no real industry standards until the early 1930s, so older records played at a variety of speeds, from 60 to 130 rpm. Vintage 78s are made of shellac mixed with dyes, fillers, and other materials, and they come in a range of sizes all the way up to 16" in diameter. Some are laminated and will come apart if they get wet. Alcohol will dissolve shellac, and even too much humidity will hurt it.

Vinyl LPs, whether mono or stereo, play at 33 1/3 rpm, and singles play at 45 rpm or 78 rpm. Yes, way back in the olden days there were 78 rpm singles; for example, these were favored by Disney in the early 1960s. You might also find some 45 rpm LPs. Two main differences between these and vintage 78s is they are made of vinyl rather than shellac and they are cut in microgrooves rather than wide grooves. The coarse-groove records require a 3 mm stylus, while microgroove records use a 1 mm stylus. You can play old monophonic LPs and singles with a modern stereo cartridge and stylus, but not vintage records. There are modern cartridges and styli that are made for playing these old records, such as the popular Shure M78S.

I'm no expert on vintage 78s, but if you need more information on the correct ways to store, handle, and play these old-timers, there are a lot of great resources both online and in the real world. There are many vintage phonograph record experts, aficionados, and traders, so it's not hard to find some expert guidance.

Once you have all the hardware and safe handling sorted out, there are a few things you need to do differently in Audacity. Open the **Edit** > **Preferences** > **Devices** dialog and set the number of recording channels to 1 (mono). Then go to **Edit** > **Preferences** > **Import/Export** and select "Use custom mix." The reason for doing this is to mix down to two channels from your mono track so you'll hear music in both speakers on your stereo system. If you don't do this, you'll get playback from only one speaker. Figure 3-10 shows you what Audacity's mixer panel should look like: Move the slider at the bottom to create two output channels, and then click "Audio Track" (or whatever name you gave your track) and "Channel: 2" to link them together.

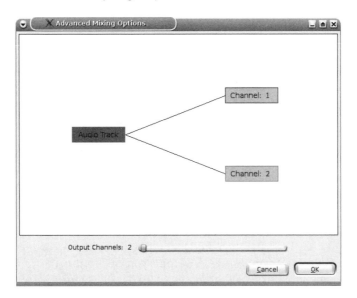

Figure 3-10: Mixing down a mono recording to two channels for playback on stereo systems

Connecting Legacy Devices to Your Computer

There are several ways to connect turntables and other legacy components to your computer. First let's talk about connectors. The terms *plug, port, socket*, and *jack* are thrown around willy-nilly these days. Just to keep it clear and simple, I shall call the connecters on cables and adapters *plugs*, and the things they plug into (like the RCA and TRS sockets on amplifiers) are *jacks*. Also, in the interest of honoring standard terminology, I shall refer to plugs and jacks according to gender, male and female. This is especially important with gender changers, which are adapters for changing from one connection type to another.

In the olden days everyone used 1/4″ (6.3 mm) TRS plugs, and life was easy. Then manufacturers started making 1/8″ (3.5 mm) mini-jacks and plugs and the even dinkier 3/32″ (2.5 mm) micro-minis. It doesn't matter what your devices have because there are adapters to fit any situation. In fact, it's common for devices with mini-plugs to include 1/4″ adapters, and you can also get adapters to fit 1/4″ plugs into mini-jacks. Just make sure you have a correctly matched adapter, either mono or stereo. Mono TRS plugs have one black insulator ring, and stereo plugs have two.

RCA audio connectors, fortunately, are still the same as they have always been. RCA plugs come in a rainbow of colors, and each color has a meaning: Red means right channel, white means left channel or mono channel, and the other colors are for different surround sound channels. They're all the same, so it doesn't matter if you use the "wrong" colors. There is only one size. They are also called *phono* plugs. Figure 2-7 on page 37 shows an assortment of TRS jacks, adapters, male and female RCA connectors, and a dual-RCA-to-single-stereo-plug adapter. Adapters are inexpensive, and you always need them, so get a grab bag for all occasions.

My favorite way to digitize legacy media is to connect a stereo amplifier or receiver to an analog-to-digital/digital-to-analog converter (ADC/DAC), which then connects to the computer. Then every component that connects to the amp—turntable, tape deck, radio tuner, VCR, CD, DVD—is available to record in Audacity. (CDs and DVDs can be played and copied directly on your computer; see Chapter 5 to learn how to do this.)

You probably already have an ADC/DAC on your computer—your computer's sound card. If it has a Line In port, you should use that. These are light blue 1/8″ stereo jacks. Depending on your amp or receiver, you should have a pair of standard RCA outputs you can connect to your sound card, usually called *record out* or *line out*. Flip back to Figure 2-2 on page 34 to see the back of my treasured old Pioneer amplifier.

So, connecting my amp to an internal computer sound card requires a two-RCA-to-1/8″ stereo mini-plug adapter, as in Figure 3-11.

On surround-sound home theater receivers, consult your manual to figure out the best recording outputs. For example, I have an Onkyo 5.1 system with a pair of RCA tape outputs, just like my old Pioneer amp. You have to use the remote control to select the correct output channels, and then it records whatever is currently playing.

Figure 3-11: Because of the proliferation of 1/8″ mini-plugs, this is the workhorse of many a conversion studio.

My favorite recording interface is an M-Audio MobilePre USB, which is a combination microphone preamp and ADC/DAC. This replaces an internal computer sound card. The MobilePre supports a number of different connectors, so I could use the two-RCA-to-1/8″ adapter or a two-RCA-to-two-1/4″ TRS adapter, as in Figure 3-12.

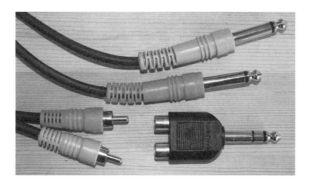

Figure 3-12: A two-RCA-to-two-1/4″ TRS adapter. Note that the Y-adapter (bottom right) is not needed for connecting the MobilePre to the Record outputs on the amplifier. The Y-adapter comes in handy when I need to use a headphone jack for my recording source.

Connecting a Turntable to Your Computer

There are several ways to connect a turntable to your computer in addition to connecting through your amplifier connected to your computer. A popular method is to use a USB phono preamp that lets you connect any turntable, even cherished old ones, directly to your computer. In fact, you might want to look for a good old turntable instead of a modern one, because it's hard to match the quality of those old turntables without spending a mint. You can pick up decent USB phono preamps for cheap, such as the ART USB Phono Plus V2 for around $100. It includes a gain control, a clipping indicator, a monitor port, a USB port, RCA inputs and outputs, optical ports, and an S/PDIF port. The ADC/DAC operates at 16/44.1 and 16/48. It even includes a phono ground connector, which is a must-have for turntables that have ground wires. If you don't ground them, you'll get an annoying hum.

You need a phono preamp and not just any old preamp, because phono preamps apply the RIAA equalization curve correction. This is very important. The *RIAA equalization curve* is an industry standard for attenuating bass frequencies (below 500 Hz) on a vinyl LP and boosting frequencies above 2,120 Hz. Vinyl LPs have to be recorded this way or the bass grooves would take up most of the album, resulting in short playing time, and the higher frequencies would barely be audible. When you play a vinyl record, your integrated amplifier or receiver corrects this imbalance with a built-in phono preamp that reverses the RIAA curve. It sounds tinny with hardly any bass, and you can hear this by turning off your speakers and placing your ear close to the cartridge while a record is playing.

The RIAA equalization curve became widely adopted starting around 1955, so records from before then may have different equalization curves. If you want to fuss with making your own handcrafted equalization corrections, you can do this in Audacity. Audacity also has a number of prefab equalization curves, such as Columbia LP, AES, Decca, and RCA. Use an ordinary preamp instead of a phono preamp to get an uncorrected signal, copy your album into Audacity, and then apply your own equalization. Figure 3-13 shows what the RIAA curve equalizer looks like in Audacity.

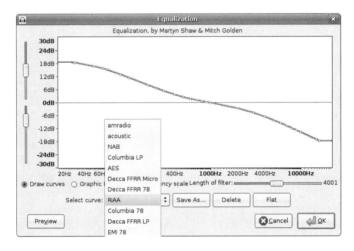

Figure 3-13: The Equalization effect allows you to fine-tune equalization any way you want, and it supports creating custom presets.

A good way to connect a turntable to your recording interface, as mentioned earlier, is to connect your turntable to your stereo receiver or amplifier in the usual manner and then connect your receiver to your computer's recording interface.

One more option to consider is buying a USB turntable with its own built-in phono preamp. These are becoming popular as more people want to try converting their own albums to CD. It's a great concept and convenience, but a lot of them are not very good quality, so shop carefully.

My own personal turntable is an Audio-Technica AT-PL120. This is not a sweet decades-old turntable but a shiny new direct-drive three-speed with its own internal phono preamp. That's right, 33 1/3, 45, and 78. It's designed to be a DJ turntable, so it comes with an elliptical stylus for playing records both frontward and backward. (The horror! As if I would do that to a perfectly good LP!) It has adjustable speed, pitch, antiskate, and feet levelers, and it's weighty and solid as a good turntable should be. The internal preamp is switchable, so you can either connect it directly to a recording interface or switch off the internal preamp and connect to an external phono preamp. If you want to play vintage 78s, you need to purchase a special cartridge and stylus, such as the Shure M78S wide-groove monophonic cartridge.

NOTE   *Our excellent technical consultant Alvin notes that radio DJs used direct-drive turntables so they could rotate them backward: "You manually adjust the record so that you know where the song begins, then turn the record back one quarter of a turn. When you hit "play" on those record players, the turntable is at full speed in the one quarter turn."*

Figure 3-14 shows my own setup at home. I have both recording and playback routed through my M-Audio MobilePre USB.

Figure 3-14: From the right to left: nice old Pioneer stereo amp, Audio Technica three-speed turntable, color printer, M-Audio MobilePre, screen, headsets, three-core CPU wedged into salvaged E-Machine case

Connecting a Tape Deck

Tape decks can connect directly to your computer. Just connect their RCA output plugs to your recording interface with the appropriate adapter. Your recording interface might already have RCA inputs.

Which Is Better: Vinyl, Tape, or CDs?

There are endless debates over which has superior sound quality, vinyl LPs or CDs. I've been a serious music fan since I was a wee tot way back in the days of reel-to-reel tapes and vinyl LPs. My dad was a symphony musician and music teacher, and to this day I don't believe he has acknowledged any music made after the 18th century. (Kidding, Dad! Hugs!) I think CDs are the bee's knees.

In the olden days before CDs, a lot of music lovers who wanted to preserve their vinyl played a new LP only once, to copy it to tape. It was no use purchasing commercially recorded cassettes because of their inferior quality. They used the cheapest tape and were plagued with hiss, narrow dynamic range, and overall cruddy tone. By the early '70s, commercially recorded reel tapes were pretty much gone from the market, so if you wanted good-quality tape recordings, you had to do it yourself.

This might sound like a lot of fussiness to readers who are not familiar with audio tapes and LPs, but there were shortcomings with both media, and neither one provided a completely satisfactory solution. It's easier to skip tracks on an LP and they're easier to handle than reel tapes, but it's nearly impossible to keep them clean and undamaged. Neither one holds very much music. A vinyl LP holds 16 to 24 minutes per side; modern dance music LPs hold 12 minutes or less because of the extreme thumping bass, which creates wider grooves. Don't even suggest using a record changer—those are for people who like having mangled records. A 1,200-foot, 7-inch reel of 1/4″ tape, which was common for home recording, holds 64 minutes per side at 3.75 inches per second (ips) and 32 minutes at 7.5 ips. (In comparison, professional recordings were made at 15 and 30 ips.) Neither one is easily portable, and you can't play them in cars.

Cassette tapes revolutionized home and portable audio. They were good compromises among sound quality, portability, and cost, and they were a lot more rugged than reel tapes or LPs. You can stop a cassette tape at any point and remove it from the machine; you can't do that very easily with reel tapes. Cassettes for the home market travel at 1 7/8 ips, and their tapes are 0.15″ wide. Sound quality isn't equal to that of LPs and reel tapes, but if you have a good recorder and use good-quality Type II or IV tape, it is pretty nice. Whenever I bought a new vehicle (new to me, that is), the first thing I did was put a good sound system in it. I made a lot of long trips because I liked going places, and having a big box of music tapes made those trips even more splendid. Cassette tapes came in a variety of sizes, and I liked 90-minute cassette tapes because I could get two LPs on one tape. A dual-well cassette player with auto-reverse delivered 180 uninterrupted minutes of music. Larger sizes, such as 120-minute cassettes, were too thin and fragile to use. Thinner tapes stretch; 60-minute, high-quality tapes are thickest and suffer the least amount of stretch.

Cassette recorders were the salvation of music lovers. My friends and I liked to make and exchange mix tapes, because even in my youth oh so long ago commercial radio was pretty horrible, just the same Top 20 dreck played over and over, with more commercials than music and annoying DJs interrupting the music. So, trading mix tapes was a great way to discover new music. Another cool thing was we could copy just the songs we wanted and not suffer through the filler that plagued so much popular music. Given the continual failures of the music industry to deliver what would please its customers, it's amazing that it survives at all. The bosses at the big labels should give thanks every day to determined customers who figure out workarounds that let them enjoy commercially produced music, rather than giving up on it entirely.

A Quick Tip About Tape

Alvin recalls that tape is manufactured very wide and very long: "The outermost edges, and the first and last lengths of the tape, are the poorest and used for the lowest-grade audio tape. The sections that are higher-grade become the higher quality audio tape, and the very best became the digital tape for computing. Because of this you can use most computer tape for audio, which I do. The large quarter-inch cartridge (QIC) tapes that have gone bad are fantastic reel-to-reel tapes. I have an ancient solid-state Ampex home audio recorder, circa 1969 (transistors, point-to-point wired like the old vacuum tubes). With no noise reduction, 1 7/8-, 3 3/4-, and 7 1/2- inch speeds, with RadioShack's cheapest tape and slowest speed, it sounds better than cassette metal tape and Dolby C noise reduction."

Cassette tapes are also given credit for spreading Western pop music, especially punk and rock, in developing nations and Eastern bloc countries.

There isn't much nostalgia for cassette tapes. They served a purpose, and some people still like them. But it's not easy to find good cassettes anymore because manufacturing quality has declined.

Neither tape nor vinyl ages well. Tape is a magnetic medium, so it can be ruined by stray magnetic fields. Tape is less prone to collect dust and scratches than vinyl, but both suffer physical wear and tear. Both will last decades if they are handled and stored carefully, but the sad fact is the more you play and enjoy them, the more they will wear out. They won't suddenly become unplayable; they tend to lose the high frequencies first and fade over time like a garment that is washed too many times.

The Digital Advantage

Lovers of vinyl claim that it sounds warmer, sounds more true to life, and has a wider and more accurate dynamic range. CD fans claim that LP aficionados are nostalgic for all the ambience that goes along with playing a vinyl record: the sounds made by the turntable, the addition of surface noise from dust and scratches, flipping it to hear the other side, and all the fussiness required to keep LPs in good condition. I miss the cover art, posters, and generously sized booklets that came with LPs—you just can't do much with a tiny CD case. But no matter how careful you are with keeping LPs clean, handling them carefully, keeping your stylus clean, and keeping your tonearm optimally balanced and tracked, it is impossible to avoid causing wear or even damage merely by playing them, because you're scraping a diamond stylus with a Mohs' scale hardness rating of 10 over a surface with a Mohs' hardness of 1.

Some LPs survive in better condition than others because they are better engineered. Vinyl LPs begin life as master tapes. These are copied to the master disk, which is made of metal or lacquer. Cutting a record is an exercise in compromise. Quiet passages can't be too quiet or they will be lost in noise, but if they are too loud, the grooves will overlap and create skips. Louder volume also results in less playing time, so there is as much artistry in the engineering as there is the in music itself. Unfortunately, all LPs are not created equal. As the industry matured, a multitude of demands were placed on the master recording engineers, who were often told to make the master tapes also serve as masters for cassettes, and butchered for radio play. The vinyl itself became thinner. In other words, the lowest common denominator reared its mediocre head. Older LPs are beloved because they're better made.

CDs have most of the technical advantages. The biggest advantage of digital audio is that copies are equal to the originals. This is not true of analog audio, which loses something with each generation. By the time you get to a copy of a copy of a copy, you know it's a long way from the original.

A CD offers as much as a 96 dB dynamic range, whereas the best vinyl delivers maybe 75 dB and, more typically, in the 50s. So, the CD offers a superior signal-to-noise ratio, plus something that even the best LP system is hard-pressed to deliver, and that is absolute silence in the silent passages. True, this absolute silence is largely theoretical because some sound will probably be created somewhere in your audio chain—a bit of hum, a touch of electrical interference—but the CD itself is dead silent. Vinyl wins on frequency range, sort of—if you have good enough equipment (which would make you a rare, wealthy, and elite audiophile indeed), it will capture frequencies as high as 70 to 75 kHz, up there where the bats fly. More typically it falls into the 10 Hz to 25 kHz range.

Down here in the real world, most audio hardware is designed with upper limits of 20 to 30 kHz in mind. The human ear can detect frequencies up to 25 kHz, and the range of sensation is 50 kHz. If you have something blasting away at 115 dB sound pressure level at a frequency of 45 kHz, you'll feel the pain but not know why. Some folks believe that very high frequencies are still perceived in some manner and add to the listener's enjoyment. What they might be talking about are the harmonics. If you have a sound at 100 Hz, there are harmonics of that sound at 25 Hz, 50 Hz, 200 Hz, and so on. If you clip the harmonics, the sound tends to sound a little dead on the high end.

I have compared some of my favorite music on both CD and LP, and it's the extra noise on LPs that sets them apart. I can really tell the difference in a symphony—the quiet passages on a CD are unmarred by scratches, hiss, or rumble, and the loud bits are loud and accurate, without distortion. If you want to make your own comparisons, make sure you have LPs and CDs that have been recorded with skill and care. An awful lot of them are junk, and the trend with modern popular music is simply to crank all levels on a CD to the maximum, with no regard for dynamic range, distortion, nuances, or balance. Pianos and organs are great for testing the quality of

Wire Recordings

The original master "tapes" were made on wire recorders, which used spools of steel wire as the recording medium. Wire recorders were in wide use until the 1960s, when they were supplanted by magnetic tape recorders. Old music, like the original Carter Family recordings of the 1920s, were recorded on wire recorders. Wire rusts, and the fidelity is nothing to get excited about, but it is very durable. Even so, most of those old recordings are lost.

But not all! *The Live Wire: Woody Guthrie in Performance 1949* won the 2008 Grammy for Best Historical Album. It was restored from wire recordings and is believed to be his only recorded live performance. Like a lot of wire recorders, these recordings were made on a home-built device, which complicates any restoration process. But restored they were, and now you can enjoy Woody Guthrie live on CD.

your audio system because their sounds are difficult to reproduce accurately, they have monster dynamic and frequency ranges, and you can tell pretty easily if they sound right. Try "Toccata and Fugue in D Minor" by Johann Sebastian Bach; this covers the full range of the pipe organ, the big kind you see in cathedrals. At one point, a bass pedal is held so long your speakers may visibly distort. Pink Floyd's "Time" from the *Dark Side of the Moon* exercises the sound separation among left, right, and true center. Jimi Hendrix's *Electric Ladyland*, if you can find the original double LP and not some bad CD remaster, is an amazing piece of studio and artistic wizardry that will exercise your audio system and reward careful listening.

CDs win hands down for convenience. They're sturdy, they don't get damaged from being played, you don't have to continually fuss with them, and they are portable. Most CD players have remote controls, and you can play the tracks in any order or shuffle. You can load multiple CDs in a CD changer without harm and bliss out for hours.

Despite the efforts of the music industry to foil our fair use rights and desire to enjoy music the way we want to, it's as easy to create custom-mix CDs as it was to create our own mix tapes. And for most of the same reasons: to package music the way we want and to discover new artists. (Chapter 5 tells how to make compilation CDs.) However, we now have two marvelous new options that we didn't have back in the olden days, and that is satellite radio and Internet radio. Neither one is high on the audio quality scale, but you can't beat them for variety and discovering new artists. Commercial broadcast radio is worse than ever, which I didn't believe was possible.

CDs also win on cost. A hundred dollars buys a perfectly satisfactory CD player. Even in the olden days, a good-quality turntable, cartridge, and stylus cost several hundred dollars, and they haven't gotten any cheaper. Oh, and

CD Players

You can spend a little or a lot on a CD player. Ideally, you'll be able to test them with your own sound system before making a purchase, especially if you're going for a higher-end model. As with all digital audio, the quality of the digital-to-analog converter determines how good it sounds, so spending more can make a difference. If you are connecting your CD player to a receiver or amplifier that has its own DAC (you'll see optical or coaxial digital inputs), that gives you two DACs to try. Using the digital connector means the CD player sends a digital signal to your receiver and does not use its own DAC. Instead, the receiver performs the conversion to analog. Using your CD player's RCA connectors means your CD player will do the conversion and send an analog signal to your receiver. If you have a high-end CD player, you probably don't want your receiver mucking with its output, so use the analog RCA connectors. Of course, it's not always that simple, because in some modern A/V receivers, the integrated preamp converts all incoming signals with no regard for whether they are analog or digital, which is dumb, but there it is. This is not always documented, so you might have to pester your vendor to find out what you have.

don't forget the dust cover, which was always an overpriced add-on. And a stylus-tracking force gauge, and cartridge alignment tool, and special cleaning accessories, and so on.

So who wins, vinyl or CDs? Easy—whichever one you like better. Don't get hung up on specs; it's the music and your enjoyment that matters.

Longevity

Longevity is still an open question. The current state of digital storage is not encouraging for the long term, so you better plan to periodically transfer your archives to fresh media. There are several problems with long-term digital storage: One, the physical media may not last for more than a few years without deteriorating. Two, think of all the closed, proprietary file formats that have come and gone in the past 10 or 20 years and are no longer readable. Three, if your media survive and the files are still readable, will you have a hardware device that can read your media? If someone handed you a 5.25″ disk, a Zip disk, a 3.5″ diskette, or a super floppy disk, would you have any idea what to do with it? Currently we take CDs, DVDs, USB sticks, and 3.5″ hard drives for granted, but they are all just a few years old, and we do not know what the future holds.

NOTE *There might be a business opportunity in old drives and software. Alvin notes, "There's a market for those who can transfer from the ancient media to current. I have a Viper QIC tape drive for the DC300 tapes, a Bernouli drive, a Questech 40MB drive (it was a favorite of Apple Macintosh's), a TEAC digital audio cassette drive (205MB storage), Zip and Jaz drives, 250MB Colorado QIC, and other floppy tape drives."*

Commercial CDs are pressed rather than burned like home-created CDs and will outlive most home-burned CDs because they are built of sturdier materials and have deeper grooves. CD-Rs will outlive CD-RWs; don't use CD-RWs for anything that you want to last more than a year or two.

There are significant differences in brands. Taiyo Yuden is the top-of-the-line manufacturer of CD and DVD blanks. Taiyo Yuden blanks appear under their own name and under different brand names, but the secondary vendors change their suppliers often, so you can't count on the names to tell you what you're getting. Genuine Taiyo Yuden blanks are made only in Japan. There are fakes, so search online to learn how to identify the real deal.

Verbatim, TDK, and Sony are also considered to be good brands, though they use multiple suppliers. You can read the disk ID after purchase with diskDVD Identifier and DVDInfo for Windows, DVD Media Inspector for Mac, and cdrecord and dvd+rw-mediainfo for Linux.

4

CREATING AND EDITING LIVE TRACKS FOR CD

 CDs are great for storing and distributing your own recordings, and you can use Audacity to prepare your tracks for copying to a CD.

Suppose you have some long tracks recorded in the studio or from a live performance. You might want to split them into individual songs or cut out material between songs and knit them together to sound like one long, unbroken live track. Maybe you're cutting and pasting the best of several different recording sessions. Perhaps you have multitrack recordings that need to be downmixed to two-channel stereo for CD. You want to clean it all up and make it sound as good as possible.

Recording live shows is challenging. I'll talk about several different ways to do this, from inexpensive and easy to more expensive with ultimate control over the final mix. Then we'll move on to using Audacity to prepare your recordings for CD.

NOTE *Please review Chapter 1 if you need to review how to use Audacity.*

The workflow goes like this:

1. Record stuff.

2. Apply cleanups and fixes in Audacity.

3. Create song titles and metadata for individual songs.

4. Export to two-channel 16/44.1 WAV.

5. Copy to CD and enjoy!

The most time-consuming part is fix-its and cleanups. If you don't need to do a lot of fixing, it goes fast.

Making Good Live Recordings

In Chapter 2, we learned about putting together a recording studio and how to turn your computer into a digital audio workstation. Making good live recordings is harder than making good studio recordings because so many things are out of your control. However, that's okay, because you're not necessarily after some sort of technical perfection but rather capturing the excitement and energy.

Getting good two-channel stereo recordings is pretty easy, because nearly all audio equipment supports two-channel stereo. If you want multichannel recordings of live shows (for more control of the mix), then you'll need more expensive equipment.

One of the biggest potential hurdles relates to who controls the venue's sound system. If it is you, then you can do whatever you want. If the performers or venue have their own system and technicians, then you'll need their cooperation.

Remember to record some audience noise in case you need to add a bit more live flavor. You should also record a few minutes' worth of various background and audience noises to use later for noise removal. You want good samples of noise not mixed with music, or anything you want to keep, for best noise removal.

Portable Digital Recorder

A little portable digital recorder just might surprise you with how well it can capture a live performance. The Zoom H2, which is my favorite compact digital recorder, has four built-in microphones. You can use either the front pair or rear pair or all four at once to create a spatial, three-dimensional sound. The Zoom comes with a little stand to put it on any flat surface and a handle that fits into a mic stand so you can easily position it anywhere (Figure 4-1). It's unobtrusive and even looks like an old-fashioned microphone.

Figure 4-1: The Zoom H2 on a microphone stand.

The Zoom has a 1/8″ stereo line input, which means you can connect it directly to a mixer. Usually in live shows all instruments and vocalists are connected to a single sound console, and even the most low-budget console should have a pair of stereo RCA recording outputs. The Zoom uses a two-RCA-to-1/8″ stereo TRS adapter, as shown in Figure 4-2.

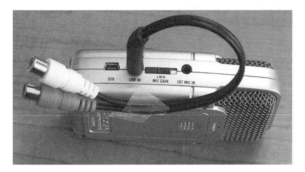

Figure 4-2: Zoom H2 with a two-RCA-to-1/8″ stereo adapter for connecting to a mixing console

Whatever you hear through headphones connected to a monitoring port on the sound board is how your recording will sound, so ideally there will be a good person at the sound board keeping all the channels balanced and sounding good. Because everything is already mixed down to two channels, your editing options are limited, so it needs to be right during recording.

The Zoom also has a USB 1.1 port to connect to your computer, so you can record directly to your computer if you prefer, rather than recording to the Zoom's SD storage card.

You don't have to use the Zoom H2 just because I like it—there are dozens of different great portable digital recorders to choose from, with all kinds of feature sets.

Laptop with Audacity

Fix up a laptop with Audacity and a decent recording interface, plug into the sound console at the show, and you can edit and make CDs on the spot. Copy the raw tracks to a USB stick for performers who want to do their own editing. If the internal sound card in your laptop does not suit you, try a nice external USB recording interface like the one in Figure 4-3, which shows a ThinkPad and M-Audio MobilePre USB all ready to go to the show.

Another option is to use a higher-end PCMCIA sound card like the Digigram VXpocket v2. The Digigram costs about $500. It works on Linux, Windows, and Mac; provides two channels at full duplex; and supports S/PDIF and XLR connectors.

Figure 4-3: ThinkPad and M-Audio MobilePre

Multitrack Recording of a Live Performance

Suppose you want more editing and mixing control, and you want to make a multichannel live recording. How do you do this? With the right knowledge and a big enough budget to support all the necessary equipment. Audacity records as many tracks at one time as your recording interface supports, starting with version 1.3.9. Older Audacity releases support a maximum of 16. (See Chapter 9 to learn more about making good multitrack recordings with Audacity.)

Don't try this without really knowing what you are doing, because connecting things the wrong way will result in bad sound or even damaged equipment. If you do not have control of the PA system at the venue, then you will need the cooperation and help of the resident sound engineer. Here are four different ways to approach making live multitrack recordings.

One option is to supply your own microphones and mic every performer and instrument separately from the venue's sound system. Although this means a lot of microphones and cables everywhere, this lets you use your own recording equipment independently of the main sound board.

A more common option is to use microphone and instrument cable splitters to make each mic and instrument cable do double duty. This is how many professionals record live concerts; they share mics that are run through splitters, and each team controls its own recording console. Sometimes these are tucked away backstage, and sometimes they have long cable runs running outside to mobile recording trucks. This setup has a lot of flexibility, and you can add your own mics as you see fit. For example, it seems to be a rule that no two people can agree on the correct way to mic drums, so they will set up their own drum mics.

You'll need splitters, transformers, maybe some resistors and patch panels, and cables, and you'll need to know how to connect everything. You'll need to know the ins and outs of dealing with phantom power and who supplies it, connecting and disconnecting in the correct order, getting along with the other stage and sound crews, and lots more.

One more option is to connect directly to a mixing console that supports multichannel outputs. (A good word to know is *busses*—the more busses a mixer has, the more flexible its signal routing options.) Then you don't need redundant mics or splitters and long cable runs. Look for *direct outs, aux sends*, or *subgroup outs*. Some outputs send signals that are affected by the mixer controls, so they'll have fades and special effects as applied by the console technician. If you want a straight unprocessed signal, that will depend on the features of the sound console and what the sound tech can let you use.

If you are the sound engineer and get to use your own equipment, consider getting a multichannel digital mixer, like the PreSonus Studio-Live 16-Channel FireWire Digital Mixer. Then you don't need a separate ADC/DAC, and you don't have to puzzle out how to make analog consoles designed for live shows also make good digital recordings. Sadly, the Studio-Live is not supported on Linux, but it has excellent software bundles for Mac and Windows. This is a super nice, new generation mixer that is designed to support multichannel recording, both in the studio and in the performance hall. It costs about $2,000, plus you'll also need an amplifier for powering live shows.

Be Nice to the Sound Crews

Be nice to the venue's sound engineers and crew. They are skilled professionals who have to combine both science and artistry, and they will make or break your recordings. Don't act like you know everything, because they won't be fooled. In my experience, sound crews at live shows are nice people who share their expertise generously as long as you listen carefully, are helpful, and keep out of their way.

Audacity Settings for Recording

Let's run through the appropriate recording settings in **Edit** > **Preferences**. (Please visit Chapters 13 and 14 to learn how to tune your PC for audio recording and managing your sound devices.)

First, open a new Audacity project and use **File** > **Save As** to save and name your new project. You can't save changes while Audacity is recording, so you might take advantage of short breaks to stop recording, press CTRL-S or use **File** > **Save Project**, and then pick up where you left off with SHIFT-Record.

Set your recording and playback devices on the **Edit** > **Preferences** > **Devices** tab and set the number of channels you are recording. Audacity will show only the number of channels that your recording interface supports. Windows users, always select **Windows DirectSound** and never MME for the Host, because MME is the antiquated generic Windows sound interface. You could select **Primary Sound Driver** for your recording and playback devices if you have only one sound card. If you have more than one, then select the specific recording interface from the drop-down Recording Device menu (Figure 4-4). (Your selections will be different, unless you have the same audio interfaces that I have.)

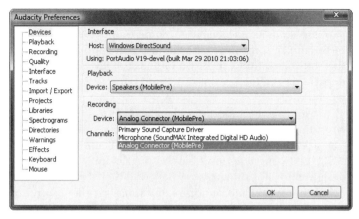

Figure 4-4: Setting the correct recording and playback devices in the
Edit > **Preferences** > **Devices** *dialog on Windows*

Figure 4-5 shows how it looks on a Linux PC:

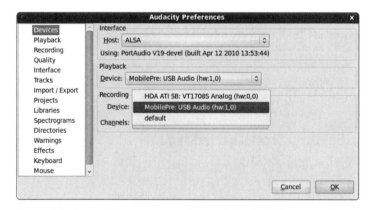

Figure 4-5: Setting the correct recording and playback devices in the
Edit > **Preferences** > **Devices** *dialog on Linux*

You'll probably want to review your recordings during breaks in the show, so set your playback device to something that outputs to headphones.

On the Recording tab, uncheck "Overdub," "Software Playthrough," and "Sound Activated Recording." Leave your Latency settings alone unless you experience dropouts. Dropouts mean your CPU can't keep up, so increase the Audio to buffer value until the dropouts stop (Figure 4-6).

The settings on the Quality tab (Figure 4-7) depend on what your analog-to-digital converter supports. Let's say you have an analog mixer connected to a high-end sound card that supports up to 24/96 (24-bit depth, 96 kHz sampling rate); if you have enough hard drive space, you could record at 32-bit depth and 96,000 Hz sampling rate for ultimate high quality. (*Bit depth* is called *Sample Format* in this menu. Bit depth is the correct term.)

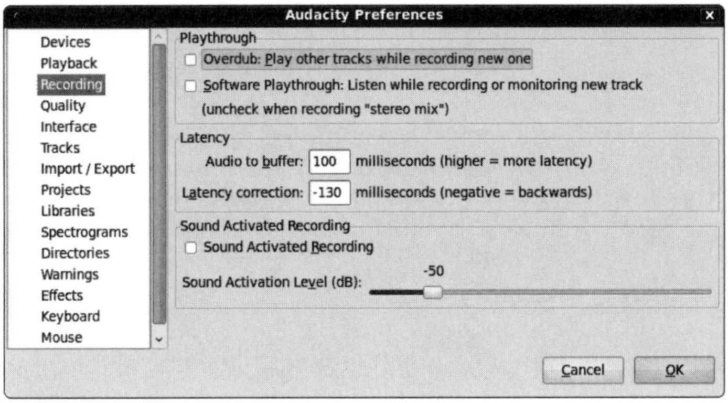

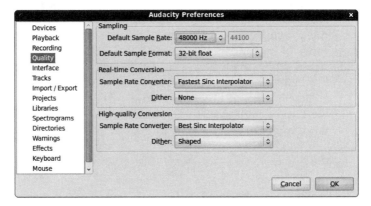

Figure 4-6: Entering settings on the Recording tab

Figure 4-7: Settings in the Quality tab are determined by what your recording interface supports and your preference.

My MobilePre maxes out at 16/48, so I set Audacity to 32-bit float/48 for recording. It's no good setting a higher sampling rate (upsampling) than your recording interface supports because there is no magic quality infusion. It wastes disk space and bogs down your CPU, and upsampling hurts audio quality. But there are benefits to recording at 32-bit float even on 16-bit sound cards, which is explained in Chapter 1. (See "16/44.1, 24/96, 32-Bit Float" on page 27 to learn more about quality settings.)

If you are recording from a digital mixer or a mixer with its own digital output, then that will determine your maximum bit depth/sampling rate. For example, the Behringer Xenyx X2442USB 24-Channel Mixer is an analog mixer with a built-in ADC that delivers a 16/48 digital signal via USB. It plugs right into your computer, so you don't need a sound card. So you could set Audacity to record at 32-bit float/48 for maximum quality. If 16/48 isn't good enough, you could connect an outboard ADC that supports higher bit depths and sampling rates to the Xenyx's RCA analog recording outputs.

Don't Switch Your Quality Settings Until You've Finished!

It is best to stick with the same quality settings throughout recording and editing, until your final exports. Changing bit depths and resampling are not good for audio quality, so the fewer times a recording is resampled or exported to a lower bit depth, the better. I record and edit at 32-bit float/48 and then export to different quality levels as I need them, such as 24-bit WAV and FLAC for highest quality or the lower-quality Ogg Theora or MP3 formats. If you prefer recording and editing at lower quality levels, such as 16/44.1 (which is CD quality), the same principle applies: Use 16/44.1 from recording to final edit, and then if you want lower quality levels, select them as needed at export.

There isn't much difference between a 44.1 kHz sampling rate and 48 kHz. The sampling rate determines your frequency range, which is about half the sample rate. 44.1 kHz covers the range of human hearing. Sometimes I can hear a small difference in recordings made at 48 kHz compared to 44.1 kHz recordings, but I have to be listening for it on a good sound system. There is a more noticeable difference between 16- and 24-bit recordings. Start with a high-quality recording, and then you can export to any number of lesser-quality formats as you want.

Setting Recording Volume Levels

Set your recording levels before you start by clicking the **Input Level Meter** (Figure 4-8). Because digital recording has such a high signal-to-noise ratio, which is also called a *low noise floor*, you can set a conservative peak level to allow for the unpredictability of a live performance. It's not like recording

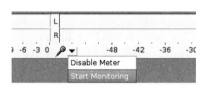

Figure 4-8: Turn on the recording monitor to set your peak recording levels before starting recording.

on tape where we had to push recording levels as high as possible to keep noise levels at acceptable levels; you don't want to go over zero in digital audio because that causes distortion. I aim for a peak level of −24 dB for live shows. The Meter toolbar has a little handle on the right to make it longer or shorter, and the handle on the left is for dragging it anywhere you want, even outside of Audacity.

Starting, Stopping, and Pausing Recording

When you're ready to start recording, just click the red **Record** button. Click **Pause** to stop and then **Record** to continue on the same track. Clicking **Stop** and then **Record** starts new tracks, so if you stop when you meant to pause, pick up again on the same track by pressing SHIFT-Record.

Monitoring Your Live Recording

The best way to monitor your recording is by plugging headphones into a monitoring port. For example, the MobilePre has a zero-latency monitoring port, and there are always monitoring ports on mixers. The better recording interfaces have zero-latency monitoring ports, which is a good thing to look for when you're shopping.

Editing Live Recordings

Well, that was fun! You heard a great show, or had a wonderful studio session, and recorded everything successfully. Now how do you get all that goodness onto a CD?

If you used a digital recorder, you need to copy the files from the recorder into your Audacity computer. I prefer to use a separate storage card reader rather than connecting the recorder to the computer because it usually works better and faster, especially on non-Windows PCs. Any SD or Compact Flash card should be seen by your PC as a generic USB storage device, but manufacturers love to infest devices that use them with weird Windows-only file transfer managers. This does not make sense to me, since Windows has a perfectly good built-in USB storage device manager. Many of them also have a fondness for using USB 1.1, and not the full-speed 12Mbps but the agonizingly slow 1.5Mbps version, which is super fun when you fill a multigigabyte SD card.

However you do it, once your recording is transferred to your Audacity PC, open Audacity and use **File** > **Open** to import your recording into Audacity. Then save this new Audacity project with **File** > **Save Project As** and give it a different name than your audio filename. Audacity will warn you that "Project depends on other audio files" (Figure 4-9) and ask whether you want to copy all audio into your project. Click **Copy All Audio into Project (Safer)**. Now you have your original and a copy, and whatever you do in your Audacity project does not touch the original file. (See "Saving Your Work" on page 13 to learn more.)

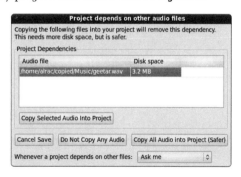

Figure 4-9: Making a copy of your original recording to preserve it

If your recording has multiple files, create a separate Audacity project for each one. I like to use related project names like Fiddle-Festival-1, Fiddle-Festival-2, and so on.

If you made your original recording in Audacity, you can work from your original project file, which will change it, or you can make a copy and work from that. To make a copy, click **File** > **Save Project As** to save it with a different name.

Editing and Downmixing Multitrack Recordings

You can skip this section if you are working from a two-channel stereo recording.

This section is a short review of multichannel downmixing, so please visit Chapter 9 to learn about multitrack recording and mixing in detail.

If you made a multitrack recording, which is three tracks or more, you have a lot more great editing options than with a two-channel stereo mix. One track per vocalist or instrument gives you ultimate control, and even if you had to settle for subgroups because of limitations of the mixer, this is still a feast of flexibility.

Starting in Audacity version 1.3.8, you can use the sleek new Mixer Board to adjust the pan and gain on each track by selecting **View** > **Mixer Board**. The playback in Audacity is exactly how your mix sounds, so you get an accurate preview of your mix.

Of course, you can still use the Pan and Gain controls on the Track panels of each track if you prefer.

Editing and fixing your tracks is the same whether you have a stereo mix or a multitrack recording, which we'll cover in the following sections. There are some special hazards with multiple tracks. One is keeping them synchronized. Be careful with deletions and additions, because this changes the length of the tracks. Another is downmixing to two-channel stereo combines tracks so they get louder and might create clipping. Third is the Link Tracks button, which first appeared in Audacity 1.3.9. This keeps label tracks synchronized with the audio tracks. Having a label track at the top of your project is useful for making notes, and it does not link to the tracks below it. But a label track that lies underneath your audio tracks, which is where new label tracks always appear when you create new ones, creates a track group that includes all the audio tracks above it. Link Tracks is enabled by default, so if it gets in your way, just click the **Link Tracks** button to turn it off. Newer Audacity versions display chain links that appear when you make any selection or Time Shift tracks to indicate that Link Tracks is active (Figure 4-10).

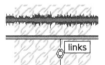

Figure 4-10: Chain links appear when the Link Tracks button is active.

There are two ways to downmix. This first method is clicking **Tracks** > **Mix and Render**, which creates a new stereo track in your Audacity project. You can then make further adjustments before export, such as creating labels, fixes, and other edits. It will sound just like the playback in Audacity sounds, so when it sounds right in Audacity, it's ready to go. First set your left, right, and mono channel assignments in the Track menus. Left is channel 1, right is channel 2, and mono tracks are mixed down to both.

When you click **Tracks > Mix and Render**, your tracks are replaced with a new stereo track. If you would rather have Audacity create a new stereo track without replacing your original tracks, use the keyboard combination CTRL-SHIFT-M. I prefer the second method because I want to save my original tracks. Then I copy the new stereo track into a new project, finish editing, and then export.

Downmixing combines tracks, so they get louder. Make sure **View > Clipping** is activated so you can quickly find clipped passages. You might reduce the amplitude of all your tracks before downmixing with **Effect > Amplify** to −9 or −12 and then apply **Effect > Normalize** after downmixing to bring the volume back up where you want.

The second downmixing method opens a custom mixer, which is really a channel mapper, at export. Open **Edit > Preferences > Import/Export**, and select "Use custom mix." Then select **File > Export**, and you'll get a simple mixer (Figure 4-11) that allows you to control your channel mapping. This is how you control which tracks go to the right channel, left channel, or both. Channel 1 is always the left channel.

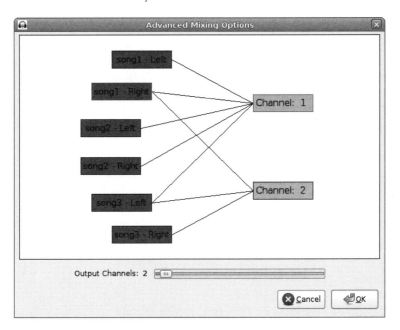

Figure 4-11: Downmixing a multichannel recording into two stereo tracks

This does not work with **File > Export Multiple**, so if you want to divide your downmixed track into individual songs, you'll have to import it back into Audacity.

Special CD Settings in Audacity

The next thing you need to do is go to the Selection toolbar and change the timing to CD frames, which is 75 frames per second (fps). This ensures that any cuts you make will start and end on a CD frame. Any audio that lands outside of these frames will be lost and will possibly create clicking noises. Figure 4-12 shows what this looks like. You can choose either hh:mm:ss + CDDA frames (75 fps) or CDDA frames (75 fps). The former shows the time plus CD frames, and the latter displays only CD frames. Check the "Snap To" box to ensure that stops and starts are always on the CD frame boundaries.

Figure 4-12: Setting the correct frame rate for CD audio in the Selection toolbar

While you're at the Selection toolbar, set the Project Rate value to 44,100 Hz. Audio files for CD must be 16/44.1 WAV files. (The bit depth will be selected at export.)

Trimming

Now it's time to do some housecleaning on your recording. Remember that you have a lot of different views to choose from, such as **View > Fit in Window**, **View > Fit Vertically**, and the Zoom tool. Pressing CTRL-2 returns to Normal view. **View > Zoom to Selection** is a great little time-saver that expands your selection to the width of the window. Remember also that Audacity has nearly unlimited undo, even past saves. You don't lose your undo history until you close your project.

A good starting point is to trim away any excess. When you select unwanted segments for deletion, leave a little extra. You can always trim more, but it's harder to put it back. The shaded area in Figure 4-13 is a bunch of people speechifying and is not something I want to save, so it's gone all in one swoop. There doesn't appear to be anything at the beginning or in between the songs to trim right now, so I'll leave those alone until later.

Another way to trim a lot of excess is to select what you want to keep and then click the **Trim** button. This keeps your selection and deletes the rest.

Splitting Stereo Tracks for Surgical Repairs

Sometimes there will be a defect on just one channel of a two-channel stereo track. If you split this into two tracks, then you can apply repairs to just the one channel and rejoin the tracks. There are a couple of advantages to this: The second track helps to mask a less-than-perfect fix, and the fix that you apply to the defective portion probably won't help the other channel sound any better and may even hurt the quality.

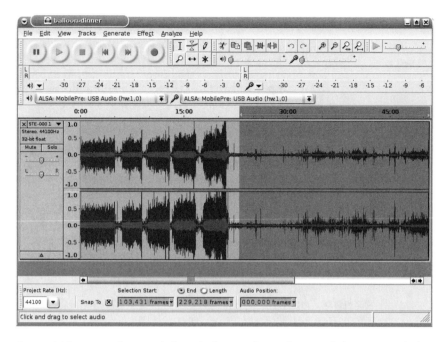

*Figure 4-13: Using **View** > **Fit in Window** to do rough cuts with the entire track displayed*

To divide a stereo track, go to the Track menu and click **Split Stereo Track**. To rejoin the tracks, use the Track menu in the track that is on top and click **Make Stereo Track**. The two tracks must be adjacent to each other.

Fixing Clipping and Too-Loud Passages

Hunt down any clipping and too-loud passages and fix them. These throw off the volume levels for the whole track and shock listeners, so it's always a good idea to fix them.

Find any clipping quickly by selecting **View** > **Show Clipping**. This marks any clipped passages with red bars. Zoom in on the clipped segments until you can precisely select the parts that are too loud and then use a negative value, such as −3 dB, in **Effect** > **Amplify** to lower the volume. Rerecording clipped segments is better, but since you probably won't have that opportunity with a live show, making them less noticeable is the next best thing. Click the **Preview** button to see whether it sounds right, and if it doesn't, change the Amplification value until it does. Then click **OK** to make it permanent.

NOTE   *Adjust the length of previews in **Edit** > **Preferences** > **Playback**. The default is three seconds.*

Look for any extreme peaks that are not clipped, which could be a drum beat, sudden audience noise, something dropped, a bump of the mic—whatever it is, check it out and decide whether it needs to be toned down.

If any clipped or too-loud passage is so obnoxious you want to remove it entirely, select it and select **Edit** > **Silence** (or CTRL-L) to make it totally silent. You might not want to delete it because that shortens the track, which would be a problem on a multitrack project. If it is so long that silencing it would be too noticeable, try patching the annoying part with a clip from somewhere else. To do this, first delete the offending bit with **Edit** > **Split Cut**. This leaves a gap in place of the deleted portion. Then carefully paste into the gap a segment of the same length copied from another part of the track, or even from a different track; you can use anything as long as it sounds all right. This can be finicky work, so remember to zoom in so you can see what you're doing. The Envelope tool is good for smoothing transitions with careful fades, or try the Draw tool to apply some careful interpolation.

Noise Removal

Audacity's Noise Removal tool is pretty good, though it can take a few tries to get it right because noise removal is always a compromise with its side effects—removing noise also affects the sounds you want to keep. If the sounds that you want to keep have similar volume and frequencies as the noise, you might not get very good results. Noise removal works best when the noise is distinctly different from what you want to keep.

First you need to create a profile of the unwanted noise. This is why you recorded various audience and background noise samples at the live show, so you would have good samples to create a profile from. Create a noise profile by selecting a 5- to 30-second segment of noise, then go to **Effect** > **Noise Removal** and click **Get Noise Profile**. (If your samples are not long enough, double them up by copying and pasting them into the same track.) Then select the part of the track you want to remove the noise from, go back to **Effect** > **Noise Removal**, and click the **Preview** button to hear how it sounds (Figure 4-14).

The Noise Removal effect has three adjustable settings: Noise reduction, Frequency smoothing, and Attack/decay time. Noise reduction controls how much the volume of the noise is reduced, so a value of −10 turns it down by 10 decibels, and −50 will nuke it into silence. For both Frequency smoothing and Attack/decay time, moving the slider to the left is more aggressive, and moving it to the right makes gentler changes. A larger value for Frequency smoothing means it changes a wider range of frequencies. Remember: Attack refers to how hard a note is hit, and decay is how long it takes to fade away. Smaller values are more abrupt, and larger values are more gradual.

When the Preview sounds good, click **OK**. If you don't like it after pressing OK, press CTRL-Z to undo, or use **Edit** > **Undo**, to try again.

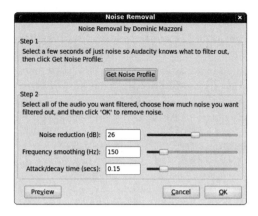

Figure 4-14: Using the Noise Removal effect to tone down unwanted background noises

You can build your noise profile with noise samples from the Freesound Project (*http://www.freesound.org/*). This is a collaborative database of Creative Commons—licensed sounds. You can find just about anything here, including samples of white, pink, and brown noise; buzz from a bad TRS plug connection; pool hall noise; and lots more. You can contribute your own samples to the project, too.

Compressing Dynamic Range

Using dynamic range compression wisely is an important skill in audio editing. For example, in podcasts that have more than one person talking, it's a kindness to your listeners to make sure that the volume levels of the various people speaking are all the same. Compression is also used to change the character of sounds. For example, drums are mostly rapid peak sounds, so a bit of compression is used to give them a fuller, richer sound. Compression can make a vocalist or instrument "pop" out of the mix and make it sound more vivid. Compression can also help level out an erratic performer, such as a singer with bad mic technique or an instrumentalist who doesn't have good volume control but is loud and soft at the wrong times.

What you can accomplish with compression will be limited by your recordings. If you have multitrack recordings with every performer and instrument on their own tracks, or usefully subgrouped, then you have all kinds of editing flexibility. If your recording is two-track stereo, then you can't edit very surgically, but you can apply compression to the whole recording to make it sound better in noisy environments, such as vehicles and workplaces. Controlling it yourself means you can measure out just the right amount.

There are several places in the audio chain where compression can be applied. Was a compressor used during recording? If it was, be careful about applying any more because that can make your track sound fake or weird.

I'm conservative when it comes to using compression. If something needs to be louder or quieter, I prefer to adjust it with the Envelope tool or Amplify effect. In the olden days of tape, compression techniques like Dolby noise reduction were used to minimize tape hiss. Music was compressed in the recording and then expanded on playback to lower the noise floor. Digital audio has such a high signal-to-noise ratio, this isn't necessary.

Now let's learn how to use Audacity's Compressor effect (Figure 4-15).

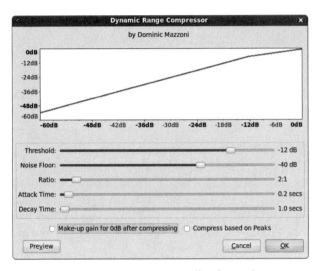

Figure 4-15: Audacity's Compressor effect for applying dynamic range compression

Select what you want to apply compression to, part of a track or a whole track, and then click **Effect** > **Compressor** to open the Compressor effect. You can make the Compressor window larger and expand the decibel scales by dragging the corners.

The Threshold setting determines the starting point, in decibels, where the gain of the audio signal is reduced. A threshold of −60 dB means everything with an amplitude of −60 dB and above will have reduced gain, which in most cases is too much, since that will be everything. A threshold of −10 dB means the loudest 10 dB of your track will have its gain reduced.

The Noise Floor setting prevents background noise from being amplified during pauses by keeping the gain constant until the signal comes back up to the Threshold level; it does not allow the gain to increase in quiet passages that are below the Noise Floor decibel setting. If there are no quiet pauses in your audio, then this setting won't help much, and you should move the slider all the way to the left, −80 dB, to make it have no effect.

The Ratio setting controls how much compression, or reduction in gain, will be applied to sounds that are higher than your Threshold setting. A higher ratio, such as 4:1, means more compression. An input signal of 4 dB higher than your threshold will be reduced to 1 dB higher than the threshold, so it applies a 3 dB reduction. Try gentler ratios first, starting at 2:1, and then listen to the preview. If it's not enough, try a higher ratio. Audacity's compressor has a maximum ratio of 10:1, which is a lot. Other compressors go as high as 60:1.

Attack Time determines how quickly compression is applied, and Decay Time determines how long it takes to phase out the compression. A too-short Attack Time might result in some audible distortion, and a too-long Decay Time might miss some short peaks. The Preview button helps you try different settings quickly.

Compression makes your audio quieter, so you may need to amplify or normalize it after applying compression. The Compressor effect has a "Make-up gain for 0 dB after compressing" checkbox, which is another way of saying apply normalization to 0 dB. I don't use it because I prefer to control normalization separately, and I don't always normalize to 0 dB, but it's there if you want to save a step.

There is also a "Compress based on Peaks" checkbox. When this box is unchecked, which is the default, the compressor reduces the gain on sounds above the Threshold level using RMS values. "Compress based on Peaks" raises the gain on quieter sounds that are above the Threshold level.

Be careful with compression because it is easy to overdo it. In much of modern popular music, there is virtually no dynamic range; it's all rammed into the same narrow 5 dB or even smaller range with no quiet passages, no contrast, and just one big shouting blob all boosted to the maximum, sometimes even into distortion. Any emotional impact and artistry are destroyed. You're trying to make it more comfortable for different listening environments or improve how a vocalist or instrument sound, not kill the recording entirely.

Visit "Compress Dynamic Range" on page 240 to learn more about dynamic range compression and how to use the excellent Chris's Dynamic Compressor.

Cutting a Single Long Track into Individual Song Tracks

Do this when you have a single stereo track in your Audacity project and have already done all of your other cleanups and fixes. A single stereo track in an Audacity project can contain a number of songs, but to Audacity it's all one long, unbroken track; it doesn't know where the song breaks are, so you have to make them yourself. There are two different approaches you can take. One is the usual collection of separate songs with a few seconds of silence dividing them. Another is marking the song breaks so you can skip around, but with no breaks between them, like a live concert album.

Whichever you prefer, just do as shown in Figure 4-16: Figure out where you want each song break; then press CTRL-B to mark the spot and create a *label*. This is where you type in the name of the song. Labels go at the beginning of the songs, so when you start, first press the **Home** key on your keyboard to make sure you're at the very beginning.

Figure 4-16: Creating song titles and breaking up a long track into individual songs with a label track

If you need to move a label, grab it by its moving handle, which is the little round dot (Figure 4-17).

The angle handles are for extending labels to mark sections of your track. These are called *region labels* (Figure 4-18). Learn all about labels and label tracks in "Creating and Managing Labels" on page 173.

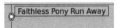

Figure 4-17: The little round dot in the label handle is for moving the label.

Figure 4-18: Drag the angle handles to use labels to mark out sections of track.

In Audacity versions 1.3.9 and newer, beware the Link Tracks button. This keeps audio and label tracks synchronized and can get in the way by forcing tracks to be aligned when you don't want them to be. Turn off Link Tracks if it gets in your way, though this is less likely to be a problem for a single stereo track. Link Tracks probably won't appear in the first 2.*x* Audacity release but may appear later when the kinks are worked out. Learn more about Link Tracks in "Link Tracks and Track Groups" on page 176.

Creating Graceful Breaks Between Songs

Creating silence between songs, with graceful fades in and out, is easy in Audacity. There are several tools to choose from. First, let's try the Envelope tool. Figure 4-19 shows it in action, creating about a 2.5-second fade-out to silence and then fading back in. The little, white squares are the *node control points*. Create these by clicking the track, and then you can move them to make adjustments. Each node has four control points—one inner pair and one outer pair. Control

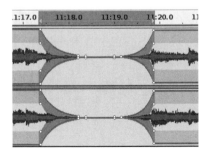

Figure 4-19: Using the Envelope tool to create fade-ins and fade-outs

points move both horizontally and vertically. To get rid of a node, grab a control point and drag it outside the track's boundary.

Envelope tools are standard in most audio-editing applications. It takes a bit of practice to get the hang of them, but once you figure them out, you gain a high degree of control over fades and amplitude.

You may also try selecting **Effect** > **Fade Out** and **Effect** > **Fade In**, which is fast and easy. All you control is the length of the fade. First select the segment that you want to fade and then apply the effect. Figure 4-20 shows how to create a nice 10-second fade-out.

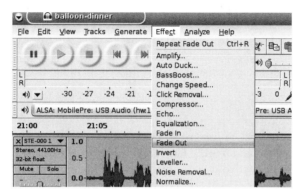

Figure 4-20: First make a selection 10 seconds long and then apply **Effect** > **Fade Out**.

Suppose you want two seconds of silence between songs, but there isn't that much space between them—no problem, you can insert as much silence as you want by selecting **Generate** > **Silence**. Use the Selection tool to mark where you want the silence to begin, select **Generate** > **Silence**, set it to two seconds, and click **OK**.

NOTE   *Beware of CD-writing applications that automatically insert two-second breaks between songs. This should be a configurable behavior.*

Normalization

One of the last steps to perform is to apply normalization to raise the volume level of your track. Select the whole track, and then select **Effect** > **Normalize**. Check both "Remove any CD offset" and "Normalize maximum amplitude to." The highest value you can use for the maximum amplitude is zero, which is a good value to use for a two-channel stereo track.

Optional Track Metadata

You have the option to write track metadata using the **File** > **Open Metadata Editor** dialog. Before export, fill in information common to all the tracks: artist name, album title, genre, date, and comments. Audacity will automatically fill in the track names from the labels or track names and number each track automatically. You can see a preview for each track at export if you open the **Edit** > **Preferences** > **Import/Export** dialog and check "Show Metadata Editor prior to export step." Uncheck this to skip the per-track preview.

WAV format does not support CD text or metadata. (Other audio file formats do, such as Ogg, FLAC, and MP3.) This is not the same as CD text. CD text is a nonstandard extension to the Red Book CD Audio format that displays song titles on CD players that support it. Most software CD players support CD text, and so do newer home and car CD players. Most CD-writing software supports CD text, so you can enter the individual song titles when you are authoring the CD. Some CD-writing programs (such as Nero, which runs on both Linux and Windows) extract song titles from the file-names, which is a lovely time-saver.

The metadata are always preserved in your Audacity projects.

Final Export

This has been a great journey, from recording to editing, and now you are two steps away from creating CDs of your great recordings. The second-to-last step is to export your recordings to the correct format for CDs, which is 16/44.1 two-channel WAV. This is also the step where your tracks are broken up into individual song files. (If your project has more than two tracks, please see "Editing and Downmixing Multitrack Recordings" on page 88.)

If you have not already set the sampling rate for your project to 44.1, do so now. Change the Project Rate setting to 44,100 Hz on the Selection toolbar. Then select **Tracks** > **Resample**, set the rate to 44,100, and click **OK**. This will take a few minutes on long tracks.

Now click **File** > **Export Multiple**. Enter the directory you want to save your audio files in and select both "Split files based on: Labels" and "Name files: Using Track/Label Name."

Click the **Options** button to set the correct export format. Choose Header: WAV (Microsoft) and Encoding: Signed 16 bit PCM (Figure 4-21).

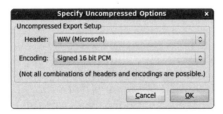

Figure 4-21: The correct export format settings for CDs

Your track will be exported as a bunch of individual WAV files, one per label.

Writing Your Songs to CD

Now you have a batch of nice individual WAV files, one file per song. Use your favorite CD-burning program to put your tunes on a CD. Be sure to create an audio project and not a data project, because CDs must be in the Red Book Audio format to play in all CD players. Set your burn speed to half the maximum as coaster insurance. Some CD-writing programs, like Nero, automatically grab the song titles from your WAV filenames, which is a nice time-saver. Most CD-writing programs create a default two-second gap between songs, so watch out for this. You can make a live album that sounds like one long, unbroken track by eliminating these gaps and still have individual song tracks so you can skip around.

Labeling Your CD

Don't use sticky paper labels on your CDs, because these degrade the disc over time. There are better ways to create nice-looking labels. You can get special CD blanks that are made to be printed on by inkjet printers that support printing on CDs. These are different from ordinary printers by having a special tray to hold the disc.

Another type of printable CD requires a special thermal printer. These are not expensive, usually around $100.

A third type is the *LightScribe* CD, which requires a special CD writer and CD blanks. These cost about the same as ordinary CD/DVD writers, around $50.

There are many software programs for designing your CD labels and making them look nice and professional.

Mass CD Duplication

You might want to make CDs to distribute, and you can do this without spending huge amounts of money. There are many laser CD duplicators that are like your computer's CD burner, only faster and with multiple trays. These range from about $400 for simple duplicators with manual feeds to several thousand dollars for automatic feeds and local data storage.

There are also commercial duplication services with varying levels of service, such as cover art and design. These can be cost-effective and save you time and hassle. The best CDs are pressed rather than burned. A duplication service that uses a press rather than a laser duplicator costs more and usually requires larger runs. But your discs will last longer.

"Do I need to buy a special audio CD?" is a common question. No, you do not. All CDs are exactly the same type, but it is worth sticking with good brands like Taiyo Yuden (my favorite). Verbatim, Ridata, and MAM-A are also reliable brands. Always get CD-R; don't bother with CD-RW except for experimentation. See "There Is Not a Special Audio CD" on page 102 for more information.

Combining Songs from Different Recording Sessions, Fix-its, and Special Effects

There are a few different ways to combine songs from different recording sessions onto a CD. Please see Chapter 5 to learn how to do this.

Chapter 11 covers special effects, and Chapter 12 has more details on fix-its and cleanups.

5

AUTHORING A COMPILATION CD

You can make custom-mix CDs just like we used to make custom-mix tapes back in the olden days. There are many reasons for making your own custom-mix discs: to make your own song collections, to make your own greatest hits samplers, to combine your best live performances, to make party discs, to make a promotional CD of your own music, to weed out songs you don't care for, to condense several CDs or LPs into fewer discs . . . whatever your reasons, it's easy to do with Audacity.

This newfangled digital era is the best: You can make copies that are perfect clones of the originals, and it's faster and easier to edit files on a computer than on tape. Creating your own custom CD goes like this: Collect the audio tracks you want to use in Audacity, apply cleanups and edits, write your track metadata, export to your desired format, write to a CD, and you're done.

Audio CDs

There are two types of audio CDs that you can make, and which type you choose is determined by your playback devices. The standard CD that plays on all CD players is encoded according to the Red Book CD Audio standard. This is what commercially recorded CDs use, and this is what you want to use to make a universally playable disc. That is no big technical deal, because all you do is choose "Create an audio CD" in your CD-writing program. You must always create 16/44.1 WAV files for Red Book CDs.

The second type of CD you can make is written to the Orange Book standard to play on a computer. Again, this is no big technological deal; it's just an ordinary data CD, and in your CD-writing program you'll choose "Create a data CD." On this type of disc you may use any audio file format you want, such as FLAC or 24-bit WAV for higher quality or lossy, compressed formats like Ogg Vorbis or MP3 to cram more songs onto a disc. You are limited only by your choice of software media player, and these days it's a rare software media player that doesn't support everything under the sun.

You should verify CD-R and CD-RW support in your CD player. CD-RWs are great for creating temporary collections for parties and special events, but some CD players don't handle them very well. Some don't even handle CD-Rs well, but that is pretty rare anymore. Some newer CD/DVD players support non–Red Book formats such as MP3, WAV, and WMA.

NOTE *Alvin, our excellent technical reviewer, explains why older CD players have problems reading newer discs. "The older azide-based discs had a very large difference in reflectance, and the sensitivity of the player was set to this large difference. With CD-RW and the pthalocyanine (silver)–based discs, the difference in reflectivity of the 0 and 1 (burned vs. unburned) disc is much smaller."*

There Is Not a Special Audio CD

I've said it before, and I'll say it again: All blank CDs are exactly the same type; there is no such thing as a special audio CD, even though you see them in stores. The only special things about them are a pressed data flag that is part of the Serial Copy Management System (SCMS) to control copying protected material and a copying tax that goes to the Recording Industry Association of America (RIAA) or its equivalent in other countries. The SCMS encoding controls three states: copy allowed (00), copy once (11), and copy prohibited (10). It might get in the way if you try to use the kind of CD player that attaches to your stereo system to copy a copy of a commercial CD. But you can copy the original all you want, and computer hardware and media are exempt from being SCSM-compliant.

There are quality differences among brands, and different materials are used to make the discs. Taiyo Yuden makes its own discs; they are very good and promise the most longevity. Mitsui, Phillips, Kodak, Verbatim, and TDK are all reliable as well. The price difference between the good brands and the not-so-good brands isn't significant. There is no point in pinching pennies because you'll just create more coasters with the lesser-quality brands, so you won't save any money. See Andy McFadden's CD-Recordable FAQ (*http://www.cdrfaq.org/faq.html*) to learn all about CD media.

Convert MP3s to Red Book CD

A commonly asked question is "How do I copy my MP3s to a CD that will play on every CD player?" They must be converted to 16/44.1 WAV files and then Red Book–encoded. To do this, use Audacity to convert MP3s to 16/44.1 WAV format, and then in your CD-writing program select "Create an audio CD." It won't give you WAV quality; it will still be lo-fi, lossy MP3 quality. You won't get more than 80 minutes of music on your disc even with the smaller file sizes. But you'll have a standard CD that will play anywhere.

CD Writers and Software

These days, most consumer-level CD/DVD burners are pretty good and not very expensive, about $40 to $90. External USB burners are portable, and some are bus powered so you don't need a power cord.

CD-writing software is everywhere. For basic CD writing, you shouldn't have to pay money because there are dozens of freebies. There is built-in CD/DVD-writing software in Windows, though it's pretty limited. Nero and Roxio are decent and offer inexpensive editions. For more advanced tasks, Sony's Creative Software CD Architect (Windows only) is a decent value in a CD-mastering program at less than $100, with professional features such as cross-fades, cue sheets, indexing long live tracks, previews, dithering, resampling, karaoke, and DJ mixes.

Linux users have three good graphical open source applications to choose from: Brasero, Gnome CD Master, and K3b. All are graphical frontends to powerful command-line apps such as wodim, cdrdao, and various encoders and converters. They, of course, can be used on their own without the pretty graphical interfaces.

Gapless burning is a common problem in do-it-yourself audio circles. This means creating a CD that plays one long, unbroken track, like a live show, with no breaks between songs. This can be put together from multiple audio files or from a single long WAV file. You need a CD burner that supports gapless burning, which now should be all CD/DVD burners. Look for session-at-once (SAO) and disc-at-once (DAO) support. Track-at-once (TAO) means the laser pauses at the end of each track. SAO burns your whole session in one pass with no pauses and leaves the CD open so you can add more tracks, while DAO closes the disc. Use SAO or DAO for gapless burning of audio CDs.

An extra challenge for CD-authoring software is creating a track index for a long, unbroken performance. Create a long WAV track in Audacity, and then create CD text and a track index in your CD-writing program so you can navigate the disc just like on a CD with multiple song tracks. (You can't create this in Audacity.) You should end up with two files: a *.bin* file, which contains your audio, and a *.cue* or *.toc* file, which contains the disc index. Some CD-authoring applications use their own weird nonstandard cue sheet formats; beware of these, because other CD-writing programs won't be able to use them, and they might confuse playback devices.

Roxio, CDRWin, Sony's Creative Software CD Architect, and higher-end suites by Steinberg and Minnetonka are some programs that can do this for Windows users. Brasero and Gnome CD Master do the best job for Linux users. K3b can index long tracks, but its interface for doing this is rather cumbersome.

Three Ways to Author a CD Compilation in Audacity

There are several ways to create a CD compilation in Audacity. One way is to copy each song into a single Audacity project, each on its own separate track. Edit and apply fixes to each track individually, and then normalization across all tracks is a single step. Give each track its own name, and there are your song titles. This is a good method for creating a typical audio CD with multiple song tracks and a short, silent gap between each one.

Another way is to copy all of your songs into a single stereo Audacity track, apply fixes and edits, and then create a label track to divide them into individual songs. You can use this to create a CD that appears to be a single long, unbroken track by creating nice smooth transitions between each song and then making sure there are no gaps between the songs when you burn your CD.

With the first two methods, your final result is a batch of WAV files, one file per song.

A third method is to copy all of your songs into a single stereo Audacity track and apply edits and fixes. Export it as a single 16/44.1 WAV file, and then use your CD-writing program to create song titles and divide it into individual song tracks with two-second gaps, or index the track so that it remains unbroken but still navigable.

Each method has its advantages, so let's look at each one in detail.

One Track per Song Project

I like this method for creating CDs with multiple song tracks and a standard two-second silent gap between each one. You can normalize all tracks at once and edit each one individually without worrying about inadvertently changing something else. When each song in your project is on its own track, it looks like Figure 5-1.

Your first step is to create a new Audacity project by selecting **File** > **Save Project As**. Next, configure Audacity with the following settings for creating CD-ready WAV files.

Set the frame rate to CD audio in the Selection toolbar, as shown in Figure 5-2. This ensures that any splits you make will start and end on a CD frame. Any audio that lands outside of these frames will be lost and possibly create clicking noises. You can choose either hh:mm:ss + CDDA frames (75 fps) or CDDA frames (75 fps). The former shows the time plus CD

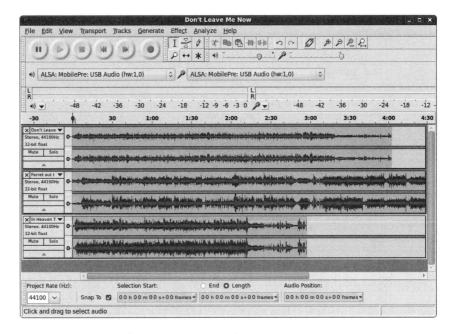

Figure 5-1: Putting each song on its own track

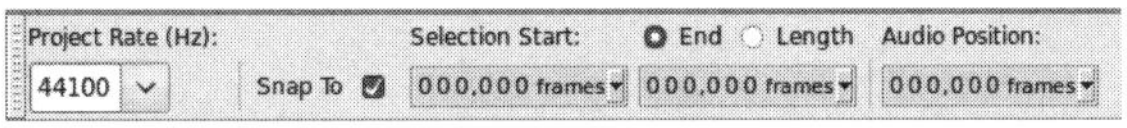

Figure 5-2: Selecting the CD frame rate and project rate in
the Selection toolbar

frames, and the latter displays only CD frames. Check the "Snap To" box to
ensure that stops and starts are always on the CD frame boundaries. Set the
Project Rate value to 44,100 Hz.

Now open the **Edit** > **Preferences** > **Recording** dialog and make sure
that "Overdub: Play other tracks while recording new one" and "Software
Playthrough: Listen while recording or monitoring new track" are not
checked.

In the **Edit** > **Preferences** > **Devices** dialog, set Channels to 2 (Stereo).

Now add some audio files to your project. To add audio files in WAV,
FLAC, or some other format, select **File** > **Import** > **Audio**. If you want to
copy tracks or clips from another Audacity project, open the other project in
a new window and copy and paste.

Name each track with the song name in the Track menu. (At export,
each track will be exported into individual WAV files that use the track names
as filenames.)

Next, apply edits and repairs. (See "Fixes and Cleanups" on page 111.) I
like to put one second of silence at the beginning and end of each track and
normalize all of them to 0 dB. Then as I build my CD-ready WAV collection,
they're all ready to go and don't need any more processing in Audacity.

Make sure that your Project Rate setting is still 44,100 Hz. If the first track you opened or imported was at a different sampling rate, then that would have become the project rate. It doesn't matter if you have mixed sampling rates, because everything will be resampled to the project rate at export.

An optional step at this point is to enter some metadata by opening **File** > **Open Metadata Editor**. You can enter information such as the album title, year, genre, and comments. This is saved only in your Audacity project because WAV files do not support metadata. (Other audio file formats do, such as FLAC, MP3, and Ogg Theora.) Audacity will automatically fill in each track title from your track names, the track number, and everything you entered in the Metadata Editor.

If you want to review the metadata for each song as it is exported, open **Edit** > **Preferences** > **Import/Export** and check "Show Metadata Editor prior to export step."

Now you are ready to export your tracks for CD recording. Flip back to "Final Export" on page 98 if you need a refresher on exporting multiple tracks. Be sure to click the **Options** button to set the correct export format.

Click **OK** and then **Export**. You will see a confirmation for each song and a summary when it is finished as in Figure 5-3.

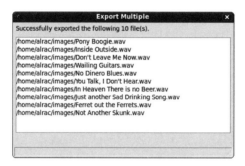

Figure 5-3: A successful multiple export

Now you have a batch of CD-ready WAV files. Use your favorite CD-writing program to create an audio CD and be sure to create an audio project, not a data project. Most CD software supports CD text and adjusting the gaps between the songs. Beware of default two-second gap settings, which will add to any gaps you created in Audacity.

Single Audacity Track Compilation Project

For this method, your Audacity screen will look something like Figure 5-4 when you are finished editing and ready to export. Why do it this way? I think it's easier to control fades and transitions between songs, and I like having everything in a single track. This is my favorite way to create live CDs with no breaks between songs.

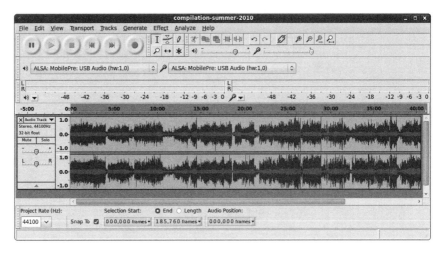

Figure 5-4: This compilation includes songs from various sources, all knit into a single Audacity track.

Your first step, as always, is to create a new Audacity project with **File > Save Project As**. Next, configure Audacity with the following settings for creating CD-ready WAV files, just as you did in the previous section.

Set the frame rate to CD audio in the Selection toolbar, as shown in Figure 5-2. This ensures that any splits you make will start and end on a CD frame. Any audio that lands outside of these frames will be lost and possibly create clicking noises. You can choose either hh:mm:ss + CDDA frames (75 fps) or CDDA frames (75 fps). The former shows the time plus CD frames, and the latter displays only CD frames. Check the "Snap To" box to ensure that stops and starts are always on the CD frame boundaries. Set the project rate to 44,100 Hz.

Now open the **Edit > Preferences > Recording** dialog and make sure that "Overdub: Play other tracks while recording new one" and "Software Playthrough: Listen while recording or monitoring new track" are not checked.

In the **Edit > Preferences > Devices** dialog, set Channels to 2 (Stereo).

Now you can put some audio tracks in your project. If you want to copy some tracks from another Audacity project, open this in a separate Audacity window with **File > Open** or **File > Recent Files**, and copy and paste. To add audio files such as WAV, FLAC, Ogg Theora, and so forth, select **File > Import > Audio**. Each new import will open in its own track, so you will have to cut and paste it into your compilation track and then delete the extra track.

When you have all the songs you want, apply edits and repairs (see "Fixes and Cleanups" on page 111). If your songs vary in volume and you want them all the same, you'll have to adjust each one individually using **Effect > Amplify**. Select each song one at a time, and then bring them up to your desired peak amplitude, no more than zero.

Now create a label track. This is how each song gets a title and how this one long track will be split into a bunch of separate song files. Start by pressing the HOME key to make sure you are at the very beginning, and then press CTRL-B to create the label. Type in the song title and press the RETURN key. Click at the beginning of the second song, make another label, and keep going until you're finished labeling all the songs (Figure 5-5).

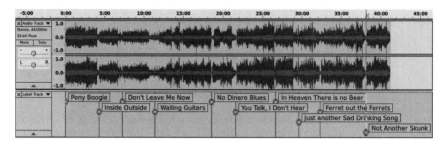

Figure 5-5: Creating a label track

Make sure your project rate in the Selection toolbar is still 44,100. Any clips that have a different sample rate will be resampled to the project rate at export.

If you'd like, you can enter some metadata, but remember that the information is saved only in your Audacity project—WAV files do not support metadata. To export your project for CD recording, see "Final Export" on page 98. When you are finished, you will see a confirmation for each song and a summary as in Figure 5-3.

Single Audacity Track + CD-Mastering Program

This third method requires a good CD-authoring program that supports CD text, track splitting, and control of the spacing between tracks. The idea is to create a single long Audacity track with all of your songs and do your cleanups and fixes in Audacity. Then export it as a single 16/44.1 WAV file and use your CD-writing program to create song titles, to divide the track into individual songs and adjust the gaps between songs, or to create an index without breaking up the track.

There are many CD-authoring applications that can do this, such as Roxio, CDRWin, Sony's Creative Software CD Architect, and higher-end suites by Steinberg and Minnetonka for Windows users. Brasero and Gnome CD Master are best for Linux users.

Let's use Brasero to illustrate how to do this, because it has the simplest interface. First, create your new audio project and load your audio file. Then right-click your file and click **Split File**. This opens Brasero's Split Track window (Figure 5-6). Select Method: Split track manually, click the **Play** button to hear your track, and click **Slice** to mark a song break.

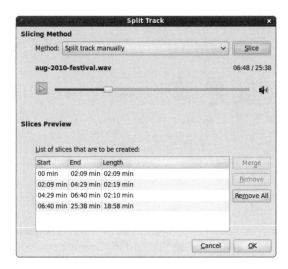

Figure 5-6: Using Brasero to split a long track

Drag the Play slider back and forth to find split points quickly, or just kick back and listen, clicking the **Slice** button as the appropriate breakpoints come along.

When you're finished, click **OK**. This takes you to a window like Figure 5-7 where you can enter your track titles, and then you can either create a disc image and cue sheet that you can use in any CD-writing application or go ahead and burn to disc.

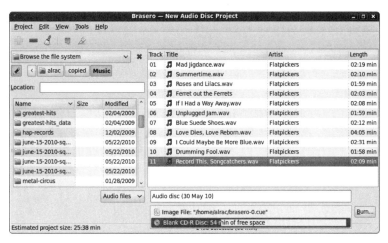

Figure 5-7: Entering song titles and getting ready to burn to disc, or creating a .bin image and .cue file that can be used by any CD-writing program

This example creates a long track with no breaks between songs. What if you want song breaks? No worries: Just right-click any track to insert a two-second pause (Figure 5-8).

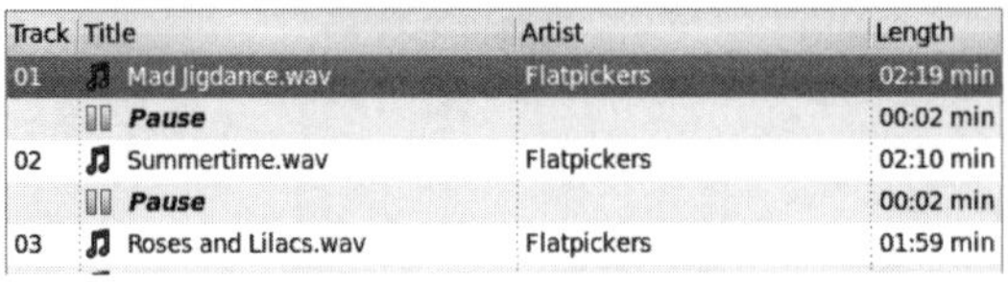

Track	Title	Artist	Length
01	♫ Mad Jigdance.wav	Flatpickers	02:19 min
	▊▊ *Pause*		00:02 min
02	♫ Summertime.wav	Flatpickers	02:10 min
	▊▊ *Pause*		00:02 min
03	♫ Roses and Lilacs.wav	Flatpickers	01:59 min

Figure 5-8: Using Brasero to insert breaks between songs

If your long track is a compilation of songs with the usual silent breaks between each song, try selecting Method: Split track for each silence. Then it will split it automatically.

Of course, the other CD-authoring applications do things their own way, but this should give you an idea of the basic steps.

CD Cue Sheets and BIN Files

Cue sheets are used in conjunction with *.bin* image files, which contain your audio, that any CD-writing software can use to burn a new CD. The cue sheet contains the table of contents for the disc, like this one created by Brasero:

```
FILE "/home/alrac/winding-road-1.bin" MOTOROLA
TITLE "Audio disc (26 June 10)"
TRACK 01 AUDIO
        TITLE "Guitar Summit"
        PERFORMER "Winding Road"
        INDEX 01 00:00:00
TRACK 02 AUDIO
        TITLE "Gone Away Again"
        PERFORMER "Winding Road"
        INDEX 01 02:50:24
TRACK 03 AUDIO
        TITLE "Tennessee Waltz"
        PERFORMER "Winding Road"
        INDEX 01 06:45:63
TRACK 04 AUDIO
        TITLE "Montana Two-Step"
        PERFORMER "Winding Road"
        INDEX 01 14:30:72
```

Cue sheets are used on both CDs and DVDs. If you're into ripping commercial CDs and DVDs, you probably already know about cue sheets, because some ripping software can create them from the table of contents (TOC) on the CD. You can create and edit these yourself, though I'm lazy and prefer to have some nice CD-authoring software do it for me. Here are the most commonly used fields, including some not used in the Brasero example:

PERFORMER   The artist or group

FILE   The name of the corresponding disc image file, with the file type. MOTOROLA is a type of binary file. Other options are BINARY, WAVE, AIFF, and MP3.

TITLE   The disc title

TRACK   The track number and data mode, which is AUDIO

TITLE   The track title

INDEX   The number 01 marks the start of the track. The time values are minutes, seconds, and CD frames. (Remember, in Audacity we always set the time parameter to CDDA Frames in the Selection toolbar.) An INDEX value of 00 creates a hidden track, which is a gimmick you've probably experienced on some of your own CDs.

PREGAP   How many seconds of silence to insert before a track starts; for example, 00:02:00 is two seconds.

POSTGAP   How many seconds of silence to insert after a track ends.

You don't have to use cue sheets. You don't even have to know anything about them. They're just another optional item in your CD- and DVD-authoring toolkit to help you control what goes on your discs. There are all kinds of free how-tos all over the Internet if you're interested in learning more.

Fixes and Cleanups

Chapter 4 included a bunch of information on cleaning up live tracks, and a lot of that applies to cleaning up compilation CDs too. We'll review the basics here along with explanations of a few other fixes that may come up when you make your compilation discs. We'll talk about splitting stereo tracks for more precise editing, normalization, adjusting the gaps between songs, and graceful fades. See Chapter 12 to learn more about fix-its and cleanups such as noise removal; dynamic range compression; and fixing clicks, pops, clipping, and other defects. Chapter 11 is all about applying special effects.

Splitting Stereo Tracks for Surgical Repairs

Sometimes there will be a defect on just one channel of a two-channel stereo track. If you split this into two tracks, then you can apply repairs to just the one channel and then join the tracks back together. There are a couple of advantages to this: The second track helps to mask a less-than-perfect fix, and the fix that you apply to the defective portion probably won't help the other channel sound any better and may even hurt the quality.

To divide a stereo track, go to the Track menu and click **Split Stereo Track**. To rejoin the tracks, use the Track menu in the track that is on top and click **Make Stereo Track**. The two tracks must be adjacent to each other.

Normalization

Normalization, or raising all your different songs to the same volume levels, is a common audio-editing task that can be done in CD-writing software. But again, in Audacity you have a lot more control.

Before normalizing, you should review your tracks for any unusual peaks that could indicate some kind of defect, such as a bumped mic, a cough, something dropped, or anything that is so loud it doesn't sound right. Normalization doesn't change the dynamic range, so one too-loud peak means normalization won't have much effect, and you could end up with a track that is too quiet overall. To lower the volume on any too-loud peak, zoom in until you can select it precisely, and then open **Effect** > **Amplify**. Enter a negative value, like −3 dB, to lower the volume. You can use the Preview button to help adjust it. When it sounds right, click **OK**, and move on to the next one.

If you put your whole project into a single Audacity track, you'll have to select each song carefully and raise it to your desired maximum volume level. You should do this before creating any fades. Another way to handle this is to use the Envelope tool so you can fix it all with one tool.

When every song is on its own individual track, it's easier—select all tracks (CTRL-A or **Edit** > **Select All**), and then click **Effect** > **Normalize**. Check both "Remove any CD offset" and "Normalize maximum amplitude to," and enter your maximum volume level up to 0 dB.

Making Graceful Fades and Song Breaks

Creating breaks between songs, with graceful fades in and out, is easy in Audacity. Many CD-writing programs can do this too, but you have more control in Audacity. There are three Audacity tools that I like to use: the Fade In/Fade Out effects, the Envelope tool, and the Silence generator.

The Fade In/Fade Out effect is fast and simple; all you control is the length of the fade. First, select the segment that you want to fade, and then select **Effect** > **Fade Out** or **Effect** > **Fade In**.

If you need to insert an interval of pure silence, use the Selection tool to mark where you want the silence to begin, click **Generate** > **Silence**, set it to whatever duration you want, and click **OK**.

The Envelope tool gives you more control of both the duration and the degree of fades. Figure 5-9 shows it in action, creating about a 2.5-second fade-out to silence and then fading back in. The little squares are the *node control points*. Create these by clicking the track, and then you can move them both horizontally and vertically. To get rid of a node, grab a control point and drag it outside the track's boundary. Envelope tools are standard in most audio-editing applications. It takes a bit of practice to get the hang of them, but once you figure out how to make them go where you want, you gain a high degree of control over fades and amplitude.

What about cross-fades, you ask? A cross-fade is when one track fades out and another fades in at the same time, with some overlap and no break. Cross-fades are used all the time in soundtracks and music. Some Audacity plug-ins for creating cross-fades are included in the standard add-on plug-in packages, but they're pretty limited. I think it's easier and better to use the Envelope tool. Someday Audacity will have a good cross-fade tool. Meanwhile, Figure 5-10 shows my preferred method.

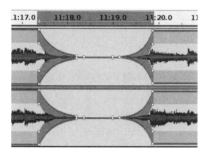

Figure 5-9: Using the Envelope tool and the Time Shift tool to create fade-ins and fade-outs

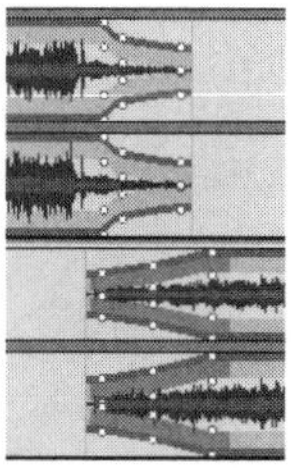

Figure 5-10: Creating a cross-fade with the Envelope tool

This shows two Audacity stereo tracks. Let's call the one on top Song1 and the one on the bottom Song2. Use the Time Shift tool to position Song2 for the desired length of overlap; then use the Envelope tool on each track to set the length and degree of fade. When it's just the way you want, you'll have to mix down the two tracks into a single stereo track. If you want to create a lot of cross-fades in a project, use two separate Audacity tracks as in Figure 5-11. Then you'll have to mixdown only once.

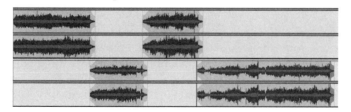

Figure 5-11: Creating cross-fades between every song by using the Time Shift tool and the Envelope tool

Click **Tracks** > **Mix and Render** to mix your tracks down to a single new stereo track in your Audacity project, replacing your original tracks. You can then make further adjustments before export such as creating labels, making fixes, and performing other edits. It will sound just like the playback in

Audacity sounds, so when it sounds right in Audacity, it's ready to go. Channel assignments are controlled in the Track menus: Left, Right, and Mono. Left is channel 1, Right is channel 2, and Mono tracks are mixed down to both. (Remember to use CTRL-SHIFT-M if you want Audacity to create a new stereo track without replacing your original tracks.)

Keep in mind that combining tracks makes them louder, so click **View** > **Show Clipping** to quickly find any clipped passages. If the mixdown creates clipping, undo it, use the Normalize or Amplify effects (Effect menu) to reduce the amplitudes of your tracks, and try it again. If you go too low, you can always raise the volume on your final, mixed-down track using **Effect** > **Normalize** or **Amplify**.

See Chapter 9 to learn more about multitrack editing and mixing.

Configuring Audacity for Orange Book CDs

Orange Book CDs are ordinary data CDs without any special audio encoding. These will play on any computer but not in most standalone CD players like in your car or stereo system. You can mix up audio file formats on these and get a lot more minutes of music on a CD.

In the **Edit** > **Preferences** > **Devices** dialog, select 2 channels (stereo).

In the **Edit** > **Preferences** > **Recording** dialog, uncheck "Overdub: Play other tracks while recording new one" and "Software Playthrough: Listen while recording or monitoring new track."

In the Selection toolbar, select CDDA Frames (75 fps) and check the "Snap To" box (Figure 5-2).

Putting an Orange Book CD Collection Together

If you already have a batch of audio files all ready to copy to a CD, you don't need Audacity at all. Just open your CD writer and create a new data CD project. Copy your files to the CD, enter CD text if you want, burn the disc, and you're done.

There are a couple of different ways to assemble an Orange Book CD project in Audacity. Remember, your audio files are treated as ordinary data files, so you can use any audio file format that is supported by your media player. If the CD will contain all the same formats and quality settings, such as all FLAC or all Ogg Vorbis or all MP3, you can follow the same steps as for a Red Book CD, which is to create a single Audacity project containing all of your songs. Export to your desired format and quality. Then in your CD-writing program, select "Create a data CD" instead of creating an audio CD. If you created track metadata, it will be displayed in CD players that support it (except for WAV files, which do not support storing metadata).

The first audio file you open will set the project rate. You can resample audio files to different sampling rates, but this can hurt audio quality. Upsampling doesn't add more quality, just more bits. Downsampling throws away bits. A good tactic is not to mix up files in Audacity but rather to edit files that have the same sampling rate in a single Audacity project. After export, you can mix and match them all you like.

You won't be able to apply normalization or adjust the breaks between the tracks in your CD-writing program because it won't see the files as audio files. Apply normalization in Audacity and make sure every track is normalized to the same level, like 0 dB or whatever you prefer. Adjust the gaps between songs in Audacity in the usual way, with fades and silences.

Figure 5-12 shows what the metadata look like when you play a CD in Amarok, which is an open source cross-platform media player. The compilation includes a mix of FLAC, WAV, and MP3 files, which Amarok handles with ease. Pretty much any computer media player should do the same thing. FLAC format gives you WAV quality in one-third to one-half the file size, and it supports metadata.

Figure 5-12: A mixed FLAC, MP3, and WAV CD compilation in Amarok

File Formats and Quality Settings

There are many different audio file formats; WAV and FLAC are great choices for highest quality, and Ogg Vorbis and MP3 are good lossy, compressed formats when you need to save space.

An Orange Book CD supports all WAV files, so you can use 16- or 24-bit and whatever sampling rate you prefer.

Online music services such as Magnatune, Pristine Classical, and Grooveshark offer downloads in FLAC format because it is equal in quality to WAV in a smaller file size.

FLAC supports both 16- and 24-bit depths and has nine compression levels, from 0 to 8 (Figure 5-13). The default is 5, and that is a good one to stick with, though nobody will mind if you experiment with the others. The different settings are different levels of compression, with 0 being the least compression and 8 the most. FLAC is lossless, so there is no difference in quality, only in how much the files are compressed. The value 8 takes several times longer to encode than 5 with not much additional benefit. Decoding FLAC files that have been maximally compressed doesn't take any longer than decoding ones that have been lightly compressed, so the degree of compression won't affect playback.

Ogg Vorbis is also an open and unencumbered format. It has 11 quality settings in Audacity, from 0 to 10 (Figure 5-14). The value 3 is roughly equivalent to a 128Kbps MP3, which is pretty lo-fi. I think 6 is good for music. Ogg Vorbis uses channel coupling for all levels up to 5, which means that redundancies between two stereo channels are combined to save bandwidth, so you might notice a loss of stereo imaging. Channel coupling is not used at levels 6 and up. I don't perceive any gain in going greater than 7, though your ears may tell you differently.

Figure 5-13: FLACs are lossless and a great choice for Orange Book CDs.

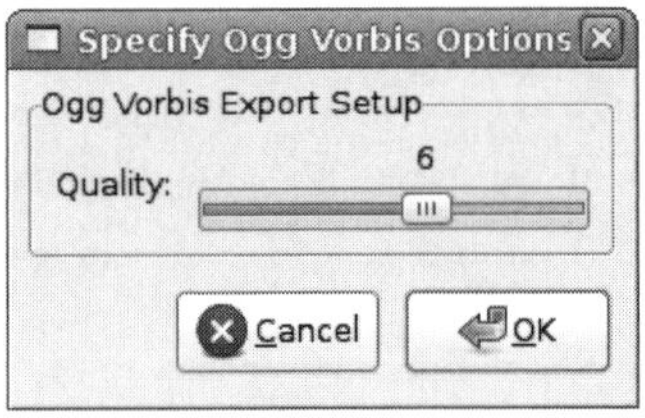

Figure 5-14: Ogg Vorbis is a good-quality lossy, compressed audio format.

MP3 is a closed, proprietary format with patent encumbrances, though I have not heard of small-time musicians getting sued for royalties. Nobody will know what you use on your own personal music discs anyway.

MP3 supports both variable and constant bitrates. Constant bitrates are best for Internet streaming. Variable bitrate MP3s are good for a Orange Book CD because they often sound better than constant bitrate files. A constant bitrate means the same fixed bitrate is used throughout the file, even if it needs more or fewer bits in certain passages. Variable bitrate operates within a range that you select, using more or fewer bits as needed. For my ears, a variable 170 to 210Kbps MP3 sounds as good as higher-bitrate MP3s, and it sounds better than the lower bitrates (Figure 5-15). Naturally it is your ears that must be happy.

Computer Media Players

Software media players will play any audio file format you throw at them. Windows users could try Windows Media Player, Winamp, or VLC. Linux users could start with VLC, Rhythmbox, Mplayer, Songbird, Xmms, or

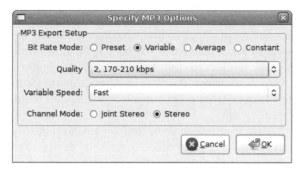

Figure 5-15: MP3s at 170 to 210Kbps sound okay to me, better than lower bitrates and as good as higher bitrates.

Amarok. There are dozens, maybe even hundreds, of software media players, so you should be able to find one you like.

Ripping CDs

It's easy enough to copy and paste into an Audacity project from your own digital audio file archives, but what about plucking songs off CDs? The audio tracks on a CD are written using a special format, the Red Book CD Audio standard, so you can't just copy the songs off a CD but must use a special digital audio extractor, or *CD ripper*. Some CD-writing programs include rippers, such as Nero (Windows and Linux) and K3b (Linux). There are multitudes of standalone CD rippers for all platforms. For example, Windows users can try Windows Media Player, Audio Grabber, or the excellent Exact Audio Copy. Exact Audio Copy has a bit of a learning curve, but once you get it set up for your system, it is fast and accurate, and it handles damaged CDs better than any of the others. Linux users have, among many others, the excellent Grip, KAudiocreator, and VLC Media Player.

CD rippers extract tracks directly from the CD, so you don't need a sound card. This how you make a true, 100 percent faithful clone of the original. You could also intercept the playback signal in various ways and record that, such as connecting your CD player directly to a recording interface using its RCA connectors, using the line or headphone port on your stereo amplifier, or even holding a microphone in front of your speakers. But these techniques won't produce a perfect copy; they might introduce some flaws, lose a bit of fidelity, or introduce some alterations such as a different treble/bass curve. This is called the *analog hole*, which is yet another silly ogre invented by people in the entertainment industry who seem to have no understanding of audio technology. You don't need to be an audio engineer to understand that the ultimate fate of the digital bits on a CD is to be converted into an analog signal that we can listen to and that anything that we hear can be recorded.

Different tactics have been tried in futile attempts to "close the analog hole," such as introducing deliberate distortions and signal degradations to foil copying, getting laws passed to cripple the functionality of audio and video players, keying playback to watermarks so that only signals bearing the correct, approved watermarks will play back at all, and putting backdoors in devices that allow vendors to shut them down remotely or control them in other ways. It's a losing arms race because anything that is invented can be circumvented, and customers are unwilling to leap tall buildings just to hear their music.

Audio CDs are rarely copy-protected anyway, and the few attempts that have been made were public failures. Sony BMG was rather severely embarrassed when it was discovered that its copy protection secretly installed rootkits on Windows PCs, which violated laws in various countries and opened security holes. In the United States, Sony BMG admitted that it violated federal law and had to deal with a number of civil lawsuits. This so-called copy protection did not work on anything but Windows PCs, so Linux and Mac users and owners of standalone CD players and mass CD duplicators were not affected.

Rippers are useful for recovering tracks from your own CDs and from deteriorating out-of-print commercial CDs.

NOTE *In this era of "intellectual property" protection craziness (at least in the United States), the principle of fair use has taken a beating. I'm not going to offer legal advice because I'm not qualified, and it would deteriorate into a rant anyway. I do want to offer a gentle reminder that the other extreme of disregarding copyrights is just as wrong, and no, we are not entitled to everything for free. And it doesn't require legal genius for a person to recognize when they're taking unfair advantage.*

Specialized CD rippers cater mainly to the MP3 crowd, so watch your file formats. Most CD and DVD rippers support exporting to a number of different audio file formats, such as Ogg, WAV, FLAC, AAC, WMA, and MP3. For best quality, always rip the native format, which for Red Book CDs is always WAV. Once you have ripped your tracks, you can then edit them in Audacity just like any other digital audio file and export to any other formats you want.

Ripping DVDs

If you want to extract the audio tracks from DVDs, then you need a DVD ripper. Some good DVD rippers for Linux are K9copy, K3b, dvd::rip, and VLC Media Player. HandBrake and DVDFab are good Windows rippers, and VLC also runs on Windows. Try VLC first; it is open source, is free of cost, and has the most features. With VLC, you can extract and transcode your DVD audio tracks into almost any format. Again, you'll get best quality by ripping to the native format and then can use Audacity to export to other formats if you need to do so.

6

AUTHORING SUPER HIGH-FIDELITY AUDIO DVDS

CD audio is a universal music medium just like vinyl LPs were. There are multitudes of playback devices, and audio quality is excellent even on inexpensive CD players. But when you want higher fidelity or larger storage capacity than an audio CD (how about seven CDs' worth on a single DVD?), what do you do?

You may feel like you are being shunned because all the attention is being given to newer and better video formats and the only audio lovers getting any attention are MP3 consumers. Lossy formats and tiny portable devices with lo-fi earbuds are getting all the glory, while audiophiles are stuck with aging formats and technologies that haven't advanced in years. Adding insult to injury is the never-ending parade of ineffective, hostile DRM (which stands for *digital rights management* or *digital restrictions management*—take your pick) follies that are infesting new video and audio playback technologies, like termites in new houses.

Fortunately, there are some options for the golden-eared digital audiophile. In this chapter, we're going to look at DVD-Audio. DVD-Audio is a special digital audio format for DVD; it is not the same as the audio formats used in DVD movies. You'll sacrifice some portability because it is not as well supported as CD audio, but a number of home and vehicle DVD players support it.

CD audio supports only two-channel 16/44.1 sound. DVD-Audio supports very high-resolution audio, all the way up to 24/192 and up to six-channel surround sound. Audacity, from version 1.3.3, also supports these features.

If you don't want super-duper high fidelity, you can store a passel of music on a DVD. You don't need any special hardware to create DVD-Audio disks; you need just an ordinary computer DVD writer and blank DVD media. You do need special authoring software to create the correct type of DVD disk image, and you have to use PCM-type audio file formats such as FLAC, WAV, and AIFF. I like FLAC because it's an open, high-quality lossless, compressed format that creates files that are 30 percent to 50 percent smaller than WAV and AIFF.

Some examples of DVD-authoring software are DVD-AUDIO Solo Plus (Windows), Minnetonka Audio Software discWelder (Mac and Windows), Steinberg Wavelab (Windows), and DVD Audio Tools for Linux. See "DVD-Audio Authoring Software" on page 129 for more information.

NOTE   *You may want to review Chapters 1 and 2 for refreshers on using Audacity and for recording studio basics.*

What Are WAV, AIFF, and FLAC?

Let the iPod and Zune set have their tiny, overpriced lo-fi devices, for there is a whole world of high-fidelity digital audio to explore. As we discussed in Chapter 3, digital audio has many advantages over analog audio. Audacity has native support for three high-quality PCM audio formats: WAV, AIFF, and FLAC. WAV and AIFF are pretty much the same thing.

Waveform Audio Format (WAV) was developed by IBM and Microsoft from the Interchange File Format (IFF), which was developed by Electronic Arts (EA) and Commodore-Amiga in the mid-1980s. IFF can carry text, image, or audio data, and it was intended to be a generic wrapper for exchanging different types of data across diverse platforms.

Audio Interchange File Format (AIFF) was developed by Apple, and it is also based on IFF. There are small technical differences between WAV and AIFF because they were developed to run on different operating systems, but these days both are well supported by most software media players.

Free Lossless Audio Codec (FLAC) is a high-quality lossless compressed format. It is an open and unencumbered standard. Online music services such as Magnatune, the Philadelphia Orchestra online music store, and Linn Records offer downloads in FLAC format because it is equal in quality to WAV in a smaller file size. FLAC is well supported and growing in popularity.

FLAC, WAV, and AIFF are linear pulse-code modulation (LPCM). Linear means *integer*, which we'll discuss in detail in "Creating High-Quality Recordings in Audacity" on page 122.

All three are excellent choices for both your studio masters and your final exports. You can make perfect copies of them for archiving and backups, and you can generate lower-resolution copies in lossy formats such as Ogg Vorbis and MP3. Your workflow looks like this:

1. Source material, such as live recordings or copies of legacy media, is converted to high-resolution masters in Audacity.

2. Generate files for playback in FLAC, WAV, or AIFF.

3. Use special authoring software to write tracks to DVD.

DVD-Audio Overview

DVD-Audio is a digital audio format for DVDs. It is not the same as the audio formats used in DVD movies but is a different format just for audio. DVD movies use various compressed, lossy audio formats to preserve disk space, which even on a DVD is at a premium when you combine movie-length video and multichannel surround sound. DVD-Audio supports professional studio master audio quality, which is 24/192. If you're content with CD audio (16/44.1 stereo), you can cram about seven hours' worth onto a single standard 4.7GB DVD. At 24/192, you'll get about 75 minutes of music on a standard DVD. Some DVD-authoring software supports writing to 8.5GB double-layer DVDs, so you can really pile in the tunes. The DVD-Audio standard also supports still pictures and video menus.

NOTE   *Sometimes home-burned double-layer DVDs are not reliable on different playback devices. Stick with the good-quality brands of DVD blanks and make sure that your DVD player supports both double-layer DVD-R and DVD-Audio. Your particular DVD writer may work better with specific brands of blanks, so use what your manufacturer recommends.*

DVD-Audio is an LPCM format like WAV and AIFF. It supports bit depths of 16, 20, and 24 and sampling rates up to 192 kHz. Audacity supports 16- and 24-bit depths and pretty much any sampling rate you want. If the rate you want isn't in the **Edit** > **Preferences** > **Quality** dialog, just enter your own in **Edit** > **Preferences** > **Quality** > **Default Sample Rate** > **Other**.

DVD-Audio has a theoretical dynamic range of 144 dB, though the limitations of audio hardware mean your maximum dynamic range is always about 120 dB. Dynamic range in this context isn't about cranking the volume or blasting your listeners with sudden extreme peaks; the advantages of an extremely wide dynamic range are loads of headroom for recording and processing and a very low noise floor.

DVD-Audio supports a range of stereo and surround channel combinations at 24 bits: 1.0 mono and 2.0 stereo at sampling rates of 44.1 kHz, 48 kHz, 88.2 kHz, 96 kHz, 176.4 kHz, and 192 kHz.

These all support sampling rates of 44.1 kHz, 48 kHz, 88.2 kHz, and 96 kHz at 24 bits:

- 2.1 stereo   (left, right, LFE)
- 3.0   (left, right, surround)
- 3.1   (left, right, surround, LFE)
- 4.0   (left, right, center, surround)
- 4.1   (left, right, center, surround, LFE)
- 5.0   (left, right, center, surround right, surround left)
- 5.1   (left, right, center, surround right, surround left, LFE)

The *low-frequency effects (LFE)* channel deserves a bit of explanation. It's often assumed to be the subwoofer channel, but this is not quite right. The LFE channel is a special channel that carries sounds in the 3 Hz to 200 Hz frequency range, and the LFE signal can be sent to any speaker capable of handling this range.

Uncompressed DVD-Audio has a bitrate limit of 9.6Mbps, so you can have glorious 24/192 two-channel stereo. But you're not going to get uncompressed 5.1 surround at full 24/192 resolution because 9.6Mbps is not enough bandwidth for full resolution on all of those channels. The best you'll get is 24/96 in 5.1. You can have different resolutions on different channels, such as 24/96 for the two front channels and 16/48 on the surround channels. You need compression to get higher resolution for 5.1, and the only compression supported by the DVD-Audio standard is the proprietary Meridian Lossless Packing (MLP) lossless compression. A license for MLP is expensive, usually more than $2,000, and available only for Windows and Mac authoring software.

Creating High-Quality Recordings in Audacity

Your starting point is the highest-quality audio files you can create. This does not necessarily mean recording at the highest possible sampling and bitrates, but using good recording techniques to produce the best-sounding recordings. As we discussed in Chapters 1 and 2, a lot of factors affect the quality of your audio recordings: background noise, microphone placement, the quality of your mics, preamp, analog-to-digital converter, and the power of your computer.

Audacity supports up to 32/192 recording, so let's see what the pros and cons are of using higher resolutions.

More Power

You need a stout CPU to handle high-resolution recording. I have one PC with an Athlon LE-1620 2.4 GHz and 4GB of RAM. It is a single-core CPU, and it bogs down at sampling rates higher than 48 kHz. Multicore CPUs are wonderful for audio production. Audacity is not designed to take advantage of multiple cores, but you'll still see a significant performance improvement because your operating system will use those extra cores for other tasks, which frees up CPU cycles for Audacity. I also have a system with a three-core CPU (AMD Phenom X3), and it handles eight channels at 24/96 with no trouble (using a Focusrite Saffire Pro 26 I/O FireWire recording interface).

I haven't noticed any advantage in having more than 4GB RAM, but memory is so cheap it doesn't hurt to load up. (See Chapters 13 and 14 to learn about tuning your computer for best audio performance.)

What Bit Depth Is Best?

The Audacity documentation recommends recording at 32-bit float and then downsampling to your desired bit depth for your final export. So even though your final product is 24 or 16 bit, starting from 32-bit float results in higher quality than recording in 24- or 16-bit integer. This is true even if your recording interface supports only 16 bits. You will always downsample because there are no 32-bit playback devices; you must always export to 24-bit or lower integer (also called *linear*) formats. 32-bit float is always an intermediate step, not the final result.

Let's talk about what 32-bit float is, since it is rather misunderstood. Integers are whole numbers, and *float* means floating decimal point. A 32-bit float number is a 24-bit mantissa plus an 8-bit exponent. 32-bit float means great precision and very high resolution. You get a smoother, more accurate response curve across the whole range of your analog-to-digital conversion.

Bit depth controls dynamic range, and in audio production dynamic range is very important. Each bit equals about 6 dB dynamic range. So, 16-bit has a dynamic range of 96 dB, 24-bit is 144 dB, and 32-bit float is about 1,500 dB; 32-bit integer is 196 dB. There are limitations in electronic hardware that limit actual dynamic range to a maximum of about 120 dB, and most people don't care to listen to music with a dynamic range greater than 50 dB, which is quite a lot. So what's the point of having very wide dynamic range? The value of all that dynamic range is abundant headroom for editing, lowest noise, less risk of clipping, and lossless exports to lower bit depths.

Those extra eight bits make all the difference when you're doing a lot of manipulation and effects. You can mangle your 32-bit files to your heart's content and when you're finished make a lossless 24-bit export. If you started from a 24-bit file, applied a lot of processing, and finished with a 24-bit export, you would likely introduce some noise and experience some loss of quality.

We dinosaurs from the analog era have a habit of pushing recording levels as close to the red line as possible, because there were good reasons for doing so. Even the best analog tapes and recorders created a bit of hiss and had a relatively narrow dynamic range, so we had to push the limits of signal to noise to minimize this. Going a bit over the red line didn't matter very much with analog audio because it was a gradual effect—at +2 or +3 the distortion was bothersome only to the fussiest of listeners. At +4 or +5 you were a cool rock band. In digital audio it's all or nothing—when a signal passes 0 dB, everything over zero is discarded, or clipped. You might hear an audible click or something similar to the familiar analog distortion buzz. It's easy to hear for yourself. Just plug in a mic, crank up the gain, and talk loudly. Or use **Generate** > **Tone** to create a sine wave, and then use **Effect** > **Amplify** to crank it way up over zero. You can find clipped segments easily by selecting **View** > **Show Clipping**, which uses red bars to mark clipped passages.

Some documentation says that recording at 32-bit float means virtually no distortion, even if you go over 0 dB. But there are several variables that affect any sounds that go over 0 dB, mainly the software processing your sounds. Different Audacity plug-ins, or any other software that you might use, will process sounds over 0 dB in different ways, so you could still get clipping and create distortion. It's not necessary to push your recording levels that high anyway since you have dynamic range to burn.

The short story is that the 16-bit, 24-bit, and 32-bit depths all offer more dynamic range than you'll ever be able to use, so you'll have plenty of headroom with any of them. When you're recording at 24-bit depth, you can handily afford to throw away the top 12 dB. At 16 bits you can set your peaks to −6 or −9 dB and have no worries. Audacity's 32-bit float means you can record to a peak of −24 dB, which is helpful at a live show to allow for unexpected peaks.

Of course, there are downsides to recording at high bit depths and sampling rates. Higher resolutions eat up disk space and require more CPU power (Table 6-1).

Table 6-1: How Much Disk Space per Stereo Minute Is Used by Different Bit Depth/Sampling Rate Combinations

Bit Depth/Sampling Rate	Disk Space per Stereo Minute
16/44.1	10MB
16/48	11MB
24/48	17MB
24/96	33 MB
24/192	66MB

If you overload your CPU, you'll get dropouts, which sound terrible. If you like skips, pops, and fuzz, it's better to add them on purpose as special effects.

Consider the complexity of what you're recording. Simple voice recordings, such as an audio book or podcast, don't benefit much from super-high resolutions. A solo singer or instrumentalist or a small band can be captured perfectly at 16/44.1, while a symphony orchestra will use everything you have.

So the answer to the question "Which one is best?" once again is "It depends." If you have enough computer power and storage, recording at 32-bit float with any sampling rate gives you loads of elbow room for all kinds of editing and exporting. You can always go downward, but you can't go upward. On the other hand, if you are careful and skilled, all the links in your audio chain are good quality, and your own ears are pleased with the results, then lower resolutions are plenty fine. The fun part is you can do this any way you want.

What Sampling Rate Is Best?

Now that we've thoroughly thrashed out bit depths, what about sampling rates? As we learned in Chapter 1, sampling rates determine frequency range. The frequency range is about half the sampling rate. The best human hearing has a range of about 20 Hz to 22 kHz, so a sampling rate of 44.1 kHz should cover the range of human hearing. The better audio hardware has an upper limit of 20 to 30 kHz.

But it's not quite that simple. Some studies seem to indicate that very high frequencies are still perceived in some manner and add to the listener's enjoyment. What they might be talking about are the harmonics. If you have a sound at 100 Hz, there are harmonics of that sound at 25 Hz, 50 Hz, 200 Hz, and so on. When you limit the frequency range, you also limit the harmonics.

If you have good hearing and are fussy about your music, I wager you'll be happier with 24 bits than 16. In my experience, bit depth makes a more obvious difference than sampling rates. I record at 32-bit float/48 and export to 24/48 when I want best quality. Don't upsample, because all that does is add bits without adding quality, and most likely it will sound a little worse.

Saving Your Masters

Audacity project (*.aup*) files are not quite adequate for archiving, because every time you edit a project they change. They are fast and efficient workspaces. But project files have been known to be fragile; if a project becomes corrupted, you have only Audacity's automatic recovery mechanism to fix it. If that fails, game over. A good way to archive your studio masters is to export them as WAVs or FLACs. The highest quality is a 32-bit float WAV. (Select **File** > **Export** > **Options**.) Then you won't lose so much as a bit and will always have a high-quality master. FLAC maxes out at 24-bit integer, which is still a lot of bits, and FLAC files are smaller than WAV.

Multitrack recordings take a bit of care to preserve as WAVs or FLACs, because the Audacity track names and channel mappings get lost at export and are preserved only in your Audacity project files. If you export a big multitrack project as a single file, you'll get all your tracks back but without their track names. Instead, they will all have the filename. If you select **Export** > **Multiple**, which exports each track into an individual file, the track names will become the filenames.

I save both Audacity project files and 32-bit float WAV masters. "Saving Your Work" on page 13 goes into more detail on making backups.

Creating 5.1 Surround

Audacity 1.3.8 and newer can record as many tracks at the same time as your sound card supports and your computer can handle. Older Audacity versions support a maximum of 16 tracks at once. Set the correct number of tracks in **Edit > Preferences > Devices**. If your recording interface supports fewer channels than you want to record, you'll have to lay them down in multiple sessions (see Chapter 9).

Audacity 1.3.3 and newer come with a simple multichannel mixer interface for mapping your tracks to the correct surround channels, as Figure 6-1 shows. Make sure the slider at the bottom is set to the correct number of output channels.

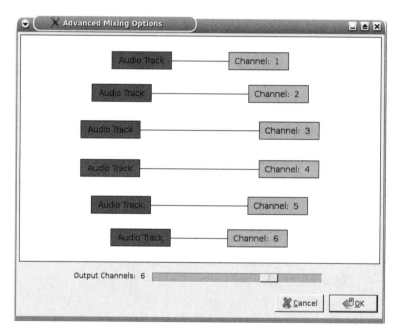

Figure 6-1: Simple mixer and channel mapper

This mixer appears automatically when you export files if you open the **Edit > Preferences > Import/Export** dialog and select "Use custom mix." Unfortunately, Audacity doesn't tell you what track is going to which channel. So use this guide, which details the DVD-Audio channel-numbering convention:

Channel 1	Front Left
Channel 2	Front Right
Channel 3	Center

Channel 4   Low Frequency Effects (LFE)

Channel 5   Surround Left

Channel 6   Surround Right

To keep from driving yourself crazy, name your tracks so you know what they are (using the Track menu), as Figure 6-2 shows. You can name them whatever you want.

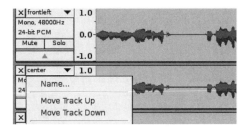

Figure 6-2: Using the Track menu to give your tracks helpful names

Then you'll see the track names in the mixer. However, in Figure 6-3 the two front channels are in the wrong order. No problem—just click them to remap them to the correct channels and make them look like Figure 6-4.

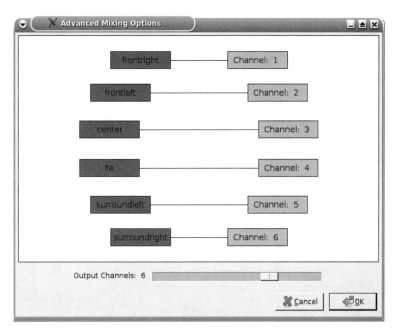

Figure 6-3: Your track names show up in the mixer.

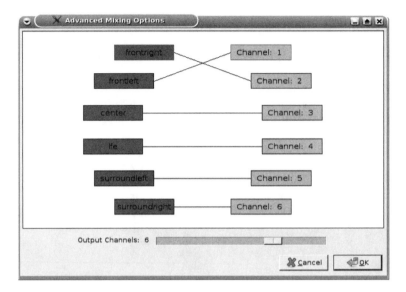

Figure 6-4: Fixing out-of-order tracks

What if you want stereo from a multichannel project? No problem—just change the mixer settings. Follow the example in Figure 6-5 to map six channels to two stereo channels, first making sure the output slider is set to two channels. Tracks can be mapped to more than one channel.

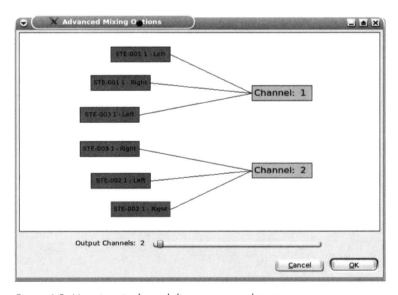

Figure 6-5: Mapping six-channel discrete surround to stereo

Exporting to 16-Bit

You might try applying some *dithering* when downsampling from 32 or 24 bits to 16. This is set in the **Edit** > **Preferences** > **Quality** > **High-quality Conversion** drop-down menus. Dither is deliberately adding noise to smooth the rough edges for a cleaner sound. *Shaped* dither is considered to give the best results, but it is also the most CPU-intensive. *Triangular* is a good compromise between quality and CPU cost, and *rectangular* is lightweight and makes the smallest alterations. Dithering isn't needed on 24-bit files, though I won't complain if you want to experiment and hear for yourself.

DVD-Audio Authoring Software

Once you have your FLAC, WAV, or AIFF audio files all ready to copy to a DVD, all you need are plain old normal DVD blanks, an ordinary computer DVD writer, and special DVD-Audio authoring software. Here are some examples:

DVD Audio Tools for Linux   Linux has only one DVD-Audio authoring application that I know of, and that is DVD Audio Tools (*http://www .dvd-audio.sourceforge.net/*). It has both a command-line interface and a nice graphical interface. It runs on both Linux and Windows, and it is free software (licensed under the GPL) and free of cost.

DVD Audio Tools is simple and streamlined—the first time you use it, you should have a playable DVD in an hour. It accepts both FLAC and WAV files. You can also use it to "rip" audio tracks from unencrypted DVDs. DVD Audio Tools only creates a disk image, so you'll need to burn the disk with your usual favorite DVD-writing application.

DVD-AUDIO Solo Plus   Cirlinca's DVD-AUDIO Solo Plus (*http:// www.cirlinca.com/products.htm*) is a nice Windows program that supports just about everything you would want to do: It supports multichannel surround, 8.5GB dual-layer discs, gapless playback, and unencrypted CD/DVD ripping. Currently, it retails for about $45. Cirlinca does not offer Meridian Lossless Packing (MLP) licenses. (MLP is a patented method of lossless compression for DVD-Audio.)

Minnetonka Audio Software discWelder   discWelder for Windows (*http://www.minnetonkaaudio.com/*) comes in three editions: Bronze, Chrome, and Steel. Bronze is priced at $99, Steel is $595, and Chrome wants $2,995 to follow you home. Another $2,000 gets you MLP. Bronze is comparable to DVD-AUDIO Solo Plus. Steel supports 8.5GB dual-layer disks and slide show graphics and gives you complete control over mixing and mapping. For that price Chrome should cook your breakfast and clean your house, but it doesn't. Instead, it adds support for animated graphics, lets you have both stereo and surround streams, and exports to DLT tape. There are also Mac versions.

Steinberg Wavelab   Steinberg's Wavelab 7 (*http://www.steinberg.net/en/products/wavelab.html*) comes in two editions: Wavelab 7 for about $500 and Wavelab Elements 7 for about $100. These come with bales of features for audio editing, mastering, special effects, multichannel surround, and, of course, DVD-Audio.

After you spend all that money and go to all that trouble, you don't want grotty old hand-scrawled disk labels, do you? No, you don't, and that is why you are going to spend a few bucks on a new LightScribe DVD burner. These cost the same as ordinary old-fashioned DVD burners, which is $50 or less, and you can burn fancy disk labels right into the disk. You have to purchase LightScribe DVD blanks, which currently cost a small bit more than the ordinary kind. Both Linux and Windows have software for creating the labels.

Another option is to purchase inkjet-printable DVD blanks, and then you can make color labels. You'll need an inkjet printer with a special CD/DVD tray to use these.

A plain old felt pen is also perfectly fine for writing your disk labels.

Remember, you don't want to use sticky paper disk labels, because the glue degrades the disk over time.

Transferring Legacy Media

In Chapter 3, we learned how to convert legacy analog media to digital formats. Tapes and vinyl records require jumping through some extra hardware hoops to get everything connected. CDs and DVDs are easier, because you can do everything on your computer. First copy the CD, DVD, or legacy media to your computer. The popular term for copying CDs and DVDs is *ripping*, and this is done with special, easily obtained software. Some good DVD rippers for Linux are K9copy, dvd::rip, and VLC. You need *libdvdcss* to rip encoded DVDs. libdvdcss is available in many Linux distributions and should be easy to find.

HandBrake is one of the best Windows DVD rippers, and it even has a command-line-only version for Linux. VLC also runs on Windows, and DVDFab Platinum is very good. All of these let you select just the audio tracks. Try VLC first; it is open source and free of cost, and it has the most features. With VLC you can extract and transcode your DVD-Audio tracks into almost any format.

CD rippers are legion. Linux users can also try K3B, KAudioCreator, Brasero, Asunder, SoundJuicer, and Grip. Windows users can also try Windows Media Player, Audiograbber, and Winamp.

A good archive format for CDs ripped to a hard drive is 16-bit FLAC, and 24-bit FLAC is appropriate for most DVD-Audio tracks. It makes a perfect copy and saves disk space. If you think you're going to edit your ripped tracks, consider archiving them as 32-bit float WAV masters to give yourself some headroom for future editing.

What About SACD?

Music lovers are always asking "What about Sony/Phillips's Super Audio CD (SACD)?" SACD is not an option for the home or small studio because the recorders are very expensive, plus you must pay format license and patent fees, which is a shame, because it's a real breakthrough. SACD takes one-bit samples at a 2.82 MHz sampling rate. That's right, 2.82 million times per second. That is a tad more than the standard Red Book CD sampling rate of 44.1 kHz. On paper, it's closer to an analog waveform than any other digital format. SACD does not use pulse code modulation (PCM) but a new method of recording and playback that is called Direct Stream Digital (DSD). PCM requires interpolation and oversampling filters, while DSD employs a more direct, less-complex signal path. SACD has a potential dynamic range of around 100 dB.

It seems that vendors of both SACD and DVD-Audio became bogged down in DRM nonsense, rather than marketing these high-quality formats in a pleasing and attractive manner, so both have been slow to gain traction in the marketplace. I think they are both going to fade away eventually.

Learn More

Please see Chapters 1 and 2 to learn the basics of using Audacity and setting up a recording studio, Chapter 9 for multitrack recording, and Chapter 12 for fix-its and cleanups.

7

CREATING PODCASTS

Thanks to the Internet, everyone who is anyone is making podcasts. Now anyone with a little bit of recording gear and an Internet connection can create an audio broadcast to share with the world. You can tell stories, report news, and share how-tos. Your podcast can be just you talking, you interviewing another person, you and a cohost, or you and a gaggle of cohosts and guests. You can add a music track or special effects. Making podcasts with Audacity is easy and fun.

Once you have created your masterpiece, you need a website to host it and make it available to your eager audience. The Internet is full of free and inexpensive podcast hosts. If you have enough bandwidth and want to be your own server admin, you can be your own host thanks to the multitudes of free and open source streaming server software.

The term *podcast* used to refer to downloadable MP3-encoded recordings for iPods. Apple made a brief, ferocious attempt to own the word *pod* and sicced lawyers on a number of small businesses who dared to use the word, such as TightPod (laptop-protecting covers), Profit Pod (data collector for vending machines), Spodradio (a German online broadcaster), and

Podcast Ready (another online broadcaster). Fortunately, it seems that the attack lawyers have moved on to something else, and it is safe to say "pod" again. So, that is what we are going to do: pea pod, pod of whales, pod people. Open the pod bay door, Hal.

Audacity is a dandy tool for making podcasts. You can use a digital recorder and then dump the recording into Audacity for editing, or you can record directly into a computer. A USB microphone or headset connected to a netbook makes a great lightweight portable recording studio. Or, you may indulge in using an entire studio full of fancy expensive gear; it's entirely up to you.

Up until now in this book I've been nattering on about high-quality audio and not using lossy, compressed audio file formats. With podcasts we're going the other way: smaller file sizes and lossy, compressed formats. You still want to start with creating a high-quality master, but it's not necessary to treat your podcast the same way as an ultimate audiophile music recording, because it is going to be trimmed down for Internet streaming and fast downloads.

You may want to review Chapter 1 and Chapter 2 first to learn the fundamentals of using Audacity and how to set up your recording gear.

The Short Story

Making a simple podcast takes just a few steps:

1. Make your recording.
2. Edit it in Audacity: trim, repair, normalize—the usual cleanups and fixes.
3. Export to a playable compressed format such as Ogg Vorbis or MP3.
4. Upload to a site where your fans can download and enjoy your podcast.

Let's take a look at the finer points of making a good podcast.

NOTE   *Audio terminology is a bit confused when it comes to defining* track. *Track can be a single mono track, a stereo track, and even a sound track. In Audacity, it is helpful to think of a track as any single editable unit, which is any mono track or stereo track. Any edits that you make, such as deletions, additions, special effects, and so on, will be applied equally to the left and right channels in an Audacity stereo track.*

Making a Simple Voicecast

The simplest podcast is just you talking. As simple as this sounds, speaking into a microphone takes a bit of practice. You might practice speaking into a microphone without creating unwanted noises such as smacks, pops, loud breathing, clicking dentures, or any other unpleasant sounds. Beware verbal ticks like "uh, um, you know." Practice gauging the optimal distance between your mouth and the microphone, and set it up so that you can stand or sit comfortably. Using a mic stand is better than hand-holding, and if you're using a lavalier mic, clip it where your clothing won't rub on it. I prefer a good-quality USB headset. Speak past the mic as though you have an audience in the room, rather than into the mic; this will help you energize your voice and project it in a way that will reduce unwanted side effects. A windscreen or a foam windsock is essential.

How fast should you speak? This depends on your personality and the type of material. Usually 120 words per minute is cited as a good rate, though it will feel slow to most English speakers. This doesn't necessarily mean a speed limit of two words per second, but it means relaxing and using carefully timed pauses to allow listeners a chance to absorb what you're saying.

I use a Plantronics stereo USB headset for voice recordings (Figure 7-1). It's comfortable and easy to use, and the sound quality is good. USB recording interfaces have their own analog-to-digital converters, so you don't need a sound card. They also eliminate the risk of picking up internal computer noise, which is sometimes a problem with internal sound cards.

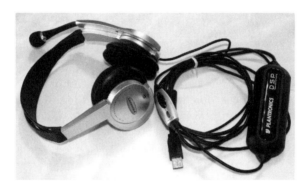

Figure 7-1: A good USB headset is a great tool for making voice recordings.

It takes a lot of practice to speak well without a script or rehearsing, so don't feel bad if you need them. It's better to make as clean a recording as possible than to clean up a recording all full of bad stuff, and your listeners will appreciate a crisp, focused presentation.

Audacity Settings

First create a new Audacity project with **File** > **Save Project As**.

Then set your recording and playback devices in the **Edit** > **Preferences** > **Devices** dialog, and set your channels to however many you are recording at one time. If it is just you with a mono microphone, set one channel. If you are using a stereo mic or headset, that is two. Beware of cheapo onboard sound chips, like the ones used in laptops—the microphone input is often mono even if they claim it's stereo.

In the **Edit** > **Preferences** > **Quality** dialog, set a default sample rate of 44,100 and a default sample format (which is really *bit depth*; Audacity has a few terminology quirks) of 32-bit float. (See Chapter 1 for more information on bit depths and sampling rates.) You can record at a higher audio resolution if you prefer, but for a simple voicecast, those extra bits aren't going to make any difference. In fact, you could use 16/44.1. It saves disk space, sounds good, and exports to lower-quality formats like MP3 and Ogg Vorbis just fine.

Now go to the **Edit > Preferences > Recording** dialog, make sure that "Overdub: Play other tracks while recording new one" and "Software Playthrough: Listen while recording or monitoring new track" are not checked.

Leave the Preferences menu and click the Input Level Meter to start monitoring and to set your recording level (Figure 7-2). This might take a bit of trial and error, depending on how much variation there is in your voice. Record to a peak of −9 or −12 dB to give yourself a good safety margin, and you'll still have a very good signal-to-noise ratio. Never go over zero; that results in clipping, which creates distortion. The blue lines mark the highest peak for the session, and the red lines mark the highest peak in the

Figure 7-2: Setting the recording level

last three seconds. The dark red bars indicate peak levels, and the light red bars show the average amplitude.

Most USB headsets come with Windows software that lets you control both the input and output volumes. Linux users may have to rely on ALSA (see Chapter 13) to set the volume levels. The Audacity Mixer toolbar (Figure 7-3) works with audio interfaces if their drivers support volume controls. Many don't. This is why I love recording interfaces with ordinary, old-fashioned knobs to twiddle.

Figure 7-3: The Audacity Mixer toolbar

And now, the moment you've been waiting for—click the **Record** button and start talking! Figure 7-4 shows a voice recording in progress.

Click **Pause** to stop recording, and **Record** to append to your existing track. If you click **Stop** and then click **Record**, you will create a new track. If you click **Stop** by mistake, pick up where you left off with SHIFT-Record.

Cleaning Up Your Recording

Once you have recorded your deep thoughts, you can go back and clean up your recording. First, delete anything you don't want to keep; just do a rough cut on your first pass and leave a bit extra. You can always delete more, but you can't put back very easily. If you have more than one track, be mindful of keeping them synchronized (though if they do get out of sync, there are simple ways to get them back together).

Then select **View > Show Clipping** to highlight in red any clipped segments. If you find some, there are a number of ways to fix them.

If it is a very brief clip, less than a quarter second in duration, zoom in until you can precisely select the clipped part and delete it. When it's a fraction of a second, no one will notice.

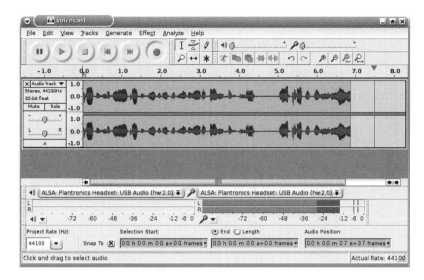

Figure 7-4: At last, we're making our recording!

Another way is to re-record the clipped segment at the correct recording level in a second track or Audacity window and then copy that over the clipped segment. It's not easy to replace a short segment surgically, so you might select a longer section to replace. Look for natural breaks so you can patch the new part in gracefully, as in Figure 7-5. The selection in Figure 7-5 is about four seconds long, even though the clipped portion (indicated by the three vertical peaks between the six-second mark and the six-and-a-half–second marks) is less than a half second in duration.

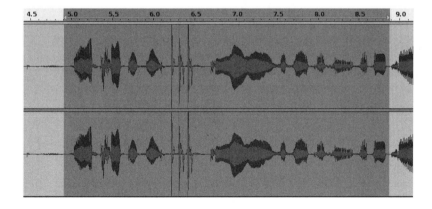

Figure 7-5: Making a smoother patch by selecting a segment to replace at natural breaks

Now here is a cool trick that I like because it helps me keep track of where I am editing. If you have used Audacity very much, you know that a slip of the mouse or accidentally hitting a hotkey will lose your place, and if it's a long track, it's a pain to get back to where you where. So, don't delete your selection but instead use **Edit** > **Split Delete**. This replaces the selection with an empty gap, as in Figure 7-6. This also keeps your track at the same length, which you might want if you have two or more tracks to keep synchronized.

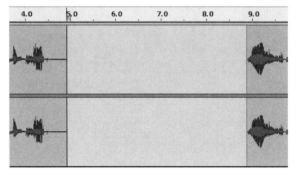

*Figure 7-6: Using **Edit** > **Split Delete** to leave a gap marking your deletion*

Now you can go ahead and make your rerecording. Don't worry about making the recording levels exactly the same as in your original project because that is easy to adjust with **Effect** > **Amplify**. When it is satisfactory, with nary a belch, bump, or cough, copy it and paste it into the gap (Figure 7-7). The edges may not exactly match, but we can fix that.

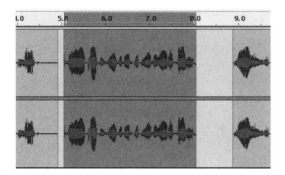

Figure 7-7: Paste the new segment into the gap you left when you deleted the bad bit.

There are a number of ways to deal with the empty parts on either side of the new segment. The simplest is to delete them. If you don't want to shorten the track, use **Generate** > **Silence** to fill the gaps.

Another way is to use the Time Shift tool to move everything together. The edges will match exactly when you see the Snap Guide appear, which is a yellow vertical line that appears when borders are perfectly lined up. Click to mark the place where the borders join, and then zoom way in until you can use the Repair effect to smooth over the edge of your patch. This operates on a maximum sample size of 128 samples, so zoom way in until you can make a selection that small. The Zoom tool centers on wherever you click. Then click **Effect** > **Repair**, which uses interpolation to make a seamless join.

One more fun Audacity trick for stretching out a patch is to use **Effect** > **Change Tempo** to slow down your patch without changing the pitch. You can measure the exact length required by selecting the "Length" radio button in the Selection toolbar and then make a selection from the beginning of your patch to the end of the gap. The yellow Snap Guides will appear when you are exactly on your borders. The example in Figure 7-8 needs to be 60 seconds long.

Then select just your patch, click **Effect** > **Change Tempo**, and enter the new length, as shown in Figure 7-9. Click the **Preview** button, and if it doesn't sound too weird, click **OK**, and you're done.

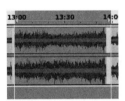

Figure 7-8: Figuring out how long your patch needs to be

Figure 7-9: Using **Effect** > **Change Tempo** to stretch out a patch

Reducing Too-Tall Peaks

You should also look for any disproportionately tall peaks in your waveform (Figure 7-10, at 2.7 to 3 seconds), even if they aren't clipped, and review them to decide whether they need to be reduced. In this example, I was speaking too loudly from the excitement of making a podcast, so I used **Effect** > **Amplify** to reduce the amplitude. Yes, it says "amplify," but if you give it a negative value (such as −3 or −6 dB), it will attenuate.

You can use trial and error to figure out how much reduction in volume to apply, or you can use the Waveform (db) view to get an idea of how much you need. Change the waveform display to Waveform (db) in the Track menu (Figure 7-11), and then expand the width of the track (grab the border with the mouse and pull) until you see the decibel scale on the left (Figure 7-12). In this example, it looks like the loud part could be as many as 12 decibels too loud, so that gives me a starting point of −12 to try. Remember, Audacity gives you nearly unlimited undos (**Edit** > **Undo** or CTRL-Z), so it's safe to use trial and error.

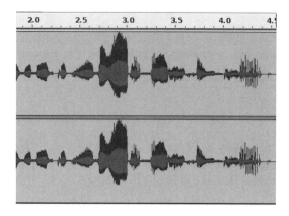

Figure 7-10: The portion from 2.7 to 3 seconds is too loud.

The decibel scale in the Track panel is adjustable in the **Edit** > **Preferences** > **Interface** dialog, from 0 to −36 to 0 to −145. This lets you adjust the display to whatever is useful for you. I usually keep it at −60 because that gives me plenty of detail without making the scale too large.

Figure 7-11:
Changing the
waveform display to
Waveform (dB)

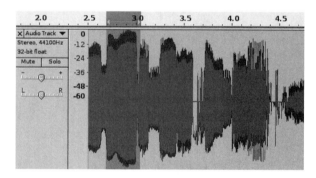

Figure 7-12: This selection could be as many as 12 decibels too loud.

Fades

There are two ways to control fading in and fading out. The easy way is to select the track segment you want to fade in or out and then click **Effect** > **Fade In** or **Fade Out**. All you do is control the length of the fade.

For finer-grained control, use the Envelope tool. Click the waveform to create control nodes, and then drag these around to make different parts of your track louder or quieter. Drag nodes past the track boundary to get rid of them.

Normalization

When you have your track all trimmed and cleaned up, the last step is to apply **Effect > Normalize**. Make sure both boxes in the Normalize dialog are checked ("Remove any DC offset" and "Normalize maximum amplitude"). DC offset refers to the mean amplitude; if this is not zero, then normalization won't be applied correctly because the amplitude levels will be off balance, and it might even create a bit of distortion. Figure 7-13 shows an example of DC offset, before and after correction. In the top track, you can see how the whole waveform is not quite centered on zero, and then in the bottom track it is.

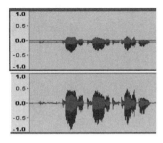

Figure 7-13: The waveform before normalization (above) and after (below)

Export to MP3 or Ogg?

Now that your recording is all cleaned up, it is time to export it to a compressed lossy format, either Ogg Vorbis or MP3 (MPEG-1 Audio Layer 3, not MPEG-3). (Refer to Chapters 13 and 14 to learn how to enable MP3 support on Linux and Windows.)

MP3 is the universal portable digital audio format: Everything supports MP3. As we discussed in Chapter 1, there are differences between Ogg Vorbis and MP3. Some listeners claim that Ogg Vorbis delivers higher quality than MP3. At low bitrates, neither one sounds very good to me; rather, they sound flat and without character or depth. At higher bitrates, both sound acceptable, though I think Ogg delivers a more accurate, natural sound. MP3s sound a bit too-bright and crunchy.

Ogg Vorbis supports multichannel surround, while MP3 supports one or two channels. MP3 is encumbered by patents held by several different patent holders in different countries, and the last one expires on 2017. Does this mean you'll get a visit from attack lawyers if you distribute your work in MP3 format? I don't know. It seems that a lot of artists distribute their work as MP3s without paying license fees and don't get in trouble. Ask a lawyer who specializes in these issues.

Even if your listeners all have megamondo broadband, it's a good practice to maintain a frugal attitude. And they don't all have fat pipes; estimates of US dial-up users range from 25 to 45 percent. Don't forget that the Internet is international, so your potential audience includes countries that rely on dial-up and low-speed wireless. Even for broadband users, network congestion and queuing gum up streaming media, so the moral is that streaming audio is still more reliable at lower bitrates.

As always, there are trade-offs. If your podcast host allows it, you can offer your listeners a choice of listening options at different quality levels and both streaming and downloadable files.

Ogg Vorbis Quality Settings

Ogg exports are easy in Audacity. You might have read how-tos that say to use a variable bitrate (vbr) rather than a constant bitrate (cbr). Although this is good advice, it is unnecessary because Ogg Vorbis does not support cbr. Select **File** > **Export** > Save as type: Ogg Vorbis Files, and then click the **Options** button (Figure 7-14). Exporting to Ogg Vorbis is simple: Pick a number. 0 is the lowest quality and smallest file size, and 10 is the best quality and largest file size.

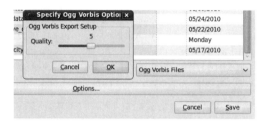

Figure 7-14: Setting Ogg Vorbis quality level

A variable bitrate means that simple passages will have a lower bitrate, and more complex passages will have a higher bitrate. This delivers better quality than a fixed bitrate. You won't be able to calculate file sizes precisely, but the fine folks who invented Ogg Vorbis don't think much of measuring quality by bitrates anyway. To give a basis for comparison, a quality setting of 3 results in an average bitrate of around 112Kbps, and Ogg fans claim it sounds better than a 128Kbps MP3.

Ogg Vorbis uses *lossy channel coupling* up to level 5. Redundancies between the left and right channels are combined to save space. This might affect the stereo imaging, so if this bothers you, use a quality setting of 6 or higher because channel coupling is turned off at this level. I use 6. My ears can't tell the difference between 7 and up. Your ears, of course, may tell you a different story.

For a simple voicecast, you can go all the way down to 0, and it still sounds acceptable.

MP3 Quality Settings

On both Linux and Windows, you may have to install an MP3 encoder separately. Use the LAME MP3 encoder because it is high quality, free of cost, and open source. Linux users can install it from their usual package repositories, and Windows users should follow the instructions at the Audacity downloads page (*http://audacity.sourceforge.net/help/faq?s=install&item=lame-mp3*).

NOTE   *Windows users should visit the OSSwin project (*http://osswin.sourceforge.net/*) to find links to hundreds of excellent open source applications for Windows.*

I don't know if audio geeks love to argue for the sake of arguing or simply have strong passions about everything, because MP3 quality settings are minefields of controversy. Just follow this simple rule, and you'll be fine: I, your author, am right (except when your own ears tell you differently).

In Audacity you have four categories for setting the MP3 bitrate: Preset, Variable, Average, and Constant.

Preset gives you four different prefab combinations that are recommended by the LAME developers: Medium, Standard, Extreme, and Insane. Standard is fine for music, but you can go lower for a simple voicecast. Medium, Standard, and Extreme all use *variable bitrates (vbr)*. Variable bitrate means the bitrate varies according to the complexity of the sounds, which results in better audio quality. In the olden days, variable bitrates gave MP3 players fits because they were designed for *constant bitrates (cbr)*. But that was a long time ago, and these days variable bitrates shouldn't present any problems. Variable bitrates are always defined within a range, like the 170Kbps to 210Kbps of the Standard preset.

Insane uses the maximum constant bitrate, 320Kbps. In my experience, the Standard setting (170Kbps to 210Kbps) is about as good as MP3 can deliver, and anything over that doesn't make a noticeable difference.

Variable has a range of 10 quality settings. Quality setting 5 is 110Kbps to 150Kbps, which is fine for simple voicecasts.

Average is, in my opinion, not worth bothering with. It is a compromise between Variable and Constant bitrates. You set a constant bitrate, but since it's an average, a little bit of fluctuation is allowed. So the quality is not quite as good as Variable, and it's a little better than Constant bitrate.

Constant bitrates are supposed to work better for streaming audio over the Internet, and you get a predictable file size. If you want to use constant bitrates, Audacity gives you a full range to choose from.

Set Variable Speed: Standard. Standard gives better quality, and it takes a tiny bit longer to encode.

Figure 7-15 and Figure 7-16 show the MP3 export menus and the various quality settings.

Leave Channel Mode: Stereo, because you have to be desperate for storage space to even think of using Joint Stereo. If you are desperate for storage space, to the point that you're thinking of encoding your MP3 files at a bitrate of 112Kbps or lower, then give it a try. The term *joint stereo* is a poor name that does not describe what it does. A popular misconception is that it joins the two stereo channels and destroys the stereo separation. As always with audio engineering, it's more complex than that. Here is a new audio term for you: *human psychoacoustics*. Isn't that a splendid phrase? No, it doesn't mean psycho like a crazy person with a big knife, sorry. It means engineering audio in a way that takes into account how the human ear perceives sounds, instead of adhering to a strictly mathematical model, which does not correspond to how human hearing really works. It is quite sophisticated, and if you don't like the way joint stereo sounds, it's easy enough to do over.

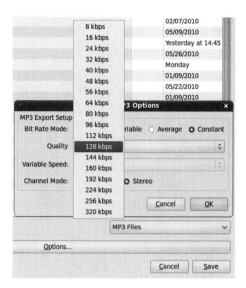

Figure 7-15: Audacity supports a wide range of MP3 bitrates.

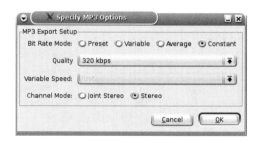

Figure 7-16: Audacity offers a range of MP3 quality settings and presets.

What is joint stereo? In the MPEG-1 Audio Layer 3 standard, it means using any of several techniques to reduce bitrate while preserving an acceptable level of quality by merging redundancies in the left and right channels. These "redundancies" are frequencies that the human perceives as less directional, which are the upper frequencies. It should improve how recordings at low bitrates sound because more audio data are preserved at the expense of stereo imaging.

Other Lossy Formats

There are other lossy, compressed audio formats that generate small file sizes, such as AAC, WMA, and RealPlayer. Audacity supports these via the FFmpeg library on Linux and Windows and has some nice export presets. You may also use the external encoder of your choice, which you can access via the Save as type drop-down menu in the Export dialog (Figure 7-17).

Figure 7-17: Using the "external program" option to export with any installed audio encoder.

NOTE *See Chapters 13 and 14 to learn how to install FFmpeg and MP3.*

AAC wasn't very popular until Apple chose it as the default format for its iTunes Store and all of its audio devices. WMA is the Windows Media Format, and RealPlayer is . . . well, RealPlayer. AAC, WMA, and RealPlayer are all closed, proprietary formats that are encumbered with various unpleasant features such as digital rights management (DRM), tracking software, and patent guff.

Exporting Your Podcast

Once you have decided what format or formats to export your podcast to, select **File** > **Export** to make your actual exports. You can make all kinds of exports from the same Audacity project. Note that you can export part of a track by selecting part of it and then selecting **File** > **Export Selection**.

Two-Person Podcasts

Say you don't want to be a lone pontificating hermit but instead want a cohost or want to interview another person. The easiest and best way is for each person to have their own mono microphone going to a separate recording channel. This makes it a lot easier to make edits and repairs. Be kind to your listeners and try to make both voices as close to the same volume level as you can. Let your ears be your guide more than the waveforms, because even when the waveform says both voices have equal volume, some people sound louder. (There's that psychoacoustic thingie again.)

If you're using a netbook or laptop with a real stereo microphone port, you can use a splitter for plugging in two mono mics.

Editing a Two-Track Recording as a Single Stereo Track

When you record two channels, Audacity creates a single stereo track no matter how you are set up. You can use two separate mono mics or a single stereo mic, and the default is a single stereo track. Figure 7-18 shows how this looks. (Notice how the waveform indicates that each person has politely taken turns to speak.)

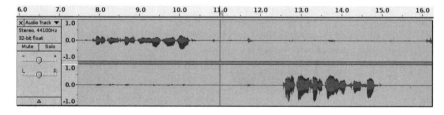

Figure 7-18: Recording with two mono microphones, one left and one right, in a single Audacity stereo track

You can make adjustments in the relative volumes of the left and right channels by using the cool new Mixer Board, which first appeared in Audacity 1.3.8 (Figure 7-19.) Use the Mixer Board to adjust the gain, or volume level, of the track, and use the Pan slider to adjust the relative volume of the left and right channels. These adjustments do not change the project file; you will hear the changes in playback in Audacity and in your final export, but your Audacity project files will not be altered. The Mixer Board controls are all or nothing; they apply to the whole track and can't be applied only to sections of the track.

This is pretty easy, and if you want more control, you can split your recording into two mono tracks.

Figure 7-19: The Mixer Board

Editing a Two-Track Recording as Two Mono Tracks

Splitting your stereo track into two mono tracks gives you a lot more control. Click the drop-down arrow in the Track menu, and select **Split Stereo Track** (Figure 7-20). Now you have two separate tracks and can make whatever changes and fixes you need to each one individually.

Figure 7-20: Split a stereo track into two mono tracks for easy editing.

You should name each track (also by using the Track menu) so you will always know what they are.

NOTE   *Here is a cool trick for the Mixer Board: If you use certain words in your track names such as* guitar, vocals, piano, *and even some abbreviations, the icons will match the names. See "Customizing the Mixer Board" on page 189 to see a complete listing of keywords.*

After splitting your stereo track into two mono tracks, edit each track separately, making the usual fixes and matching the volume of your two speakers as well as you can. By default, Audacity plays all tracks at the same time when you hit Play. Look on the Mixer Board for the Mute and Solo buttons to control which ones you want to hear. Solo automatically mutes all tracks except the one you want to hear; Mute silences one track at a time.

If your two people talk at the same time, you can separate them by adding silence. For example, if there is five seconds of overlap where they are both yakking at once, add five seconds of silence to one track to push them apart. Position the cursor where you want the silence to begin, click **Generate** > **Silence**, and enter how many seconds of silence you want. You may have to do this several times on both tracks to keep them lined up, especially after making changes.

When you have everything cleaned up and ready to export, rejoin your tracks by using the Track menu in the upper track and clicking **Make Stereo Track**.

Adding a Background Music Track

Now that you're aces at producing multitrack podcasts, adding a music track is as easy as falling over. Just like when you make a solo podcast, your soundtrack should be in a two-channel stereo track even if it is a mono recording. Then your listeners will hear music in both channels. You can create a two-channel track from a mono track by copying the track, pasting the copy below the original, and selecting **Make Stereo Track** from the upper track's Track menu.

You can add a music file to your podcast project by opening the **File** > **Import** > **Audio** dialog or by copying and pasting from another Audacity project.

You can adjust the music volume with the Gain slider. Remember, the Gain slider does not alter your project file, so it's a quick way to tune your mix without making a lot of changes that might mess up your project for future editing. Another option is to use the Envelope tool to vary it from pleasant background to thrilling crescendo. The Envelope tool does change the project file.

There is an even cooler way to manage the volume on your background music track, and that is with **Effect** > **Auto Duck**. This is perfect for recordings with a background music track because it automatically lowers the volume when the foreground track cuts in and raises it when the foreground cuts out. In Figure 7-21 we see the setup: A background music track is on top, and the bottom track is the voice track. When the voices start, I want the music volume to decrease, and when the voices stop, the music should get louder. The tracks have to be in this order: the background track on top and the foreground, or *control track*, underneath.

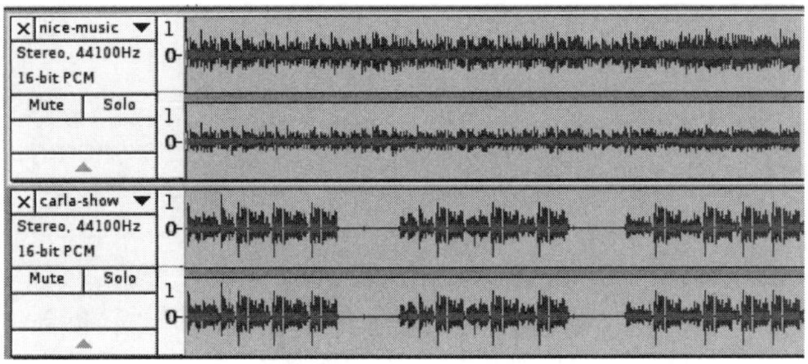

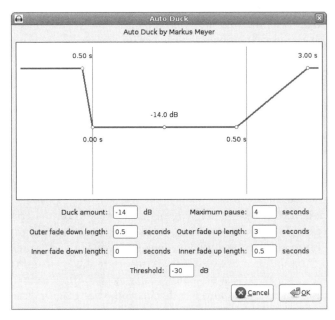

Figure 7-21: To use Auto Duck, your background track must be on top and the foreground, or control track, underneath.

Select the background track and hit **Effect** > **Auto Duck**. You'll see a control panel like the one in Figure 7-22, which shows the settings I like to use. These settings create a fast fade-out and a gradual fade-in. The background track ducks out of the way fast and gracefully glides slowly back in with just a little bit of overlap with the voice track.

Figure 7-22: My suggested Auto Duck settings for a fast fade-out and slow fade-in

Figure 7-23 shows the result.

Figure 7-23: Auto Duck has been applied; compare these to the tracks in Figure 7-21.

Duck Amount is how much volume reduction you want on the background track.

Maximum Pause determines how long the total fade-in and outs will take. The values for Outer fade down length and Outer fade up length cannot total more than the maximum pause.

The Outer fade down length setting determines how quickly the background track will fade before the voice on the control track comes back. Anything outside the two vertical lines happens when the control track is below your threshold. The Inner fade down length setting determines how much overlap there will be with the control track.

The Outer fade up length setting sets how fast the backing track fades back in when the voice on the control track stops, and the Inner fade up length setting controls the overlap. A half second of gently rising music over the voice isn't a lot; I think it makes a nice bit of a transition.

The Threshold setting controls the sound level for triggering the Auto Duck effect.

When you are finished, you need to mix and render your tracks together into a single stereo track. If you press CTRL-SHIFT-M, this mixes your project down into a new stereo track underneath your original tracks. This is how I prefer to mixdown because it saves my original tracks, and then I copy the new stereo track into a new Audacity project for final tweaks and exports. If you use **Tracks** > **Mix and Render** instead, your original tracks are replaced by the new stereo track.

Sometimes combining multiple tracks makes them too loud, so undo Mix and Render (CTRL-Z or **Edit** > **Undo**) and use the Gain controls to turn them down a bit. Then export again. (When you have odd problems with track volume, such as unbalanced sound, check your Gain sliders.)

Now your podcast with its background music track is ready for export.

Visit Chapter 11 to learn more about Audacity's special effects, Chapter 12 for fix-its and cleanups, and Chapter 9 to learn more about multitrack recording and mixing.

8

BECOMING AN ONLINE STAR

So you want to distribute your own recordings and maybe even make some money selling them. In this wonderful Internet era, online distribution is easy and inexpensive. There are two distinct skill sets needed for succeeding at online music distribution: being technically adept at creating good recordings in various formats for downloading and streaming and understanding the business of being a professional artist, which is complex and involves tasks like customer service, contracts, and copyright issues. In the first section of this chapter, we'll learn about creating different audio file formats for various purposes, such as lower-quality promotional MP3s, streaming audio, and high-quality downloads. In the second part, we'll take a look at the business of being a recording artist, which is trickier than being a good musician and recording whiz.

File Formats and Audio Quality

With Audacity it is easy to export your audio files to whatever format you want. Let's take a look at your options. The common downloadable formats are AAC, MP3, Ogg Vorbis, WAV, and FLAC.

NOTE *Please review Chapter 1 if you need a refresher on exporting to different audio file formats, and see Chapters 13 and 14 to learn how to set up and tune your system for audio production.*

AAC is becoming popular because that is the format used by Apple's iTunes Store. Version 1.3.6 of Audacity introduced support for importing, exporting, and converting non-DRM AAC files via FFmpeg. These have the M4A (*A* for audio) file extension. M4P files are DRM encumbered. (No, it's not *P* for Pooey, but Protected.)

Creating files in AAC format in Audacity is easy: Select **File** > **Export** > Save as type: M4A (AAC) Files (FFmpeg) and click the **Options** button. In the Options dialog, you have a range of quality settings from 10 to 500, with 500 being the highest quality. This range represents Fair, Okay, Good, Better, and Best. The 256 setting is good for a more complex recording. A very simple recording, such as one-voice spoken-word piece, sounds decent at 50 (Figure 8-1).

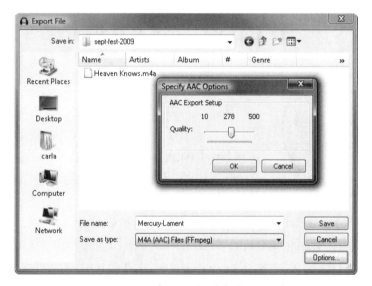

Figure 8-1: Exporting to AAC format (the default iTunes format) creates a file with an .m4a extension.

Audacity supports many different MP3 options, and you can read all about them in Chapter 7. Let's review the ones that are most practical to use. MP3 supports both constant bitrates and variable bitrates. Variable bitrates deliver better quality. Your online distribution sites will have specific requirements, and with Audacity, you can easily tailor your tunes to meet them.

The 128Kbps constant bitrate MP3 is the lowest common denominator in the United States. This will play on every digital audio player, and some distributors require constant bitrate MP3s for streaming. In Audacity, click **File** > **Export** > **MP3 Files** > **Options** > **Constant** > **128Kbits/sec**.

The Options dialog gives you a wide range of constant bitrates, from 8Kbps to 320Kbps. Although 320Kbps is often touted as CD-quality, it isn't. Your own ears may tell you differently, but I can't hear any improvement over 192Kbps.

NOTE *Some low-bandwidth carriers may require bitrates as low as 32Kbps for streaming Internet audio. While this may not sound wonderful, it expands your potential audience. Half of Internet users in the United States are still on dial-up, and many other countries still rely on predominantly low-bandwidth Internet services.*

Your best Audacity options for variable bitrate MP3s are in the **File** > **Export** > **MP3 Files** > **Options** > **Variable** dialog. Choose your desired quality setting, set Variable Speed: Standard and Channel Mode: Stereo (Figure 8-2). There are 10 bitrate options in this menu, from 45Kbps to 85Kbps to 220Kbps to 260Kbps. I like 170Kbps to 210Kbps as a good level for music, and I like 110Kbps to 150Kbps for simple spoken-word pieces. The Variable Speed option limits the variable bitrate to a set range so you can get both better quality and some predictability.

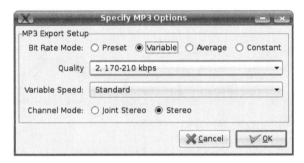

Figure 8-2: Using variable bitrate settings for MP3s in Audacity

If your distributor supports it, you should also offer Ogg Vorbis files for users who don't care for MP3. They may prefer the higher quality of Ogg, or they may using prefer open source, patent-unencumbered formats. Ogg Vorbis can be streamed or downloaded just like MP3. It delivers high quality at low bitrates and supports multichannel surround, while MP3 supports only one or two channels. MP3 is a closed, proprietary standard chock-full of messy, confusing patent conflicts. I haven't heard of any of the patent holders coming after anyone who uses an open source encoder like LAME, which is the preferred MP3 encoder to use with Audacity, and I haven't heard of any small-time users getting in trouble for distributing their work in MP3 format. Just be aware that it is an issue for some of your fans, and there is a possibility it could turn into a problem for you.

Audacity supports Ogg Vorbis, and it is easy to choose your quality level. Go to **File** > **Export** > **Ogg Vorbis Files** > **Options**. You get a menu with a little slider that lets you choose from 11 quality settings, from 0 to 10. A value of 3 is roughly equivalent to a 128Kbps MP3. A value of 5 is pretty nice for music, with one possible drawback: Ogg Vorbis uses channel coupling for all levels up to 5. This means that redundancies between two stereo channels are combined to save bandwidth, so you might notice a loss of stereo imaging. Channel coupling is not used at levels 6 and up. I don't perceive any gain in going above 7, though your ears may tell you differently. Ogg Vorbis support is growing fast, and a lot of playback devices support it (Figure 8-3).

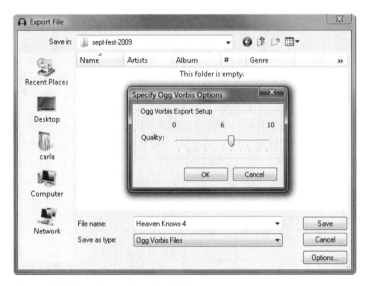

Figure 8-3: Exporting to Ogg Vorbis format

FLAC is a wonderful lossless, compressed format that gives WAV-quality audio in a smaller file size. FLAC files are typically around a third smaller than WAVs. FLACs are great for fans who play music from their computers or have computer-based music servers, and an increasing number of music players, both home and portable, support FLAC. FLAC cannot be streamed but must be downloaded and then played.

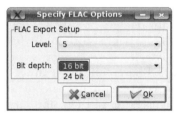

Figure 8-4: FLAC supports both 16- and 24-bit.

FLAC supports both 16- and 24-bit depths and has nine compression levels, from 0 to 8 (Figure 8-4). The default is 5, and that is a good one to stick with, though nobody will yell at you for experimenting with the others. The different settings are different levels of compression, with 0 being the least compression and 8 the most. FLAC is lossless, so there is no difference in quality, only in how small the files are compressed. A value of 8 takes several times longer to encode than 5 with not much additional benefit. Decoding FLAC files that have been maximally compressed doesn't take any longer than ones that have been lightly compressed, so the degree of compression won't affect playback.

WAV is the standard for high-quality uncompressed audio. File sizes are large and cannot be streamed, but they are wonderful for your fans who want a high-quality file that can easily be converted to other formats, such as CD and lower-quality portable formats. And, of course, to enjoy for itself. Go to **File** > **Export** > **Other uncompressed files** > **Options**. In the Uncompressed Export Setup dialog (Figure 8-5), select Header: WAV (Microsoft), and then choose your encoding. Select either Signed 16 bit PCM or Signed 24 bit PCM. 16-bit is CD quality, and 24-bit is DVD and studio master quality. Select 24-bit only if your original recording is 24-bit or higher.

Figure 8-5: WAV settings should be either signed 16-bit or 24-bit.

Signed means positive integer, which we learned about in Chapter 1. You want signed 16- or 24-bit integer because those are playable formats outside of Audacity. 32-bit float is an intermediate editing format used internally by Audacity and other audio editors.

The Business of a Recording Artist

You're becoming serious about distributing your own recordings. You've heard all the horror stories about how artists are ripped off by the entertainment industry and have memorized Courtney Love's wonderful speech to the Digital Hollywood online entertainment conference on May 16, 2000, "Courtney Love Does the Math" (*http://salon.com/technology/feature/2000/06/14/love/*):

> Today I want to talk about piracy and music. What is piracy? Piracy is the act of stealing an artist's work without any intention of paying for it. I'm not talking about Napster-type software.
> I'm talking about major label recording contracts.

Frank Zappa and Janis Ian have also written or given talks in this vein, which you should be able to find online.

Or maybe you aren't worried about possible unpleasant experiences from signing with a major label, but you want to retain control of your own destiny and your own work. You want to release recordings engineered to your specifications and tailored for different uses, rather than dumbing everything down for the lowest common denominator. You want to work when and where you feel like it and not have other people telling you what to do. When someone actually wants to buy your work, you want to make it as easy as possible and then keep the money. So, what do you do?

I can't help you with attaining fame, glory, and groupies. Getting noticed is still the hardest part. But I can point you to resources for online distribution and tell how to package your recordings for different uses such as high-quality audiophile, lo-fi promotional MP3s, streaming audio, and CDs.

Establishing an Online Presence

Distribution and promotion used to be the big hurdles for recording artists, and that was why they needed to make deals with record companies. Now distribution is easy, thanks to the Internet. An Internet distribution strategy has two parts: your own personal website and as many music distribution and broadcast sites as you can manage. Always have your own personal site with photos, contact information, and links to where fans can hear and purchase your music. This increases your search engine presence, and it makes it easy for fans to find you. Do please resist the urge to make this a typical overproduced site full of special effects and animations and dark, barely readable color schemes; this guarantees you will chase away your visitors. Make it clean, simple, readable, and easy to navigate, because nobody cares how self-indulgent your web designer is. They want to know about you and how to hear your music, and they don't want to jump through hoops to get there.

You should have a consistent online identity. The first step to building your online identity is to register your own domain name. Don't have an email address or domain name that promotes someone else's business, like carlarockstar@gmail.com or guitarcarla@hotmail.com. Free email addresses are seriously uncool anyway. Domain names are cheap, about $15 per year. If you change web hosts and email service providers, your domain name will always travel with you. Suppose you have a band—let's say you're The Bandits—and your domain is *http://thebandits.com/*. Now you can do all kinds of creative things with the domain name. Everyone in your band can have their own email address, such as drummer@thebandits.com, diva@thebandits.com, or rockgod@thebandits.com. No matter what music distributors, hosting services, or social networking sites you try, *http://thebandits.com/* will always be there for your fans to find you.

There are all kinds of domain name registrars such as Dotster, GoDaddy, Register.com, Tucows, and many more. Most web hosting services also include domain name registration, but I would keep the two separate. Web hosting is a brutal business full of fly-by-nights that come and go, and a bad registrar can make it difficult to transfer to another registrar, or you can even lose your domain name. The Internet Corporation for Assigned Names and Numbers (ICANN) oversees domain names and maintains a list of accredited registrars (*http://www.icann.org/en/registrars/accredited-list.html*). This doesn't guarantee that their customer service or prices are any good, just that they are legitimate registrars. WebHostingTalk (*http://www.webhostingtalk.com/*) is a great source of real-world information on hosting services and registrars.

Think carefully about what kind of contact information to put on your sites, because thanks to the magic of the Internet, communications can turn into a deep time sink. If you don't want to spend a lot of time answering emails, Tweets, forum posts, and so on, then limit how people can reach you. A web form protected by a captcha is a good way to allow fans to talk to you without getting buried by spam. Captchas that use simple arithmetic problems or multiple-choice questions ("If you are a human, click the picture of the puppy.") are easy and effective. The kind that obscure text are annoying and hard for everyone but spammers.

Who is a good web designer? Someone who listens to you; who can explain what they do in plain English (or language of your choice); and who favors clean, fast, navigable site design over fancy show-off stuff that chases your fans away. Always test your sites on a dial-up connection and on a smartphone. Broadband is far from universal, and mobile Internet use is exploding, so you need to be tuned in to how your site looks and performs on slow connections and on tiny screens.

NOTE   *Remember to also factor in accessibility for vision-impaired fans. The United States has an aging population, so it's good business to welcome all of your fans, and accessible design is good design for all visitors. If your website designer doesn't want to bother with making your site friendly to all visitors, look for a different designer.*

Consider having a rented snail mailbox. It's reliable, it weeds out the casual stream-of-consciousness Twitter/email communiques, and it ensures that anyone who really wants to talk to you can do so.

What about MySpace and Facebook? Go for it; they're free, and you'll probably be pleasantly surprised at who finds you there. Budget some time to keep them current. You don't have to log in every day to have deep, meaningful conversations with fans, but definitely make sure that links and information about all of your recordings and performances are current. It takes time to build a following, so be patient and read all of the helpful information that tells you how to get the most benefit out of MySpace and Facebook. There are no fast, magic solutions, and you shouldn't believe anyone who tries to sell you some.

Never ever spam. Do not believe "marketers" who claim they sell genuine guaranteed opt-in mail lists full of people who are happy to hear from you. This is a lie. You should carefully build your own mailing lists. The right way is to have a confirmed opt-in, which means when someone signs up, they have to respond to an email that is sent to confirm their registration. Make opting out easier than signing up; the lesson that marketers and spammers refuse to learn is you can't force people to like you.

Do be careful—there is no such thing as privacy online. Everything you say is a public performance and recorded forever.

You'll have to measure your own tolerance for texting, Twitter, and whatever other newfangled communication tools come along. They can be powerful and effective, and they can drive you crazy.

Online Music Distributors

Hooking up with an independent online music store that handles sales, gives you a fair cut, and doesn't try to glom your copyrights is no longer a fantasy, and you have many to choose from. Here is a sampling of sites with different approaches to distributing music and compensating artists.

Magnatune's (*http://www.magnatune.com/*) motto is "We are not evil." They have another motto that I like better: "You get great music, musicians get 50%." That's 50 percent of sales, not profits. Magnatune distributes music in several DRM-free formats: streaming only, which is like listening to the radio, downloads in various formats, CD, and licenses for commercial use. All music is try-before-you-buy, and customers can either select what songs and albums they want to hear or listen to various streams. Magnatune customers can also get a streaming membership for $15 per month, which purchases unlimited listening and downloads with no commercials.

Magnatune supports MP3, WAV, FLAC, AAC, and Ogg Vorbis formats. WAV and FLAC are the highest quality, and WAVs can be written to CDs. 128Kbps MP3s are the lowest quality and are licensed under Creative Commons "Attribution-NonCommercial-ShareAlike" license. This grants liberal rights for noncommercial uses: sharing, remixes, sampling, and covers. Any commercial use is expected to pay money. There is a lot of information on the Magnatune website, and they have live humans to talk to.

You retain all copyrights to your own work and can make deals with other distributors. Magnatune pays artists every six months, provided they have earned at least $100.

CD Baby (*http://www.cdbaby.com/*) sells both DRM-free CDs and MP3 downloads and partners with a number of online stories like iTunes and Amazon. It also does bulk CD duplication and artwork. CD Baby charges a $35 setup fee per album; this covers digitizing the CD, converting tracks into various formats, scanning the cover art, and doing other housekeeping chores. You set your own CD pricing. CD Baby keeps $4 per disc and 25 percent of download sales. Artists are paid weekly. Your CDs will be available through a multitude of stores such as Borders and Amazon.

CD Baby offers a nice service for live shows—its Credit Card Swiper Program. This is a credit/debit card terminal that you can take to shows and set up on your merchandise table. CD Baby takes a 12.8 percent cut. This sounds like a lot, but having your own merchant credit card account is expensive. It will cost you a monthly fee whether you sell anything or not, plus a percentage of every sale, usually around 2.5 to 3 percent per swiped transaction. If you sell your CDs on your merchandise tables, CD Baby takes 12.8 percent instead of the usual $4 cut.

CD Baby offers a number of other artist services such as Host Baby (web hosting), stickers and cards, and a booking service.

eMusic (*http://www.emusic.com/*) is a well-regarded DRM-free MP3 on-line music store that is a treasure trove of good indie bands and mainstream popular music. However, they don't accept just anyone; they work with es-tablished music labels, so you need to already be signed on with someone. eMusic is all corporate and lawyerly and full of bureaucracy. It's probably a better deal for music fans than for little-known musicians, though it never hurts to check it out.

TuneCore (*http://www.tunecore.com/*) has a flat-rate system. You pay $9.99 per song plus a $9.99 annual maintenance fee, or $49.99 per album the first year and $19.98 for each year thereafter, plus $19.98 annual mainte-nance. This gets you into 19 online stores including Amazon MP3, eMusic, Rhapsody, and Spotify. They also have an Amazon: Disc On Demand op-tion for selling CDs. There is a two-month lag on sales reporting from most stores, and TuneCore reports twice per month. After that, you can withdraw your funds any time. (It requires a PayPal account.)

iTunes (*http://www.apple.com/itunes/content-providers/faq.html*) is the big show. There are significant hoops to jump through, but nothing ventured, nothing gained. CD Baby, TuneCore, and SongCast all partner with iTunes, which is easier than applying directly to iTunes.

The Independent Online Distribution Alliance (IODA) (*http://www .iodalliance.com/*) acts as a collective agent and aggregator, using the power of collective bargaining to give independents a stronger business voice. In return for a percentage of artists' royalties, it handles rate negotiations, re-porting, distribution of works, distribution of royalties, and other grotty but necessary business chores.

Independent online distribution is a growing business, and you can find many more distribution sites. Promotion is up to you, though every site provides useful tools and advice to help you. Don't be a typical clueless artist and sign your life away or hook up with some rip-off artist. Research-ing distributors is as easy as sitting down at your computer and doing some web searches. Don't forget the gnarly business of taxes and reading the fine print. When will you get paid? How can you verify sales and payment records? Copyrights, DRM, closing your account, making changes, getting help from real live humans, and dispute resolution are all important things to look at.

Consider choosing distributors by genre, rather than popularity. Sure, iTunes and Amazon are the big gorillas, but if your niche is sophisticated jazz, dance music, world music, or some such, look for a distributor that spe-cializes in your type of music.

It is good to maintain a professional, businesslike approach and remem-ber mundane details such as keeping your word; contact information; cor-rect spelling, grammar and punctuation; readable fonts; and nice-looking artwork. Nobody cares how much you artistically suffer.

Self-Hosting

Another option is to self-host, which means running your own servers. These here modern times are not like the olden days of Bulletin Board Services (BBS) when thousands of people ran their own BBS servers from PCs in their bedrooms. Maintaining a website, hosting your own downloads, and offering streams of your work are all feasible for the do-it-yourselfer but are not for the faint of heart or the technophobe. Bandwidth is the biggest problem: If you want to house your servers in your home, first find out whether you can get adequate bandwidth for a reasonable price and whether your Internet service provider will even allow you to run servers. Then you are responsible for your own security, software, hardware, and system and network administration. It is satisfying to be the boss of your own servers, but it does require a lot of skills.

A better option is to use a good hosting service that has all the tools you need and gives you a good deal on bandwidth. It's hard to beat a good hosting service on bandwidth cost, since they buy in bulk and spread the cost over many customers. Then the hosting service handles hardware problems, Internet connectivity, security, and backup power. Plans range from free for a basic low-traffic site to inexpensive shared hosting (which means one server with a limited amount of Internet bandwidth serves many customers) to paying for your own dedicated, unshared server. You can get started cheaply and upgrade as you become more successful.

NOTE *Remember WebHosting Talk* (http://www.webhostingtalk.com/) *for learning which hosts are good and which ones to avoid.*

The free/open source software world has everything you need for running your own websites. Use the Linux operating system because it is robust and secure. Then there are bales of great servers to choose from:

- Drupal, Joomla, Mambo, and Plone are all examples of excellent open source content management systems (CMS). These are the frameworks for the content that you want to put on your site so you can easily organize and post articles, photos, calendars, news, forums, and links.

- Icecast and Campcaster are excellent open source streaming Ogg Vorbis and MP3 servers that you can embed on your website.

- Shoutcast is a closed, proprietary streaming server, and Shoutcast Radio is a fast and free Internet broadcast service for hosting your streams. You can also embed Shoutcast streams in your other sites.

Many web hosting services offer Icecast and Shoutcast streaming and, of course, many other streaming media servers. Any hosting service offers a big bundle of server software and a nice graphical control panel for everything. If they don't have a particular piece of software, ask whether they will install it, and if the software is free-of-cost open source, they probably will. Most hosting services rely heavily on open source software because it is free or inexpensive and because it is good.

Selling Stuff Online

Selling things online can be as simple as having a website and a PayPal account for accepting payments or a mailing address for checks and money orders. Check and money order fraud are rampant to the point that it may not be worth accepting either one. PayPal is easy and popular; just be sure you understand its fee structure so you don't get surprised at the myriad ways it nibbles away chunks of your money. Google Checkout has lower fees than PayPal and doesn't have PayPal's reputation for inconsistent, unfair dispute resolution. You can use both, which will capture more customers since many of them will not want to sign up for one when they already have an account at the other.

Processing online credit card payments requires a sophisticated infrastructure. You don't want to be one of those shops that makes headlines when some teenager hacks your customer database and steals all the information. Consider using a prefab storefront that has all the payment processing already in place. Start at Amazon.com (*http://www.amazonservices.com/content/sell-on-amazon.htm*); it is reputable and reliable, and it posts all of its prices and policies, so it's a good starting point for research and comparisons. Amazon does not directly sell independent music but partners with music distributors like CD Baby and TuneCore. Having an Amazon storefront might be a good venue for your band swag and getting more visibility and another way to generate CD orders.

You can avoid payment hassles by hosting only free downloads and streaming on your personal site and then linking to your wares on CD Baby, Songcast, or whatever distributors you are hooked up with.

The one piece that almost everyone forgets is customer service. How are customers going to contact you when they have questions or problems, phone? Email? Who is going to respond, and can you count on them to respond quickly and in a way that keeps customers happy? If you are selling physical items like CDs, DVDs, T-shirts, and other branded merchandise, who is going to pack and ship them and how fast? Customer service is everything. It costs at least ten times more to acquire a new customer than to keep an existing customer happy, no matter how great your artistic genius.

To DRM or Not to DRM?

Digital rights management (DRM), or as some prefer to call it, digital restrictions management, means copy protection, and the various technologies designed to prevent illegal copying. The concept might sound good, since the idea of people copying your music for free sounds like a rip-off. But in practice it's a nightmare. It doesn't even slow down big-time pirates who reproduce and sell thousands of copies of movies and music CDs. It doesn't stop the clever kids who want something for nothing. It mainly gets in the way of legitimate paying customers.

It adds an intolerable overhead burden to online distribution, because this requires always-available authentication servers. Already this is falling apart after just a few years. Wal-Mart announced in September 2008 that it was going to shut down its DRM authentication servers, which meant that customers would not be able to play their DRM-"protected" music that they had purchased if they tried to move it to a different machine or restore from a system failure. Wal-Mart's remedy was for customers to copy their DRM-"protected" tracks to CDs, which would then play anywhere. There was such an outcry that they changed their plans and still maintain their DRM servers. Even though they have moved to DRM-free distribution, that old DRM baggage is going to haunt them for a long time.

Apple's iTunes store went DRM-free in February 2008, and existing DRM-protected files can be converted to DRM-free versions for 30 cents per song or 30 percent of the album price. (Thank you for the opportunity to pay twice.) Yahoo! and Rhapsody have also moved away from DRM. Amazon and EMI moved in and captured a dominant chunk of the music market by offering DRM-free tracks from the beginning.

There are a sizable number of doofy DRM schemes that make me wonder why some people get paychecks for coming up with these brainstorms, while we sensible people have to scramble for our daily bread. Sony BMG got busted not once but twice for sneakily installing cloaked rootkits on Windows computers from "protected" music CDs. Not only was this a trespass that would have been criminally prosecuted if it were some kid instead of a globalcorp, it opened big security holes in these computers. Other brilliant DRM ideas that went over like lead balloons were time-bombed music tracks that became unplayable after a certain number of days, attempts to count and limit the numbers of copies that could be made, and downloads that became unplayable when subscriptions expired. All of these depend on some kind of central authorization and control, which to my way of thinking requires unwarranted intrusions into our personal business and a level of reliability that few service providers can sustain. I have vinyl LPs that are older than me—how long do you think digital tracks will survive even without DRM monkeyshines? I can't fathom the mind-set that can come up with these sort of hostile, self-defeating Big Brother tactics.

On the other hand, having your work poached is no good either. Recording artists have a right to get paid for their recorded works; I don't think much of the folks who say, "Give your recordings away and earn money giving live performances." Apparently they have never performed or created a good recording. I don't have any wisdom to offer except to treat your paying customers as well as you can. In real life, and not the bizarro world inhabited by the entertainment industry barons, most people will treat you fairly if you treat them fairly and do the right thing because it's the right thing, not because they are forced to.

Copyrights and Legal Issues

Copyright law is in a seriously weird place right now in the United States and some other countries as well. The rights of copyright owners keep getting extended, while fair use is taking a beating, and minor infringements are escalated into major crimes. Creators are pushed out as the rights holders to their own works, though that is an old, chronic problem. As Courtney Love said in "Courtney Love Does the Math":

> . . . a congressional aide named Mitch Glazier, with the support of the RIAA, added a "technical amendment" to a bill that defined recorded music as "works for hire" under the 1978 Copyright Act.
>
> He did this after all the hearings on the bill were over. By the time artists found out about the change, it was too late. The bill was on its way to the White House for the president's signature.
>
> That subtle change in copyright law will add billions of dollars to record company bank accounts over the next few years—billions of dollars that rightfully should have been paid to artists. A "work for hire" is now owned in perpetuity by the record company.
>
> Under the 1978 Copyright Act, artists could reclaim the copyrights on their work after 35 years. If you wrote and recorded "Everybody Hurts," you at least got it back to as a family legacy after 35 years. But now, because of this corrupt little pisher, "Everybody Hurts" never gets returned to your family, and can now be sold to the highest bidder.
>
> . . . By the way, which bill do you think the recording industry used for this amendment? . . . How about the Satellite Home Viewing Act of 1999?

That charming little provision was overturned retroactively in The Work Made for Hire and Copyright Corrections Act of 2000. But you see what you're up against. One way to take matters into your own hands is to release your works under a Creative Commons license. There are several of them, and you can read all about them at *http://www.creativecommons.org/*. These allow you to define different degrees of permissions for reuse and distribution, from permissive to restrictive. When you look for legal advice, be sure that you find an attorney who is well versed in all aspects of copyright law, including Creative Commons.

Note that I said, "when you look for legal advice," not "if." The Internet is already full of nonlawyers trading legal advice, so do yourself a favor and find a real lawyer to advise you. You can find all kinds of information online and at the library, and then when you meet with an attorney, you'll be well prepared. Unfortunately, this is a necessary part of being an artist in these modern times. You can live on beans and rice, you can patch old clothes, and you can drive an old car held together with wire and tape. But undoing legal messes is difficult, expensive, and often not possible; prevention is much cheaper and considerably less stressful.

Learn More

Please refer to Chapter 4 to learn more about putting live performances on CD. Chapter 6 goes into detail on producing very high-fidelity audio files, and Chapter 9 is all about multitrack recording and mixing in Audacity.

9

MULTITRACK RECORDING

Editing and mixing multiple tracks is a whole lot easier in the digital realm than it is in the analog world. No waiting for tapes to rewind, no physically cutting and pasting tapes—it's all just pointy-clicky bit shuffling. Although Audacity isn't the most sophisticated application for heavy-duty multitrack recording and editing, you can make excellent mono and stereo recordings with it and even 5.1 and 7.1 surround sound. It's the real deal, with discrete tracks.

NOTE   *That's* discrete *as in separate, not* discreet *as in able to keep a secret. Discrete is an important term in audio because it tells you when you're getting the real deal, and not something simulated. For example, a surround sound hi-fi system will emulate 5.1 sound from a stereo recording, which has only two discrete channels. Real 5.1 has six discrete channels.*

What is Audacity missing? It doesn't have per-track recording level meters, and you can't make edits while tracks are playing. When you're using a multichannel recording device, you can't control which input goes to which track. Multichannel surround mixing is still rather rudimentary: You can export to 5.1 and 7.1 surround, but Audacity gives you no help mapping the channels. Audacity's strengths lie in recording, editing, and mixing for mono and stereo playback. Ardour might be a better choice for Linux and Mac users who want to perform heavy-duty studio wizardry, perform multichannel surround, and have maximum control, and of course Windows and Mac users have great thundering herds of other high-end audio production suites to choose from.

So, what can Audacity do? It will record as many channels at one time as your recording interface supports and your computer can handle. Some examples of multichannel recording interfaces are the M-Audio Delta 1010 PCI sound card (10 × 10), the Edirol FA-101 FireWire audio interface (10 × 10), the RME Hammerfall sound cards, and the M-Audio NRV10, which is a useful combination of an analog mixer and 10-channel FireWire DAC/ADC.

Audacity has no hard limit for the total number of tracks in a project; you can keep adding tracks until your computer keels over. Audacity supports all of the basic multitrack editing and mixing functions: mix and match clips, time-shift and synchronize, layer multiple copies of the same track or clip, do fix-its and special effects, and mixdown to any number of channels from 1 to 32 (WAV, AIFF, and Ogg Vorbis; other file formats support fewer channels). In real life, mono, stereo, and 5.1 surround (6 channel) are your likeliest options.

Tracks, Channels, and Clips

Let's take a moment to be sure of our terminology. A single track in Audacity is represented by a single waveform, as in Figure 9-1. I call this a mono track to make it clear that it's not a stereo track. However, the definition of *track* is a bit fuzzy in audio and also in Audacity because it treats a stereo track the same way it treats a mono track—even though there are two channels with two different waveforms, Audacity sees a stereo track as one track, and everything you do to it is applied equally to both channels. A track is also a single song in a track, CD, LP, or tape that contains several songs.

Figure 9-1: This is what a single mono track looks like—one waveform, no matter how many voices or instruments are recorded on the track.

Channel refers to audio inputs and outputs. When you record using a single mono microphone, that is a single input channel even if you have an entire orchestra playing and choir singing. Multichannel recording interfaces let you use more microphones and instrument plug-ins, which creates more tracks.

NOTE   *The number of input channels in **Edit** > **Preferences** > **Devices** must match the number of your physical input channels.*

You get the ultimate flexibility and control by giving every voice and instrument its own mic. Studio recording is nothing like live recording—sometimes every performer is in a separate soundproof cubicle, or recorded at different times and different locations, so the various band members might never even be physically present at the same time. It's a common practice to use multiple mics on a single performer and then manipulate the resulting multiple tracks to create absolute perfect wonderfulness (or an overproduced glop, as the case may be).

Be careful with the physical recording inputs that you plug your mics and instruments into—some are mono, some will be stereo, some will require phantom power, and others will be for various other purposes. Be sure you're plugging things in correctly—just because it fits doesn't mean it's right.

NOTE   *A good habit to develop is to never hotplug anything, unless you are certain it is safe to do so. Don't turn on phantom power until after your condenser mics are plugged in. Don't plug anything into your amp, preamp, mixer, and so on with the power on, or at least make sure all volume controls are at zero. Turn power off before unplugging. Most audio equipment is tolerant of a certain amount of abuse. But pops from hotplugging are annoying and may damage your equipment.*

If you use a stereo mic on a mono recording input, only one channel will record, and you'll have a stereo track like the one in Figure 9-2 with one channel blank.

Figure 9-2: This is what happens when you plug a stereo microphone into a single-channel recording input.

No worries if this happens to you; just use the Track menu to separate a stereo track into two tracks, and then delete the empty one. There are two split track options: Split Stereo Track creates a left and a right track, while

Split Stereo to Mono creates two mono tracks. (You can use this same menu to join two individual tracks into a single stereo track.) Assigning a track left, right, or mono is important when you mixdown to stereo: Left tracks go to the left channel, right tracks go to the right channel, and mono goes to both. (See "Mixdown to Stereo" on page 188 to learn more.)

Low-end onboard sound chips are notorious for claiming to have stereo microphone inputs, but then only one channel works. If you try a mono microphone on one of these, it may not work at all, so I can't resist giving the obvious warning: Test it before you need it.

NOTE *See Chapter 2 for a refresher on setting up audio hardware, and consult your product documentation. Beware anyone who wants to "help" you! It's your gear, and you don't want the help of people who don't know what they're doing, which is quite a large number of folks who think they're experts (such as professional musicians who have been on stage all their lives and rely on the old "whack it until something happens" technique). Your peace of mind and equipment are more important than their egos.*

Output channels are like input channels. If you create a 5.1 surround mix that is six discrete channels—left, right, center, surround left, surround right, and low-frequency effects (LFE)—you could take a single mono track and export it to 5.1 surround, as Figure 9-3 shows. I don't know why you would want to, but it's there if you do. Audacity supports a maximum of 32 output channels. If you have a playback device that supports 32 channels, you will have yourself one heck of a fun time. A more realistic option for all those channels is to export them to a single 32-bit WAV file, or 32 individual WAV files (using **File > Export Multiple**), and then import them into a more sophisticated mixing application for advanced mixing and studio wizardry. For example, some users like to record and edit in Audacity and then do the final mix in a different program that does things Audacity doesn't do, such as support MIDI, or that has more sophisticated multitrack mixing. Since Audacity is free, it doesn't cost anything but some time to try different workflows.

Clips are segments of tracks. You can have a lot of fun with clips, such as changing what a person says in an interview by moving the words around, making loops, or grabbing clips from different recordings and blending them together in new and different ways. You can have several clips in a single track or put each one in its own track. You can even drag clips from one track to another using the Time Shift tool (Figure 9-4).

How to Make Multitrack Recordings

There are several ways to make multitrack recordings. One way is to use a multichannel recording interface and record all of your tracks at one time. Another way is to record new tracks at different times into an existing project; this is called *overdubbing*. Another way to manage a multitrack project is to run multiple recording sessions, each in its own Audacity project, and then copy tracks from these into a single Audacity project.

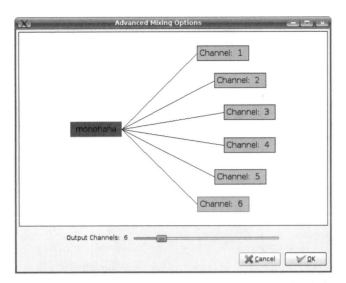

Figure 9-3: An amusing example of creating a 5.1 WAV file from a single track using Audacity's custom export mixer

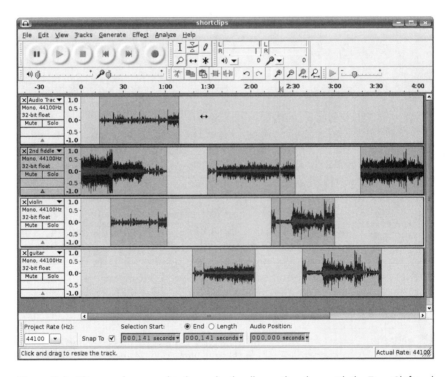

Figure 9-4: Clips can be moved independently all over the place with the Time Shift tool, even to different tracks.

For recording larger numbers of tracks at once, I have a Focusrite Saffire Pro 26, which is an excellent multichannel FireWire recording interface. It has eight microphone preamps, phantom power, two ADAT banks (16 channels), S/PDIF, 24/192 digital I/O, and a lot of other goodies. Figure 9-5 shows a four-channel recording session in Audacity using the Saffire. As you can see, it doesn't look special: It's just four channels all recording at the same time. The Saffire can theoretically handle 26 recording inputs at one time, which Audacity can handle with no problem; the only limitation is what my computer can handle. (Audacity versions before 1.3.8 are limited to 16 inputs at once.)

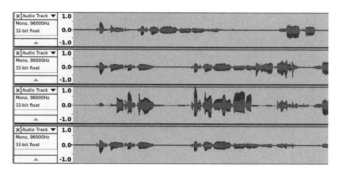

Figure 9-5: Recording four tracks at one time with the Focusrite Saffire Pro

My little M-Audio MobilePre USB can record four inputs at once. However, it is really a stereo recording interface with only two discrete input and output channels. So recording four inputs means that two are combined on each channel, and instead of four tracks that can be manipulated individually, there are only two. This once again illustrates that in the great wide world of audio, there are many ways to do things.

Many higher-end sound cards and recording interfaces are designed to be combined, and then they appear to Audacity as a single interface. Audacity does not have the ability to combine multiple recording interfaces; it must see a single device with multiple channels. Windows and Mac users get special drivers and management software to do this. With luck you can combine lower-end sound cards as well. However, in my experience, combining cheapo sound cards is painful and unreliable on any platform, so I'm going to pretend that such an option does not exist.

NOTE *Remember that Audacity supports almost unlimited undos and redos, so you can experiment safely. Undo changes with* CTRL-*Z or* **Edit** > **Undo** *and redo with* CTRL-SHIFT-*Z or* **Edit** > **Redo**.

When you want to add audio files such as WAV or FLAC to your project, import them into your Audacity project with **File** > **Import** > **Audio**.

File > Open launches a new Audacity session, and **File > Import > Audio** opens an audio file into the current project. You can't import an Audacity project into another Audacity project, but you can open two or more projects and copy tracks between them.

Get well-acquainted with the Track menu (Figure 9-6) because you will use this a lot.

There are a number of items to note here. You can split a stereo track using the Track Menu; click **Split Stereo Track/Split Stereo to Mono**. Then, for your own sanity, give each track a descriptive name.

You can join two mono tracks to make a stereo track. They have to be adjacent to each other, and you have to select **Make Stereo Track** from the uppermost track's Track menu. Then Audacity will automatically join it to the next track below. If the tracks are not together, select **Move Track Up/Down** from the Track menu or drag one with the mouse by grabbing it on the track label. (See Chapter 1 if you don't remember what all the Audacity parts are called.)

Figure 9-6: Track menu

Playback Tips and Tricks

As you recall from diligent study of Chapter 1, by default Audacity plays all tracks at once when you press the playback button. Pressing the spacebar also starts playback. To listen to one track, click **Solo** in the Track menu. To listen to some tracks but not all, click the **Mute** button on the ones you don't want to hear. CTRL-U mutes all tracks, and SHIFT-CTRL-U unmutes all tracks. Position the cursor on the Time Scale at any starting point you want; when it changes to a little hand, click to start playback at that point. You can skip all over your track this way without using the Stop/Play buttons.

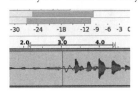

Figure 9-7: Play back a selection by creating a play region on the Time Scale.

You can quickly play a selected part of a track by creating a *play region* by clicking and dragging in the Time Scale to mark the section you want to play (Figure 9-7). This plays immediately, and then the play region disappears.

You can create a persistent selection by selecting part of the track in the usual way, by clicking and dragging with the Selection tool. Then click the **Play** button to play only that selection, or click SHIFT-Play to loop-play the selection. Press CTRL-B to create a region label for the selection (see "Creating and Managing Labels" on page 173 to learn more about region labels). Press **C** (for cut) to hear a preview of what the track will sound like with the selected part cut out. The default length of the lead-in and lead-out to the cut is one second; you can change this in **Edit > Preferences > Playback**.

A fast way to play part of a track is to click to mark a stopping point, position the cursor to the left of the mark (don't click, just hover) and press **B**. Playback will start where the cursor is positioned and stop at your mark. You can go the other way and place the cursor to the right of your mark, then press **B**, and it will play from the selection to the cursor.

Label Tracks

Label tracks are useful for keeping track of what's happening on your project tracks. You might remember labels from Chapter 3, where they were used to divide long tracks copied from vinyl LPs into individual song tracks. When you're editing multiple tracks, you can also use them for bookmarks and notes and to create alignment markers. Each audio track can have its own label track (Figure 9-8). New label tracks are created by selecting **Tracks > Add New > Label Track**. Position label tracks by grabbing the track label with the cursor and dragging them or by using the Track Menu's **Move Track Up/Down** selection.

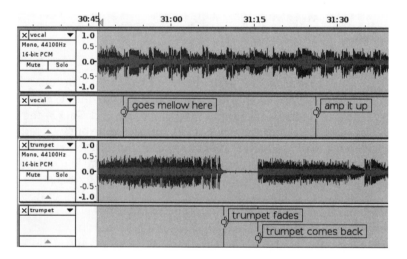

Figure 9-8: You may use as many label tracks as you like.

If you depend on label tracks, then you need to take extra care with backing up your Audacity projects, because they exist only inside Audacity. Label tracks can be exported and imported just like audio tracks, but unfortunately (as of Audacity 1.3.12), you cannot export multiple label tracks. If you try to export multiple label tracks (**File > Export Labels**), they will be merged into a single text file, and at import you'll get a single label track containing all the labels from all the tracks.

You can place a label track at the very top and use this like a conductor's score, with notes and timing marks for the whole project.

Creating and Managing Labels

There are two types of labels: *point labels* and *region labels*. In Chapters 3, 4, and 5, we used point labels to divide long tracks into individual songs. Region labels mark a selection, as Figure 9-9 shows.

Figure 9-9: Point labels mark a single point on a track, and region labels mark a section.

Point labels are easy to create. Stop playback, click in your track with the Selection tool wherever you want a new label, and then press CTRL-B. Type in your label name or whatever text you want, and hit RETURN. You can also select **Tracks** > **Add Label At Selection**. To delete a label, backspace over the label text until it disappears.

Press CTRL-M to add labels during playback; this is one of the few Audacity functions that doesn't require stopping everything first. When you have multiple label tracks, remember to first select the one you want the new label in. (Click its track label to select it.)

Take a look at the little handles on the labels, the angles, and the circle. Grab the circle to move the label. Drag the angle handles to make or resize a region label. Change a region label to a point label by dragging an angle handle until all the handles merge.

You can create region labels in several ways. One way is to select part of your audio track and then select **Tracks** > **Add Label At Selection** (or just press CTRL-B). Another way is to stretch out a point label by dragging its angle handle. The little angle and circle change how they behave when you have adjoining region labels. The little circle handle creates and moves a common border, and common borders are separated with the angle handles (Figure 9-10).

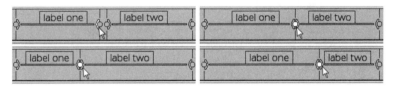

Figure 9-10: Circle handles move the whole label, and angle handles create and resize region labels. You can join region label borders and then move the border with the circle handle, and you can separate them with the angle handles.

Press the TAB key to navigate forward through your bookmarks, and SHIFT-TAB to go backward. Select **Tracks** > **Edit Labels** to edit and reorder them quickly. Labels are numbered to show which label track they belong to (Figure 9-11).

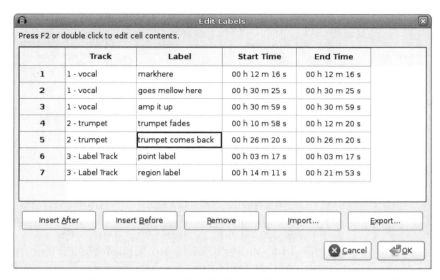

Press F2 or double click to edit cell contents.

	Track	Label	Start Time	End Time
1	1 - vocal	markhere	00 h 12 m 16 s	00 h 12 m 16 s
2	1 - vocal	goes mellow here	00 h 30 m 25 s	00 h 30 m 25 s
3	1 - vocal	amp it up	00 h 30 m 59 s	00 h 30 m 59 s
4	2 - trumpet	trumpet fades	00 h 10 m 58 s	00 h 12 m 20 s
5	2 - trumpet	trumpet comes back	00 h 26 m 20 s	00 h 26 m 20 s
6	3 - Label Track	point label	00 h 03 m 17 s	00 h 03 m 17 s
7	3 - Label Track	region label	00 h 14 m 11 s	00 h 21 m 53 s

Insert After   Insert Before   Remove   Import...   Export...

Cancel   OK

Figure 9-11: Selecting **Tracks** > **Edit Labels** puts all your labels in one place for easy editing and reordering. Note how the labels are numbered according to their label tracks, 1, 2, and 3.

Using Labels to Edit Multiple Tracks

You can use labels to mark points or segments across multiple tracks. Suppose you want to delete a 10-second chunk across two audio tracks. Mark this with a region label, and then click inside the label text (Figure 9-12).

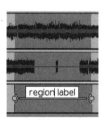

Figure 9-12: Using a region label to select track segments across multiple tracks

This turns the label text field white and selects a 10-second segment in all tracks above the label track, including other label tracks. If this includes tracks you don't want affected, deselect the extra tracks (SHIFT-click the track labels). Press CTRL-X or select **Edit** > **Cut**, and the selections will vanish. You can use this for any editing function across multiple tracks. You can move the selection or change its size simply by changing the region label.

It's not required to use region labels for operations like these, because you can use the Selection tool to make selections across multiple tracks. The keyboard works too, using the up- and down-arrow keys to move the cursor and using the SHIFT and arrow keys to size selections.

Aligning and Moving Tracks

There are many ways to move tracks around, both in time and in track order. Audacity has several good tools for moving and aligning your tracks.

One way to move tracks backward and forward in time is by using the Time Shift tool (Figure 9-13). The Time Shift tool moves an entire track forward or backward in time.

It couldn't be easier: Just click, hold down the mouse button, and drag the waveform left or right. You can even drag past the beginning of the track and move forward in time, which is indicated by little arrows in the track as in Figure 9-14. This is nondestructive, and you can drag it back out again.

Figure 9-13: Selecting the Time Shift tool

Figure 9-14: When you time-shift beyond the beginning of the track, two little arrows appear.

When you are time-shifting tracks and they become perfectly aligned with other tracks, or are exactly aligned with starting at zero, Audacity displays a vertical yellow line. Audacity calls this a *Snap Guide*. If there are multiple boundaries and they are too close together, the Snap Guide will get confused and not work. Zoom in to give it some elbow room.

As long as a track is a single unbroken waveform, the Time Shift tool moves the whole waveform. To divide a track into independent segments, click with the Selection tool to mark where you want to split it, and then select **Edit > Split** (or press CTRL-I). The selection line turns white, and now you have two segments that you can time-shift independently.

NOTE *If Link Tracks is enabled, tracks with label tracks will not split. Disable Link Tracks to change this.*

To rejoin split tracks, time-shift the segments back together. The yellow Snap Guide line will appear when they are touching. Then change to the Selection tool, make a selection spanning the join, and select **Edit > Join** or press CTRL-J. If there is a gap, selecting **Edit > Join** will fill it with silence.

Take a look in the **Tracks > Align Tracks** menu for a treasure trove of useful track alignment commands. Suppose you have been time-shifting multiple tracks and they're all over the place, so you want to reset everything and start over. Select the tracks you want to line up, select **Tracks > Align Tracks > Align Tracks Together**, and then select **Tracks > Align Tracks > Align Tracks with Zero**. Poof! Everything is reset to start at zero.

NOTE *Don't include label tracks because they always start at zero, so this will prevent audio tracks with any offset from aligning to zero. Deselect label tracks by SHIFT-clicking in their track labels.*

Align with Cursor is a fast way to shift a track by a precise amount. Here's how it works: Let's say you want to insert a time offset of 10 seconds at the beginning of your track. Click at the 10-second point to mark it, and then select **Tracks** > **Align Tracks** > **Align with Cursor** to move the start of the track to that point. Align End with Cursor lines up the end of the track with the cursor.

Align with Selection Start and Align with Selection End are similar to Align with Cursor, except the track is moved relative to a selection. For example, if you have a selection spanning the 5- to 10- seconds segment, Align with Selection End positions the track to begin at the 10-second mark. Align with Selection Start moves it the other way so that it starts at the 5-second mark.

Align End with Selection Start/End work the same way, except they are relative to the end of the track.

A slick trick with labels is to create an alignment point when you have to time-shift multiple tracks. Use a point label for this: Create your point label, click the label text, and a line will extend from the label into all tracks above it. Use the Time Shift tool, and the yellow Snap Guide will appear when the beginning or end of the track (or tracks) is perfectly aligned with your point label.

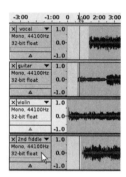

Track alignment can be also made without labels at any arbitrary point on the Time Scale. Using the Selection tool, click anywhere in a single track to mark your alignment point, and then extend the cursor up or down into the other tracks by selecting them (SHIFT-click in the track labels). SHIFT-click also unselects. You can select arbitrary tracks using this method, as Figure 9-15 shows. Then use the Time Shift tool to line up against the cursor mark or select **Tracks** > **Align Tracks** > **Align with Cursor**.

Figure 9-15: Tracks 1, 2, and 4 have been selected.

Link Tracks and Track Groups

A new (and sometimes confusing) feature that appeared in Audacity 1.3.9 is the Link Tracks button (Edit toolbar). This should be activated (depressed) by default; this keeps label tracks aligned with audio tracks through time shifts, tempo changes, cuts, pastes, and other changes. You can turn off Link Tracks when it gets in your way by clicking (raising) the **Link Tracks** button or selecting **Tracks** > **Link Audio and Label Tracks** and unchecking the box.

Label tracks are linked to the audio track or tracks immediately above them, until there is another label track; these are called *track groups*. Create a new label track with **Tracks** > **Add New** > **Label Track**. It will appear at the bottom of the existing tracks, and you can move it by grabbing the track label and dragging it or by selecting **Move Track Up/Down** from the Track menu. You can insert blank label tracks to separate track groups from other tracks.

When you use the Time Shift tool in a track group, every track in the group moves as a unit. When you delete part of one track, a corresponding segment is deleted from every track in the group. When you paste a segment of audio into one track, the other tracks receive a corresponding length of silence. When you use **Effect** > **Change Speed** and **Change Tempo**, the effects are applied to all tracks in the group. Labels are kept in sync through all these changes.

NOTE *Link Tracks may not be enabled in the Audacity 2.0.x series. They first appeared in Audacity 1.3.9 and should return in the Audacity 2.1.x beta series. Their behavior may change, so check your Audacity release notes.*

Time-Shifting Multiple Tracks at the Same Time

What if you want to time-shift multiple tracks the same amount, all at the same time? SHIFT-click the track labels to select the tracks you want to time-shift, or press CTRL-A to select all of them and then use the Time Shift tool to move them (Figure 9-16).

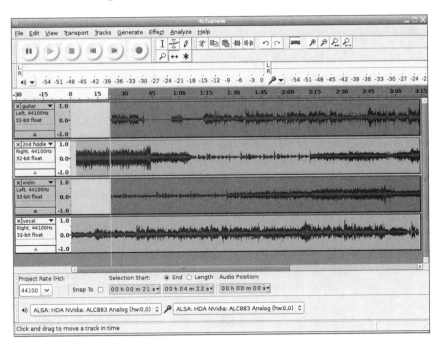

Figure 9-16: Time-shifting multiple selected tracks. Note that the selected tracks (1 and 3) are darkened.

If your Audacity version includes the Link Tracks feature, disable it, or time-shifting the tracks won't work right.

Splitting Tracks

Splitting tracks is how you break a long track into independent clips that you can move around as you need. Sometimes you need to move a section a second or two to match it up to the other tracks or to separate two people talking at the same time. Sometimes you want to split a track into a bunch of short clips. To create clips, position the Selection tool where you want to make the split, and then press **Edit > Split**. Now you have two clips and can use the Time Shift tool to move them around.

Select **Edit > Split Cut** to cut a selected portion of a track and leave a gap so the track length is unchanged. The cut portion is placed on the clipboard and can be pasted (CTRL-V or **Edit > Paste**) into another location.

Selecting **Edit > Split Delete** deletes the selected portion.

Selecting **Edit > Split New** creates a new track and moves the cut portion to it (Figure 9-17).

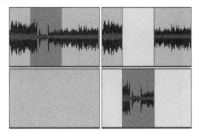

Figure 9-17: Selecting **Edit > Split New** creates a new track with the cut segment.

Working with Clips

If you're working with short clips, rather than the long tracks we've seen so far, it looks like Figure 9-4. You can have multiple separate clips on the same track. Each one can be time-shifted independently and even dragged to other tracks with the Time Shift tool. You can perform edits on the individual clips, such as changing the amplitude, applying effects, removing or pasting in additional material, and fixing defects. The one thing you cannot do is control the channel mapping when exporting individual clips that share the same track because this is done per track, so any clips you want to control this way need to be on their own tracks.

Figure 9-18: Audacity's Snap Guide feature

Audacity's Snap Guide feature is helpful when you want to select a clip precisely, because you'll see the yellow lines appear when you are exactly on its borders (Figure 9-18).

Selecting multiple clips is a bit tricky. Press CTRL-A to select all tracks. To move a selected batch of clips, first use the Selection tool to mark out a segment on the time line that crosses all the clips you want to move. Then use SHIFT-click in the Track panels to select tracks, and then use the Time Shift tool to move them. It's rather clunky, and you can't skip around and select an arbitrary batch of clips (Figure 9-19).

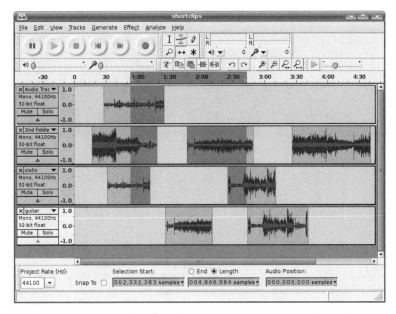

Figure 9-19: You can only select clips in a common region on the timeline. In this example, the clips with the darkened areas in the first three tracks will all time-shift together.

Time-Shifting Inside Tracks

The Time Shift tool is good for moving an entire audio segment forward or backward in time, but what if you want to insert a break in the middle of a track or time-shift a portion of a track? Audacity has a number of different ways to do this. My favorite method for creating a break or padding a track is to select **Generate** > **Silence**. This avoids splitting the track or deleting anything; all it does is insert a period of absolute silence of whatever duration you want. Position the Selection tool where you want the silence to start, select **Generate** > **Silence**, enter the duration of the silence, and click **OK** (Figure 9-20).

Figure 9-20: Generating silence

As Figure 9-21 shows, you have multiple options for timing the length of the silence: hours, seconds, milliseconds, and various frame rates, which I'll explain in the next section.

Days, hours, seconds, and milliseconds are straightforward, and I admire anyone who is working with audio files with durations measured in days. *Samples* displays the number of audio samples according to your project's sampling rate; for example, when your project's sampling rate is 44,100 Hz, one second's worth of audio is 44,100 samples.

Another way to do this is to split the track into two or more segments and then move them apart to create a break of whatever duration you need.

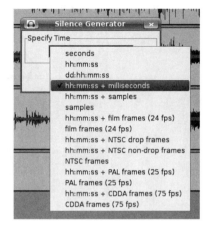

Figure 9-21: Audacity gives you a lot of different values to choose from for the duration of your silences.

See "Aligning and Moving Tracks" on page 175 to learn how to do this.

Metronome Track

The first and best cure for synchronization problems caused by slightly different tempos is keeping everyone in time when you make your recordings. In other words, the key is prevention. You know those big, expensive recording studios, with all the soundproofing and expensive gear? They don't rely on editing wizardry to fix defects any more than they have to. That is why they are soundproofed and do multiple takes. And that's why they use metronomes to keep all the players in time.

Metronomes don't cost much, and every recording studio should have one. Like so many other electronic widgets, they come in a monstrous array of styles, features, and prices. Just get one has both a silent blinking and an audible click beat. If it also includes a tuner, has a sine wave generator, receives weather forecasts, and makes sandwiches, those are nice bonuses.

Audacity will make a metronome track for you. It is better to use a stand-alone metronome because that doesn't use any CPU cycles, but it's there if you want it. If you've installed the C* Audio Plugin Suite (*http://www.de/dsp/caps.html*), look in the Generate menu for C* Click Metronome. You'll see a menu like the one in Figure 9-22, where you set the beats per second, volume, and duration. *Damping* accepts values from 0.1 to 0.9. Damping makes the metronome sound muted at higher damping values and more resonant at lower values.

Similar to a metronome track is a *click track*. Unlike a metronome track, it has an accented beat at the beginning of every measure. The pitch of the accented and nonaccented beats is controlled by MIDI note number values. MIDI note numbering starts at 0 and ends at 127, spanning almost 11 octaves. Number 60 is middle C, and there are 12 notes per octave (see Table 9-1 for a MIDI note number cheat sheet).

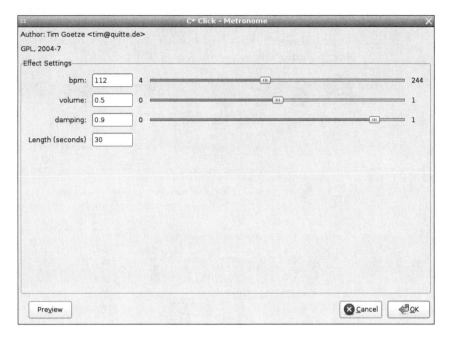

Figure 9-22: Look in the Generate menu for the C* Click Metronome plug-in.

Table 9-1: Pitches and Their Corresponding MIDI Note Number Values

Pitch	MIDI note number
C	60
C#	61
D	62
D#	63
E	64
F	65
F#	66
G	67
G#	68
A	69
A#	70
B	71

If you're wondering why no flat symbols are used, it's because there is no flat symbol on a keyboard.

Figure 9-23 shows the configuration panel for **Generate** > **Click Track**. (On Linux it's deeper in the Generate submenus, depending on what plug-ins are installed.) First create a new empty track by selecting **Tracks** > **Add New** > **Audio Track**, and then open Click Track.

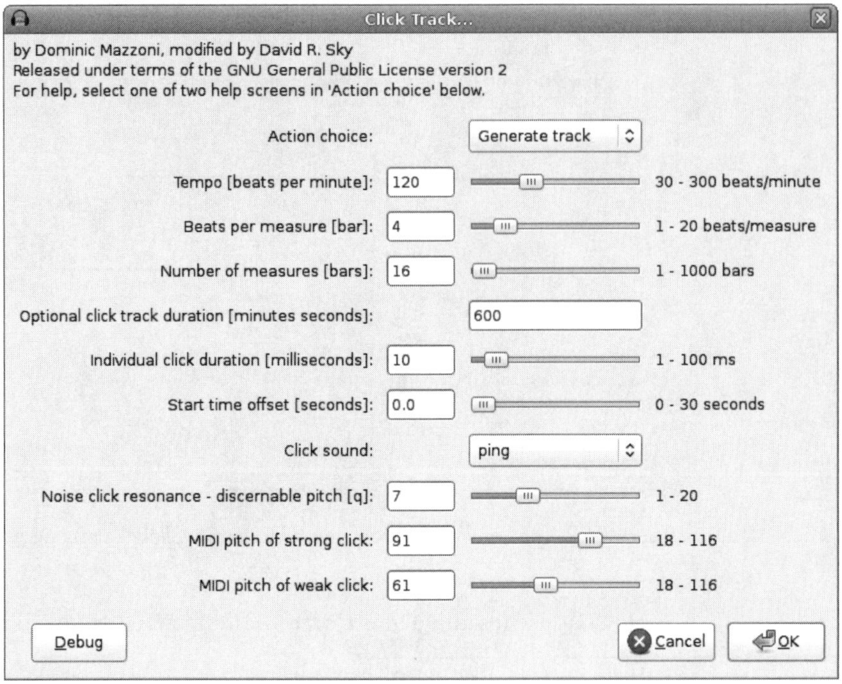

Figure 9-23: Configuring the Click Track effect

Most of the options should be self-explanatory. Number of measures determines the length of the track. Noise click resonance and Individual click duration affect the tone quality; higher values on both of these make the click tone more musical.

Overdubbing

Overdubbing is recording a new track while listening to an existing track or tracks. Overdubbing is one way to record an entire symphony by yourself, one track at a time. It's also for simpler projects, of course, such as recording yourself playing a couple of different instruments and singing, doing pretty harmony with yourself, or recording when everyone but the drummer showed up and you're going to record without her (she can record her parts later).

Let's do a quick overdub. First open an existing audio track or record a new one. Then in the Transport menu, enable Overdub (Figure 9-24). You can also enable overdubbing by selecting **Edit** > **Preferences** > **Recording**. Use the Device toolbar to route playback wherever you want it to go. Headphones are best in most circumstances, because you probably don't want microphones picking up the playback. Then click the **Record** button to record a second track. You'll hear the first track in your headphones, and you can sing or play along.

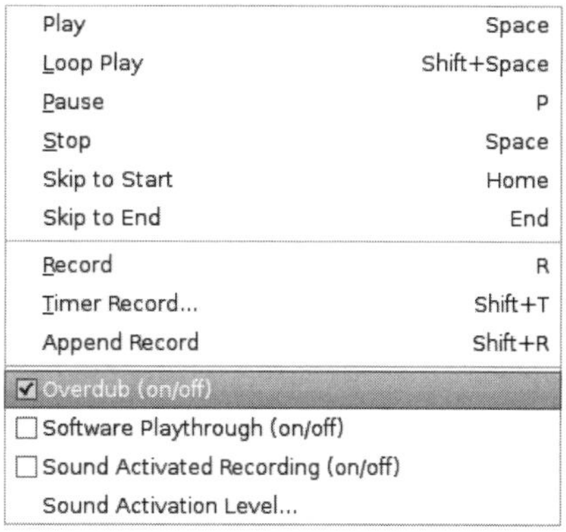

Play	Space
Loop Play	Shift+Space
Pause	P
Stop	Space
Skip to Start	Home
Skip to End	End
Record	R
Timer Record...	Shift+T
Append Record	Shift+R
☑ Overdub (on/off)	
☐ Software Playthrough (on/off)	
☐ Sound Activated Recording (on/off)	
Sound Activation Level...	

Figure 9-24: Enable Overdub so you can listen to an existing track while recording a new track.

Figure 9-25 shows a simple overdubbing session. Playback of the first track is routed to a headset, and our invisible solo performer is singing along with it on the second track.

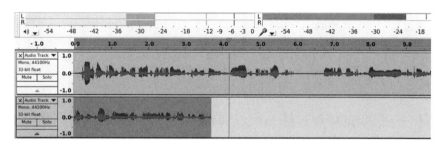

Figure 9-25: Recording a new track while listening to the first track

Measuring and Fixing Latency

Latency is a common problem when you are overdubbing, because there is always some latency in playback. Ordinarily some latency at playback doesn't matter because we're just listening, and the sound doesn't have to be synchronized with anything else. But when you're overdubbing, any latency causes the new tracks to be unsynchronized with the old tracks. An easy way to demonstrate this is to record yourself counting to 10. Then overdub a second track and count to 10 again while trying to match the first track. Play them back, and most likely the second track will not be in sync with the first track.

*Always have **Edit** > **Preferences** > **Recording** >**Software Playthrough** unchecked. Using Software Playthrough lets you monitor what you are recording, but that's the worst way to do it because it adds latency and uses CPU cycles. It is better to use a monitoring port on your recording interface.*

Audacity lets you compensate for this latency in **Edit** > **Preferences** > **Recording** > **Latency**. The default latency correction value is −130 ms, which probably is not correct for your system. You can see this correction in action when you're overdubbing a track, because when you stop recording, Audacity will time-shift the new track by whatever the latency correction value is. This time shift is indicated in the usual way with a pair of arrows on the left side of the waveform (Figure 9-26).

Figure 9-26: Automatic application of latency correction by time-shifting is indicated by the pair of arrows.

One way to get the correct latency correction value is to use trial and error. A simple method is to record a click or metronome track and then overdub a vocal track where you try to match the click track. Sure, you might feel silly saying "tick tick tick" or "ONE two three four" into a microphone, but it works. Make sure that the "Snap To" checkbox on the Selection toolbar is not checked and keep adjusting the latency value until it sounds right.

A more precise method is to measure latency using a loopback cable. This might sound exotic, but all you're doing is connecting the playback output of your recording interface back to the recording input. If it's an internal sound card, connect the line out to the line in. If it's a USB or FireWire interface, it's going to depend on your device and what kind of connectors it has, but the task is still the same—connect playback out to record in.

Then set Latency Correction to 0. Make sure that the "Snap To" checkbox on the Selection toolbar is not checked. Select the "Length" radio button, and set the time parameter to hh:mm:ss + milliseconds.

Next, generate a metronome or click track, 30 seconds long, 180 beats per second. The number of beats per second can be anything; I prefer a faster beat because it's easier to measure.

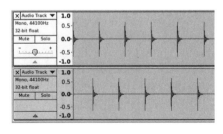

Figure 9-27: The overdubbed track does not line up with the first track because of latency.

Turn on overdubbing (**Transport** > **Overdub (on/off)**), select your recording interface for both the playback and recording devices on the Device toolbar, and press the Record button. You should see something like Figure 9-27.

When you're finished recording, zoom in until you can select the gap between a click on the top track and its corresponding click on the bottom track. If you're not comfortable using the mouse, use the SHIFT and arrow keys to mark the selection. (Use the arrow keys to move back and forth and up and down, and use the SHIFT and arrow keys to select.) You will see something like Figure 9-28.

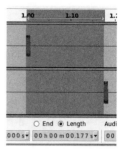

Now you have a Length value in the Selection toolbar. In my example, that is 177 ms, which is a lot. If you want, you can zoom way in to get the most precise measurement. You'll probably never get zero latency, but you can get close. Latency correction for overdubbing always takes a negative value, because the new track always lags behind the old track. If you change your recording interface, you should repeat the loopback test, because different devices have different latencies.

Figure 9-28: Select the gap from the begining of the first beat on the first track to the beginning of the first beat on the second track to measure latency

When you read up on latency, you will find many passionate discussions about it and much boasting of heroic low-latency exploits such as "I got my latency down to three milliseconds!" That is fine, if dubious, but it is good to keep a bit of perspective. It's no good going for super-low latency at the cost of stability or creating skips and stutters because your CPU can't keep up. Latency matters during overdubbing, and Audacity helps you with its configurable latency correction. It matters when you use software monitoring, which is why I prefer using recording interfaces with zero-latency monitoring ports. It matters anywhere you have additional stops in your audio chain such as outboard special-effects processors. When you play a note, you want sound to come out, not lag.

You can reduce latency in your audio production computer by using a high-speed multicore processor and streamlining your computer and tuning it for audio production. Chapters 13 and 14 tell you how to do this.

Changing Tempo

Despite your best efforts, sometimes the tempo of your tracks wanders out of sync. If you're in a punk band, it's all right, but otherwise you'll probably want to correct this. Select **Effect > Change Tempo**, which changes tempo without changing pitch. It's easy, that is, if you know what values to use, and unfortunately Audacity does not have a tempo detector. The person who writes a tempo detection plug-in will be a big hero. I use a stopwatch and count out the beats during playback. It might take a bit of trial and error, but it's usually easier than rerecording.

NTSC, PAL, and CDDA Frames

This is a simplified explanation of what frames are. If you want to make movie soundtracks, then this is just an introduction to a key concept, and you will want to learn more.

Frames values are for positioning splits exactly at video and audio frame borders. Check the "Snap To" box in the Selection toolbar, set your time value to the appropriate frame type, and then when you make splits or cuts, they will exactly match the frames. Any audio outside of the frame borders will be lost and possibly create a click.

National Television System Committee (NTSC) frames pertain to analog broadcast television in North America, some South American countries, and a few other countries. The NTSC drop frame rate is 29.97 frames per second (fps), and the NTSC nondrop frame rate is 30 fps. Audacity supports both. Why two? Why the odd 29.97 number? This is an old standard dating from the black-and-white TV era. The black-and-white broadcast frame rate was true 30 fps, but when color was added to the broadcast signal, the frame rate, for various technical reasons, was slowed down to 29.97 fps. Now pay close attention, because I am going to call on all of my mighty explaining powers to explain the difference between drop and nondrop NTSC frame rates in a way that ordinary, non-video-engineer mortals can understand. This has never been done in the history of humanity; you're seeing it here first.

NTSC drop and NTSC nondrop frame rates have only one difference: They use different *timecodes* to control the playback speed. There is no difference in the length of the program, but just a tiny difference in how fast it is played back. The term *drop* is unfortunate because it is commonly believed that video frames are dropped, but this is not true. Video time is measured by counting video frames. When you shoot one hour's worth of video at true nondrop 30 fps, your one-hour project will contain exactly 108,000 frames. If it is broadcast without first being converted to drop frame, it will run about 1 hour and 3.6 seconds, because at a 29.97 frame rate there are 107,892 frames per hour. So, at the end of an hour, there are 108 frames left over.

If you care to do the math, you'll see that there is a 1 percent difference between the two. Naturally this adds up over time, which causes woe to broadcasters. It also causes woe to film editors, who need to be able to measure cuts and scene lengths accurately.

This discrepancy is cured by inserting a bit of on-purpose amnesia and self-deceit into the drop frame timecode. With NTSC drop frame, your film is played at 30 fps, but it pretends to be 29.97 fps because that is the requirement for NTSC TV broadcast. Every video frame is counted until that 1 percent difference adds up to a whole frame. Then the timecode pretends that frame does not exist and does not count it, and continues counting on the next frame. So even though your film still has its original 108,000 frames, the forgetful timecode plays what it thinks are only 107,892 frames in one hour, but it's really 108,000. Since it has fooled itself into not seeing those other 108 frames they get played anyway, the film ends on time, and everyone is happy.

This all sounds complicated and bizarre, but in the video-engineering world, it was an elegant solution that caused minimal disruption to legacy broadcast infrastructure. The alternative, with the advent of color, was to overhaul the entire TV broadcasting system for the new color standard.

All NTSC TV broadcasters require that master tapes submitted to them use NTSC drop frame. If you're editing a film soundtrack in Audacity, you can exactly match the correct frame rate.

Phase Alternating Line (PAL) is the color TV broadcast standard for a good portion of the planet: Australia, much of Asia, South America, Europe, Greenland, and some African countries. It uses a 25 fps frame rate, which Audacity supports.

Traditional film movies are at 24 fps.

If you're making an audio track for DVD, you can use NTSC, PAL, or 24 fps. For web streaming, you can use whatever frame rates you want.

The Compact Disk Digital Audio (CDDA) frame rate of 75 fps is for audio CDs. We learned about this for converting legacy analog media to CD in Chapter 3. For example, when you copy a vinyl LP into Audacity as one long track and then split the track into individual songs, selecting the CDDA frame rate ensures that all that splits will match the CDDA frames, and you won't create clicks from the audio being out of sync with the CDDA frame rate.

Creating Loops

Some folks are totally overboard into loops. Loops are clips played over and over, such as when turning a few seconds of drumming into a long drum track, creating a backing music track from a short clip, or being hypnotically repetitious—whatever pleases you. You've probably seen low-budget documentaries that used loops to stretch a few minutes of music into background soundtracks.

A simple loop is easy. Start with a single short clip. Select **Effect** > **Repeat**. Enter how many times you want it to repeat. Audacity even does the arithmetic for you (Figure 9-29).

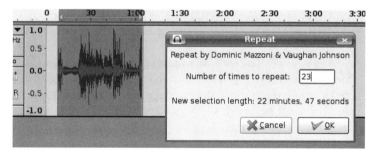

Figure 9-29: Creating a simple loop by using a short clip and selecting
Effect > **Repeat**

You can loop a clip, a whole track, or a selection in a track. The repeated parts will be appended to the original selection, so if your selection is in the middle of a track, then the repeats will also be in the middle, starting to the right of the selection.

Mixdown to Stereo

When you have done all of your edits and cleanups and are getting ready to mix your tracks down to stereo, go into the Track menus of the individual tracks and assign them to the appropriate left, right, and mono channels. Left tracks go to the left channel at mixdown, right tracks go to the right channel, and mono tracks are mapped to both channels. In Audacity, the top channel of a stereo track is the left channel, and the bottom one is the right channel.

NOTE *To learn more about cleaning up your tracks, fixing problems, and special effects, see Chapters 3, 4, 12, and 11.*

You now have the option of adjusting the pan of each mono or stereo track, which means adjusting their left-right balance to enhance stereo imaging. You can do this either with the Pan slider on the Track panel or with the Pan slider on the sleek new Mixer Board that first appeared in Audacity 1.3.8. The Pan slider does not change your project file; it only affects playback in Audacity and how your export will sound. Adjust this during playback in Audacity so you can hear exactly how your export will sound. This does not work on left or right tracks but only on mono and stereo tracks. Figure 9-30 shows how this looks.

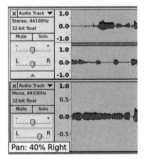

Figure 9-30: The Pan slider adjusts the left-right balance on mono and stereo tracks.

Next to the Pan slider is the Gain slider for adjusting track volume. Just like pan, gain does not change your project file but only controls how your export will sound. This is also adjustable during playback.

Audacity has several ways to mix and render your tracks down to a stereo track. First make sure that in the **Edit** > **Preferences** > **Import/Export** dialog you have selected "Always mix all tracks down to Stereo or Mono channel(s)."

Now select **Tracks** > **Mix and Render**. This replaces your tracks with the new stereo track. If you would rather not have your project tracks replaced by the new stereo track, don't select Tracks > Mix and Render but remember that nifty keyboard shortcut CTRL-SHIFT-M (Audacity 1.3.4 and newer). This mixes and renders a new stereo track that will appear below your mono tracks (Figure 9-31).

Now you have a nice stereo track all mixed and ready for more editing or to export to any number of playable formats. If you elected to use the CTRL-SHIFT-M command to mix and render, you can export just your new stereo track by selecting the track (click the track label) and then selecting **File** > **Export Selection**.

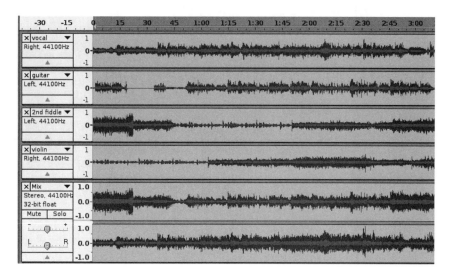

Figure 9-31: Pressing CTRL-SHIFT-*M* to mix and render preserves your original tracks and creates a new stereo track.

Customizing the Mixer Board

Here is a cool trick for the Mixer Board: You can make the icons match your track names by using certain keywords and abbreviations (Figure 9-32):

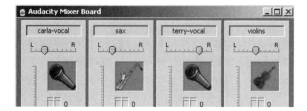

Figure 9-32: Mixer board icons match your track names.

I learned these names by browsing the source code online at *http://www .audacity.cvs.sourceforge.net/audacity/audacity-src/*. These are not documented anywhere else yet, as far as I know.

- acoustic, guitar, gtr
- acoustic, piano, pno
- back, vocal, bg, vox
- clap

- drums, dr
- electric, bass, guitar, bs, gtr
- electric, guitar, gtr
- electric, piano, pno, key
- kick
- loop
- organ, org
- perc
- sax
- snare
- string, violin, cello
- synth
- tambo
- trumpet, horn
- turntable
- vibraphone, vibes
- vocal, vox

Too Loud! Clipping!

It is important at this stage to make sure that **View** > **Show Clipping** is checked. This highlights any clipped passages in your new stereo track with red bars. When multiple tracks are combined into a single track, they get louder, so clipping is a common mixdown problem. If your new downmixed track has clipping, you need to go back, lower some volumes, and mix and render again.

Before changing anything, first check your Pan and Gain sliders. It is easy for these sliders to get moved even when you don't intend to move them. Carefully position the cursor on the slider button and click without moving it, and it will pop up the exact value. If you have trouble moving the slider, double-click it to open a little window where you can type in your pan or gain value (Figure 9-33).

Figure 9-33: Double-click the Pan and Gain sliders to open a little window where you can type in your values.

There are several ways to adjust the amplitude of your tracks. One is to change the amplitude of the tracks by selecting **Effect** > **Amplify**. Try a negative value of −3, which will reduce the amplitude by 3 decibels. So if the maximum amplitude is already at −3, this will make it −6. The value −3 is about a one-half reduction in volume. That may sound like a lot, but as the human ear perceives sound, that is about one step. About the minimum change we can detect is 1 dB. This changes your track, so you may prefer to use the

Gain slider instead. It also changes the amplitude only for mixdown and does not alter the original track. Whichever method you choose, you can preview it by clicking the **Play** button. When you're mixing multiple tracks, don't be surprised if you spend some time getting it right.

Control Your Channel Mapping

You can have more control over mixing and rendering by not using Tracks > Mix and Render but rather going straight to the **File** > **Export** dialog. This combines mixing, rendering, and exporting all into a single operation. Before you do this, open the **Edit** > **Preferences** > **Import/Export** dialog and make sure that "Use Custom Mix" is selected and that "Always mix all tracks down to Stereo or Mono channel(s)" is not. This allows you to map your channels at export, and this is when you will be grateful that you gave all of your tracks useful names (Figure 9-34). You can map tracks to more than one channel.

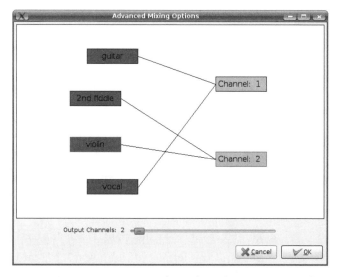

Figure 9-34: Mapping your tracks to channels at export (note the channel slider at the bottom)

Multichannel Surround

You may use Audacity to export to 3.1, 5.1, or 7.1 surround, or any multi-channel combination you want, using the Custom Mix option. How you do know which channel is for what? This handy list shows you the channel mappings for WAV:

1. Front Left
2. Front Right
3. Front Center

4. Low Frequency

5. Back Left

6. Back Right

7. Front Left of Center

8. Front Right of Center

9. Back Center

10. Side Left

11. Side Right

12. Top Center

13. Top Front Left

14. Top Front Center

15. Top Front Right

16. Top Back Left

17. Top Back Center

18. Top Back Right

Just to keep life entertaining, other file formats support different channel mappings. Table 9-2 shows some common audio file formats and their 5.1 channel mappings:

Table 9-2: Channel Mappings for Common Audio File Formats

File Format	Channel Mappings
WAV	front left, front right, center, LFE, rear left, rear right
AC3	front left, center, front right, rear left, rear right, LFE
DTS	center, front left, front right, rear left, rear right, LFE
AAC	center, front left, front right, rear left, rear right, LFE
AIFF	front left, rear left, center, front right, rear right, LFE
FLAC	front left, front right, center, LFE, rear left, rear right
WMA	front left, front right, front center, LFE, rear left, rear right

The LFE channel is commonly thought of as the subwoofer channel. This is not quite correct because it is not the same as the signal that is sent to the subwoofer port. It's a special channel for carrying sounds in the 3 to 200 Hz range, and the LFE signal can be sent to any speaker capable of handling it.

For DVD-Audio, use the WAV mappings. (See Chapter 6 for more on DVD-Audio.) Don't bother with surround sound for CDs because they only support two-channel stereo.

There are some special problems with creating multitrack surround audio in Audacity. Audacity is very good at creating high-quality stereo and mono tracks, but its abilities to manage multitrack surround are rather limited. You must know the correct channel mappings yourself for different file formats because Audacity does not tell you, and when you import a multichannel audio file into Audacity, it loses the track names and channel mappings even if the file was created in Audacity.

You can test your channel mappings after export by playing your new audio file on your computer, if your computer has a multichannel surround sound card and it is already set up and working correctly. See Chapter 13 to learn how to set up and test surround sound playback on Linux computers. Windows users will find configuration and testing tools in the Sound module of the Control Panel, and Windows Media Player supports surround sound.

Another way to test your new surround sound file is to burn it to a DVD and play it on a surround hi-fi system. Yet another way is to play the file on a digital music server that serves a surround hi-fi system.

10

MAKING YOUR OWN RINGTONES

I'm a cheapskate, and I think that paying money for ringtones is silly. Why should I, when I already own mass quantities of CDs and my own recorded music? I don't even like cell phones. When I leave home, I don't want an electronic leash. If I crash into the ditch, someone will find me eventually, and who's to say if I could even reach a phone when I'm hanging upside down in a mangled vehicle? It's really okay to be unconnected once in a while.

But fortunately for you, excellent readers, this book isn't about only what I like. Mobile phone owners love to have customized ringtones and to use their mobile devices as music players (that they can play loudly on their tinny lo-fi speakers in public places and annoy grumps like me). Most mobile service providers make it a matter of personal honor to charge customers for every last thing they can do with their phones, including ringtones and file transfers. So, you might say to yourself, fine, I'll just search online for free ringtones. Be careful—most of the "free" sites are come-ons for pay services and sometimes malware. There are some legitimate online sources for free ringtones; some of them are mediocre amateur efforts, and some are good. In this era of the Wild Wild Internet, shop carefully and be on guard.

Since the point of this book is doing your own audio production, how hard can it be to make your own ringtones and phone-friendly tunes? Not hard at all. Making the actual audio files is easy. The hard part is figuring out what audio file formats your phone supports and then how to transfer files into it. So let's use Audacity to create phone-friendly audio files and then look at different ways of transferring files into your phone. You're going to need your phone's manual or any relevant technical information you can dig up. If you don't have a manual, look on your phone manufacturer's website.

Please refer to Chapter 1 if you need a refresher on the basics of using Audacity.

Customizing Audio for a Mobile Phone

First import the audio file into Audacity that you want to use: Either open an existing Audacity project or click **File** > **Import** > **Audio** to start a new project with a WAV, FLAC, MP3, Ogg, or other audio file. Save it as a new project because you're going to make a lot of changes.

If it is a stereo file, first convert it to mono with **Tracks** > **Stereo to Mono**. Unless your phone supports stereo, of course. In **Edit** > **Preferences** > **Import/Export**, make sure that "Always mix all tracks down to stereo or mono" is checked.

If you need to create a ringtone of a specific length, such as 20 to 30 seconds, select a 20- or 30-second portion of the track to use. Here is a slick trick for precisely measuring your selection length: Position the Selection tool at the beginning of your clip. Go to the Selection toolbar, select the "Length" radio button, make sure "Snap To" is not checked, and enter how many seconds long you want your clip to be. If you're a bit shaky with the mouse, you can use the arrow keys on your keyboard to move the cursor. Figure 10-1 shows how to use this method to create an exactly 20-second clip.

Leaving your clip selected, select **Edit** > **Trim** (or press CTRL-T) to cut away the excess. Do any other edits you want, such as fixing problems, boosting the volume, applying special effects, or whatever you desire. A good trick is to fire up Audacity's equalizer to shorten the tone curve because your phone speaker has a limited frequency range, which you can find in its specs. Equalizing your audio file to match your phone speaker's frequency range will make it sound fuller and less tinny. This also makes it sound better in earbuds and Bluetooth headsets.

For example, suppose your phone speaker has a range of 500 to 10,000 Hz. In comparison, the full range of human hearing is about 20 to 22,000 Hz. Reduce the frequencies outside this range by 24 dB using **Effect** > **Equalization**. The equalizer has two sets of controls; you may use either the graphical curve or the interface that looks like a hi-fi equalizer. Select "Graphic EQ" to display the equalizer (Figure 10-2). The equalizer sliders

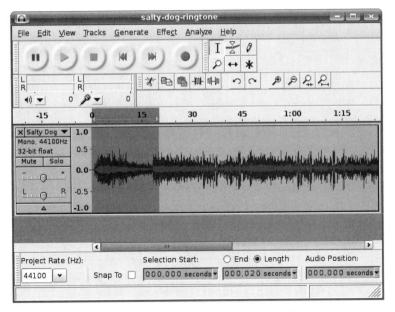

Figure 10-1: Using the Selection toolbar to create a clip of an exact duration (in this example, 20 seconds)

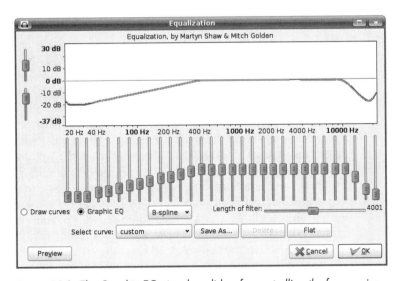

Figure 10-2: The Graphic EQ view has sliders for controlling the frequencies.

max out at a 20 dB range, while the curve has a range of 120 dB. A reduction of −60 dB is well beyond what we can hear and is as good as absolute silence.

In Figure 10-3, I manipulated the curve by clicking the line above 500 Hz to create a control point, clicking at 20 Hz to create another control point, and then dragging the 20 Hz control point down to −24. Then I did the

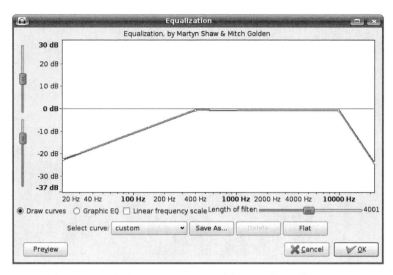

Figure 10-3: Here is the Draw curves view of the equalizer, showing a curve to match the frequency response of a telephone speaker.

same on the other end starting at 10,000 Hz. To make changes, grab and move the control points, which you can move in any direction. Gradual curves sound better than abrupt transitions.

You can enlarge the equalizer window both vertically and horizontally; making it wider exposes more of the frequency scale. The sliders on the left increase or decrease the size of the decibel scales. The equalizer has no undo function, but if you mess up incurably, you can hit the Flat button to reset to zero. Remove control points by dragging them off the graph.

You can increase amplitude by going over zero, because this is not the same zero as on the Zero Decibels Full Scale that we use when we're recording or playing back in Audacity. It does not mark the point at which clipping occurs. Rather, anything over zero in the equalizer is simply an increase in amplitude, and anything under zero is a decrease. You can still cause clipping or make it too quiet, so the Preview button will help you with this. The Preview button will preview the first three seconds of your clip by default. You can change this duration in the **Edit** > **Preferences** > **Playback** dialog.

You might save your customized ringtone equalization curve with the Save As button, and then you can apply it to all of your ringtones.

The "Linear frequency scale" checkbox, when you're in Draw curves view, changes the scale from the default logarithmic view to linear. Use the logarithmic view when you want to see the lower frequencies in more detail.

The Length of filter setting controls how many samples Audacity processes at a time. The default is 4,001 and should be fine most of the time. You can adjust this either by moving the slider with the mouse or by using the arrow keys on your keyboard. It is normal for Audacity to display a green line that follows the blue line of your equalization curve. This shows the curve that Audacity will actually use, which is affected by the limitations of the equalization algorithm. If the green line and blue line diverge significantly, increase the Length of Filter setting or smooth out your curve to make the transitions more gradual.

When you're finished editing, your ringtone is ready to export, and you need to know what file format and specification your phone requires. For example, suppose your phone requires 192Kbps constant-bitrate MP3 at 8,000 Hz sampling rate. No problem. If your project sampling rate is not already 8 kHz, click **Tracks** > **Resample** to resample it to the correct rate. The Track panel will then show the new sampling rate. Then open the **File** > **Export** > **MP3 Files** > **Options** dialog. Select Bit Rate Mode: Constant and Quality: 192Kbps (Figure 10-4).

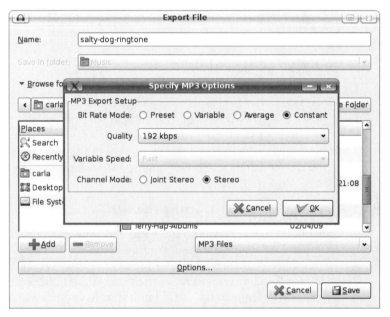

Figure 10-4: Exporting to the MP3 format and quality level required by your phone

With newer phones that support WAV files, requirements run the gamut from 8-bit depth 8 kHz sampling rate to 16/44.1. If you need to change the sampling rate, do that before export by using the **Tracks** > **Resample** dialog. Then export using the **File** > **Export** > **Other uncompressed files** > **WAV** dialog and selecting the appropriate bit depth. Figure 10-5 shows what exporting to an 8-bit WAV looks like.

Remember, resample before export and set the bit depth at export. What if your phone specs specify a bitrate, such as 64Kbps? The bitrate is always bit depth times sampling rate times the number of channels, so 8-bit depth times 8 kHz sampling rates times 1 channel equals a bitrate of 64Kbps. However, ideally your phone documentation won't make you do math and will spell it all out for you.

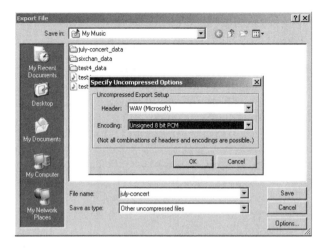

Figure 10-5: Exporting to 8-bit WAV

Keep in mind the storage available on your phone and how much hi-fi is it worth trying to squeeze into a lo-fi playback device. If you have a choice of different quality levels, it might pay to experiment with lower quality settings to find a good balance between quality and storage capacity.

Applying Dynamic Range Compression

Little phone speakers can't handle much dynamic range, so you should compress the dynamic range of your audio files to level out variations in volume. I prefer **Effect** > **Leveller** for this because it reduces the gain on the louder frequencies and raises the gain on the quieter frequencies. The Leveller effect tends to be harsh, but it sounds pretty good on little mobile device speakers. Figure 10-6 shows the settings I like to use: a Heavy level of compression and a low Threshold for Noise. The Threshold for Noise determines what frequencies it will change, so −80 db means virtually everything, while −20 dB affects frequencies at −20 dB and up.

After applying the Leveller effect, you might need to normalize your track to raise the volume as high as possible. Select **Effect** > **Normalize**, check "Remove any DC Offset," check "Normalize maximum amplitude to," and set the decibel value to zero, which is as high as you can go. Figure 10-7 shows a waveform with the first half Levelled and Normalized and the second half untouched.

Strictly speaking, the Leveller effect doesn't really behave like a compressor but more like a limiter. A limiter is like a compressor set to a high ratio, like 20:1 and higher, so rather than smoothly reducing the gain above your threshold, it squashes it most firmly.

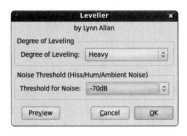

Figure 10-6: Suggested settings for **Effect** > **Leveller** *to compress the dynamic range*

Figure 10-7: The first half of the wave-form has had both the Leveller effect and Normalize effect applied. See how the highs and lows are more even than in the second part of the waveform.

Phone Audio File Formats

Ordinary audio file formats aren't weird enough; most mobile phones also support a special ringtone format called Ring Tone Text Transfer Language (RTTTL). Modern mobile phones also support MIDI, MP3, WAV, and a host of other audio file formats. Audacity does not support RTTTL or MIDI, but you can use it to prepare audio clips for RTTTL or MIDI conversion with other software. Chapters 3, 7, 11, and 12 tell all about cleaning up your audio files, using different audio formats and quality levels, and special effects.

RTTTL

RTTTL is a text language invented by Nokia that describes ringtones and is designed to be the universal cell phone ringtone language for easy ringtone transfers. This is what it looks like in written form:

```
AbbaDance:d=4,o=5,b=80:32p,2d,8c.,2d#,32d.,16c.,32a#.4,8c.,8d.,2d.
```

That is ABBA's "Dancing Queen." No, really, it is. You can download RTTTL ringtones just like any other audio file, or you can type them in using your phone keypad, if your phone includes a ringtone composer. It might be called *melody maker* or something similar. Your phone manual will tell you which keypresses to use for the RTTTL characters. The AbbaDance example shows the three required elements: the name, the default value, and data.

The *name* field is the song name, and it can't be more than 10 characters or contain a colon, because the colon marks the end of the name string.

The *default value* field defines the default duration, octave, and tempo:

d   Duration

o   Octave

b   Tempo

Any note not assigned its own duration will use the default. For example, d=4 in AbbaQueen means the default duration is a quarter note. There is a four-octave range numbered from 4 to 7. Tempo sets the beats per minute.

RTTTL describes the standard durations of musical notes:

1   Whole note

2   Half note

4   Quarter note

8   Eighth note

16   Sixteenth note

32   Thirty-second note

.   A dot equals a half-beat

You get whole notes and sharps but no flats, because there is no flat symbol on the keypad. But that's all right, because sharps and flats overlap—for example, G-sharp and A-flat are the same thing.

P   pause

A   A

A#   A-sharp and B-flat

B   B

C   C

C#   C-sharp and D-flat

D   D

D#   D-sharp and E-flat

E   E

F   F

F#   F-sharp and G-flat

G   G

G#   G-sharp and A-flat

If you really want to dig into RTTTL, you can find the spec online; just exercise your mighty "RTTTL spec" web-searching powers. There are many sites with downloadable RTTTL ringtones all ready to go.

Proprietary Audio File Formats

If your phone requires a proprietary or nonstandard audio file format not natively supported by Audacity or you prefer to use AAC, WMA, or some other format, you can use Audacity first to create and edit your audio clips, export them to WAV format, and then use a file converter application to convert the WAV into the correct format. Where do you find a converter? There are skillions of them, which you can find with a bit of web searching.

Another option is to install the open source FFmpeg encoder. This is a high-quality, open source multimedia encoder, and Audacity has FFmpeg integration built in. FFmpeg is Free software and free of cost. Visit the FFmpeg documentation page (*http://www.ffmpeg.org/documentation.html*) to learn how to download and install it on Mac and Windows. Linux users can install it from their distribution's software repositories.

The Advanced Audio Coding (AAC) audio format is a lossy, compressed encoding and compression technology that encompasses both digital audio and video as part of the MPEG-2 and MPEG-4 specifications. AAC audio is supposed to sound better than MP3, which is also a lossy, compressed format. AAC is patented, and anyone who wants to distribute AAC-encoded content may do so freely without restrictions or payment. But a patent license is required to develop and distribute AAC codecs.

AAC is the default audio container format for iTunes, though iTunes also supports WAV, MP3, AIFF, and Apple Lossless. AAC has some abilities that MP3 does not, such as support for up to 48 channels, while MP3 supports only 2, and a wider range of sampling frequencies, 8 kHz to 96 kHz, while MP3 supports only 16 kHz to 48 kHz. AAC is said to handle higher frequencies and stereo imaging better. There are some other differences that are more interesting to codec designers; the bottom line, as always, is how it sounds to you.

NOTE   *Fraunhofer-Gesellschaft, one of the original developers of MP3 and one of its many patent holders, also has a 5.1 surround-sound MP3 encoder and decoder. As most people say when they hear about this, "Why bother with cruddy lo-fi six-channel surround sound? Two cruddy lo-fi channels are plenty." But for those who are interested, it is free to evaluate on Mac or Windows only. If you like it and want to use it for anything other than personal evaluation, it will cost money.*

AAC is represented by a host of file extensions—*.m4a, .m4b, .m4p, .m4v, .m4r, .3gp, .mp4,* and *.aac*—which include both video and audio. Audacity uses the *.m4a* extension, which Apple uses to indicate a non-copy-protected audio-only file. *.m4p* is the extension used for encrypted, copy-protected iTunes audio files.

Saving your files in AAC format in Audacity is easy, once FFmpeg is installed: Click **Export > M4A (AAC) Files (FFmpeg) > Options**. In the Options dialog you have a range of quality settings from 10 to 500, with 500 being the highest quality. This range represents Fair, Okay, Good, Better, and Best. The value 256 is a good setting for a more complex recording. A simple recording, such as a spoken-word piece, sounds decent at 50, though 100 is noticeably better (Figure 10-8).

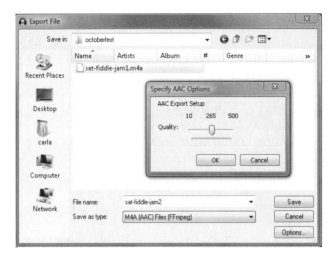

Figure 10-8: Exporting to AAC format (the default iTunes format), which creates a file with an .m4a extension

WMA is Windows Media Audio, a proprietary, lossless audio compression technology invented by Microsoft. WMA refers to both the codec and the audio file format. WMA supports a maximum 48 kHz sampling rate and two channels. WMA audio is usually encapsulated in an Advanced Systems Format (ASF) container, which contains metadata such as song name, artist name, and track number. ASF also supports Windows Media DRM (digital rights management). The file extension for DRM and non-DRM WMA files is the same, *.wma*; if you try to play a DRM file on a player that doesn't support Windows DRM, it will label it as unplayable.

In Audacity, open the **Export > WMA (version 2) Files (FFmpeg) > Options** dialog. Your only option is to select a bitrate (Figure 10-9).

How to Transfer Files to Your Phone

What most US providers want to you to do is sign up for their online services and buy all your ringtones and music from them. What if you just want a phone and not a web browser/email client with a tiny screen? Then you can order new ringtones attached to text messages. What if you don't want to pay for text services or learn to type with your thumbs? Then you must be some kind of weirdo. Wear the label with pride, and let's explore other ways to move files in and out of our phones. My preferred method is from a PC— my PC, that is, that I control and don't have to pay fees to access.

Many phones accept SD storage cards, usually miniSD or microSD cards. For less than $20, you can get any of these with a USB SD card reader or an adapter for a standard SD card reader so you can plug it into a standard USB port on a computer. These cards have several gigabytes of storage capacity.

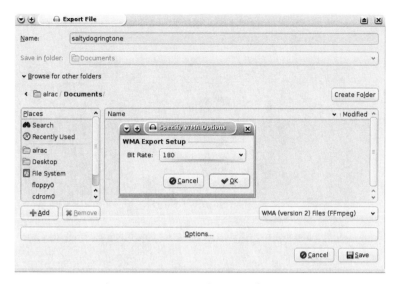

Figure 10-9: Encoding your ringtone in the WMA format

NOTE *The first time you install a new SD card in your phone, you should format it using the phone's menu. This creates the right type of filesystem for your phone. Your phone's manual will tell you how. Formatting the storage card erases everything on it.*

After formatting a card, just plug it into the appropriate card reader, plug it into your computer, copy over your new ringtones, and then stuff the card into your phone and transfer the files to the correct directory. Your phone might even have some helpful menu options to make this easy.

Bluetooth is another common option for connecting a mobile phone to a PC. It's an odd name for a useful function: very short-range wireless radio networking, from 1 to 100 feet. If your computer does not have a Bluetooth adapter, you can buy a USB Bluetooth adapter for less than $30. Get Bluetooth 2.0 because that is the newest and fastest standard. To establish a Bluetooth networking connection, follow the instructions in your camera's manual. Typically, you'll activate Bluetooth on your PC, set it to *discovery* mode, and then set up *pairing* with your phone from the phone's menu. If it asks you for a personal identification number (PIN), this is usually an arbitrary number that you invent at the time of discovery and then duplicate on the computer to complete the connection.

Some cell phone service providers disable file transfer via Bluetooth because they want to overcharge you for online services or charge you extra up front for a *data connection kit*, which is a fancy way of saying they want to gouge you for uncrippling some of the phone's built-in functions. Figure 10-10 shows a microSD card, a USB Bluetooth adapter, and accessories.

Of course, you can avoid all this business of paying to unlock phone functions by purchasing an unlocked phone. You'll have to figure out for yourself if it's better to go with a branded phone, which is subsidized by the service provider and locks you in for a year or two, or to pay full price for the freedom of an unlocked phone.

Figure 10-10: A microSD Flash storage card adapter, a wee Cirago USB Bluetooth interface, another adapter, a cute red USB microSD reader, a tiny 2GB microSD card, and a US quarter for scale

I think the easiest and best way to transfer files between a computer and a cell phone is via an ordinary USB cable, and some phones support this.

Any of these methods can be used for any kind of file transfer, and not just your ringtones. Photos, contacts, messages, any of the data stored in your phone can be backed up to a PC or transferred from a PC to your phone. There are many Windows and Apple software applications for managing your mobile phone from your computer. These usually cost a few dollars. There is a good open source, free-of-cost application worth trying that runs on Linux, Mac, and Windows: BitPim. To quote the BitPim website (*http:// www.bitpim.org/*):

> BitPim is a program that allows you to view and manipulate data on many CDMA phones. . . . This includes the PhoneBook, Calendar, WallPapers, RingTones (functionality varies by phone), and the Filesystem.

Now you know how to create and optimize your own custom ringtones and audio files for your mobile devices and how to add extra storage so you can carry around your entire music collection with you. Don't forget the earbuds. Or even some fancy, high-end padded headphones, because your phone speaker might be poo but its sound processor just might be pretty good, needing only some good headphones to come to life.

11

AUDACITY PLUG-INS FOR SPECIAL EFFECTS

Plug-ins are add-on software modules that give Audacity extra functionality: filters, analysis, tone generators, and special effects of all kinds. Plug-ins are nice because you don't have to install a monolithic program with everything in the world just to get the few extra features that you really want.

Some are bundled with your Audacity installation, and you can find many more on the Internet. Or you can even write your own. Plug-ins do not run standalone; they run on *hosts*, which are applications (such as Audacity and other audio production software) that support the plug-ins. You will find Audacity's plug-ins in the Generate, Effect, and Analyze menus.

There are three types of plug-ins that work with Audacity: Linux Audio Developer's Simple Plugin API (LADSPA), Virtual Studio Technology (VST), and Nyquist. LADSPA is mainly for Linux, though there are some LADSPA plug-ins for Windows and Mac. VST is for Windows and Mac, and Nyquist plug-ins work on all three.

Plug-ins are sorted alphabetically in the Audacity menus; there isn't a way to sort or organize plug-ins according to your own wishes, such as the ones you use the most. Finding helpful information about them, such as what they do or what the various settings mean, is often a bit of a challenge. There is some information on the Audacity wiki, and the home sites of the various plug-in projects have documentation of varying degrees of helpfulness. It's easy enough to try them and hear for yourself what they do. In this chapter, we'll cover a batch of commonly used plug-ins in detail and define some terminology. A brief audio glossary at the end of this chapter explains some of the more common terms you'll encounter for plug-ins and special effects.

Manipulation and analysis of digital and audio signals are part of the discipline of *signal processing*. We're not going to dive into the math and theory of signal processing in this book; to learn more, see the bibliography for some references.

Let's dive right into exploring and playing with some of Audacity's special effects. Your own Audacity menus may be different from those in the examples, depending on which Audacity version you are using and what plug-ins you have installed. If you don't know how to find and install plug-ins, skip ahead to the sections in this chapter on finding and installing plug-ins on Linux and Windows.

NOTE *When you can't find documentation, sometimes browsing the source code rewards you with useful information. You can see all of Audacity's source code online at* http://audacity.cvs.sourceforge.net/viewvc/audacity/audacity-src/. *Use the Sticky Tag menu to select the correct Audacity version, and then look in the* nyquist, *plug-ins,* and src/effects *directories to see the source code for Audacity's plug-ins.*

Cross-Fades

Our first effect is not even a real Audacity special effect: cross-fading. A cross-fade is when one track fades out and another track fades in with some overlap. We hear this all the time on radio and TV. Audacity doesn't have a cross-fade function, but it's easy enough to create one with the Time Shift tool.

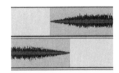

Figure 11-1: A simple cross-fade created using the Fade In/Fade out effects and the Time Shift tool

You need two tracks to do this. Apply **Effect > Fade Out** to one, and apply **Effect > Fade In** to the other. Then use the Time Shift tool to move the tracks to create the degree of overlap you want (Figure 11-1).

For finer control of the degree of fades and their duration, use the Envelope tool.

Generate Menu

The Generate menu contains plug-ins for creating new tones. Start with a new, blank Audacity session. Select **Generate** and then whatever effect you want to try. This will open a dialog with the available options for the particular tone. If all the audio in an existing track is selected, generating a new tone will replace the old one. If a portion of the existing audio is selected, the selection will be replaced. If no existing tracks are selected, then creating a new tone also creates a new track. You can also select **Tracks** > **Add New** > **Audio Track** to create additional tracks.

Sine Wave Example

Let's create a sine wave to get the hang of creating tones. Open the **Generate** > **Tone** dialog. Select a sine waveform, set the frequency (Hz) to 3,999, set the amplitude to 0.8, and set a duration of whatever you want. The default is 30 seconds (Figure 11-2).

You will see something like Figure 11-2. Zoom way in to see the classic sine waveform (Figure 11-3).

Figure 11-2: What a 3,999 Hz sine wave may look like at first

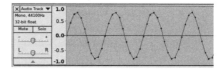

Figure 11-3: What a 3,999 Hz sine wave looks like at extreme zoom

Click the **Play** button to enjoy your new sine wave tone.

Frequency Range of Generated Tones

The available frequency range of your newly generated tones is theoretically half the project sampling rate. For example, if your project rate is 8,000 Hz, then the available range for your tones should be 0 to 3,999 Hz. But your usable range is a bit less. You will know you are at the extreme end of the range when you see either silence or a pulsing waveform instead of a nice steady waveform. Figure 11-4 shows a 3,999 Hz sine wave created with project sampling rates of 8,000, 16,000, and 32,000 Hz (from top to bottom). Figure 11-5 shows how they look when you zoom way in and how they look smoother at higher sampling rates.

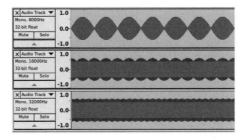

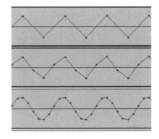

Figure 11-4: How a 3,999 Hz sine wave looks at three different project sampling rates

Figure 11-5: This shows how the waveforms smooth out at higher sampling rates.

DTMF Tones

Using the **Generate** > **DTMF tones** effect is fun, because you can use it to play any word or text string in DTMF tones. What, you ask, are DTMF tones? Those are the tones emitted by an analog touch-tone telephone: *dual-tone multifrequency*. It's called dual-tone because each keypress sends a tone that is a combination of two tones. The handy table in Figure 11-6, poached from Wikipedia (with permission), shows the tone matrix for a touch-tone phone.

Figure 11-7 shows the DTMF tone generator dialog. The DTMF sequence is a word, phrase, or any alphanumeric string. The tone/silence ratio controls the duration of the spaces between each tone.

	1209 Hz	1336 Hz	1477 Hz	1633 Hz
697 Hz	1	2	3	A
770 Hz	4	5	6	B
852 Hz	7	8	9	C
941 Hz	*	0	#	D

Figure 11-6: Analog telephone tones are combinations of two tones for each keypress. (Image courtesy of Wikipedia under the Creative Commons Attribution-ShareAlike license.)

Figure 11-7: The DTMF tone generator plays any word or phrase in touch-tones.

Figure 11-8 shows what "carla" looks like in DTMF.

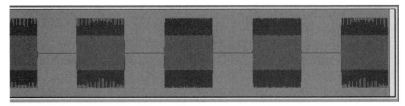

Figure 11-8: A DTMF waveform spelling "carla"

Chirps

The **Generate > Chirp** effect is another fun tone generator. Use this to generate tones that sound like slide whistles. Select a low frequency and a high frequency and duration, and the tone will slide up or down according to frequency order. You can try different waveform types to hear how they sound: sine, square (alias or no alias), or sawtooth. The Interpolation setting offers either Linear or Logarithmic. Linear gives equal time to all frequencies, while Logarithmic plays the lower frequencies for a longer period of time (Figure 11-9).

Figure 11-9: Chirp tones sound like slide whistles.

Generating Noise

The **Generate > Noise** menu item is for generating white, pink, or brown noise. Why, you may ask, would you want to do that? I'm nowhere near knowledgeable enough to get into the mathematics, which is the foundation of acoustics and which is fascinating if you care to learn. I can answer "what for": to test audio gear, to configure sound balance in music halls, to create background noise to help sleep or concentration, and to cover up annoying sounds. Figure 11-10 shows Audacity's simple noise generator.

Figure 11-10: **Generate > Noise** takes three options: type of noise, amplitude, and duration.

White noise is often used in electronic music production because it has the useful property of cutting through other noises. It is called white noise because it is analogous to white light, which is an equal combination of all light frequencies. White noise is a combination of all audible audio frequencies, so one way to think of it is 20,000 tones all playing at once at the same amplitude. However, this isn't strictly accurate, since it is usually generated by random noise generators in which all frequencies are equally probable, rather than all played at once. Human hearing is more sensitive to higher frequencies, so even though the amplitude is the same at all frequencies, we notice the higher frequencies more. White noise sounds like steam hissing.

Pink noise sounds similar to white noise, but instead of having the same amplitude at different frequencies, it drops off by 3 dB per octave as frequencies climb, with equal amplitude across each octave. So, lower frequencies have more power than higher frequencies, and pink noise sounds more like a roar than a hiss.

Brown noise is also known as red noise. It is called brown for Brownian motion, not for color, and if you're interested in why, I shall leave it as your homework assignment to find out. (More math.) Brown noise decreases in amplitude by 6 dB per octave as frequencies increase, so it has even more bass emphasis than pink noise. Pink and brown noise are closer to how human ears perceive amplitude across the frequency range than white noise.

Figure 11-11 shows what white, pink, and brown noise look like in Audacity. The bottom three tracks are in Spectrum view, which gives you a nice picture of the relative energy (amplitude) at different frequencies. Red is "hotter," or higher amplitude, and blue is "cooler," or lower amplitude. It's just like the light spectrum where the red end of the spectrum is hotter and blue is cooler. If the image were in color, you would see that the white noise spectrum is uniform, the pink noise spectrum ranges from red to red-with-blue, and the range from red to blue is more pronounced in the brown noise spectrograph. Of course, you can easily create these in Audacity and see the colors.

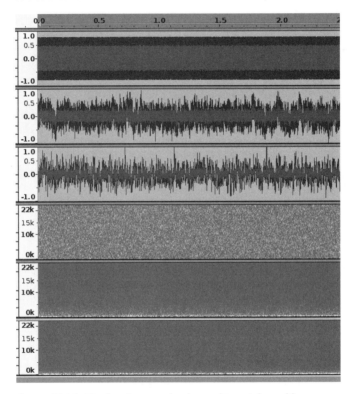

Figure 11-11: The first three tracks show white, pink, and brown noise in linear waveforms. The second set of three tracks shows them in Spectrum view.

Several other types of noise "colors" are not supported in Audacity, unless you find or write a plug-in. Purple noise is the opposite of brown noise because amplitude increases 6 db per octave as frequency increases. Blue noise is the opposite of pink noise: Amplitude increases 3 dB per octave.

We've used **Generate** > **Silence** several times in this book. It creates a completely silent interval of whatever duration you want. This is handy for aligning tracks that are off by a little bit, evening out the spacing in a podcast with two speakers so they don't talk at the same time, and making sure that the intervals between songs are absolutely quiet. It's also useful for testing how silent your playback system really is.

Test Tones

Selecting **Generate** > **Tones** is a fun way to test the limits of your cheapo (or nice) sound card and to give yourself an ad hoc hearing test. You can create tones with *sine, square, sawtooth,* or *square, no alias* waveforms. Zoom way in to see the waveforms like you see in books and articles about waveforms (Figure 11-12).

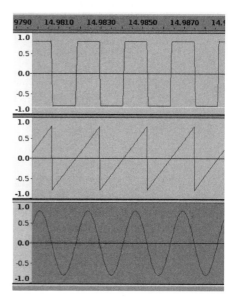

Figure 11-12: Square, sawtooth, and sine waves

A *sine wave* can be thought of as a pure tone without harmonics, so when you want a pure tone, you want a sine wave. A sine wave alternates smoothly from positive (above the median, or zero line) to negative (below the median line) and back again. More complex tones can be represented by combinations of sine waves. Sine waves are all around us: Ocean waves, the Slinky, alternating current, and light waves are a few examples. In audio, a sine wave represents *frequency*, which is measured in *hertz* (cycles per second), *amplitude* (loudness or volume), and *phase*. Figure 11-13 shows what these look like in Audacity.

You can think of phase in terms of Audacity's Time Shift tool; when the phase is nonzero, that means the waveform is moved forward or backward in time. A negative value is backward, and a positive value is forward. This is called *linear phase* because all frequencies are affected equally. Sometimes we don't notice a linear phase shift because there is nothing to compare it to. An example of this is playing a CD—the music is delayed a little bit by passing through the digital-to-audio converter, but we don't care because we don't notice it. On the other hand, this is a real problem for overdubbing because new tracks will be out of sync with old tracks, so we have to compensate for it. (See Chapter 9 to learn more about overdubbing and synchronization.)

Two waveforms deliberately phase-shifted relative to each other will create new sounds. A common effect is creating a pleasing echo by duplicating an audio track and then mixing the two tracks with the second track a little bit out of phase. Now you know the secret of overproduced commercial vocals: They use way too many phase-shifted layers. (If you like echo, try selecting **Effect** > **Echo**.)

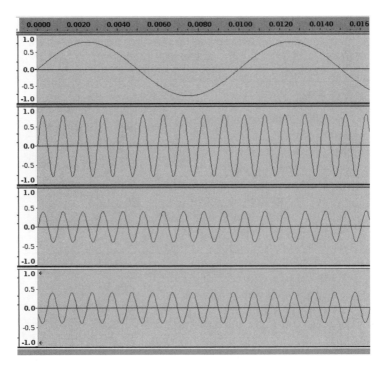

Figure 11-13: The top track is a 100 Hz sine wave, and the second track is 1,000 Hz, showing what different frequencies look like. Both have the same amplitude. The third track is half the amplitude of the top two, and the fourth track is a copy of the third track, shifted slightly out of phase.

Phase shift also describes synchronization between two or more waveforms. Two waveforms that are exactly in phase combine amplitudes and sound louder. Two waveforms with varying degrees of being in or out of phase produce all kinds of different sounds. Two identical waveforms that are inverted 180 degrees relative to each other cancel each other out. Noise-cancellation devices do this, with varying degrees of effectiveness.

A *square* waveform pertains to digital electronics. (The square wave is sometimes also called the Rademacher function.) Rather than the nice smooth curve of the analog sine wave, a square waveform represents the instant transitions of digital circuits. Just like everything digital, it's all binary—ones or zeroes, on or off. Unlike a sine wave, which represents a pure tone with no harmonics, square waveforms are chock-full of harmonics. You can hear a distinct difference when you create a sine waveform and a square waveform in Audacity and compare them. Square waveforms contain only odd-integer harmonics, such as first, third, and fifth harmonics.

A *square, no alias* waveform is a dandy demonstration of the distortion caused by aliasing in digital audio. Create a square tone and a square (no alias) tone of the same frequency and duration side by side and zoom in. You'll see something like Figure 11-14, and there should be an audible difference when you listen to them, with the no-alias tone sounding smoother and purer. This is also a great way to experience the effects of different sampling rates; you'll notice that lower sampling rates have higher distortion.

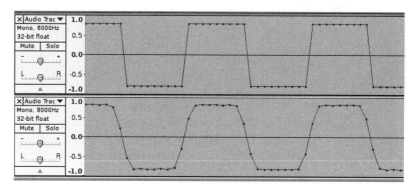

Figure 11-14: The top waveform is aliased, and the bottom waveform is not.

A *sawtooth* waveform has both even and odd harmonics, so it is used for synthesizing complex musical sounds such as stringed instruments.

Click Track

The Click Track effect is a useful plug-in that may not come with your default Audacity installation (see "Linux Plug-ins" and "Windows Plug-in" near the end of this chapter for information on finding and installing more plug-ins). It works on Linux, Mac, and Windows. Click tracks are like metronome tracks, with one difference: The first beat of each measure is accented (Figure 11-15).

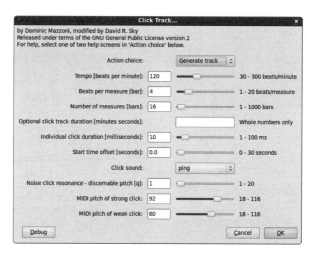

Figure 11-15: The Click Track effect creates a beat track at configurable tempo, duration, and tonal qualities.

The different click types are *ping, noise,* and *tick.* The Noise click resonance setting makes them sound crisper or mushier, with higher values being crisper.

Click Track uses two different default tones: C above middle C for the first beat of each measure, which is represented by MIDI number 72, and middle C for the remaining beats in each measure, which is MIDI number 60. For example, if you select a waltz beat, which is three beats per measure, you'll hear "TICK tick tick TICK tick tick." There are 12 notes per octave, including flats and sharps. Figure 11-16 is handy table listing all the MIDI note numbers.

Octave	Note Numbers											
	C	C#	D	D#	E	F	F#	G	G#	A	A#	B
-1	0	1	2	3	4	5	6	7	8	9	10	11
0	12	13	14	15	16	17	18	19	20	21	22	23
1	24	25	26	27	28	29	30	31	32	33	34	35
2	36	37	38	39	40	41	42	43	44	45	46	47
3	48	49	50	51	52	53	54	55	56	57	58	59
4	60	61	62	63	64	65	66	67	68	69	70	71
5	72	73	74	75	76	77	78	79	80	81	82	83
6	84	85	86	87	88	89	90	91	92	93	94	95
7	96	97	98	99	100	101	102	103	104	105	106	107
8	108	109	110	111	112	113	114	115	116	117	118	119
9	120	121	122	123	124	125	126	127				

Figure 11-16: Your handy MIDI note table for selecting MIDI pitches for a click track

NOTE   *Just for fun, sing the "Do Re Mi" song from* The Sound of Music *to refresh your memory of the seven whole notes—do, re, mi, fa, so, la, ti, do. (If you've forgotten, that covers one octave plus one note: A, B, C, D, E, F, G, A.)*

Pluck

Another interesting add-on plug-in is Pluck. It's pretty simple: Choose your MIDI note, set the duration, and configure a gradual or abrupt fade-out. A higher note like 96 sounds like the slide-advance tone in old-fashioned slide shows. (Grade school in the 1960s, back in the last millennium . . .) A low-frequency note sounds like a sci-fi sound effect (Figure 11-17).

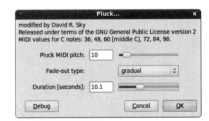

Figure 11-17: The Pluck effect generates tones at different frequencies with short or long fade-outs.

Risset Drum

The Risset Drum effect creates a nice tone that at lower frequencies sounds like a deep bass drum, or any large resonant drum with a fat tone, and at higher frequencies sounds metallic like a cowbell or a triangle (Figure 11-18).

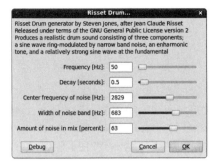

Figure 11-18: The Risset Drum effect

The Risset Drum effect is named for the inventor Jean-Claude Risset, who created a lot of amazing effects with electronic audio. A Risset pattern creates the illusion of a rhythm in reverse: It sounds like the tempo is increasing when it is really decreasing, and the other way around. A Risset rhythm gives the illusion of a rhythm that is always accelerating even as it stays the same.

This is a good effect to use for creating a 2/4 or 4/4 percussion beat. The settings I used in Figure 11-18 create a deep, booming bass drumbeat at two beats per second. The Decay value sets the length of the beat, so 0.5 makes two beats per second. This creates only a single beat, so you can preview how a steady repeated beat will sound by clicking SHIFT-Play. Click the **Stop** button when you've had enough. When you're ready to create a drumbeat track, select the beat and then click **Effect** > **Repeat** to create a loop. This opens a dialog with one option: how many times you want it to repeat. It even does the arithmetic for you and tells you how long it will run (Figure 11-19).

Figure 11-20 shows what your new drum track will look like.

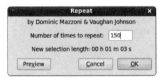

Figure 11-19: Looping your Risset beat with the Repeat effect to create a drum track

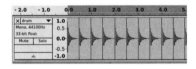

Figure 11-20: A drum track created with the Risset Drum and Repeat effects

What if the tempo you created isn't quite right? That is easy to fix with the Change Tempo effect, which changes the tempo without changing pitch. First undo the Repeat effect so that you are back to your original, single drum beat. Then click **Effect** > **Change Tempo** and enter your new Beats per Minute value. In Figure 11-21, it changes from 120 beats per minute to 150. But of course it is still just a single beat, so go back to **Effect** > **Repeat** and create a loop again, and there is your new, faster drum track.

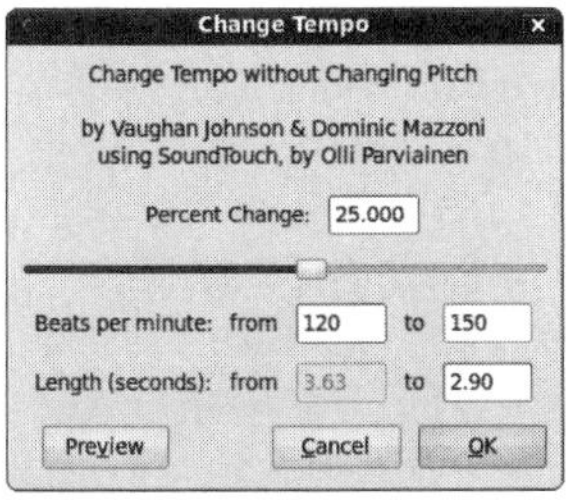

It is best to change the tempo of your single, original beat because applying the Change Tempo effect to your whole loop track will change where each beat starts, and most of

Figure 11-21: Use the Change Tempo effect to change tempo without changing pitch.

them will be off-tempo. Though this could be interesting enough to use, it's up to you.

Effect Menu

The effects in the Effect menu don't create new tones but modify existing tones. A good way to get the hang of the Effect menu plug-ins is to apply them to tones created in the Generate menu. A sine wave is great for experimenting with effects because it is a simple tone and you can hear exactly what the effect does. Another good test tone is a simple recording of your own speaking or singing voice.

NOTE *Note the Repeat Last Effect (CTRL-R) command at the top of the Effect menu. This is a fast way to reapply the same effect with the same settings.*

Reverberation

Probably the most popular effect in audio editing is *reverberation*. You have probably listened to commercial music recordings where the reverb was laid on too thick and it sounds like the singer is being crushed under layer upon layer of reverb or like the recording was made in an empty swimming pool. A little reverb goes a long way. The usual purpose of reverb is to better simulate a live sound, but of course you can do whatever you like. Reverb can sound ethereal and distant and be evocative of things half remembered.

Audacity's Gverb plug-in is cross-platform and has a Preview button so you can easily try different settings. You should preview reverb settings on monitor speakers rather than headphones, because the channel separation in headphones will lessen the reverb effect.

NOTE *The default preview in Audacity is three seconds; you can change this in the **Edit** > **Preferences** > **Playback** dialog.*

There are several ways to approach applying reverb to your audio tracks. A common technique is to work from a duplicate wet track rather than your original, unmodified dry track. When you have tweaked your reverb satisfactorily, mix the wet track together with a copy of the dry track. Keeping an original, 100 percent dry track means you can make several reverb tracks with different settings and control the final results in the mix.

You can also edit just a duplicate track, keeping the original for insurance in case the copy becomes a muddled mess. If you are daring, you can work without a net and operate on your original. Audacity has nearly unlimited undo, so this isn't all that daring, but bad things can happen and then you have extra work.

First select a portion of audio or the whole track. To start from neutral with Gverb, push all sliders all the way to the left (Figure 11-22), except the Dry signal level, which should be at zero.

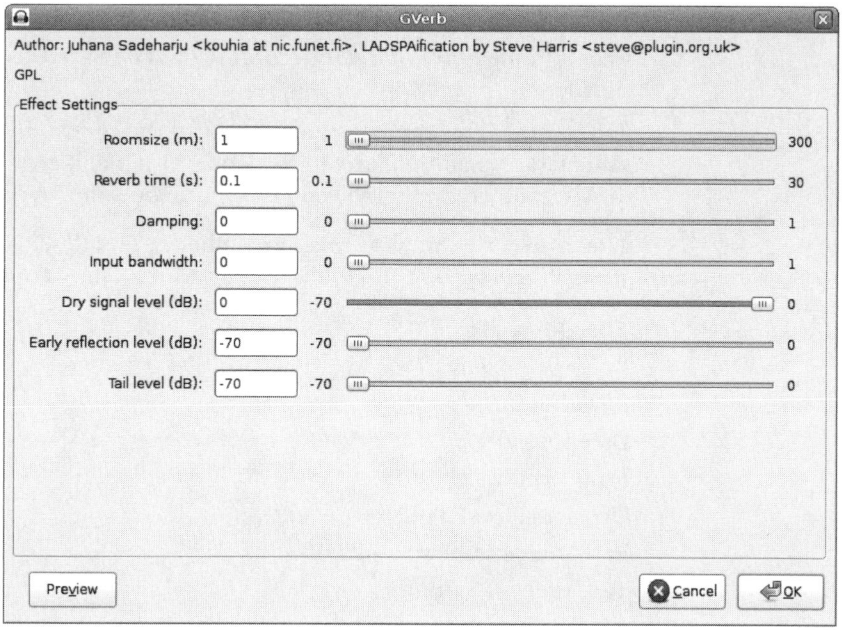

Figure 11-22: Gverb with all the settings at neutral, or no reverb

Now you can try the settings and hear what they do. The most notice-able changes come from the Early reflection level and Dry signal level settings. Next give Tail level a go, keeping it at an equal or lesser value than Early reflection level, and then try changing Reverb time. This is what each setting does:

Roomsize   This is supposed to simulate different room sizes, in square meters, and it operates mainly on the Early Reflection and Tail Levels. To my ears it doesn't seem to do much; your mileage may vary. Other reverb plug-ins and gadgets seem to do this better.

Reverb time   This controls the duration of the reverb in seconds, with larger values giving longer duration.

Damping   The higher the Damping value, the less intense the reverb. This simulates different room sizes and surfaces, like a small room with hard surfaces making a bright sound or a large room with absorbent surfaces creating a softer, darker effect.

Input bandwidth   This is a tone control, with higher values emphasizing higher frequencies and sounding brighter.

Dry signal level   This controls how much of the original signal is altered; 0 is none, and −70 is all of it. However, even at zero you will still hear some changes. The overall volume is reduced along with lower dry signal levels, so you may need to apply normalization after applying your reverb.

Early reflection level   This simulates how sound is reflected off the walls and furniture. Early reflection is always delayed compared to a dry signal.

Tail level   This controls the intensity of the reverb. If you make this value larger than the Early reflection level value, it gives an interesting distance affect, as though you're listening outside the concert hall.

The Audacity manual suggests a number of prefab settings to try (*http:// wiki.audacityteam.org/index.php?title=GVerb*), which I have copied here:

- **The Quick Fix**
  Roomsize: 40 m^2
  Reverb time: 4 s
  Damping: 0.9
  Input bandwidth: 0.75
  Dry signal level: 0 dB
  Early reflection level: −22 dB
  Tail level: −28 dB

- **Bright, small hall**
  Roomsize: 50 m^2
  Reverb time: 1.5 s
  Damping: 0.1
  Input bandwidth: 0.75
  Dry signal level: −1.5 dB
  Early reflection level: −10 dB
  Tail level: −20 dB

- **Nice hall effect**
  Roomsize: 40 m^2
  Reverb time: 20 s
  Damping: 0.50
  Input bandwidth: 0.75
  Dry signal level: 0 dB
  Early reflection level: −10 dB
  Tail level: −30 dB

- **Singing in the Sewer**
  Roomsize: 6 m^2
  Reverb time: 15 s
  Damping: 0.9
  Input bandwidth: 0.1
  Dry signal level: −10 dB
  Early reflection level: −10 dB
  Tail level: −10 dB

- **Last row of the church**

  Roomsize: 200 m^2

  Reverb time: 9 s

  Damping: 0.7

  Input bandwidth: 0.8

  Dry signal level: −20 dB

  Early reflection level: −15 dB

  Tail level: −8 dB

Freeverb is an older reverb plug-in that is a bit simpler to use, and to my ears it sounds better (Figure 11-23). The Room Size slider has a wide and obvious range, and there are both Wet and Dry sliders. Width mimics speaker spread. Check the "Freeze Mode" checkbox to play the preview dry without changing your Freeverb settings so you can quickly compare it to the modified signal.

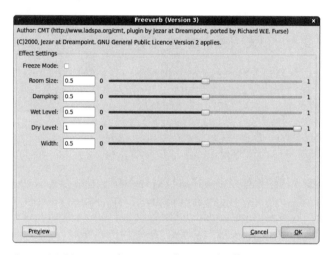

Figure 11-23: Freeverb is an another reverb effect.

If Freeverb doesn't come with your Audacity installation, visit the Free-verb3 home on SourceForge to get both source code and binary files (*http:// freeverb3.sourceforge.net/*).

Now let's look at the built-in Audacity Effect plug-ins.

Amplify

I use the **Effect** > **Amplify** effect a lot for both reducing and increasing amplitude. Don't check "Allow clipping" or go over zero unless you know you really want to, because anything greater will be clipped and distorted. An increase of 3 dB is double, and 1 dB is about the smallest change we can perceive. Enter a negative value, such as −3 dB, to reduce amplitude. Amplify can be applied to a selection, a whole track, or a group of tracks.

Auto Duck

This is a great effect for recordings with a background music track, such as a podcast, because it automatically lowers the volume when the foreground track cuts in and raises it when the foreground cuts out. In Figure 11-24, we see the setup: On top is a stereo background music track, and the bottom mono track is a spoken-voice track. When the voice starts, I want the music volume to decrease, and when the voice stops, the music should return to its former volume level. They have to be in this order: the background track on top and the *control track* underneath.

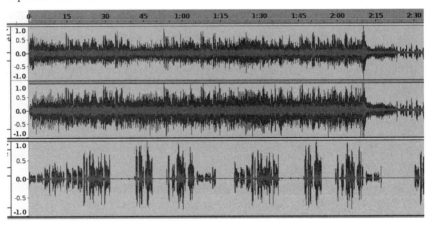

Figure 11-24: Using Auto Duck, with your background track on top and your foreground, or control track, underneath

Select the background track, and click **Effect > Auto Duck**. You'll see a control panel like the one in Figure 11-25, which shows the settings I like to use. These settings create a fast fade-out and a gradual fade-in. The background track ducks out of the way fast and gracefully glides slowly back in with just a little bit of overlap with the voice track.

Duck amount is how much volume reduction you want on the background track.

Maximum pause determines how long the total fade-ins and fade-outs will take. The Outer fade down length and Outer fade up length values cannot total more than the Maximum pause value.

The Outer fade down length setting determines how quickly the background track will fade before the voice on the control track comes back. Anything outside the two vertical lines in the graph happens when the control track is below your threshold. The Inner fade down length setting determines how much overlap there will be with the control track.

The Outer fade up length setting controls how fast the backing track fades back in when the voice on the control track stops, and the Inner fade up length setting controls the overlap. A half second of gently rising music over the voice isn't a lot; I think it makes a nice bit of a transition. Figure 11-26 shows what these tracks look like after the Auto Duck effect is applied.

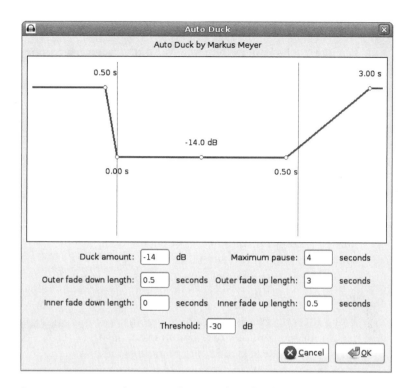

Figure 11-25: Example Auto Duck settings for a fast fade-out and slower fade-in

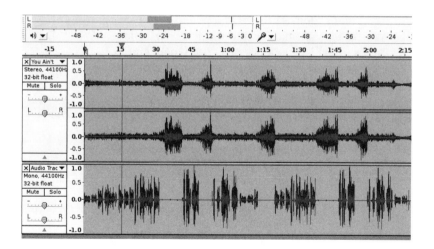

Figure 11-26: Auto Duck has been applied; compare this to Figure 11-24.

The Threshold setting controls the sound level for triggering the Auto Duck effect.

Change Pitch

Change Pitch changes the pitch without changing the tempo, so you can adjust your audio higher or lower in pitch without speeding it up or slowing it down. I've used this on tracks that were a little bit out of tune, and it does a nice job. The Change Pitch effect will do its best to detect the current frequency and pitch of your selection, and then you can go up or down from there (Figure 11-27). There are all kinds of digital tuners for instruments and voice that do this and even fancy rackmount units that automatically correct the pitch for you.

Figure 11-27: The Change Pitch effect serves up several ways to measure pitch changes.

Phaser

Using **Effect** > **Phaser** splits the signal into two parts (one wet and one dry), applies your settings to the wet track, and then combines them back into one. Its primary purpose is to create an oscillating or vibrato effect, and thanks to the wonder of modern electronics, you can apply a multitude of extra effects to it. Try it on a recording of your own voice or a plain sine wave to get an idea of what it can do. The *phaser* (phase shifter) is a popular effect used in all kinds of music: to create a soaring effect on electric guitars, to sweeten keyboards, and to make all kinds of spacey science-fiction noises (Figure 11-28). (A similar effect is the *flanger*, which you get when you install the extra plug-ins from the Audacity website.)

Figure 11-28: The Phaser effect creates a multitude of fascinating and eerie sounds, from soaring vocals to space aliens.

The Stages setting determines the number of filters used at one time, from 2 to 24. Higher values create a more complex, layered tone, with multiple oscillations.

The Dry/Wet balance accepts values from 0 to 255, with 0 being completely dry and 255 completely wet.

An LFO frequency is a *low-frequency oscillation* that creates a pulsing rhythm or vibrato-type effect. In the Phaser dialog, the available LFO Frequency range is from 1 to 40 Hz, or 1 to 40 pulses per second. Increasing the value of this setting can have a dramatic effect, depending on the other settings and how it interacts with them. For example, try setting both LFO Frequency and Depth to their maximums and see what happens. You know how ripples in a swimming pool spread out, bounce off the sides, bounce back, and collide with each other? Sound waves do the same thing, and you can't always predict the results. It may help to keep in mind that sound waves are three-dimensional, so they're all over the place and not just on a fairly flat plane like water ripples.

LFO Start Phase determines the phase shift of your signal, from 0 to 359 degrees. That's right, just like a circle. The degree of phase shift is most easily explained by looking at Figure 11-29. A sine wave alternates smoothly between positive and negative voltage; positive voltage is above the center line, and negative voltage is below. Where the waveform crosses the center line is the *zero crossing point*, be-

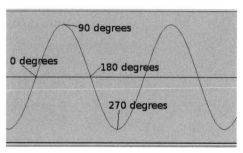

Figure 11-29: Phase shift is measured in degrees of a circle.

cause that is the point of zero voltage. The starting point of the sine wave is zero rising to positive; 180 degrees is at zero crossing into negative. When it gets back to zero from negative, that is a full 360 degrees.

You might recall from earlier in this chapter how this affects your audio signal: Two waveforms at a phase shift of 180 degrees from each other cancel each other out, and varying degrees of phase shift combine to create different sounds, from a simple echo to weird space alien noises.

You can also illustrate this three-dimensionally with a Slinky. That's right, Slinky is more than a toy—Slinky is a physics teaching tool. Slinky is a helix, and Slinky represents audio phase in three dimensions. Slinky ripples in longitudinal waves just like sound and in traverse waves that are like the stretched strings of musical instruments. Slinky illustrates harmonics and amplitude. Slinky is amazing, and researching "physics of Slinky" will lead you to all sorts of fascinating knowledge (Figure 11-30).

Depth usually refers to how much the pitch is bent, from 0 to 255, with higher values producing a more pronounced vibrato effect. However, Audacity's phaser seems to bend the amplitude rather than the pitch, which makes a signal that fades in and out quickly. Crank this up along with the Stages value to get some neat space alien sounds.

Finally, Feedback is the familiar distortion effect that adds crunch and texture. A higher percentage equals more distortion. Set the Dry/Wet balance and Feedback value to the maximum to generate some really weird sci-fi sounds like they used in old movies.

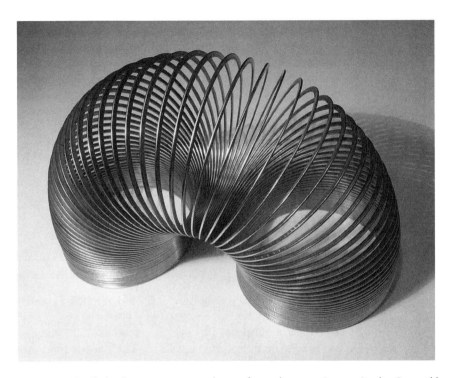

Figure 11-30: Slinky illustrates many attributes of sound waves. (Image Credit: Created by Wikipedia user Roger McLassus, released under the GFDL.)

Reverse

Reverse is a simple effect with no options—it turns your audio around backward. Back in the 1970s when disapproving pruney-lipped people were playing LPs backward to find the Satanic messages, this would have saved them a lot of trouble. It was a waste of time anyway, since records with devil messages played them frontward.

Sliding Time Scale/Pitch Shift

This is a fun new effect that changes tempo or pitch, or both. But that's not all—it also has a sliding effect so you can go from slow to fast, lower to higher pitch, both at the same time, and the reverse. I know, all of these effects have been done before in the wonderful Looney Tunes and Merrie Melodies cartoons. But they had to do it the hard way with expensive equipment.

Checking the Dynamic Transient Sharpening checkbox seems to result in a wider dynamic range with a bit less distortion. Overdoing Sliding Time Scale/Pitch Shift will create distortion, and it's a horsepower hog—on old, slow PCs it will take a long time.

WahWah

Just like the name says, this makes your signal go "wah-wah." Maybe I'm easily amused, but exaggerated WahWah effects applied to nice, ordinary music tracks crack me up every time. On a more serious note, the WahWah effect makes an instrument sound like a voice. One of the most famous uses of this effect is on *Frampton Comes Alive* for the song "Do You Feel Like We Do." (Admit it, you still own the vinyl double set and take it out and play it once in a while. Don't be embarrassed; it's a great album, and Mr. Frampton is a fine guitarist.) Another standout use of WahWah is in Steely Dan's "Haitian Divorce" on the *Royal Scam* album, which gives the lead guitar a sarcastic voice.

WahWah is similar to phase shifting. It uses LFO to set the oscillations per second, from 0.1 to 4 Hz. That's right, point one to four, a lot slower than the Phaser effect.

LFO Start Phase and Depth are just like the settings in the Phaser effect.

Resonance accentuates the higher frequencies; 1 is least effect, and 10 is the most pronounced.

Wah Frequency Offset emphasizes the lower frequencies at lower percentage settings and emphasizes the higher frequencies at the higher settings. It will cause clipping if you go too high (Figure 11-31).

The WahWah effect adjusts the phase of the left and right channels on a stereo track, making the track sound as though it travels back and forth between the speakers.

Now let's take a look at finding and managing Audacity plug-ins in Linux and Windows.

Figure 11-31: The WahWah effect makes instruments "talk" and plays tricks with left-right channel balance.

Linux Plug-ins

There are two types of Audacity plug-ins that work in Linux: LADSPA and Nyquist.

Linux LADSPA Plug-ins

There are several specialized Linux distributions for multimedia production, such as 64 Studio, dyne:bolic, Planet CCRMA (which is a special set of packages for Fedora and CentOS), and Ubuntu Studio. There are two ways to install LADSPA plug-ins. One way is to use your Linux package manager. 64 Studio includes a bundle of more than 300 plug-ins. Debian and Ubuntu break them out into separate packages. Here are some of the LADSPA plug-in packages in Debian and Ubuntu:

- blepvco (LADSPA anti-aliased, minBLEP-based, hard-sync-capable oscillator plug-ins)

- blop (Band-limited wavetable-based oscillator plug-ins for LADSPA hosts)
- caps (C* Audio Plugin Suite)
- cmt (Computer Music Toolkit LADSPA plug-in collection)
- ladspa-sdk (useful LADPSA tools for users and developers)
- swh-plugins (Steve Harris's LADSPA plug-ins)
- tap-plugins (Tom's Audio Processing LADSPA plug-ins)
- vamp-examples (audio analysis plug-ins)

Look in the Sound section of the download repositories to find these. Install them via your favorite graphical package manager, or use a command-line tool like aptitude, for example `aptitude install blepvco`, or whatever package name you want.

Here are some of the plug-in packages in Planet CCRMA:

- ladspa-blop-plugins (Band-limited wavetable-based oscillator plug-ins for LADSPA hosts)
- ladspa-swh-plugins (Steve Harris's LADSPA plug-ins)
- ladspa-cmt-plugins (Computer Music Toolkit LADSPA plug-in collection)
- ladspa-mcp-plugins (by Fons Adriaensen; currently contains a phaser, a chorus, and a moog vcf *(voltage controlled filter)*)
- ladspa-fil-plugins (four-band parametric equalizer)
- ladspa-rev-plugins (reverb based on gverb, plus new features)
- ladspa-tap-plugins (Tom's Audio Processing LADSPA plug-in)
- ladspa-vco-plugins (anti-aliased dirac pulse oscillator)
- ladspa, ladspa-devel (useful LADPSA tools for users and developers)

Fedora has a graphical package manager, or you can run yum from the command line, as in `yum install ladspa-blop-plugins`.

You can also install individual plug-ins by simply copying them either to */usr/lib/ladspa/*, which makes them accessible to all users on your system, or to your personal home directory, such as */home/carla/.ladspa*, which means they will be available only to you. All LADSPA plug-ins have an *.so* extension, for example *gong_1424.so*.

LADSPA stands for Linux Audio Developer's Simple Plugin API. This is a framework for writing universal plug-ins that work in any Linux audio application by giving application developers a common, simple, well-documented application programming interface (API) to support. As a result, a large number of Linux audio applications support LADSPA plug-ins: Audacity, Ardour, ReZound, Rosegarden, GNU Sound, and many others.

There are several popular LADSPA plug-in projects:

- Steve Harris's plug-ins (*http://www.plugin.org.uk/ladspa-swh/docs/ ladspa-swh.html*)

- Tom's Audio Processing plug-ins (TAP) (*http://www.tap-plugins .sourceforge.net/*)

- CAPS, the C* Audio Plugin Suite (*http://www.quitte.de/dsp/caps.html*)

- Computer Music Toolkit (CMT) (*http://www.ladspa.org/cmt/*)

Naturally this list shows just a few; there are many more.

LADSPA Version 2 (LV2) is the successor to LADSPA. It is more extensible and more flexible. The Linux version of Audacity supports LV2 as of version 1.3.6. Visit *http://www.lv2plug.in/* to get current information on LV2 plug-ins, such as Steve Harris's LV2 plug-ins (*http://www.plugin.org.uk/lv2/*) and other active LV2 projects.

You can get detailed information on individual LADSPA plug-ins by installing the *ladspa-sdk* package. This is the package you need to learn to write your own LADSPA plug-ins, and it also includes some useful commands for getting information about plug-ins. listplugins shows all your installed plug-ins, as this snippet demonstrates:

```
$ listplugins

/usr/lib/ladspa/sine.so:
        Sine Oscillator (Freq:audio, Amp:audio) (1044/sine_faaa)
        Sine Oscillator (Freq:audio, Amp:control) (1045/sine_faac)
        Sine Oscillator (Freq:control, Amp:audio) (1046/sine_fcaa)
        Sine Oscillator (Freq:control, Amp:control) (1047/sine_fcac)
/usr/lib/ladspa/noise.so:
        White Noise Source (1050/noise_white)
/usr/lib/ladspa/triangle_1649.so:
        Bandlimited Variable Slope Triangle Oscillator (FASA) (1649/triangle_fasa_oa)
```

analyseplugin gives detailed information on individual plug-ins, as in this abbreviated example:

```
$ analyseplugin gong_1424.so

Plugin Name: "Gong model"
Plugin Label: "gong"
Plugin Unique ID: 1424
Maker: "Steve Harris <steve@plugin.org.uk>"
Copyright: "GPL"
Must Run Real-Time: No
```

```
Has activate() Function: Yes
Has deativate() Function: No
Has run_adding() Function: Yes
Environment: Normal or Hard Real-Time
```

Linux Nyquist Plug-ins

Nyquist plug-ins also work on Linux and have an *.ny* extension. You can download some from the Audacity site (*http://www.audacity.sourceforge.net/download/nyquistplugins*), and a web search will find hundreds more. Install these by copying them to */usr/share/audacity/plug-ins/* for systemwide usage or to *$HOME/.audacity-files/plug-ins* to keep them all to yourself. The Nyquist programming language (*http://www.audacity.sourceforge.net/help/nyquist*) is freely available and open source, so you can write and distribute your own Nyquist plug-ins to your heart's content.

Windows Plug-ins

Three plug-in types run on Windows: VST, LADSPA, and Nyquist.

Steinberg's Virtual Studio Technology (VST) is a plug-in standard invented by Steinberg for its Cubase line of MIDI and audio recording and production software. Steinberg licenses VST to third-party developers so they can create VST plug-ins for any host; consequently, VST is the most widely used plug-in standard. Audacity comes with a basic set such as Gverb, Tremolo, and Vocal Remover.

VST plug-ins have a *.dll* extension. The Audacity download page (*http://www.audacity.sourceforge.net/download/plugins*) has links to more, plus a directory of VST plug-ins known to work well with Audacity. Installing these means simply copying them to *\Program Files\Audacity\Plug-ins*.

You'll also find LADSPA plug-ins that work in Windows on this page. Nyquist plug-ins work in Windows as well; again, just copy them to *\Program Files\Audacity\Plug-ins*.

The Internet is full of audio plug-ins, and you can use the plug-ins that come with other audio production software.

Audio Effects Glossary

Audio effects have their own terminology, so let's take a look at some of the more common terms you're going to encounter with audio plug-ins.

All-pass filter   A filter that passes all frequencies equally and applies phase shifting. Reverberation effects use all-pass filters.

Decay   Decay controls how quickly or how slowly a sound fades away.

Delay   This controls the degree of reverberation and how it sounds, whether it's just a bright lively touch or an overdone muddy mess. In the olden days, this was done with tape loops and changing the spacing between the recording and playback heads on tape recorders. Now all you do is move a slider or type a numeric value in seconds or fractions of seconds.

Four basic audio waveforms   A waveform is a visual representation of a sound, and the four basic waveforms that are important to audio are *sine, square, sawtooth,* and *triangle.* Figure 11-32 shows them side-by-side, thanks to Wikimedia. Their shapes pertain to all sorts of advanced math, which is definitely beyond the scope of this book and my own tiny math knowledge. These waveforms are not unique to audio but are used in many disciplines such as math, physics, electrical engineering, and all different kinds of signal processing.

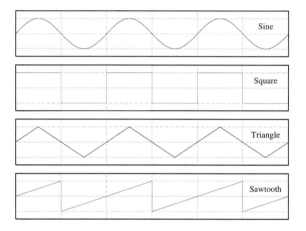

Figure 11-32: The four basic waveforms

Harmonics   Harmonics can be thought of as overtones, though some textbooks say they are not the same and then use a boatload of advanced math to show why. We'll keep it at the training wheels level: When you play a note on a musical instrument, that is the *fundamental frequency.* This note may also be accompanied by harmonics, which are other notes that are integer multiples of the fundamental frequency. So, a fundamental frequency of 100Hz can have harmonics of 200 Hz, 300 Hz, 400 Hz, and so on. These are numbered in order: fundamental frequency, 2, 3, 4, and so on. Square waveforms contain only odd-numbered harmonics, while sawtooth waveforms have both even and odd.

One reason to preserve a wide frequency range (which is controlled by the sampling rate) is to preserve the harmonics, because even if you can't hear the full frequency range, you can hear the harmonics. Narrowing the frequency range loses some harmonics in the range you can hear.

High-pass filter   This passes high frequencies unaltered, while attenuating lower frequencies that are below the *cutoff* point. So, you could use this to tone down boomy bass or unbalanced midrange frequencies.

Low-pass filter   This allows low frequencies to pass unaltered and attenuates higher frequencies above the *cutoff* point, which you set. Use this to tone down recordings where the higher frequencies sound too bright or where there is noise such as tape or stylus hiss.

Low-pass filters are also used in hi-fi electronics to route low-frequency sounds to subwoofers or to whatever speakers can handle them.

Reverberation   Reverberation is one of the most commonly applied effects; it tries to simulate a live sound like we hear in a concert hall or stage show. Reverb is echo, or sound reflections, that occur too quickly to be perceived individually. This is what gives a piece of music a "live" sound: When we attend a live performance, the music is reflected from innumerable surfaces all around us. A recording studio is usually a deliberately "dead" environment, so there is no natural reverb. So, reverb is applied to recordings to enliven them and make them sound more realistic. It is used in live shows to create a bigger, more spacious sound. You can't control the acoustics where you perform, but you can do a lot with your electronics to overcome bad acoustics and to tailor your sound to simulate different environments.

Stiffness   This tries to replicate the sound of physical objects at different levels of stiffness, such as woodwind reeds, cymbals, and gongs.

Wet/dry balance   A *dry* signal has not yet had any special effects applied to it; an audio signal becomes *wet* after effects are applied. Most plug-ins and hardware special effects mixers allow only a proportional adjustment; if your wet balance is 45 percent, then your dry balance is 55 percent.

12

FIX-ITS AND CLEANUPS

Audacity has a number of tools for fixing defects and cleaning up recordings. As I keep saying, your best approach is to make the cleanest recordings you can, because that is a lot easier than fixing them. There is no TV crime-show magic; there are limits to what you can do.

However, there is a lot you can do to fix problems, so we're going to learn how to do that in this chapter. (If you need a refresher, Chapter 1 covers the basics of using Audacity, and Chapter 2 goes into building a simple recording studio.)

Split Stereo Tracks

Oftentimes only half of a stereo track will have a defect. So, you should split the track (**Split Stereo Track** in the Track menu), apply repairs to each track independently, and then rejoin them with **Make Stereo Track** from the Track menu. Then you'll have the advantage of the good half helping to mask imperfect repairs.

Repeat Last Effect

Note the Repeat Last Effect (CTRL-R) command at the top of the Effect menu. This is a fast way to apply the same effect with the same settings over and over. The Effects menu is a bit inconvenient because the effects go away when you click OK, so when you need the same effect over and over, it gets a bit tedious to wade through the whole menu again and again.

Noise Removal

There is no Hollywood magic wand like those used by the TV-crime lab techs who take a damaged lo-fi recording, clean it up, separate all the different elements, and magically isolate a voice print of the bad guy from way in the background . . . or match the exact waveform of the engine noise of the getaway vehicle and identify the make and model, identify the rare custom shoes from the sound of footsteps, or any of the other fanciful things TV writers come up with. It just isn't so. Trying to separate multiple sounds on a single track is like trying to decompile a mixed drink; once everything is mixed together, there really isn't a practical way to separate it again. Noise removal is always a compromise with its side effects, and that is why recording studios use multitrack recorders in soundproofed rooms—because getting a clean recording is always better than trying to clean up a mucky one.

However, sometimes unwanted noises sneak in, and you don't have the luxury of redoing the recording. Audacity's Noise Reduction effect works pretty well when the noise is distinctly different from what you want to keep and you have a sample of pure noise to build a noise profile. A common example is the stylus hiss or turntable rumble from a vinyl record album. These are easy to clean up: First select a section of just the hiss or rumble, then click **Effect** > **Noise Removal** > **Get Profile** to create a profile of the noise. Make sure nothing but noise is selected and make it as long as possible, up to 30 seconds. Even 5- to 10-second profiles will work, but longer ones are more accurate. When Audacity is finished building the profile, the Noise Removal panel will disappear.

The next step is to select the track segment you want to fix, select **Effect** > **Noise Removal**, and click **OK**. It is better to apply Noise Removal as surgically as you can because it alters your recording. The difference might not be obvious unless you're listening for it, but it does make perceptible changes to the parts you want to keep.

If you don't like the results, press CTRL-Z to undo, change some settings, and try it again. The default noise reduction level is −24 dB, which means frequencies identified as noise are attenuated by −24 dB. If this removes too much of the recording, set a higher decibel value, such as −20 dB, and try it again. A trick that often works well to reduce bad side effects is to go back to your noise sample, decrease its amplitude a few dB, create a new profile, and try again. Chances are you won't be able to erase the noise completely because doing so may erase things you want to keep, but you can lower it to where it's not so noticeable.

The Frequency Smoothing slider is more surgical at smaller values and affects a wider range of frequencies as you move the slider right to set larger values. Try smaller values first, because they'll affect less of your recording.

The Attack/decay time slider determines how fast the Noise Removal effect responds to change in the audio signal. For noise that is fairly steady, use a larger value. If the noise fluctuates rapidly, then use a smaller value for a faster response time (Figure 12-1).

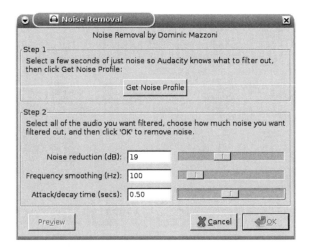

Figure 12-1: This shows some gentle Noise Removal settings: Frequencies identified as noise are reduced by 19 dB, frequency smoothing is narrow, and attack and decay times are moderately slow.

Normalization

The Normalize effect (**Effect** > **Normalize**) is the workhorse of many a digital recording studio, because it is common to record to a peak of −12 dB or lower, sometimes all the way down to −24 dB. Normalization is usually the last step before export to bring your recording up to a higher peak volume level. Digital audio has such a wide dynamic range that you can record to conservative peak levels to avoid distortion and then later normalize your tracks to bring the peak levels up to a comfortable playback level.

Normalization is also used to bring multiple tracks up to the same peak volume level. Do not use Normalize if you want to preserve the relative volume levels of different tracks. For example, if you have one track that peaks at −6 dB and another one that peaks at −12 dB and you want to keep the 6 dB spread, don't use Normalize; use Amplify. With Amplify you can raise or lower them a set amount, for example +3 dB, which would raise them to −3 dB and −9 dB, respectively. But if you want both tracks raised to a peak of −3 dB, then Normalize is the tool for the job.

Always leave "Remove any DC offset" checked, because DC offset is not something you want to keep. If there is any DC offset, this indicates that your mean amplitude is not zero. A little bit of offset is no big deal, but if the offset is big enough, it will mess up your dynamic range, and it could even cause some distortion (Figure 12-2).

DC offset is short for *DC offset from zero*. DC originally meant direct current, but now it applies to any waveform representing any type of signal. Figure 12-3 shows the before and after: The track on top is the original, unnormalized track with a bit of DC offset, and the bottom track is normalized and has no DC offset.

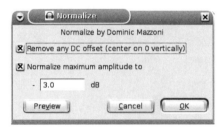

Figure 12-2: Always check "Remove any DC offset" and "Normalize maximum amplitude to" and set a maximum decibel value of zero or less.

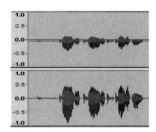

Figure 12-3: Before and after: a bit of DC offset on an unnormalized track on top; corrected DC offset and normalized on the bottom

Remove Clicks and Scratches

Audacity offers a couple of fast ways to clean up a scratchy recording of a vinyl LP. Digital recordings can also pick up clicks from various sources. The first of these is Click Removal: It's not as reliable as manually correcting scratches, but it's fast and pretty good.

Click Removal

The Click Removal effect (Figure 12-4) looks for spikes in the waveform that are typical of pops caused by scratches, deletes the scratch, and then does a bit of interpolation to reconstruct the waveform. The Select Threshold setting determines the sensitivity for deciding when a spike is a scratch; it uses an algorithm that compares the audio on both sides of the spike to figure out what part is the scratch and what part is the good audio. Its value is the square of the required ratio between the amplitudes inside and outside the loud section. In other words, smaller Select Threshold

Figure 12-4: The Click Removal effect takes only two settings.

values are more sensitive, and larger values are less sensitive. Higher sensitivity means it may alter peaks that are not clicks, and a too-low Select Threshold will miss some clicks. The Max spike width determines the maximum length of a segment, in milliseconds, that the Click Removal tool will operate on.

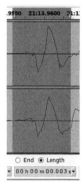

To get an idea of the Max spike width value to use, first set the Selection Start value on the Selection toolbar to Length, and set the time parameter to hh:mm:ss + milliseconds. Then zoom in on a click in the waveform and select it, and you'll have its length in milliseconds. The Max spike width should be large enough to include some good audio samples on both sides of the click so that it will have enough good audio to compare to. Figure 12-5 shows a spike that is less than 3 ms long. I usually stick with the default of 20 ms, which gives good results most of the time.

Loud, obvious scratches are the easiest. The Click Removal effect doesn't handle sections of light, crackly static very well; the Noise Removal effect is better for this. Click Removal is fast and pretty good, but it's not 100 percent, and it may mistake percussion effects for scratches.

Figure 12-5:
Here is a click that is less than 3 ms long.

Repair

The Repair effect is my preferred tool for fixing scratches. It has to be applied manually, one scratch at a time, but it does a great job. Zoom in until you can precisely select a region no more than 128 samples long, and then select **Effect > Repair**. It will delete the selection and then use interpolation to smoothly fill the gap. It's a great tool for all kinds of surgical fixes: clicks, scratches, pops, and short clipped segments. Figure 12-6 shows a before and after repair of a clipped segment.

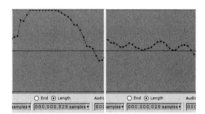

Figure 12-6: A brief clipped segment smoothed over with the Repair effect

Draw Tool

The Draw tool (Tools toolbar) gives you ultimate control of repairs at the sample level. First zoom in far enough to see the individual audio samples. The cursor changes to a little pencil, and then you can use it to smooth out the contours of the defect to make it less noticeable. The sound itself doesn't change because you're just making it quieter, as Figure 12-7 shows.

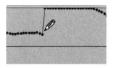

Figure 12-7:
Smoothing out a click with the Draw tool

Truncate Silence

What if you have a long recording that you want to trim by a few minutes, without losing any audio? Perhaps you have a recording with a lot of silences you would like to trim. The pauses between songs are too long, your deep thoughts are interspersed with long pauses, or you have a sound-activated recording with a lot of dead air. The Truncate Silence effect will automatically find and shorten those silent intervals.

Don't use the Truncate Silence effect after you have created fade-ins and fade-outs, because it will wreck them.

Effect > Truncate Silence has four settings: Min silence duration, Max silence duration, Silence compression, and Threshold for silence. The simplest way to use this effect is to set the min and max duration to the same values and adjust your threshold so that it catches only silent passages. In Figure 12-8, any silent passages (-40 dB or quieter) greater than 800 ms long will be shortened to 800 ms. (1,000 ms is 1 second.)

Don't set Max silence duration to zero because it might crash or do some other unpredictable behavior. The min-

Figure 12-8: These settings for Truncate Silence look for silent passages longer than 800 ms and then shorten any silence of -40 dB or quieter to 800 ms.

imum I have found to be reliable is 5 ms, though some folks push it down to 1. If you want no silences at all, you'll have to delete them manually, though to my ears 1 ms is as good as zero.

Threshold for silence tells it what threshold to use to mark where the silent passages begin. A value of -35 or -40 dB works well when the silent passages are really silent; when they're noisy like on an LP, with stylus noise between songs or turntable hum, you might have to kick it up to -25 dB.

The Silence compression setting configures a ratio, rather than a fixed length of silence duration, so that your silences will vary in length. You might want to use this to preserve the natural cadence of a speaking voice or to make a live performance sound more realistic. Suppose your min duration is 100 ms and your max duration is 5,000 ms. If you set the silence compression to 4:1, a 10-second silence will then be reduced to 2 seconds. The results will vary according to the difference between your max duration and your longest silences. To get a predictable result, you can use Truncate Silence to shorten the longest silences to whatever maximum you want and then apply it again using silence compression.

Change Tempo

The Change Tempo effect is a great little fix-it when you're mixing multiple tracks and the tempo is off by a small bit on any of them. It changes tempo without changing the pitch. You can apply it to selections, whole tracks, or multiple tracks. There are a couple of ways to approach this. One is by trial and error; just fiddle with the Percent Change setting until it sounds right.

Some folks have great ears and can do this quickly. You can also set the Beats per Minute (BPM). If your other tracks follow a known BPM, then use this. If you don't know the correct BPM, play a minute of a track with the correct tempo and count the beats. I do this with a stopwatch, and it works great when no one else is around to bother me and interrupt my counting.

Finally, there is a setting for Length in seconds. If you know exactly how long your track or selection is supposed to be, this is a fast and easy way to set it right (Figure 12-9).

Figure 12-9: Change Tempo gives you three ways to correct the tempo, as well as a Preview button.

Change Pitch

This changes the pitch without changing the tempo, so it's a great little fix-it when a performer is off-key. You can apply it to selections, whole tracks, or multiple tracks. As you can see in Figure 12-10, it offers several different settings: You can change keys, for example from A to C, or by semitones (half steps), exact frequency, or a percent. If you have a good ear, the Percent Change slider and Preview button are probably fastest.

How do you precisely measure pitch? The Change Pitch effect comes as close as it can, though you get more accuracy with an electronic tuner.

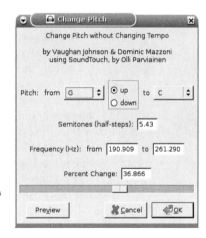

Figure 12-10: Change Pitch alters the pitch without changing tempo.

Change Speed

I'm sure the Change Speed effect has many practical applications, but I always seem to end up using it for amusement because it changes both tempo and pitch, just like messing around with turntable speeds. So, you can speed up your audio to play fast and high, like an over-caffeinated Alvin and the Chipmunks, or low and slow like Samuel Ramey, the famous bass-baritone opera singer, on tranquilizers. It supports the standard turntable speeds of 33 1/3, 45, and 78 RPM and a range of arbitrary speeds controlled by a slider or by typing in a percentage value (Figure 12-11).

Figure 12-11: Change Speed changes both pitch and tempo.

Compress Dynamic Range

This is a dynamic range compressor, not to be confused with file compression. Dynamic range compression is commonly thought of as "make the loud bits quieter and the quiet bits louder." Most compressors only reduce gain; they narrow the dynamic range by attenuating the louder parts so that the range between the soft and loud parts is reduced. It is overused and abused in commercial recordings, which is a shame because it is a useful effect when it is used carefully and with good purpose. My preference is to use compression as little as possible, because I think many "fixes" done with compression are better worked out during recording, with the Amplify or Normalize effects, or with the Envelope tool.

You can use compression to improve the balance of recordings by reducing the dynamic range of tracks that are supposed to be more in the background and not drawing attention to themselves. Apply some compression to level out changes in volume and maybe lower their overall volume, and they become good little supporting players. You can tailor recordings for different playback devices and environments. You can apply compression to an entire recording or to individual tracks or parts of tracks.

For example, if you want background music for playing in a noisy environment, compressing its dynamic range will make it easier to listen to because you'll have a more consistent volume level, rather than having unexpected peaks interspersed with inaudible passages. A podcast with several different people speaking will benefit from careful volume control and compression, especially when you're recording people who are not experienced with talking into microphones and who don't speak at a consistent level. For this kind of recording, you'll get best results by manually adjusting the amplitude until it's as consistent as you can get it (the Envelope tool is great for this) and then applying some careful compression to the final mix for a last bit of polish. Adjusting voice tracks can take a fair bit of finessing, because some voices sound louder even when they're not. You should also keep in mind how your audience is likely to listen to your recording—if they're at work or listening on earbuds or listening to something designed to soothe them to sleep, be kind and don't surprise them with sudden spikes in volume.

Compression can smooth out uneven volume levels caused by an inexperienced performer or one who is having a bit of an off day. For example, your bass guitar player is tired and hits some notes too hard and some not hard enough. Or your singer has bad mic technique and moves around too much, so she fades in and out. Maybe you have a vocalist or other soloist who needs to stand out from the mix, so applying a bit of careful compression to their track and then increasing the amplitude will push them to the front.

Most compressors make your selection quieter, so you may have to use the Amplify or Normalize effect after applying compression.

NOTE   *Apply dynamic range compression conservatively, because when it is overdone, it can create a bellows effect, with the volume rising and lowering on a regular beat. Another side effect is raising your noise floor, because noise becomes relatively louder along with the quieter passages. Yet one more side effect is giving greater emphasis to background sounds, such as audience noise. Too much compression can introduce distortion.*

How Much Dynamic Range?

So, what is a good dynamic range to aim for when you're applying dynamic range compression to a recording? The definitive answer is "It depends." First let's talk about what is possible and what we hear, and then we'll look at some examples for various situations.

Human hearing can perceive a range of roughly 120 dB. The maximum real-life dynamic range in digital audio is about 115 dB. The dynamic range of a CD is about 96 dB. Vinyl LPs can deliver as much as 60 dB. A live symphony might encompass 80 dB. A comfortable listening range for most folks is going to be narrower than that, more like 20 to 30 dB, which is still a nice wide range. What works for you might take some trial and error. My own rule of thumb is under ideal listening conditions, at home using my good stereo hi-fi, without distractions or people talking to me, I'm comfortable with a dynamic range of no more than 50 dB. And that's when I'm in the mood for a dramatic opera or symphony or a raucous live rock show. Most of the time I prefer something a little quieter.

Sometimes you hear new things in familiar recordings when you narrow the dynamic range, because this "raises" the quiet parts. (It's all relative; reducing the gain on the louder frequencies makes the quieter ones sound louder.) You might hear feet hitting piano or drum pedals, performers muttering asides, more nuances in quiet parts—you just don't know until you try.

You can easily experiment in Audacity to get a feel for different dynamic ranges by recording a simple test file and then using **Effect > Amplify** to set different parts of it at different dB levels. Figure 12-12 shows a simple recording where, starting at −50 dB, each 10-second segment is 10 dB louder until it reaches the maximum of 0.

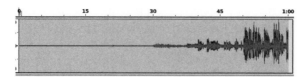

Figure 12-12: A simple dynamic range test: Starting at −50 dB, each 10-second segment is 10 dB louder.

Modern popular music is typically mashed into a 5 dB or even smaller range, at peak amplitude or over, which is a horrible thing to do to good music. In many modern recordings and remastered old recordings, the dynamic range is so narrow that it's like pushing everything to the redline. There are no quiet passages, no nuance, and no contrast; it's just one loud schmear. It destroys nuance and flavor. The reasons for doing this are a splendid combination of simplicity and stupidity—when we hear two recordings at different volume levels, our initial impression favors the louder one as sounding better. It's also used to make a track stand out from the pack when it's played on radio or TV or in a public place. But that hardly works anymore since they all do it.

The end result is compressing the life out of a recording. It's aural junk food—sure, that first hit of a candy bar or potato chip, or whatever your particular favorite goody is, is mighty nice. But you can't live on junk food, and it soon becomes unsatisfying. It's the same way with overdone compression; that first impression might be "the louder one is better!" But after a few minutes of listening, most folks change their minds and prefer a better-engineered recording. Even if you're not consciously aware that a recording has been butchered beyond hope with compression, you'll likely experience fatigue and get tired of listening. A web search on *loudness wars* will return a lot of interesting information.

You can see this as well as hear it by ripping a song from a music CD, importing it into Audacity, and viewing the waveform. Figure 12-13 shows a selection from Rickie Lee Jones's "The Magazine"; compare this to any Top 40 contemporary CD. "The Magazine" is a wonderful work that rewards attentive listening on a good sound system, and you can see in the waveform that it has not been compressed into a useless tiny dynamic range, nor have all the levels been maxed out. In fact, it doesn't come anywhere near the red line. I prefer recordings made with the assumption that I know what to do with a volume knob.

I won't give any horrid examples because I'm too chicken to point fingers, but you can find plenty with a quick web search and probably in your own music collection. It's that same old race to the bottom, the familiar battle of quality and artistry against pandering to the lowest common denominator. In this modern era, that is lo-fi MP3s played on tiny, lo-fi portable devices and computer speakers, and loud systems with horrid powered subwoofers that are to music what hot sauce is to food—a little bit adds punctuation and contrast; a big whacking overdose kills off all the flavor and enjoyment and turns it into an act of aggression.

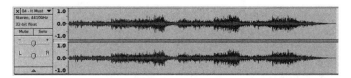

Figure 12-13: "The Magazine," by Rickie Lee Jones, was engineered with some actual dynamic range. Note how the peaks are nowhere near zero, and there is a fair spread between the quietest and loudest parts of the waveforms.

One more horrid example of dynamic range compression abuse is television commercials. They are supposedly not allowed to be louder than the programming, but they get around this by having no dynamic range at all but with everything pushed to the maximum. (I think they are louder, too.)

Compressor Settings

That's enough complaining about the state of the world. Let's fire up **Effect > Compressor** and learn what the different settings do (Figure 12-14). Most times, using compression is two steps: Apply the Compressor, and then raise the volume level of the compressed segment back up to where you want it.

This is a simple compressor with only four settings. The pros use expensive hardware compressors, and Audacity's Compressor does not quite match these in ability. But it's good enough for performing basic compression chores.

The Threshold setting determines the starting point, in decibels,

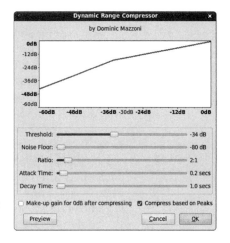

Figure 12-14: Audacity's Compressor effect is simple, with just a few settings.

where the audio signal is attenuated. A threshold of −50 dB means all parts of the signal with an amplitude of −50 dB and above will be attenuated. This on most recordings will be everything. Usually you don't want to compress everything; you get better results with a light touch and tailoring it for a specific purpose.

The Noise Floor setting holds the gain at a constant level on audio below the Noise Floor setting. If your track has a lot of quiet sections, this keeps them from being amplified.

The Ratio setting determines how much compression will be applied. A 4:1 ratio means an input signal of 4 dB higher than your threshold will be reduced to 1 dB higher than the threshold. A ratio of infinity brings everything down to the threshold level. In Audacity's Compressor effect, the maximum is 10:1. Other compressors go up to 60:1, which in practice is the same as infinite. The graph in the Compressor gives you a nice visual of this, showing that low ratios are more gentle and higher ratios result in greater gain reduction.

Again, my approach is "Less is better." It's easy to experiment with this in Audacity and listen to how your audio quality is affected by different settings. I use compression sparingly, rarely going over a −20 dB threshold or a 4:1 ratio. If I'm thinking a recording needs more than that, I stop and think about what it really needs—some careful adjustments with the Envelope tool? Rerecording?

Attack Time determines how quickly the compressor reaches its maximum effect, and Decay Time determines how long it takes to phase out the compression. A too-short Attack Time setting could result in some audible distortion, and a too-long Decay Time might miss some short peaks. You can get some different effects with different attack times. For example, a longer Attack Time setting such as 0.5 seconds will not catch and attenuate a sharp drumbeat, so this adds some punch. A fast Attack Time dampens percussion and other sharp peaks. You probably want the fastest Attack Time for vocalists, which is 0.1 seconds, unless you're trying for some unusual effects.

A slower Decay Time can create a long, almost soaring fade-out. This is a common technique used to extend a guitar note. Audacity's Compressor is medium good at this, and it goes up to 10 seconds. If you're going for a natural sound, a fast Decay Time is better. Play around with it to see what it does to different instruments and vocals. For example, a drum track with a fast Attack Time setting and a slow Decay Time setting will sound interesting, almost backward or echoey, because the beats are not allowed to decay naturally but are held longer at a louder level.

A common side effect of compression is *pumping and breathing*. This happens when you select a high Threshold setting and there is a lot of variation in the track. The fluctuation of the compressor causes the attack/decay to become audible. Sometimes this is fun to do on purpose.

Sometimes some odd-sounding artifacts will be appended by the Compressor to the end of your recording. This is a normal by-product of compression, so deal with it by padding the end of your recording with something you can delete after applying compression.

"Make-up gain for 0dB after compressing" saves a step if you were going to normalize to zero anyway.

There is a checkbox for "Compress based on Peaks." When this box is unchecked, which is the default, the compressor reduces the gain on sounds above the threshold level. "Compress based on Peaks" raises the gain on quieter sounds that are above the threshold level. I don't think that it sounds very good; to me, it's harsh, and the pumping effect is hard to avoid. But then it's your ears that have to be pleased, not mine.

Chris's Dynamic Compressor

There is another compressor, Chris's dynamic compressor (*http://pdf23ds .net/software/dynamic-compressor/*), that is tailor-made for compressing classical music in a pleasing way. I think it works great for all kinds of audio and better than the stock Audacity Compressor effect.

The author, Chris Capel, was inspired to write this compressor because he often listened to classical music in noisy environments. After spending a lot of time fiddling with the volume controls, which wasn't very rewarding, he decided that applying some dynamic range compression to his recordings was the solution. But the compressors he tried didn't sound good enough, so he wrote his own Nyquist compressor plug-in for Audacity. Since it is a Nyquist plug-in, it will work on Linux, Mac, and Windows; just download and copy it to your plug-ins directory. It will appear in the Effect menu as "Compress dynamics." It has good instructions right on the plug-in itself, as Figure 12-15 shows.

Mr. Capel is continually changing and improving his plug-in, so you can keep up by visiting his website. Figure 12-15 shows the simple view. There is also an advanced view that displays all the options, shown in Figure 12-16. To get the advanced view, open the plug-in file *compress.ny* and follow the instructions. This exposes the advanced parameters Attack and Release speed and Attack and Release exponent. It's super easy, because all you do is move a few semicolons.

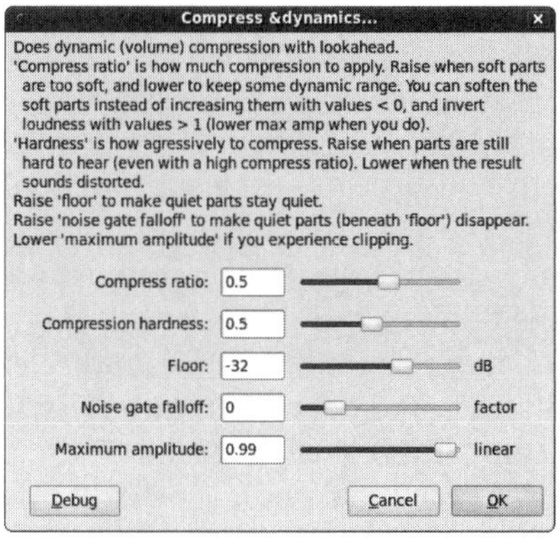

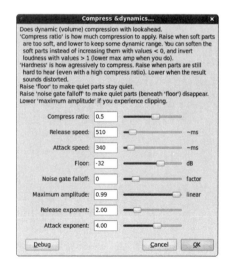

Figure 12-15: The default simple view of Chris's compressor

Figure 12-16: The advanced view of Chris's compressor, showing all options

What sets Chris's compressor apart is that it looks ahead and adjusts the gain in anticipation of what is coming next. Most compressors do not do this but rather react to changes in volume, so there is always a bit of lag. Sometimes this results in a loud peak abruptly reduced or, worse, some distortion. Chris's compressor operates more smoothly and handles percussion and other loud transient events gracefully. It is worth reading the comments on his web page, and he includes some audio samples. The source file, *compress.ny*, is a plaintext file and contains useful information.

Chris's compressor is a nice piece of work, so let's review its options.

Compress ratio operates differently from compression ratio settings on most other compressors. It works two ways: *dynamic compression* and *dynamic expansion*. Values range from −0.50 to +1.25. Negative values make the quiet frequencies quieter, which is called *dynamic expansion*. Positive values reduce the gain on the louder frequencies, which is called *dynamic compression*.

The default of 0.5 is pretty nice. It preserves a lot of the original dynamic range and sounds natural. According to some posts in the Audacity forums, 0.77 matches the NPR radio station KPCC Pasadena. So if you want to be like KPCC Pasadena, now you know how.

Release speed is like the Decay Time setting in the Audacity compressor, controlling how quickly the compression is phased out. Values are in milliseconds, so fewer milliseconds equal a faster release speed.

Attack speed is similar to the Attack Time setting in the Audacity compressor, controlling how quickly the compression is applied, until it reaches its peak ratio. If your recording has a lot of rapid peaks, you probably want a faster attack speed to catch them. However, you can add some punch to drumbeats, for one example, with a slower attack time so that they are not compressed as much. Generally, music has faster increases in volume than decreases, so to keep pace with the music, attack times should be faster, and release times should be slower.

The effects of the release and attack speeds are more subtle than their counterparts in the Audacity compressor and less prone to introducing typical compression artifacts.

Compression hardness controls how quickly compression is applied and released. A higher hardness value equals slower attack and release speeds, and a lower value is a faster, more aggressive attack and release. This appears only in the simplified view and is like a shortcut for setting the release and attack speeds, except you can't adjust them individually.

Floor sets a floor, or *noise gate*; the default is −32 dB, which means nothing below −32 dB is changed. Use this setting to define a range of the quieter frequencies that won't be changed. You might want to do this if you have a some low-level background noise you don't want amplified or you just don't want the quieter frequencies altered.

Noise gate falloff takes values from −2 to 10. Positive values reduce the gain on everything below your Floor setting, and higher values reduce the gain to a greater degree. Negative values do the opposite and boost frequencies that are below your Floor setting. I usually leave this at zero so it does nothing, though occasionally I will use it to boost the lower frequencies a little bit.

Maximum amplitude raises the amplitude after compressing, so you can save a normalization step. It is not a decibel scale, so it may take a bit of trial and error to get it right. (I think it's easier to just apply normalization.)

Attack and Release Exponents take values from 1 to 6, with 1 meaning do nothing and 6 meaning do the most. What do these do to your recording? They work in concert with your Attack speed and Release speed settings to control the responsiveness of the compressor. Mr. Capel advises that the default values of 2.00 and 4.00 should give pleasing results most of the time.

Chris's Compressor doesn't remember your last settings after you close Audacity but instead reverts to the defaults in *compress.ny*. If you figure out some different settings that you like better, you can make those the defaults by editing *compress.ny*. Here are some settings as they appear in the file:

```
;control compress-ratio "Compress ratio" real "" .5 -.5 1.25
;control floor "Floor" real "dB" -32 -96 0
```

The first numbers are the defaults, and the second set of numbers are the minimum and maximum values. So if you prefer 0.6 as the default for the Compress ratio and −25 for the Floor setting, change them like this:

```
;control compress-ratio "Compress ratio" real "" .6 -.5 1.25
;control floor "Floor" real "dB" -25 -96 0
```

Leveller

The Leveller effect is a sort of dynamic range compressor that reduces loud frequencies and amplifies quiet frequencies (Figure 12-17). Careful manual adjustment of amplitude, compression, and normalization gives better results than using the Leveller effect. Leveller is simple and fast, but it also introduces noticeable distortion as you apply higher degrees of leveling. Why use it? It's fast and easy. It sounds decent on spoken-word recordings and works best on ringtones. For ringtones, try a Moderate degree of leveling and a Threshold for Noise setting of −40 dB. This will flatten the whole waveform nicely, so it will sound richer and fuller on tiny phone speakers.

Figure 12-17: Here is the Leveller effect at moderate settings: a Moderate Degree of Leveling, which reduces loud parts and amplifies quiet parts, and a Threshold for Noise of −20 dB, which is very conservative.

Equalization

An equalizer gives you control over amplitude according to the frequency. Instead of the usual bass-midrange-treble controls we're all used to, the Equalization effect is like having nearly infinite tone controls.

NOTE   *The modern trend in tone controls on less-expensive playback devices is to do away with bass-midrange-treble knobs and replace them with presets like Rock, Classical, Jazz, and Live. I hate these. I want knobs to twiddle, by dang, not cheapo microchips with a limited set of somebody else's notions of what sounds good.*

The Equalization effect has useful prefab options and many custom tweak options. It has preset equalization correction curves for old vinyl and acetate records, such as RCA 1938 and 1947, Columbia LP and 78, Decca, and several others. Recordings made before 1955 didn't follow any industry standards; only then did the RIAA equalization curve become widely used and eventually the industry standard.

Equalization curves were invented to overcome the physical limitations of vinyl and acetate recordings, because the lower frequencies occupy more physical space on the records. Without applying an equalization curve, the recordings would be very short, and the record would be mostly bass grooves with barely perceptible treble. To compensate, the lower frequencies are attenuated, and the higher frequencies are amplified so much that the uncorrected signal sounds tinny, with hardly any midrange or bass.

NOTE   *When you play a record, you can hear the uncorrected signal by putting your ear close to the stylus.*

Your phono gear compensates for this by applying equalization correction, which is exactly the reverse of the original equalization curve: Lower frequencies are amplified, and higher frequences are attenuated. This is why turntables require a special phono preamp. Adopting the RIAA curve industrywide meant that all phono gear could then apply the same equalization correction.

For contemporary LPs and 45s, all you need is a standard phono preamp. This is the phono plug-in on your hi-fi amplifier or computer recording interface. For older records or for custom tweaks on modern vinyl, you can use a standard nonphono preamp to get the uncorrected signal and then apply the appropriate equalization curve using the Equalization effect. Or customize it to suit your own tastes. Once you have a custom curve tweaked to your satisfaction, use the Save As button to preserve it.

Try some of the equalization presets to get different effects. For example, some folks love that old AM radio sound, and now you have an easy way to replicate it with the *amradio* curve. Figure 12-18 shows what it looks like, and as you can see, it must be nostalgia driving the fondness for that old AM radio sound, because it discards everything outside the 100 Hz to 6,800 Hz range.

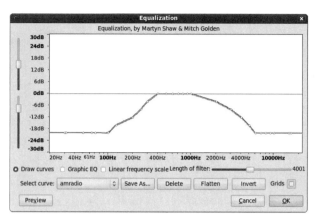

Figure 12-18: The AM radio sound, still beloved by many, is a very squished equalization curve.

The Equalization window opens small, so you might want to lengthen and widen it to expand the scales and give yourself some working room. The sliders on the left let you zoom in on the decibel range you want to work in. Figure 12-19 shows the Draw curves view, and Figure 12-20 shows the Graphic EQ view. Draw curves gives you a dynamic range of 120 dB to play with, while Graphic EQ is limited to 20 dB. If you mess up and want to start over, click the **Flat** button.

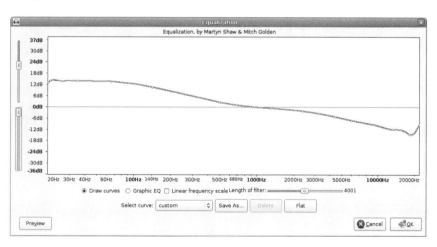

Figure 12-19: The Draw curves view of the Equalization effect, with decibel scale on the left side and frequency scale across the bottom

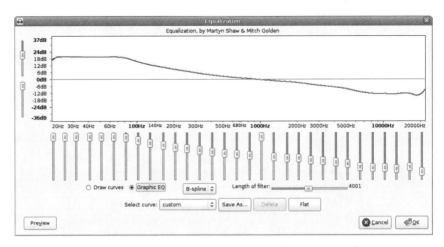

Figure 12-20: The Graphic EQ view, with sliders like a hardware equalizer

Using Draw curves is similar to using the Envelope tool. Click the blue line to create a control point, and then drag the control point. Drag it outside the frame to get rid of it. Control points can move in any direction.

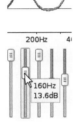

Figure 12-21: You can move the sliders in precise increments with the keyboard, and hovering the cursor displays the exact values.

The Graphic EQ sliders can be moved in several different ways. You can grab them with the mouse. You can click above or below the slider knob, and this moves it first 8 dB and then in 4 dB increments. Using the arrow keys moves it 1 dB at a time, and SHIFT-click moves it 0.1 dB. Hovering the cursor over the knob shows your precise frequency and dB values (Figure 12-21).

The Linear frequency scale setting, when you're in the Draw curves view, changes the scale from the default logarithmic view to linear. Use the logarithmic view when you want to see the lower frequencies in more detail and the linear view when you want to see all frequencies represented equally. The logarithmic view is closer to how we actually perceive sounds.

There are two colored lines in the graph: a thick blue line and a thin green line. The blue line is the one that you manipulate, and the green line shows the actual equalization curve. If they diverge, that is because you are trying to make your curve too steep. Either adjust your curve or try a larger length of filter. This controls the number of samples that Audacity operates on at a time. The default value of 4,001 should work fine most of the time. A smaller value produces a smoother curve and might sound better, though you'll need good ears and good gear to hear the difference.

You can go over 0 well into the +dB range, and this is okay because it's not the same scale as in the track waveforms. It shows how many decibels of gain you're applying (or attenuation). The RIAA curve applies nearly 19 dB of gain to the 20 to 40 Hz range, for example, with no ill effects. But you must still be careful to not create distortion by going too high, and only trial and error will show you where this is on a particular recording. Click **View > Show Clipping** in the track you're working on to quickly see whether you overdid it, because this will mark any clipping with red bars.

Fix Timing and Latency Errors

When you use the Time Shift tool, it's easy for tracks to become unsynchronized. Suppose your tracks are all over the place and you want to reset all them to start at zero. Select all the tracks, and then select **Tracks > Align Tracks > Align Tracks Together**. Then select **Tracks > Align Tracks > Align With Zero**. You could also select **Tracks > Align Tracks > Align With Cursor** to line them up at any arbitrary point.

This won't work if you have Link Tracks activated, which is indicated by a depressed Link Tracks button. Link Tracks may not be present in your version of Audacity; see the table of toolbuttons in Chapter 1 to learn more.

The Time Shift tool is a fast and easy way to move a track or a clip forward or backward in time. Simply click the Time Shift button in the Tools toolbar, and the cursor changes to a double horizontal arrow; drag your tracks or clips right or left. You can also drag clips to other tracks.

Another way to move a track or clip a precise amount is to prepend it with silence. Click at the point you want the silence to start, select **Generate > Silence**; enter the duration in seconds, milliseconds, samples, or frames; and then click **OK**. This will push the track to the right, which is like moving it backward in time.

When you are overdubbing, latency is always a problem. Audacity automatically time-shifts overdubbed tracks to compensate for latency. The default latency correction value is −130 ms, which probably is not correct for your system. You can adjust the latency correction value in the **Edit > Preferences > Recording > Latency correction** dialog.

How do you know the right latency correction value to use? One way is trial and error. A more precise method is to use a loopback cable. You need a cable to connect your playback output to your recording input. On an internal sound card, this is easy—line out to record in. For other recording interfaces, such as USB or FireWire, you'll have to find the correct type of cable and sort out your outputs and inputs.

Then set Latency Correction to 0. Make sure that the "Snap To" checkbox on the Selection toolbar is not checked. Select the Length radio button on the Selection toolbar and set the time parameter to hh:mm:ss + milliseconds.

Next, generate a metronome track 60 seconds long, 180 beats per second.

Then in the Transport menu, check the "Overdub" checkbox, select your recording interface for both the playback and recording devices on the Device toolbar, and press the **Record** button. You should see something like Figure 12-22.

When you're finished recording, zoom in until you can select the gap between a click on the top track and the its corresponding delayed click on the bottom track. If you're not comfortable using the mouse, use the SHIFT and arrow keys to mark the selection. (Use the arrow keys to move back and forth and up and down, and use SHIFT and the arrow keys to select.) You will see something like Figure 12-23. This shows a latency of 177 ms, which is a lot.

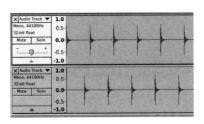

Figure 12-22: Generating a loopback overdub to make a good latency correction measurement

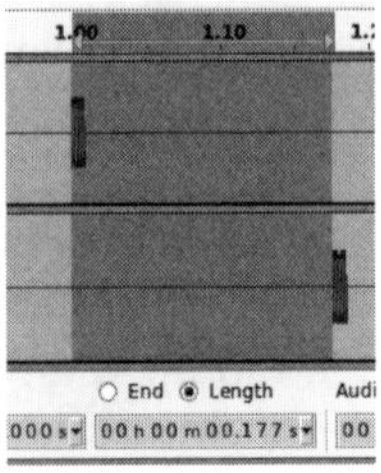

Figure 12-23: Measuring the latency between the two clicks on the click tracks

If you change your recording interface, you should repeat the latency tests, because different devices have different latencies.

Analyze Menu

The Analyze menu contains tools for analyzing your audio. I'll go over two of them that I think are fairly useful, Plot Spectrum and Silence Finder.

Plot Spectrum makes a nice colored graph showing the amplitudes of different frequencies. It has all kinds of different algorithms and functions to choose from. I ignore most of these and use a Hanning window, Spectrum algorithm, and 512 or 1024 Size. A smaller Size value shows more details. The option that is meaningful to me is Axis. Axis offers the standard choices of Logarithmic or Linear view. When I use Plot Spectrum, I'm looking for obvious indicators, not molecule-sized differences.

One handy use of Plot Spectrum is to measure your ambient noise. You can get an idea of your ambient noise level with the Input Level Meter in the main Audacity window, but Plot Spectrum gives you a lot more information. Set up your mics as usual, and then select **Transport > Timer Record** to record a 20-second sample. Plot Spectrum analyzes only 23.8 seconds at a time, so you could even set the timer to record 23.8 seconds. Figure 12-24 shows a graph of an ambient noise recording; hovering the cursor over any point shows the exact frequency, the note, and the decibels both at the cursor and at the nearest peak, which are displayed under the frequency scale.

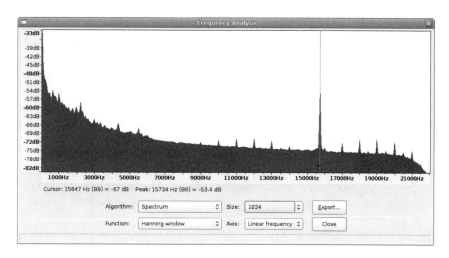

Figure 12-24: This Plot Spectrum of ambient noise shows the background noise covers a wide frequency range from 43 Hz to 22,000 Hz, from −32 dB to −82 dB, with the lowest frequencies being the loudest.

The peaks in Figure 12-24 indicate some kind of regular noise, and note how the loudest parts are in the lowest frequencies. Remember, this measures amplitude per frequency, not time, so don't read this like a waveform. It's showing you which frequencies are the loudest. Since the lowest frequencies are the loudest, I can switch to Logarithmic view to get a more detailed look at the lower frequencies (Figure 12-25).

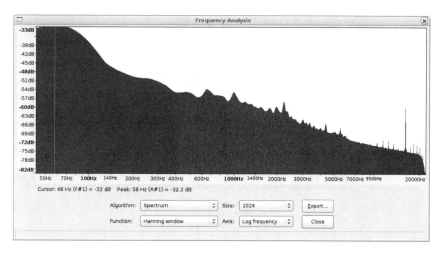

Figure 12-25: Logarithmic view shows the lower frequencies in more detail.

Anything over −40 dB is probably going to be noticeable in a recording, and now I know to look for the source of low-frequency noises. That turned out to be the subwoofer of the living room hi-fi. A pretty good level to aim for is −50 dB, and −60 dB guarantees that no background noises will be audible on your recordings.

Another good use for Plot Spectrum is to get a more precise idea of the dynamic range of a recording that you are going to apply compression to. Take readings of several of your highest peaks and lowest lows, and then you'll have some actual numbers to help you figure out what threshold to use. A good starting point is to split the difference: If your highest peak is −5 dB and your lowest is −35 dB, try a Threshold setting of −20 dB. Your own ears will tell you what works; this just gives you a reasonable place to start.

It can be helpful to generate sine waves at different frequencies just to get the hang of reading the Plot Spectrum graphs and to try the different algorithms and windows. Figure 12-26 shows what a 8,000 Hz sine wave at 0.8 amplitude looks like.

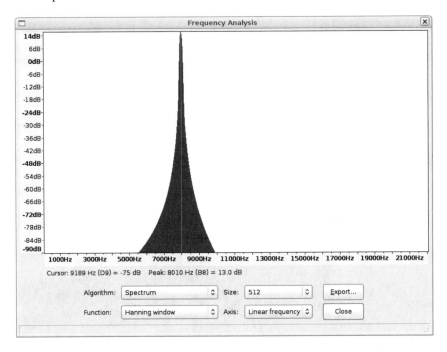

Figure 12-26: This "pure" 8,000 Hz sine tone actually includes frequencies from 6,000 to 10,000 Hz, and the frequency range narrows as amplitude increases.

As you can see, our "pure" tone isn't all that pure, with frequencies ranging from 6,000 Hz to 10,000 Hz. The frequency range narrows as amplitude increases, from 7,500 to 8,500 at −48 dB to 7,800 to 8,100 Hz at 0 db.

Silence Finder might be useful when you have a lot of songs on a single track and want to find the song breaks and create labels at the breaks automatically. Then you can select **Export** > **Multiple** to break up the track into individual songs. If you want to use the song names for labels, you will still have to type them yourself. It doesn't work very well if the silences are not clean and well defined. For example, Silence Finder would be a handy time-saver when you are converting vinyl LPs to CDs, but vinyl records often have enough noise in the song breaks to confuse it.

You can use Plot Spectrum to get an idea of the volume level in the song breaks and then set the Treat audio below this level as silence value with less trial and error. There is a funny little gotcha with this: Don't enter a minus sign, because that seems to be applied automatically (Figure 12-27).

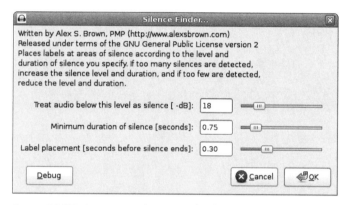

Figure 12-27: Some example settings for the Silence Finder

13

CONFIGURING LINUX FOR BEST AUDIO QUALITY

Linux audio is rather messy yet powerful. This chapter is a guide to getting everything working correctly for high-end audio production. Linux is a wonderful multimedia platform: It is stable, it is flexible, and if you use a lightweight graphical environment, you'll get better performance out of modest hardware. Although Linux audio has some rough edges, it is advancing rapidly, and it has its own universe of sophisticated audio software.

You can use whatever Linux distribution you want, because you can customize any Linux distribution to serve as your recording studio, depending on what hoops you're willing to jump through. The most important things you need, aside from Audacity and other audio software applications, are a real-time preemptible kernel for lowest latency and a few system configuration tweaks. You can configure and tune your favorite Linux distribution, or you can use one of specialized Linux distributions for multimedia production that takes care of the details for you.

I used Ubuntu while writing this book because it was the first distribution to bundle the FFADO drivers for FireWire recording interfaces. (I have the excellent Focusrite Saffire Pro 26 I/O for multichannel recording.) FireWire recording interfaces are great performers, but they present some special driver problems, so if you don't have one, don't worry about finding a distribution that includes FFADO. You can always add it later anyway.

NOTE   *The most important step is careful selection of your audio interface. Choose one that is well-supported on Linux. Life is too short to waste on something that doesn't want to work right. Visit the ALSA Sound Card Matrix (*http://www.alsa-project.org/ main/index.php/Matrix:Main*) to find supported sound cards. Also check out Appendix A for hardware information.*

Using Distributions with Real-Time Kernels

If your particular Linux distribution packages a *real-time kernel*, that takes care of the biggest hurdle. What is a real-time kernel? This is a kernel where *real-time scheduling* and *real-time preemption* are configured to favor audio recording for the lowest possible latency. Latency is inherent in computers because modern CPUs use *preemptive multitasking*; they perform one task at a time but switch back and forth between tasks so rapidly that they appear to be performing multiple tasks at once. Multicore CPUs smooth out this switching, but they still need help from the Linux kernel.

Because the Linux kernel continues to develop at warp speed, some folks are saying that a special real-time kernel really isn't necessary anymore because real-time features are integrated into the mainline kernel. You can get by without one if you strip your Linux system down to the essentials needed for audio production and use a modern multicore PC, gigabytes of RAM, and fast hard drives. I'll stick with real-time kernels for now, because they behave a little differently from general-purpose kernels.

Real-time preemption controls how tasks interrupt each other to get the CPU time they need. It's like a classroom of kids trying to get the teacher's attention, and the teacher can deal with only one at a time. A multicore CPU is like having more teachers. Interrupts are typically milliseconds in duration, which doesn't matter when we're typing a letter or editing a photograph but is enough to introduce defects into a recording. So, we can configure Linux to give the highest scheduling priority to audio functions.

There are latencies inherent in the inner workings of the kernel itself, which in modern kernels have become very small. So, it is possible to tune a Linux kernel for very low-latency audio recording, down to less than 10 milliseconds. Anything less than 20 is excellent.

Fedora and CentOS users should use Planet CCRMA packages (*http:// ccrma.stanford.edu/planetccrma/software/planetccrma.html*). Planet CCRMA (pronounced "karma") is a special collection of RPMs for Fedora and CentOS that includes a real-time kernel, all kinds of audio software, and up-to-date audio drivers. Just add the Planet CCRMA repositories to your system and then use Yum to install, update, and remove packages the usual way.

Arch Linux is a superior audio production platform, and it has its own special audio repository, ArchAudio. Red Hat, Mandriva, and openSUSE all package real-time kernels.

Ubuntu (and Kubuntu, Xubuntu, and all the rest of the family) provides a real-time kernel and related kernel modules; the bare minimum you need to get started with Audacity are these packages:

- *audacity*

- *linux-rt*

Once you have an rt kernel installed, add all human users who are going to be using Audacity to the *audio* group (in the */etc/group* file). Then add these lines to */etc/security/limits.conf*:

- `@audio - rtprio 99`

- `@audio - memlock 3000000`

The first line gives all members of the audio group the highest scheduling priority. The second value controls how memory is used.

- rtprio (real-time priority) values range from 0 to 99, with 99 being the most favorable priority. This is the very front of the line.

- memlock determines how much RAM the audio group locks up for itself, in kilobytes, and prevents it from writing to the much slower swap file. My system has 4GB RAM, so I set a limit of 3GB, or 3,000,000KB. Some how-tos say to set this to *unlimited.* This is a bit controversial, because it seems like common sense to leave some for system processes and nonaudio applications. A value of unlimited could also result in out-of-memory errors and interrupt your audio session. Some users report that setting any memlock value makes no difference.

Many how-tos also say to add one more line: `@audio - nice -19`. This isn't necessary because the rtprio function takes care of scheduling priority. It doesn't hurt anything to try it for yourself.

Then reboot to your new kernel. Note that if you are already running your rt kernel, all you need to do to activate your new group membership and changes to *limits.conf* is to log out and then log back in. Then verify your audio group membership:

```
$ groups
carla adm disk dialout cdrom audio plugdev lpadmin admin
```

Verify that your rt kernel is running:

```
$ uname -r
2.6.32-24-rt
```

The rt tells you this is a real-time kernel; this example is from Ubuntu 10.04. You should also keep a stock kernel installed. Using a different kernel is as easy as rebooting and choosing it from your boot menu. It will also help with troubleshooting, because you can try tasks that are giving you problems with different kernels to see whether they behave differently.

Specialized Multimedia Linux Distributions

There are several complete Linux distributions that are customized for audio and multimedia production. Some of them run from a CD, DVD, or USB stick, with a hard drive installation option. You should still verify audio group membership, */etc/security/limits.conf* settings, and a real-time kernel like we talked about in the previous section.

Here is a sampling of specialized multimedia Linux distributions:

- 64 Studio (*http://www.64studio.com/*)
- Ubuntu Studio (*http://www.ubuntustudio.org/*)
- dyne:bolic (*http://www.dynebolic.org/*)
- pure:dyne (*http://www.puredyne.org/*)
- Musix (*http://www.musix.org.ar/en/*)

64 Studio

64 Studio is a Debian-based distribution for all digital content creation, and it includes a huge assortment of audio, video, graphics, and publishing software. It supports both 32- and 64-bit architectures and runs on a wide range of PC hardware. The maintainers aim for stability rather than bleeding edge, so they issue updates conservatively. 64 Studio also builds and supports products such as the Trinity Indamixx digital audio workstation and the Lionstracs Mediastation.

Ubuntu Studio

Ubuntu Studio is akin to 64 Studio in having nearly every Linux multimedia application there is, except that it is based on Ubuntu, which in turn is derived from Debian. Ubuntu is more than warmed-over Debian; the Ubuntu development teams maintain its own patches and customizations. Ubuntu Studio uses more up-to-date packages than 64 Studio, so you get newer software releases and perhaps newer bugs. As with all things Ubuntu, there is a large and enthusiastic user base and good community support.

You can also add Ubuntu Studio packages to a regular Ubuntu system. Run $ `apt-cache search ubuntustudio` to see your options. The *ubuntustudio-audio* and *ubuntustudio-audio-plugins* metapackages should give you everything you need for audio production, with one important exception: The linux-rt kernel is not included, so you will have to install it separately.

dyne:bolic

dyne:bolic is a unique software project. dyne:bolic is not based on any other Linux distribution but is built from scratch from source code. That's just the beginning—dyne:bolic operates in its own creative ways. It uses only

Free software as defined by the Free Software Foundation. This is good news for users who want a system unencumbered by proprietary software. It runs from a CD and is optimized both for speed and low hardware requirements, requiring at a minimum a Pentium II 400 MHz computer or an Xbox game console. You can use it with either a Linux or Windows PC, you can save your data to a USB stick or local hard drive, and it has a hard drive installation option. Customization is not as simple as using Yum or Apt to install new software packages because you have to build a new CD image. It comes with good documentation and a friendly user community.

dyne:bolic is Rasta (*http://www.rastasoft.org/*) software. Jaromil, the main dyne:bolic developer, says this:

> But remember there is no Peace without Justice. This software is about Resistance in a babylon world which tries to control more and more the way we communicate and we share informations and knowledge. This software is for all those who cannot afford to have the latest expensive hardware to speak out their words of consciousness and good will. This software has a full range of applications for the production and not only the fruition of information, it's a full multimedia studio and has nothing to envy to other proprietary systems, because freedom and share of knowledge are solid principles for evolution and that's where this software comes from.

pure:dyne

pure:dyne was initially based on dyne:bolic but has evolved into a blend of Ubuntu and Debian. It runs from CD, DVD, USB stick, or a hard drive installation. It is more up-to-date than dyne:bolic and is optimized for modern i686 processors, though it will also run on older hardware. It is designed to be user-customizable and comes with tools to create customized images.

Musix

Musix is Debian based, for 32-bit systems. It comes on a live CD or live DVD, and it also has a hard drive installation option. Musix is also a 100 percent free operating system. It provides a lightweight desktop environment based on IceWM and the wonderful Rox filer, so it is suitable for modest hardware.

Building a Real-Time Kernel

If you don't want to use a multimedia Linux distribution and your favorite distro does not package a real-time kernel, you can build your own. A complete kernel-building how-to would be a whole chapter by itself, so I'm not going to try to stuff one into this chapter. You can easily find good how-tos; look for instructions specific to your distribution.

You'll need a proper build environment installed, kernel sources, and a copy of the configuration file for your current kernel. Once those are in place, you need the rt patch, which you can get from the mothership of the Linux kernel, *http://www.kernel.org/*. Go to the rt wiki at (*http://rt.wiki.kernel*

.org/index.php/Main_Page), and look for the "CONFIG_PREEMPT_RT Patch" download. It must have the same version number as your kernel sources. Once you have that, apply it to your kernel sources.

In your kernel makefile, set EXTRAVERSION equal to a value that tells you this is a real-time kernel, such as EXTRAVERSION = -rt. Then if your kernel version is 2.6.33.1, for example, your new kernel name will be linux-2.6.33.1-rt.

Now you are ready to configure your new kernel. Start with your existing kernel configuration and run the `make oldconfig` command; you don't need to start from scratch just to enable real-time preemption. Review your kernel configuration and enable Processor type and features > Preemption Mode (Complete Preemption (Real-Time)), and Processor type and features > Timer frequency (1000 Hz).

Then finish configuration, and compile and install your new kernel. That should be all there is to it, but review the rt wiki to make sure, because Linux kernel development is a fast-moving target. Keep your old stock kernel installed as well. You can have as many kernels as you want on your system, and if anything goes wrong, you'll have a good kernel to boot to.

Latency Is Not That Scary

Latency is not the great bugaboo that it is sometimes made out to be. One way to handle latency is to throw horsepower at it. A modern multi-core CPU, gigabytes of RAM, and fast hard drives can make latency almost disappear.

If that is not an option, it helps to understand when latency really is a problem and when it isn't. It matters when you are overdubbing. And even here Audacity helps with that, because it has a configurable latency correction in the **Edit** > **Preferences** > **Recording** dialog. (See Chapter 12 to learn how to measure and correct for latency.) It matters when you are playing a software synthesizer or playing any instrument through special effects plug-ins on your computer: When you press a key or strum a string, you want music to come out, not lag. It matters when you are monitoring a recording session, because you don't want what you hear to be out of sync.

In the **Edit** > **Preferences** > **Recording** dialog, there is a setting that affects latency called "Audio to buffer." Smaller buffers equal lower latency, but if they are too small for your CPU to handle, you'll get dropouts.

Latency doesn't matter so much during mixing or during multichannel recording where everything is plugged into a good recording interface that has a direct path to Audacity with no detours. It is more important to have a stable setup that doesn't crash in the middle of a recording session. If you can live with higher latencies in exchange for stability, that is a good trade. It's no good pushing latency levels down to the point of instability.

Interrupts are less of a problem when you run a clean system with everything turned off except what you need for audio production. (See "Linux System Tweaks" on page 287.)

JACK, the Jack Audio Connection Kit, has its own configuration options for latency and buffer size, which you can read all about in "Using JACK with Audacity" on page 276.

Sorting Out Linux Audio

In this book we use Audacity with ALSA and JACK. No PulseAudio, OSS, aRts, ESD, or whatever else might be lurking in the weeds.

The Linux audio landscape has been complicated for some years, with multiple subsystems and overlapping functionality, and now it is going through some significant changes. There is not a single Linux audio API that developers can target, but rather they must deal with a herd of audio servers and subsystems: the Open Sound System (OSS), the Advanced Linux Sound Architecture (ALSA), the Enlightened Sound Daemon (ESD) on Gnome, the analog Real time synthesizer (aRts) for KDE2/3, Phonon for KDE4, PulseAudio, and the JACK Audio Connection Kit.

ESD and aRts are entering retirement, so that thins the herd a bit, leaving PulseAudio (which runs on any Unix-type operating system), Phonon (KDE4) for controlling playback, and JACK for professional audio production. ALSA provides a common driver base for all of these that interacts directly with audio hardware, and it also provides a useful set of user tools, such as a mixer, device discovery, a simple player and recorder, and a speaker tester. PulseAudio is finding its way into many Linux distributions, such as Ubuntu and Fedora, and it looks like it will become the dominant desktop audio server.

PulseAudio is a sound daemon, while Phonon is a multimedia API supporting multiple audio frameworks, including PulseAudio. PulseAudio and Phonon provide playback mixers and routers and networked sound. Many Linux applications do not have audio device choosers. For example, the Firefox web browser only uses the default audio device. PulseAudio and Phonon let you control which audio device Firefox uses. I prefer to turn PulseAudio off when I'm using Audacity; "Turning PulseAudio and Phonon Off" on page 285 tells you how to do this.

What about OSS? Some folks prefer it, and you're welcome to give it a try. ALSA is better supported in Linux, and it includes OSS emulation for applications that want OSS.

NOTE *The Adobe Flash Player music player is buggy and unreliable. For example, Pandora Radio, the wonderful online music broadcaster, relies entirely on Flash. It is a great service, and I am happy to be a paid subscriber. But Flash Player is an ongoing source of trouble. It loses its connection to the audio system periodically, and it doesn't like changes in device routing, such as when changing from computer speakers to an external sound system. When it flakes out, it takes a either a browser refresh or a restart to get it going again. If you need an audio source for testing, you should look for something else.*

JACK is a professional-quality, low-latency (meaning it adds no latency to your sound chain) sound server for connecting audio hardware to audio production software. JACK does not run standalone but requires *alsa-base*. JACK supports multiple audio backends: OSS; FFADO (formerly Freebob) for using FireWire recording interfaces on Linux; PortAudio, which is a simple cross-platform audio API; and CoreAudio, the Mac OS X audio API. Audacity uses PortAudio.

Let's clear up some common confusions regarding PulseAudio and JACK. They address two different types of usage: PulseAudio is a device chooser and audio stream router for playback and recording, while JACK is an audio router for high-end audio production. JACK lets you route the output of multiple audio applications pretty much any way you want, so you can combine different synths and capture audio streams in various ways for recording. Pulse is CPU-intensive and creates too much latency for overdubbing and other latency-sensitive tasks, though both issues are improving as Pulse matures. It works fine for making simple recordings, and Audacity and JACK both support Pulse. You need the pulseaudio-module-jack plug-in for JACK support, which should be in your distro repositories.

When do you use JACK? You don't need it when your recording interface handles all the connections you need for your recording session. If everything plugs into a single recording interface, just point Audacity to it, and you're good to go. Though even here JACK can help by giving you flexible routing options, letting you mix the audio streams in different ways and making performance adjustments.

You need JACK when you are using a FireWire recording interface. You need it when you want to incorporate software audio applications into your Audacity recording session. (JACK has great MIDI support, though Audacity does not support MIDI.) A simple example that we'll go into in detail (in "Using JACK with Audacity" on page 276) is adding the excellent Hydrogen software drum machine to an Audacity recording session. If you want to use Hydrogen to create a drum track in Audacity, you need JACK to connect the two.

Using ALSA

ALSA has two parts: the low-level base that supplies sound card drivers and interacts directly with audio hardware and a higher-level interface that contains the userland tools. *alsa-base* and its dependencies should already be present, but you may need to install *alsa-utils* to get the userland tools. *alsa-utils* gives you alsamixer, aplay, speaker-test, arecord, and number of sound files for testing your speakers.

Open a terminal and type in **alsamixer** to open the mixer console, shown in Figure 13-1. ALSA runs in the console via an ncurses interface, which means it is completely keyboard controlled and does not require an X server. The top-left caption tells you a lot of useful information: your sound card and chipset, which set of functions you're viewing, and the values for the highlighted setting. Use the arrow keys to navigate back and forth. There are three views: Playback, Capture, and All. Press the TAB key to toggle between them. Pressing the ESC key closes alsamixer.

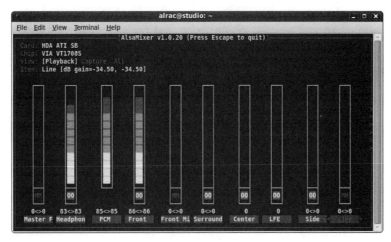

Figure 13-1: Using alsamixer *to configure onboard surround sound. On my system, all of the modules must be active—Surround, Center, LFE, and Side— for stereo sound to work, even though their volume controls have no effect.*

Press the F2 key to see detailed information on all your detected audio devices, as in Figure 13-2. Note that they are numbered from zero. Use the arrow keys to scroll up and down, and press the RETURN key to close the information window.

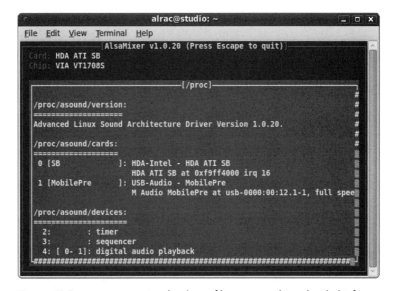

Figure 13-2: alsamixer *queries the /proc filesystem to show detailed information on your audio devices.*

Figure 13-3 shows the Playback configuration screen.

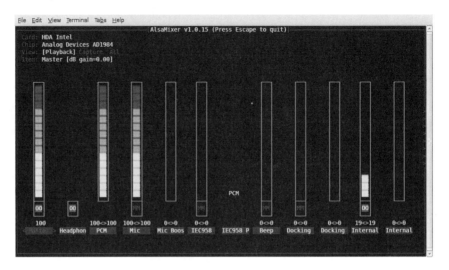

Figure 13-3: The alsamixer *playback screen controls muting and volume on playback devices.*

Setting Recording and Playback Levels in alsamixer

alsamixer only displays functions that your sound card is capable of performing. Here are the basic alsamixer commands:

- The little boxes with MM in the playback menu mean those functions are muted, or disabled. Toggle the M key to mute/unmute, and the MM turns to 00.

- 00 means zero volume, so use the up- and down-arrow keys to adjust it. PAGE UP increases volume by 5, PAGE DOWN decreases volume by 5, and END sets the volume to 0.

- When there are two channels on one slider, you can adjust each one independently. Q increases the left channel, and Z decreases it. E increases the right channel, and C decreases it.

- In the Capture screen, press the spacebar to select the active recording (Capture) device. There may be more than two options, so press it several times to see what your choices are.

- Press the F1 key to see a Help menu. F2 displays your */proc* information, which shows you what is actually detected and working, as well as device addresses.

Sometimes you will experience static or too-low volume that is caused by having unnecessary functions enabled. For example, the Playback screen for my ATI onboard sound shows a front mic volume control. When this is enabled, it causes static. When I'm using headphones, the Headphone control needs to be turned on, but changing the volume level has little effect, and I need to use both the Master and PCM volume controls. The Master volume control is not needed for the speakers, but the Headphone control is. Trial and error is about the only way to figure these things out, and lower-end sound cards are more troublesome and quirky than the better-quality ones.

Master vs. PCM

There is often confusion over Master and PCM playback settings. You usually need both Master and PCM to enable playback, though sometimes only the PCM slider has any effect. If the Master slider has no effect, this means either there is no hardware volume control built into your sound card or your sound card driver is lacking this functionality. Master is the master volume control, and PCM stands for *pulse code modulation*. Remember "Audio File Formats and Quality Settings" on page 25, where we learned about converting analog signals to digital representations? ALSA's definition of PCM sorts it out for us:

> Although abbreviation PCM stands for "pulse code modulation," we are understanding it as general digital audio processing with volume samples generated in continuous time periods.

So think of ALSA's PCM channel as a virtual sound card.

Multiple Sound Cards

If you have more than one audio interface, alsamixer numbers them from zero. For example, I have both onboard sound and the M-Audio MobilePre connected to a USB port. The MobilePre is #1, so to control it, I need to open alsamixer with this command:

```
$ alsamixer -c1
```

-c1 means "card number 1." How do you know what your card numbers are? One way is to query */proc*:

```
$ cat /proc/asound/cards

 0 SB           : HDA-Intel - HDA ATI SB
                    HDA ATI SB at 0xf9ff4000 irq 16
 1 MobilePre    : USB-Audio - MobilePre
                    M Audio MobilePre at usb-0000:00:12.1-1, full speed
```

Another way is to press F2 in alsamixer (Figure 13-2).

Adjusting Volume Levels

When you're adjusting recording and playback settings in Audacity, you can have alsamixer open at the same time, as Figure 13-4 shows. It's a fast way to tweak volume settings and to find out what the alsamixer settings actually control. In this example, a bit of trial and error showed me that the Mic Boost and the first Capture slider controlled the microphone recording volume and that this sound card has a real stereo microphone input with two channels. (Remember, the Q and Z keys raise and lower the volume on the left channel, and E and C control the right channel.)

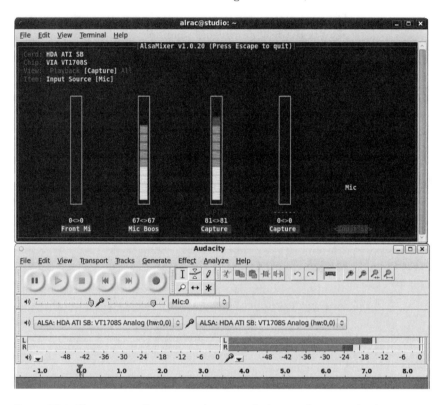

Figure 13-4: The alsamixer Capture window controls device selection and volume on recording devices. Here it is tiled with Audacity for controlling the recording volume level.

Even in a simple setup like this, there are multiple recording level controls, both in ALSA and Audacity. Keep alsamixer open for adjustments during recording.

NOTE   *If you need a good excuse to splurge on a dual-monitor setup, audio production is a great reason. You can have Audacity, JACK, and alsamixer on one screen and your other audio applications (like Hydrogen, other synths, special effects) on the second screen. Nice and tidy, and you don't have to keep moving things out of the way.*

Hardware Testing with alsa-utils

alsa-utils includes some good commands to help you troubleshoot and test your hardware. Keep alsamixer open to the sound card you are testing so you can quickly try different settings. The most common cause of no sound is because it is muted in alsamixer.

NOTE   *If you are running the JACK audio server, turn it off for these tests because these commands may not work when JACK is running. It is best to keep tests as simple as possible in any case.*

This is a quick and annoying way to verify that your default sound card and speakers work. It should generate some white noise:

```
$ cat /dev/urandom > /dev/dsp
```

CTRL-C stops it. A nicer way is to use aplay to play a WAV file of your choosing, like this:

```
$ aplay -t wav violin-summit.wav
```

-t means "file type," and your choices are voc, wav, raw, and au. wav is the default.

To see the PCM structure and a nice ASCII VU (volume units) meter, try this:

```
$ aplay -vv -t wav -V stereo violin-summit.wav
Playing WAVE 'violin-summit.wav' : Signed 16 bit Little Endian, Rate 44100 Hz, Stereo
Plug PCM: Soft volume PCM
Control: PCM Playback Volume
min_dB: -51
max_dB: 0
resolution: 256
Its setup is:
  stream : PLAYBACK
  access : RW_INTERLEAVED
  format : S16_LE
  subformat : STD
  channels : 2
  rate : 44100
  exact rate : 44100 (44100/1)
  msbits : 16
  buffer_size : 16384
  period_size : 4096
  period_time : 92879
  tstamp_mode : NONE
  period_step : 1
  avail_min : 4096
  period_event : 0
```

```
start_threshold : 16384
stop_threshold : 16384
silence_threshold: 0
silence_size : 0
boundary : 4611686018427387904
       +############## 46\%|48\%################+
```

-V stereo means "display stereo VU meter," which is represented by the hash marks. These represent the RMS volume levels (root mean square, or average volume over time), and the percentage values are the peaks. You can see that this is a stereo CD-quality file, or 2-channel 16 bits at 44.1 kHz.

What if you have more than one sound card? Use aplay -l to display the raw ALSA device information for all of your audio interfaces:

```
$ aplay -l
**** List of PLAYBACK Hardware Devices ****
card 0: SB HDA ATI SB, device 0: VT1708S Analog VT1708S Analog
  Subdevices: 2/2
  Subdevice #0: subdevice #0
  Subdevice #1: subdevice #1
card 0: SB HDA ATI SB, device 1: VT1708S Digital VT1708S Digital
  Subdevices: 1/1
  Subdevice #0: subdevice #0
card 1: MobilePre MobilePre, device 0: USB Audio USB Audio
  Subdevices: 0/1
  Subdevice #0: subdevice #0
```

ALSA devices are named in the format *interface:card,device*. Sound cards are numbered from zero. An ALSA interface is a PCM playback or recording device, a MIDI device, or a control device such as a mixer. The hw interface talks directly to the kernel, so this is the most direct way to test your audio hardware. This example sends a WAV file to the first ALSA interface, the ATI SB onboard sound chipset at hw:0,0:

```
$ aplay -vv -t wav -D hw:0,0 angeline-the-baker.wav
```

Sometimes you'll see an error message like this: Warning: rate is not accurate (requested = 44100Hz, got = 48000Hz) please, try the plug plugin. This means use plughw in place of hw:

```
$ aplay -vv -t wav -D plughw:0,0 angeline-the-baker.wav
```

hw makes no conversions of any kind—think of it as your literal playback device. It can do only what the hardware supports, so some audio files might sound weird or not play at all. plughw is a special ALSA plug-in that is like hw with extra powers; it can perform whatever conversions are necessary to play your files. aplay supports only voc, wav, raw, or au, so you might as well stick with WAVs.

This example plays a file on the second ALSA device, which in the example is the MobilePre:

```
$ aplay -vv -t wav -D hw:1,0 angeline-the-baker.wav
```

If there were a third audio interface, it would be hw:2,0.

Testing Speakers

The speaker-test command helps you determine whether your speakers are connected in the correct order. This example tests two-channel stereo:

```
$ speaker-test -t wav -D hw:0,0 -c2 -l1

speaker-test 1.0.20

Playback device is hw:0,0
Stream parameters are 48000Hz, S16_LE, 2 channels
WAV file(s)
Rate set to 48000Hz (requested 48000Hz)
Buffer size range from 64 to 16384
Period size range from 32 to 8192
Using max buffer size 16384
Periods = 4
was set period_size = 4096
was set buffer_size = 16384
 0 - Front Left
 1 - Front Right
Time per period = 2.732753
```

You should hear a pleasant woman's voice say, "Front left, front right." -c2 means two channels, and -l1 means run the test once.

This chipset supports 5:1 surround sound, so you can test this too:

```
$ speaker-test -t wav -D hw:0,0 -c6 -l1

speaker-test 1.0.20

Playback device is hw:0,0
Stream parameters are 48000Hz, S16_LE, 6 channels
Rate set to 48000Hz (requested 48000Hz)
Buffer size range from 6 to 5461
Period size range from 3 to 2730
Using max buffer size 5460
Periods = 4
was set period_size = 1365
was set buffer_size = 5460
```

```
0 - Front Left
4 - Center
1 - Front Right
3 - Rear Right
2 - Rear Left
5 - LFE
Time per period = 17.801733
```

You can test a single speaker with the -s option, like this example that tests the center speaker channel:

```
$ speaker-test -t wav -D hw:0,0 -c6 -s5 -l1

speaker-test 1.0.20

Playback device is hw:0,0
Stream parameters are 48000Hz, S16_LE, 6 channels
WAV file(s)
Rate set to 48000Hz (requested 48000Hz)
Buffer size range from 6 to 5461
Period size range from 3 to 2730
Using max buffer size 5460
Periods = 4
was set period_size = 1365
was set buffer_size = 5460
 - Center
```

Notice the clever gotcha: The speaker-test output numbers the speakers from zero, but for the -s option, you have to start from 1.

-t wav uses the included default WAV testing file; you might also try pink, which generates pink noise, and sine, which sounds like the sine wave tones from way back in the olden days of TV test screens. (Now they use infomercials. I miss the test screens.) You may specify different frequencies (in Hz) to use with the sine option, like this example that tests the subwoofer with a nice low 45 Hz tone:

```
$ speaker-test -t sine -f 45 -D hw:0,0 -c6 -s6
```

LFE means low frequency effects channel or low frequency emitter. This is the channel that handles low-pitched sounds ranging from 3 to 200 Hz. This is not the same as the physical port that you plug a subwoofer into, because the LFE signal can be routed to any speaker or speakers that support it.

Testing Recording

aplay has a companion command, arecord. Remember to check alsamixer for the correct settings, such as capture device and volume controls. If your computer has both front and rear microphone ports, alsamixer should have an option to select the correct one. In this example, two audio devices are detected:

```
$ arecord -l
**** List of CAPTURE Hardware Devices ****
card 0: SB HDA ATI SB, device 0: VT1708S Analog VT1708S Analog
  Subdevices: 2/2
  Subdevice #0: subdevice #0
  Subdevice #1: subdevice #1
card 1: MobilePre MobilePre, device 0: USB Audio USB Audio
  Subdevices: 1/1
  Subdevice #0: subdevice #0
```

This example makes a test recording with the MobilePre:

```
$ arecord -vv -fcd -V stereo -D hw:1,0 test.wav
Recording WAVE 'test.wav' : Signed 16 bit Little Endian, Rate 44100 Hz, Stereo
Hardware PCM card 1 'MobilePre' device 0 subdevice 0
Its setup is:
    stream        : CAPTURE
    access        : RW_INTERLEAVED
    format        : S16_LE
    subformat     : STD
    channels      : 2
    rate          : 44100
    exact rate    : 44100 (44100/1)
    msbits        : 16
    buffer_size   : 22050
    period_size   : 5513
    period_time   : 125011
    tstamp_mode   : NONE
    period_step   : 1
    avail_min     : 5513
    period_event  : 0
    start_threshold  : 1
    stop_threshold   : 22050
    silence_threshold: 0
    silence_size  : 0
    boundary      : 6206523236469964800
    appl_ptr      : 0
    hw_ptr        : 0
              +############## 43%|34%###########+
```

CTRL-C stops recording. -fcd means CD-quality, which is 2-channel 16-bit at 44.1 kHz. aplay plays back the test recording:

```
$ aplay -vv -t wav -V stereo -D hw:1,0 test.wav
```

ALSA Applications

ALSA creates a number of virtual interfaces for your sound card called *applications.* You can view these with aplay:

```
$ aplay -L
default:CARD=SB
    HDA ATI SB, VT1708S Analog
    Default Audio Device
front:CARD=SB,DEV=0
    HDA ATI SB, VT1708S Analog
    Front speakers
surround40:CARD=SB,DEV=0
    HDA ATI SB, VT1708S Analog
    4.0 Surround output to Front and Rear speakers
surround41:CARD=SB,DEV=0
    HDA ATI SB, VT1708S Analog
    4.1 Surround output to Front, Rear and Subwoofer speakers
surround50:CARD=SB,DEV=0
    HDA ATI SB, VT1708S Analog
    5.0 Surround output to Front, Center and Rear speakers
surround51:CARD=SB,DEV=0
    HDA ATI SB, VT1708S Analog
    5.1 Surround output to Front, Center, Rear and Subwoofer speakers
surround71:CARD=SB,DEV=0
    HDA ATI SB, VT1708S Analog
    7.1 Surround output to Front, Center, Side, Rear and Woofer speakers
iec958:CARD=SB,DEV=0
    HDA ATI SB, VT1708S Digital
    IEC958 (S/PDIF) Digital Audio Output
null
    Discard all samples (playback) or generate zero samples (capture)
```

That's a lot of applications! In ordinary use, these don't matter to the user, or to applications that send sound streams to ALSA, because everything is handled behind the scenes. You can test these the same way you tested the hw interfaces:

```
$ speaker-test -t wav -D default:CARD=SB -c2 -l1
```

```
$ speaker-test -t wav -D surround71:CARD=SB,DEV=0 -c8 -l1
```

```
$ aplay -vv -D surround51:CARD=SB,DEV=0 madbanjos.wav
```

On my system, `aplay` returned an identical set of applications for the MobilePre even though it doesn't support surround sound but only two-channel stereo. So, this works:

```
$ speaker-test -t wav -D front:CARD=MobilePre,DEV=0 -c2 -l1
```

But this doesn't:

```
$ speaker-test -t wav -D surround51:CARD=MobilePre,DEV=0 -c6 -l1
Stream parameters are 48000Hz, S16_LE, 6 channels
WAV file(s)
Broken configuration for playback: no configurations available: Invalid argument
Setting of hwparams failed: Invalid argument
```

Querying Your Sound Card

How do you know what abilities your sound card has, what bit depths and sample rates it supports, and how many channels? If you have no manual, you can query the */proc* filesystem to find out. Audio devices are in */proc/asound*. You can browse this directory in any file manager or from the command line. For example, on my system */proc/asound/card0* is the onboard ATI chipset. Reading */proc/asound/card0/codec#0* spits out a lot of information, and this snippet shows that this chipset supports high sampling rates and bit depths:

```
$ less /proc/asound/card0/codec#0
    rates 0x5e0: 44100 48000 88200 96000 192000
    bits 0xe: 16 20 24
```

The MobilePre looks like this:

```
$ less /proc/asound/card1/stream0
M Audio MobilePre at usb-0000:00:12.1-1, full speed : USB Audio

Playback:
  Status: Stop
  Interface 1
    Altset 1
    Format: 0x2 (16 bits)
    Channels: 2
    Endpoint: 3 OUT (ADAPTIVE)
    Rates: 8000, 9600, 11025, 12000, 16000, 22050, 24000, 32000, 44100, 48000
```

```
Capture:
  Status: Stop
  Interface 2
    Altset 1
    Format: 0x2 (16 bits)
    Channels: 2
    Endpoint: 5 IN (SYNC)
    Rates: 8000, 9600, 11025, 12000, 16000, 22050, 24000, 32000, 44100, 48000
```

How did I know which */proc* files to read? I tried 'em all. Do not try to edit */proc* files. */proc* is a pseudo-filesystem that exists only in memory, showing the current state of the kernel and operating system.

Using JACK with Audacity

The JACK Audio Connection Kit is a marvelous creation. Its original creator was Paul Davis, and now Mr. Davis and a team of developers support JACK. It is a professional-quality, low-latency sound server for Linux and any POSIX-compliant operating system such as Mac OS X, Solaris, AIX, HP-UX, and IRIX. Currently it runs well on Linux, Mac OS X, and FreeBSD.

NOTE *Phonon (in KDE4) doesn't get in the way when you're using Audacity, but Pulse-Audio often does, so see "Turning PulseAudio and Phonon Off" on page 285 to learn how to disable it.*

JACK acts like a switchboard to route audio signals between your audio hardware and software without adding latency. JACK can interface with only one sound card at a time, but it can interface with any number of software audio production applications, as long as they are JACK-aware. If you have a hardware device that controls all of your audio sources, then you don't need JACK. For example, in my little studio, my MobilePre can handle up to 4 inputs, and the Saffire Pro can handle as many as 26. If everything I want to record plugs into one of those, I don't need JACK. But suppose I want to use Hydrogen, the software drum kit for Linux? This is an excellent, fun drum synthesizer that is in most distro repositories, and it comes with a batch of demos so I can immediately start playing with it. How do I connect Hydrogen to Audacity? This is where JACK comes in.

The order in which you start your various applications is important. First get everything running and connected with JACK, and then Audacity always starts last. It seems we should be able to open Audacity after JACK is running, connect it to JACK, and then run whatever else we want. Sometimes this works because JACK updates new connections dynamically. But Audacity can be finicky, so I get everything else going first. Usually everything works fine on the first try, but sometimes Audacity throws out an error message about having the wrong sound device or some other unhappiness. Closing and reopening it usually takes care of this.

Let's use the MobilePre, since it is easy and simple. It has two microphones connected for vocal and a guitar, and then we'll add a nice drum track. First close all other audio applications, and then start JACK. JACK can run from the command line or the Qjackctl graphical interface. We'll use Qjackctl, which should appear in your system menu as JACK Control (Figure 13-5).

Figure 13-5: Qjackctl, the graphical JACK controller

If JACK starts up when you open Qjackctl, stop it, and then click the Setup button. You'll see a configuration dialog like Figure 13-6.

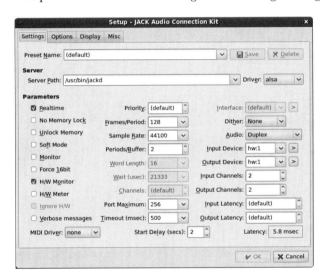

Figure 13-6: Selecting your audio devices and configuring JACK in the Qjackctl Setup dialog

1. Check Realtime in the Parameters column if you are using a real-time kernel. Otherwise, don't check it.

2. If there is a monitoring port on your recording interface, check H/W Monitor to enable it. Leave everything else in the first column unchecked.

3. In the next column, leave Priority at (default).

4. Leave Frames/Period at the default of 1024.

5. Set your sample rate and make sure it agrees with Audacity, Hydrogen, and any other audio software you are running. It must be a rate that your recording interface supports.

6. Periods/Buffer defaults to 2; leave it there for now.

7. Leave Port Maximum and Timeout at their defaults of 256 and 500, respectively.

8. In the third column, choose "alsa" as the driver.

9. Choose your input and output devices; click the little arrows to the right to display all of your sound devices.

10. Set the numbers of input and output channels, which are whatever your audio interface supports. The MobilePre has two channels for both input and output.

11. Click **OK**, and then click the **Start** button. It is normal to see a few xruns at startup. Click the Messages and Status buttons to display everything you need to know about your JACK session, both good and bad.

Now start up Hydrogen. Figure 13-7 shows what Hydrogen looks like.

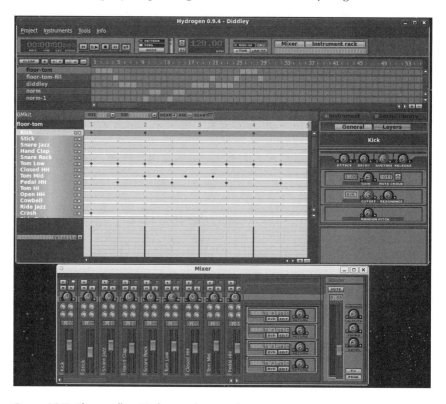

Figure 13-7: The excellent Hydrogen drum synthesizer

Hydrogen, like so many good Linux synths, lets you select which audio interface to use and which audio backend. Go into **Tools > Preferences > Audio System** and select JACK. Make sure that the Connect to Default Output Pair option is not checked (Figure 13-8).

Now go to **Project > Open Demo** and select a demo to play. Click the **Loop Song** button (to the right of the Fast Forward button) to keep it going while you're testing.

Next, click the **Connect** button in Qjackctl. Figure 13-9 is the result. The System clients are the MobilePre channels; System clients always represent your audio interface, and of course Hydrogen is labeled as Hydrogen. You should hear a drum track on the playback device selected in JACK. If you don't, connect the two Hydrogen out ports to two System playback ports. You will see lines connecting them.

Configure your playback device in JACK's Setup dialog, whether it's headphones, external speakers, or something else.

Figure 13-8: Configuring Hydrogen to use JACK

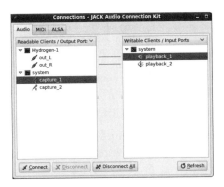

Figure 13-9: JACK and Hydrogen are running, and the Connections window shows that Hydrogen is connected to your audio interface's playback ports.

Now open Audacity. Configure Audacity to use JACK Audio Connection Kit: Hydrogen as the recording device and press the Record button. You should see something like Figure 13-10.

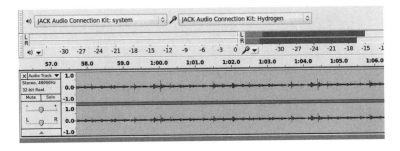

Figure 13-10: Audacity is recording the Hydrogen drum track, thanks to JACK.

Voilà! Audacity is recording Hydrogen! The JACK Connections window now displays two new PortAudio clients, which are the Audacity recording inputs (Figure 13-11).

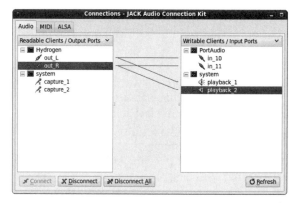

Figure 13-11: JACK connects Hydrogen and the MobilePre to Audacity. Audacity is represented by the two PortAudio clients. In this example, Hydrogen is being recorded through the two PortAudio clients and simultaneously playing back through the two system playback ports.

Usually the Connections window opens with the necessary connections in place and dynamically creates new ones on demand. If it doesn't or you want to change them, just click a Readable Client, then click a Writable Client, and then click the Connect button (or Disconnect). You can create multiple connections to each client.

The MobilePre is a two-channel recording interface that supports up to four inputs, so when I record something through the microphones, it goes into the same two-channel stereo track as the Hydrogen drum track.

In some of the older versions of Audacity and JACK, the recording device selection was not consistent. Sometimes selecting JACK Audio Connection Kit: System worked, and sometimes I had to use JACK Audio Connection Kit: <something else>, depending on what else I was using. So, you may have to try a bit of trial and error.

Connecting a FireWire Recording Interface

Figure 13-12 shows a simple example of using the Saffire Pro with JACK and Audacity. You need the ffado driver for Linux (*http://www.ffado.org/*) to use a FireWire recording interface, a FireWire adapter on your computer, and the correct cable to connect your FireWire device. There are two different FireWire plugs, 4-pin and 6-pin, and you must have the one that matches your device.

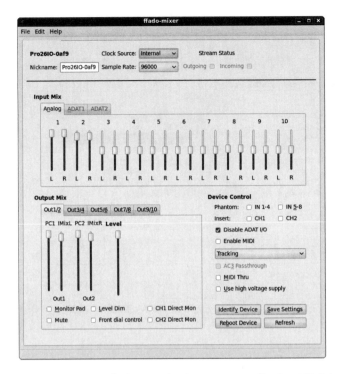

Figure 13-12: The ffado-mixer for the Focusrite Saffire Pro I/O 26

This is how I got the Saffire Pro working for this example. First I opened ffado-mixer, which comes with the ffado driver (Figure 13-12).

Then I started Qjackctl, opened the Setup dialog, changed the driver to "firewire," and changed the Interface to hw:0. Then I opened Hydrogen, set it to use JACK as the audio backend, and then started a demo loop playing. The Saffire has headphone-monitoring ports, so I plugged headphones into the appropriate port and created connections in the JACK connector to route Hydrogen's playback to the first two Saffire input ports, System playback_1 and playback_2.

Then I opened Audacity last of all. I made sure the sample rate was the same in ffado-mixer, JACK, and Audacity, and I configured Audacity to record four tracks, using the recording device JACK Audio Connection Kit: System.

Figure 13-13 shows what this all looks like: There are four PortAudio clients, which means that four recording channels are open in Audacity. Hydrogen is using two of them, and I have two mics plugged into the Saffire Pro for recording on the other two.

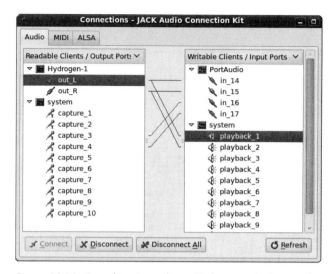

Figure 13-13: Everything is working: Hydrogen is both recording and playing back. Two mics are plugged into the Saffire Pro and are recording from Capture 3 and 4 to PortAudio 16 and 17.

Figure 13-14 shows how the recording session looks in Audacity.

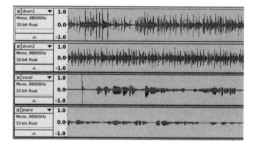

Figure 13-14: How it looks in Audacity: two Hydrogen tracks recording and two mic tracks

Creating Persistent Configurations

In the JACK Setup dialog, you can create and save multiple profiles. Make a configuration; then on the first tab enter a name for it in the Preset Name box, and then click **Save**. To open a profile, click the drop-down arrow in the Preset Name box.

The Connections window only displays your current setup and does not save it, so you must use the Patchbay to create saved connections. Get everything hooked up the way you like in Connections, open the Patchbay, and then click the **New** button. A little message will pop up and ask you if you want to save your current Connections configuration (Figure 13-15).

Click **Yes**, and this will automatically duplicate the current settings in the Connections window. You can modify this or accept it as is and save it with the Save button, giving it a unique name (Figure 13-16).

Figure 13-15: The Patchbay asks if you want to save your current Connections configuration.

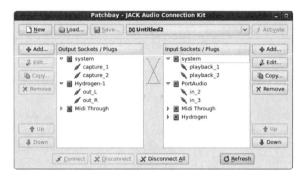

Figure 13-16: You can edit what the Patchbay captured for you or save it as is.

JACK Settings

Let's take a look at the settings in the Qjackctl Setup window in more detail.

- "Realtime" should be checked when you have a real-time kernel and unchecked when you do not.

- Leave "No Memory Lock" unchecked when you have abundant RAM, but if you're making do with a lower-end computer, try checking it if you get out-of-memory errors. This will prevent JACK from locking up memory for its exclusive use and freeing it for all processes that need it.

- Checking "Unlock Memory" helps lower-end computers by reclaiming memory slurped up by graphics toolkits like Qt and GTK, especially if you are running VST plug-ins under WINE. Leave it unchecked if you are not experiencing problems.

- Checking "Soft Mode" tells JACK to ignore xrun errors and keep running. Use this when you want JACK to keep running no matter what, for example during a live show. It's better to track down and fix the problem, but it's not always possible, and xruns don't always translate into big defects in your recording.

- You can check "Force 16-bit" when your audio interface supports only 16-bit recording. It's not required because JACK uses 32-bit internally, and it tests 32-, 24-, and 16-bit settings for your input and output devices. If your interface supports only 16 bits or you want to record at 16 bits, this will shush the routine error messages in the Messages window.

- "H/W Monitor" and "H/W Meter" enable hardware monitoring and metering for devices with support for these functions. For example, the MobilePre has a zero-latency monitoring port, so this activates it. H/W Meter is for ALSA devices only, and few recording interfaces support this feature.

- The default Priority is 10, and this maxes out at 89. Usually the default is fine. If you are running a real-time kernel, try setting it to 70 or greater to see whether it makes any difference.

- Frames/Period controls your balance between lower latency and fewer errors. The default is a buffer of 1,024 frames per second sent from JACK to your sound card, and the lowest possible value that is supported by PC hardware is 64. For lower latency, you want a lower value. If you see a lot of xruns in the Messages window, then increase this to a higher number until you have no *xruns*. An xrun is either a buffer overrun or an underrun, and xruns are audible as crackles and pops. On my system, JACK performs well at 128 frames, which results in very low latency. One audio frame is one sample times the number of channels, so a two-channel recording has two samples per frame. A *period* is a CPU processing cycle, so a Frames/Period rate of 128 results in a buffer size of 128 samples per channel, for a total of 256 samples per period for two channels. To get the buffer size in bytes, multiply Frames/Period by Periods/Buffers by 4.

- The Sample Rate setting must equal your Audacity sample rate and be supported by your recording interface. Higher sample rates put a heavier load on your CPU and may require higher values in Frames/Period and Periods/Buffers.

- Periods/Buffers is an interesting bit of memory management. JACK divides the memory buffer into periods and transfers data in units of periods. The default is two periods per buffer. More periods equals higher latency and greater stability. Try different values in combination with Frames/Period to get latency down. For example, if it takes a high Frames/Period value to get xruns down, like 2,048, try increasing Periods/Buffers to 3 or 4, and try lowering Frames/Period.

- Every input or output connection is a port. The default is 256 ports, which is more than enough for most mortals, and you can have as many as 1,024.

- Timeout controls how long JACK waits to kill an application during periods of heavy congestion. The default is 500 milliseconds.

- The driver is set to whatever driver your recording interface uses. Free-bob is the old version of the FFADO driver for FireWire interfaces, so select "firewire" since Freebob is obsolete (unless you are running an old system with actual old Freebob drivers). "dummy" is a fake driver for testing JACK.

- The Interface drop-down is active only when you select (default), meaning the ALSA default, for your Input and Output devices. Then you have a few extra choices such as */dev/dsp* and */dev/oss*. These are really not relevant in modern Linux systems, but JACK supports them if your system supports them.

- Dither can make 16-bit recordings sound better; it is analogous to anti-aliasing fonts or dithering in graphical images. Don't use dither for higher-bit depths because it is unnecessary, and they will sound worse. Think of it as blending the rough edges for a cleaner sound. Shaped dither is considered to be the best, but it is also the most CPU-intensive. Triangular is a good compromise between quality and CPU cost, and rectangular is lightweight and makes the smallest alterations. You don't have to use dithering, but it doesn't hurt to try it. Audacity also has dither, so be sure to use only one or the other.

- On the Audio menu, you can choose Duplex, Capture Only, and Playback only. Usually Duplex works fine, but you can try the other settings to see whether there are any performance improvements.

- Pick your Input and Output Devices from the drop-down menus (the little arrows on the right).

- Input Latency and Output Latency are for increasing latency. You might want to fiddle with these to bring your Input and Output streams into synchronization, especially when overdubbing or applying special effects.

Turning PulseAudio and Phonon Off

PulseAudio can be a stubborn little daemon. The man page says you can turn it off with the command `pulseaudio --kill`. But depending on your particular Linux distribution, it won't stay killed; instead, it respawns itself. This is how it works on Ubuntu 10.04: It has a normal init script to start it at boot, */etc/rc2.d/S03pulseaudio*. But when you try controlling this the normal way, it doesn't work, because running `/etc/init.d/pulseaudio stop` doesn't stop it. Removing */etc/rc2.d/S03pulseaudio* doesn't prevent it from starting at boot. Fortunately, I am even more stubborn and have figured out how to control stopping and starting Pulse. I don't want to remove it; I want it to run when I want it to run. (If you want to remove Pulse, it shouldn't hurt anything to do so.)

First look for a graphical control panel for Pulse with an option to disable it. This is missing from my Ubuntu 10.04 installation but present on Fedora and other distros. If your system has this, it might be all you need.

If there is no graphical control panel with an option to disable pulse, open */etc/pulse/client.conf*, change `autospawn = yes` to **autospawn = no**, and set daemon-binary to **/bin/true**. Make sure they are uncommented, like this:

```
autospawn = no
daemon-binary = /bin/true
```

Next, to stop it from starting at boot requires several steps. First remove the relevant /etc/rc*.d/S*pulseaudio link for your usual runlevel or rename it to a "kill" link. This prevents init from starting Pulse. On my system, that looks like this:

```
# mv /etc/rc2.d/S03pulseaudio /etc/rc2.d/K03pulseaudio
```

How do you know your runlevel? Use the **runlevel** command:

```
$ runlevel
N 2
```

That means runlevel 2, which is controlled by the links (which must be links to files in *etc/init.d*, not the files themselves!) in */etc/rc2.d/*. Your distro may have a nice graphical services manager, which is a good thing to use.

On Ubuntu 10.04, there is one more startup file to dispense with: */etc/ X11/Xsession.d/70pulseaudio*. This starts Pulse when a Gnome session starts. Move this file to a different directory, like your home directory. Don't delete it because you might want it again someday.

Other distros customize Pulse in different ways, so if these instructions don't work, then look for help specific to your distro. There is no shortage of it because a lot of users are struggling with this. Another little trick, when you find scripts that start PulseAudio, is to change the binary that they call from */usr/bin/pulseaudio* to */bin/true*. This is a nice little executable whose only job is to "do nothing, successfully." It keeps the scripts happy, and it's a convenient placeholder if you ever want to change it back.

Now that you have purged all the startup scripts, how do you stop and start PulseAudio? It's as easy as pie:

```
$ pulseaudio --kill
$ pulseaudio --start
```

Phonon is a different kettle of clams. Phonon exists only on KDE4, and it is impossible to remove because virtually all of KDE4 depends on it. It is not necessary to stop or remove Phonon in any case, because it uses only a tiny bit of system resources and adds no latency to your audio chain. It does have one annoying habit—when a sound daemon like Pulse or JACK takes control of a sound card, Phonon freaks out and emits an error message about how that sound card is missing, and it wants to remove the sound card from its menus. Just click **Cancel** to shush it.

Linux System Tweaks

Linux is a pretty efficient operating system, so you don't need to go to heroic lengths to make it get out of its own way. However, there are a few things you can do to ensure the best possible performance.

High-powered PC hardware is always good and is cheaper than high-end audio devices. My audio workstation has an AMD Phenom X3 2.4 GHz CPU, 4GB of RAM, and a terabyte's worth of SATA II hard drives. Those extra cores make a nice difference, because even though Audacity is not optimized for multicore processors, those extra cores mean faster, smoother multitasking. I also have an old laptop with a 1.4 GHz CPU, 1GB of RAM, and a slower hard drive. This handles up to four-channel 16/44.1 recording capably, but at higher bit depths or sampling rates it tends to stall. I consider a 1 GHz CPU and 512MB of RAM to be the bare minimum for music recording and editing. For podcasts and spoken-word recordings, you can go as low as 128MB RAM and a 500 MHz CPU.

Turn off your screensaver and all fancy video effects. All that Compiz-Fusion bling is pretty, but it gets in the way of good audio. In fact, you should turn off everything that is not absolutely needed: Don't run other applications, and turn off unnecessary services. There usually isn't too much cruft; Bluetooth, wireless daemons on systems without wireless devices, and Wacom tablet daemons are the most common on-by-default services that most users don't need.

Both KDE and GNOME are heavy-duty desktops that feast on CPU and memory, so you can slim your system down by using a lighter-weight graphical environment such as Xfce, IceWM, LXDE, Fluxbox, or any of the many other lightweight Linux graphical environments.

Video is the single most demanding system on your PC, so you might want to upgrade to a better video card. Many lower-end systems use shared system memory instead of a dedicated graphics processing unit (GPU). In other words, they use some of your system RAM to process video, and this is quite a bit slower because it places an extra load on your system RAM and CPU, both of which are considerably slower than a GPU. GPUs are so much faster that they are used to build clusters for very fast, very powerful, high-end scientific calculations.

Depending on your distribution, you should have a good graphical system resources monitor so you can see where your system resources are being used. The good old-fashioned top command is still a useful tool for viewing active processes and how much system resources they are using. After starting top, press 1 to see all the cores in a multicore CPU:

```
$ top

Tasks: 232 total,   1 running, 231 sleeping,   0 stopped,   0 zombie
Cpu0  :  3.7%us,  0.7%sy,  0.0%ni, 95.7%id,  0.0%wa,  0.0%hi,  0.0%si,  0.0%st
Cpu1  :  7.6%us,  0.7%sy,  0.0%ni, 90.1%id,  1.7%wa,  0.0%hi,  0.0%si,  0.0%st
Cpu2  :  0.0%us,  0.7%sy,  0.0%ni, 99.3%id,  0.0%wa,  0.0%hi,  0.0%si,  0.0%st
```

```
Mem:   4056672k total,  1602700k used,  2453972k free,   171880k buffers
Swap:  7092636k total,        0k used,  7092636k free,   655412k cached


  PID USER      PR  NI  VIRT  RES  SHR S %CPU %MEM    TIME+  COMMAND
17132 alrac     20   0  663m  35m  22m S    8  0.9  0:27.99 audacity
 2208 root      20   0  181m  83m  14m S    3  2.1 32:02.89 Xorg
10683 alrac     20   0  620m 147m  28m S    1  3.7  4:37.10 firefox
 2763 alrac     20   0  212m  10m 8276 S    1  0.3  3:00.33 multiload-apple
```

This shows that all is well. The summary at the top tells us many things: One process is running, and the rest, all 231 of 'em, are sleeping. Three CPU cores are chugging away.

All of these fields are explained in the nice man page, man top. Your version of top may display different fields, but it is still the same top command. The top section is the summary, and the bottom section is the task area.

CPU states (in the summary) are fun to examine in detail, but the main fields to keep an eye on are the us, or user field, which shows the load per CPU, and the sy, or system field, which shows the load from kernel processes. If you are seeing sy values greater than 10 percent consistently, you should track down the cause, because ordinarily it should be in the single digits.

The Mem and Swap fields tell you whether your physical RAM is sufficient. As long as Swap usage is zero and your Mem is not maxed out, that is ideal for audio processing, since RAM is many times faster than a swap file, which is on your hard disk.

Down in the task area, you see information on every process on your system. Again, don't go crazy on the minute details, but look at the biggest users at the top. This quickly reveals who the CPU and memory hogs are. Web browsers can be awful hogs in this era of lardy, script- and Flash-heavy websites, so shut 'em down. Audio processing chews up a lot of CPU cycles, so that's the main thing to keep an eye on. If you're hitting greater than 75 percent consistently, think about upgrading your CPU. The Linux kernel and most CPUs don't mind working that hard, but at that level you're probably noticing slower performance.

You can tune your swap file size a bit for better performance. If you have 512MB of RAM or less, make your swap file size at least equal to your RAM size. If you have 1GB of RAM or more, make your swap file no larger than half your RAM. But don't remove your swap file entirely—laptops need them for suspend and hibernate, and if you ever use up all of your physical memory, that swap file might save your recording session.

If you are using a PCI sound card, check your motherboard manual to find a slot that does not use shared interrupts. PCI-Express sound cards are great because PCI-E uses dedicated buses, rather than shared buses like the old PCI 2.0 standard. There are not a lot of PCI-E sound cards yet; the RME HDSPe MADI series, for one example, is first-rate and works in Linux.

Don't use networked file shares, except for storing backups of your audio files, because they're too slow.

The Tangled History of Linux Audio

The original Linux audio subsystem was Sound Blaster 16, which "just happened" because SB16 sound cards had the best support and a nice API. Those of us who are old enough to remember i386 PCs might also remember that competing brands used SB16 emulation because it was the path of least resistance. This evolved into the Open Sound System (OSS), which is portable across all Unix and Unix-type operating systems. It still exists and is maintained, and it is often confused with the OSS-compatible module in ALSA.

OSS fell out of favor as sound cards got cheaper and depended more on software to handle mixing, instead of doing the mixing in hardware. And so ESD (Gnome) and aRts (KDE) were born; these took care of mixing before sending audio streams to OSS. However, this complicated matters because Linux developers now had three different sound systems to deal with. The Simple DirectMedia Layer (SDL) was then invented as a portability layer that could use any audio backend, but it has some limitations that prevent it from ascending the throne as the Great Linux Audio Uniter. Like everything else in life, it hasn't gone away but is still used in some applications. You probably have it on your own systems.

Then OSS went closed source, and users had to pay money for it. That was the last straw for hardy Linux developers, who retaliated by inventing ALSA. So, that is how ALSA became the standard Linux audio subsystem. A good way to start a flame war is to ignite an OSS versus ALSA debate—a lot of folks still have strong passions on the subject.

OSS 4.*x* became Free software again when it was released under the GPL for Linux in 2007, and now there are two versions: the GPL version and a commercial version that includes some non-Free drivers. Some users claim that their music sounds better with OSS and that it is simpler and better and easier to use. I think a lot of that is wishful thinking, but if you like OSS, I won't think less of you.

I prefer plain old ALSA. It is the default in virtually all Linux systems, and it works. As always with Linux, do your homework before you buy to make sure you purchase well-supported hardware. The ALSA project has a supported sound cards matrix at *http://www.alsa-project.org/main/index.php/ Matrix:Main.*

ESD is the old Gnome and Enlightenment sound server, and it runs on top of ALSA. It can manage multiple sound streams and networked playback. PulseAudio has replaced ESD in GNOME.

aRts also manages multiple streams and networked playback. Don't use aRts because it increases latency beyond acceptable levels and because it is doomed—it has been unmaintained for some time now and is outdated. Phonon replaces aRts in KDE4. Phonon is not a sound server or an API but is intended to be a universal interface for all audio and video playback servers and subsystems. Phonon doesn't get in the way, so you can leave it alone.

The future of desktop playback audio for Linux is cloudy. PulseAudio is poised to become the standard sound manager for desktop Linux, but some say there are still some deeper problems to resolve that Pulse can't fix. So, don't be surprised by anything.

Sound Cards

Please visit Appendix A to learn about sound cards that are well supported on Linux, from low-budget to high-end. Remember, it is very important to shop carefully and purchase hardware that is well supported in Linux. There is a lot of great quality audio hardware that works in Linux—life is too short to waste on low-quality or poorly supported audio gear.

14

CONFIGURING WINDOWS FOR BEST AUDIO QUALITY

Microsoft Windows users are in an interesting position right now. Windows XP is still the most popular Windows version, despite being a Methuselah in computer years as it was first released in 2001. Microsoft has tried several times to retire it, but it won't go away. In July 2010, Microsoft announced an extension of support for XP SP3 through April 2014. XP will continue to be a downgrade option for Windows 7 buyers for the length of Windows 7's original equipment manufacturer (OEM) life span, which ends two years after the next Windows version ships. So, XP is going to be with us for a long time yet.

There are compelling reasons to stick with XP on your audio production computer. It is frugal of system requirements, needing less than 5GB for the operating system and service packs, and it runs acceptably with a 1 GHz CPU and 512MB RAM. Put it on a dual-core laptop with a gigabyte of RAM, and you have a capable portable recording studio.

Windows Vista didn't get much traction in the marketplace. At the time this was written, audio hardware manufacturers were finally catching up and releasing Vista drivers for their products. Audacity 1.3.*x* runs fine on Vista. But Vista is a system resources hog, eating up a good 12+GB of hard drive space just for itself. Officially, it needs a minimum of a 1 GHz CPU and 512GB RAM for Vista Home Basic or 1GB RAM for other editions, but if that is all you have, it will feel like slogging through deep sand. It needs a 2 GHz CPU and 2GB RAM just for basic chores such as email and web surfing. I recommend a minimum 2 GHz dual-core CPU and 4GB RAM for running Audacity on Vista.

Vista system requirements also apply to Windows 7. It's not very different from Vista; it's more polished, memory management is a little better, User Account Control is less annoying, and it boots up a little faster. The Sound control panel has a nice extra feature, a Communications tab with simple auto-duck settings for your playback device. You can configure it for tasks such as automatically muting all other sounds when you receive a Skype call.

Enabling MP3 Support

Because of patent encumbrances on the MP3 audio format (or more precisely, MPEG-1 Audio Layer 3), an MP3 encoder is not included with Audacity. However, you can easily get the LAME MP3 encoder, which is a high-quality, cross-platform free software MP3 encoder and decoder. One way to get it is to follow the instructions on the Audacity download page. Another way is from inside Audacity, by exporting a file as MP3. If LAME is not present on your system, you'll see a dialog like the one in Figure 14-1.

Click the **Download** button to go directly to the LAME download page. You can download either a zipped archive or an uncompressed archive. The installer is a standard Windows *.exe* file; just download it, double-click the downloaded file, and go through the installation steps. It will put LAME into *\Program Files\Lame For Audacity*. You can verify that it installed successfully by looking at the **Edit** > **Preferences** > **Libraries** dialog. Click MP3 Library: **Locate**, and it will display the full file path (Figure 14-2).

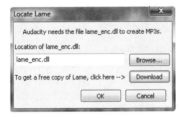

Figure 14-1: To install LAME from inside Audacity, click the **Download** button in the MP3 Export dialog.

Figure 14-2: After you install LAME, the Libraries dialog shows the full file path.

Enabling WMA, M4A/M4P Support

Audacity offers native support for open, unencumbered audio codecs and formats such as WAV, AIFF, Ogg Theora, and FLAC. But just like with MP3s, Audacity cannot ship with support for closed, proprietary, or patent-encumbered formats such as Windows Media Audio (WMA), M4A (lossy, compressed format), or M4P (M4A with DRM added). M4A and M4P are the default formats for Apple's iTunes store. They use the Advanced Audio Coding (AAC) codecs. No licenses or payments are required to distribute recordings in any form that use AAC, but anyone who makes an AAC encoder is required to purchase a patent license. Open source encoders get around this by releasing source code rather than a ready-to-use binary application and by hosting their download servers in friendly countries. Many countries do not enforce U.S. software patent laws, or even recognize the validity of software patents, and expressly allow reverse-engineering. So when it comes to figuring all this out, the Magic 8 Ball has the definitive answer: "Reply hazy, try again."

The short story is you can add support for a large number of nonfree and encumbered audio (and video) file formats by installing FFmpeg. Audacity has FFmpeg support built in, and you install it the same way as LAME. Just like LAME, it will be placed into *\Program Files\FFmpeg for Audacity*.

Both LAME and FFmpeg can be installed, and their locations on your system can be verified from **Edit** > **Preferences** > **Libraries** (Figure 14-3).

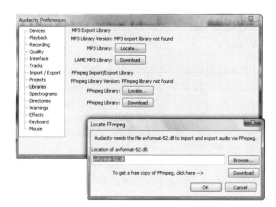

*Figure 14-3: FFmpeg and LAME can also be installed from **Edit** > **Preferences** > **Libraries**.*

Low-Latency Recording and Audio Driver Fun

Making recordings on computers means you have to care about drivers. A lot.

The standard Windows Multi-Media Extensions (MME) sound system supports two-channel 16-bit 44.1Hz recording. This is an old system that has been around since Windows 3.1. Then Microsoft developed the Windows

Driver Model Kernel Streaming (WDM/KS) and Enhanced Windows Driver Model (EWDM) drivers for Windows 2000 and newer. Audacity supports all of these. For recording more than two channels simultaneously, you want sound cards with full EWDM support. Most audio devices claim WDM support, but that doesn't always mean EWDM or WDM/KS, so they may not support recording from more than two inputs at the same time.

The Audio Streaming Input/Output (ASIO) driver is a high-quality, low-latency audio interface for Windows. Unfortunately, Audacity cannot ship with support for it because it is a closed, proprietary driver. So, you have two options: Stick with devices that support EWDM or WDM/KS, or compile Audacity with ASIO support yourself. To do this, you need the ASIO software developer's kit (SDK) from Steinberg, the company that owns the ASIO driver, and the latest Audacity source code from its CVS repository on SourceForge. You'll also need Microsoft Visual C++ 8, which is part of Visual Studio, to compile Audacity on Windows.

You'll have to register for a developer account on Steinberg.net before you can download the ASIO SDK. This is free and easy. Follow the instructions on the Audacity download page to get the latest Audacity source code. Then find the *win\compile.txt* file in the Audacity source tree, because it gives detailed instructions for building Audacity with ASIO support.

NOTE *There are some licensing issues you must be aware of. You can build your own copies of Audacity with ASIO support for personal use only: You cannot distribute them. This would violate both Audacity's license (the GPL) and Steinberg's license for ASIO. The Audacity maintainers encourage users to email Steinberg and politely request that it open source the ASIO driver.*

The cheap and easy way is to ask a friend who already has Microsoft's Visual Studio to help you. It may sound like a lot of trouble to compile Audacity to include ASIO support, but for someone who already knows their way around Visual Studio, it's pretty simple. Do you need ASIO support in Audacity? No, if you shop carefully, you can find recording interfaces with good-quality EWDM or WDM/KS drivers. Just having an ASIO driver doesn't guarantee that a device will perform well, because there are bad ASIO drivers. There are also bad EWDM and WDM/KS drivers, so do your homework before purchasing anything.

If you can find a way to enable ASIO support in Audacity, you'll have a lot more hardware and configuration options. A lot of higher-end sound cards support multiple drivers, including ASIO and the WDM family, so you can try different ones to see which ones perform the best.

Tuning Windows for Best Performance

Good audio recording requires a clean, well-performing computer that is not bogged down with unnecessary applications and services. Poor Windows is famous for getting loaded down with useless cruft, so we're going to review how to give it a good housecleaning.

A common cause of slow performance is video controllers that use shared system memory. These suck up both CPU cycles and RAM. If you have one of these, it will be worth the money to get a discrete graphics controller; the difference in performance will be large and noticeable, because the processing load will be handled by the video card. If you have cheapo shared-memory video, you should be able to upgrade, whether it's on a laptop or desktop PC. Your laptop will have very specific requirements, which you should be able to find out from your manual or the manufacturer's website. A desktop PC should offer more flexibility.

You have to match your video card to your motherboard, because there are several different types of PCI slots for desktop PC video cards: PCI, AGP, and PCI-e. You have to match both the slot and the correct voltage. Also make sure there is enough room for your new video card, because some of them are monsters with giant cooling fans. These giant beasts are for gamers, not audio production rigs. Cheap and small will work fine. You may need to go into your system BIOS to disable onboard video, if you are already using that. If all of this sounds like a foreign language to you, you might look for a knowledgeable friend to assist or even pay a professional.

Always have the latest Windows updates installed, especially service packs. Make sure you have the latest drivers for your audio devices. Run Defrag and Disk Cleanup periodically.

Turn off everything that is not essential for recording: other applications, screensaver, antimalware, system maintenance applications, firewall, web browser, email, "entertainment" crapware, adware, fancy special effects—everything. Virus checkers and Windows firewalls are notorious system resource hogs, but disabling them obviously leaves your system unprotected so you'll want to disconnect from any networks. Don't forget to turn off wi-fi and Bluetooth. Some laptops have nice physical switches to turn these off; otherwise, go into the Network Connections control panel to disable them. If you need to stay connected, you're stuck with keeping your protections turned on.

Raise Audacity's priority in the Task Manager. To bring up the Task Manager, press CTRL-ALT-DELETE. Press this combination only once, or Windows will reboot. Go to the Processes tab in the Task Manager and right-click the entry for Audacity (Figure 14-4). The default priority is normal, and you should be able to raise it to High without making other processes unhappy. Raising it to Realtime seems like the obvious choice, but it makes my system unstable. You may have better results.

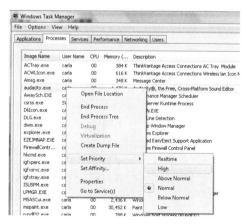

Figure 14-4: Raising Audacity's priority in the Task Manager

You can safely disable a number of Windows services that consume memory and CPU cycles with little benefit to you, and some are even security risks. Third-party software vendors love to choke Windows with all kinds of junk. You can look at the Processes tab in the Task Manager to see what is using up the most CPU and memory, and then a quick web search should tell what the service is for and whether it's something you need to keep or can evict. We'll look at some common offenders in detail in the next two sections.

Tuning Windows XP

First we'll start with some easy stuff: In Windows XP, right-click My Computer and select Properties. Click the Advanced tab, and then click the Performance **Settings** button (Figure 14-5). On the Visual Effects tab, select "Adjust for best performance." This turns off the basic Windows XP eye candy.

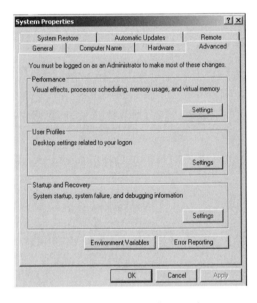

While you're still in Performance Options, go to the Advanced tab. By default the Windows paging file is dynamic and changes its size according to demand. Change it to a fixed size in the Virtual memory menu; this gives you a little faster performance. If you have 512MB RAM or less, set your swap file size to 1.5 times your RAM. For 1GB to 4GB, make it half your RAM. For more than 4GB, try a minimal size like 512MB. You want Audacity using your nice fast RAM, not slow paging files.

Figure 14-5: Fine-tuning Windows XP by turning off unnecessary and dangerous services

NOTE   *The paging file is virtual memory. If Windows runs out of RAM, it uses the paging file that is on your hard drive. Reading and writing to a hard drive are many times slower than using RAM, so it is always better to have more RAM than to have a bigger paging file.*

Now leave Performance Options and go to the System Restore tab. I recommend disabling System Restore by checking the "Turn Off System Restore on all drives" checkbox, though if you want to leave it on, that's okay. In my experience, it takes up disk space and slows down your system a little bit without being all that useful, because it seems that failures and problems are faithfully preserved in System Restore. Your best protection, as always, is keeping regular data backups on external media.

Next, go to the Automatic Updates tab and turn them off. This means you have to remember to run updates manually—don't forget! You don't want the updater to kick in during a recording or editing session because it will bog down your system, pop up messages at you, and then nag you about restarting.

On the Remote tab, disable "Allow Remote Assistance invitations to be sent from this computer" and "Allow users to connect remotely to this computer." Hello, big fat security holes anyone? And they use some system resources. You can always turn them on when you know you need them; the rest of the time they should be disabled.

We're finished with System Properties and ready to move on. Now you want to look at any services that are set to start at boot and set the ones that don't need to be running all the time to Manual or Disabled. Do this in the **Control Panel** > **Administrative Tools** > **Services** dialog. A lot of third-party software lards down your system with all kinds of unnecessary baggage. One example is the USB Audio interfaces software CD that came with my M-Audio MobilePre. Windows XP already has a perfectly good USB audio interface built in, so you don't need to install anything extra—the MobilePre works just fine without the extra guff, which is a driver installer and a rudimentary volume control panel. There's nothing to get excited about, and there's nothing particularly useful. A lot of USB audio devices do this, so try them first without installing anything extra.

Here is a short checklist of services that should be disabled because they are unnecessary or security risks, or both. It's not necessary to track down and nuke every last not-absolutely-essential service, though you're welcome to do so. TweakHound (*http://www.tweakhound.com/*) is a thorough and reliable guide to Windows system tuning, including both good tweaks and bad tweaks. It is also helpful to do web searches on specific services. Don't change anything without knowing what it does; you don't want to nuke essential Windows services. When you change a running service to Manual or Disable, you will also have to stop it. Double-click the service to open a configuration dialog.

These are some of the more common offenders:

Alerter   Sends administrative alerts. This is useless and should be disabled by default in Service Packs 2 and 3.

ClipBook   Another winner in the "Who the heck thought this was a good idea" category—ClipBook shares the contents of your clipboard with remote users. It should be disabled by default in XP Service Packs 2 and 3.

Network DDE, Network DDE DSDM   This manages Dynamic Data Exchange (DDE) network shares, which are nasty things like ClipBook. It should be disabled by default in XP Service Packs 2 and 3.

Routing and Remote Access   Turn your computer into a router and share an Internet connection. No, not while you're recording and editing. It should be disabled by default in Service Packs 2 and 3.

Error Reporting Service Phones home to Microsoft reporting gosh-knows-what information. Disable it.

Indexing Service Although building a database of files on your system for faster searches sounds good in theory, the indexer is a major hog, and I guarantee it will run exactly when you don't want it to. I've tried searches both with and without the indexer service, and I don't see much difference either way. Disable it.

Messenger Related to the Alerter service and a famous security hole. Always disable it.

Infrared Monitor Does anyone use infrared devices? If you have an infrared wireless keyboard or mouse or any other device that connects via infrared, leave this on. Otherwise, disable it.

Smart Card Is anyone using any kind of smart cards for Windows PCs? I'll eat my hat if they are. Turn this off.

Telnet Why is this even still hanging around? Telnet is completely insecure—you never ever want to enable telnet access to your PC, except under completely safe and controlled conditions when you know you really, really want to and you can be counted on to turn it off when you're finished. Disable it.

Themes "Provides user experience theme management." Whatever. This sucks up as much as 15MB of RAM. Disable it.

Terminal services This allows remote desktop sharing and administration. Disable it, and then turn it on only when you want to use it.

WebClient "The Web Client service allows . . . standard Win32 applications to create, read, and write files on Internet file servers by using the WebDAV protocol." Disable it; it's a notorious security hole that does nothing useful.

Figure 14-6 shows what the Services control panel looks like.

You may have FTP and World Wide Web Publisher services installed and enabled; disable them during recording and editing sessions. If you're not using your system as an FTP or web server, disable them permanently.

Depending on what's installed on your system, you'll find all kinds of third-party services running and bogging down your Windows PC: Norton, McAfee, TrendMicro, QuickTime, Adobe, Java, Macromedia, weird little screensaver things, newsfeeds, daily cute puppy pics, bogus system tune-up and registry cleaners, and so on; it's quite amazing what goes on behind your back. Ideally your computer will be a lean, mean, dedicated audio production machine with as little fat as possible.

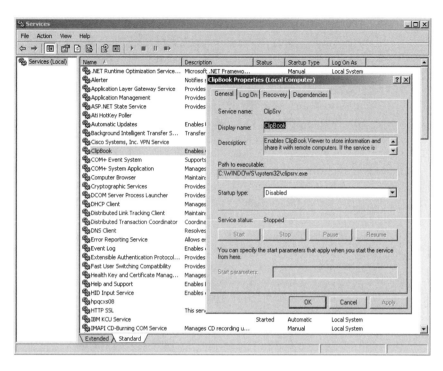

Figure 14-6: Managing services in the XP Services control panel

Tuning Windows Vista and 7

Vista and 7 have rearranged the furniture a bit. To control display and special effects settings, first open the Control Panel and set it to the Classic View. Then open **System > Advanced System Settings**. This opens the System Properties dialog, which has several tabs. Click the Advanced tab, click the Performance **Settings** button, and turn off all the bling by checking "Adjust for best performance." This turns off all special effects (Figure 14-7).

Adjust your paging file size on the Advanced tab, which is next to the Visual Effects tab. By default, the Windows paging file is dynamic and changes its size according to demand. Change it to a fixed size for faster performance; click the **Change** button under Virtual Memory. If you have 1GB RAM or less, set your swap file size to 1.5 times your RAM. For 1GB to 4GB, make it

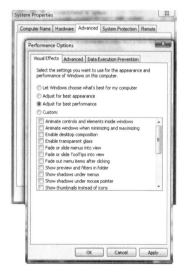

Figure 14-7: Turning off resource-hungry special effects

half your RAM. For more than 4GB, try a minimal size like 512MB. You want Audacity using your nice fast RAM, not slow paging files.

Close Performance Options and go to the System Protection tab. I recommend turning off System Restore here, though I won't complain if you want to leave it on. To disable it, uncheck all the boxes in the Automatic Restore Points box. In my experience, it eats up a lot of disk space without providing much benefit. I prefer to rely on good regular data backups, rather than hoping Windows can cure itself when there are problems.

Now go to the Remote tab and uncheck "Allow Remote Assistance connections to this computer." This is a potential security hole, and you should turn it on only when you know you're going to use it. You're done here now, so click **OK** to close System Properties.

Windows Update, Windows Firewall, and Windows Defender are all configured in **Control Panel > Security Center**. To squeeze maximum performance out of Windows Vista/7, turn off everything. Of course, when you do this, your system is vulnerable, so don't connect to any networks while you are doing audio work. Automatic Updating is especially troublesome because it will interrupt whatever you are doing whenever it runs, bother you with nag messages, and then in most cases want to reboot. Then the restart can take a long time as it applies and configures the updates. You can run the updater manually when it's convenient for you.

Vista and 7 are better than previous Windows versions at not running bales of useless and dangerous services. But you should still go through and do a bit of weeding. Don't change anything without knowing what it does; you don't want to nuke essential Windows services. A quick web search on specific services should tell you what you need to know about them, especially if they are Windows services. TweakHound (*http://www.tweakhound.com/*) is a thorough and reliable guide to Windows systems tuning.

Services are controlled in the **Control Panel > Programs and Features > Turn Windows features on or off** dialog. Your system may or may not have the following services, depending on which flavor of Windows you are running and what extras are installed.

Indexing Service   Indexes your files for supposedly faster searches. It will run when you don't want it to and gum up a great recording session. Turn it off. You won't see it on Windows 7, which replaces it with Windows Search. These should be off by default.

Internet Information Services   Are you running an SMTP or FTP server? No? Then turn this off. It should be off by default.

Microsoft.NET Framework   Microsoft keeps stuffing .NET components into every available Windows computer, whether it makes sense to or not. You may have some applications that depend on it, so leave it alone.

Tablet PC Optional components   Are you using a tablet PC? No? Then turn this off.

Telnet Client/Telnet Server   Always turn these off, except when you really want to use them. Telnet is completely insecure and should never be on by default.

Windows Meeting Space   This is touted as a collaboration tool, an update of NetMeeting. It doesn't work any better than NetMeeting. Don't turn it on except when you want to use it.

Configuring Windows Audio Devices

The ancestral Windows MME sound system, which as we already discussed is old, slow, and limited, appears in Audacity as MME: Microsoft Sound Mapper (see Figure 14-8). If you select this as your recording device, you'll get whatever is set as the default recording device in the Sound control panel. Don't choose this for your recording device—select the exact driver for your device. The correct choices for my system are the MobilePre and the onboard SoundMAX audio chipset.

Figure 14-8: Recording device picker on Windows XP—don't choose Microsoft Sound Mapper

The **Control Panel** > **Sound** control panel includes mixer panels for adjusting both recording and playback volume. You can use this to adjust recording levels while recording or playing back in Audacity. On the Playback tab, select your playback device and click **Configure** to get a simple speaker tester. This is a fast and easy way to verify that your speakers are connected correctly and working (Figure 14-9).

Note the simple little VU meter on the Recording tab, showing the recording level (Figure 14-10).

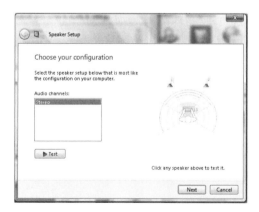

*Figure 14-9: Test your speakers in the **Playback** > **Configure** dialog. If this were a sleek 5.1 surround system, you would be able to test that each channel was routed to the correct speaker and that all speakers were working.*

Figure 14-10: Adjusting the recording volume using the Windows Control Panel

Figure 14-11 shows the Properties dialog for my M-Audio MobilePre in Vista. Vista calls it "Analog Connector"; fortunately, this can be changed if you want to give it a more informative name. Use this to enable a sound device, control the recording levels and balance, and set the recording quality level. Make sure the quality level in Windows agrees with your Audacity settings. I'm puzzled as to why the Balance setting requires an extra click and needs its own special dialog when the Levels tab has acres of empty space. But what do I know; I am not an elite software designer engineer.

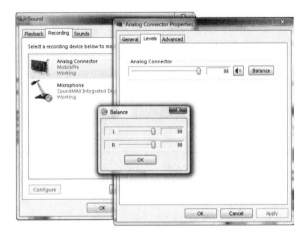

Figure 14-11: Windows offers some simple playback and recording controls.

Visit Appendix A for information on sound cards and other audio hardware.

15

CUSTOMIZING AUDACITY

Audacity has a number of configurable options in the **Edit** > **Preferences** dialog. You can improve your efficiency by setting Audacity's default options to suit your own workflow, so in this chapter we're going to learn all about them.

Audacity underwent major changes in the 1.3 series, which is the beta for the final 2.*x* release. The Audacity developers are on fire and making a large number of excellent improvements and additions. What you see in this chapter should be very close to what the final release looks like, but don't be surprised if there are some differences.

Customizing Audacity's Default Options

Audacity's default options are set in **Edit** > **Preferences**, which you can also open by pressing CTRL-P. Many of these settings can be overridden in the menus and toolbars, which is faster than opening the Preferences dialog every time you want to temporarily change a setting. Figure 15-1 shows what the main Preferences menu looks like in Windows.

Remember to have any USB or FireWire devices plugged in and switched on before starting Audacity, or Audacity will not detect them.

Let's start from the top and work our way down.

Devices

In the Devices dialog, the Host is the base sound system of your operating system. For Windows this should not be MME but Windows DirectSound. The Playback and Recording devices should be your specific devices. In Figure 15-1, I have selected the SoundMAX onboard chipset on my ThinkPad. Your sound card will probably be something else. You could also select Primary Sound Driver, which means the default recording and playback devices are selected in the Sound module in the Windows Control Panel.

Figure 15-1: Selecting the default recording and playback devices in Windows

For Linux users, the host will be ALSA, the JACK Audio Connection Kit, or the Open Sound System (OSS). The Playback and Recording device choosers can use the ALSA defaults or select specific devices (Figure 15-2). I think it's better to always choose the specific audio interfaces you want Audacity to use, rather than messing around with your system defaults.

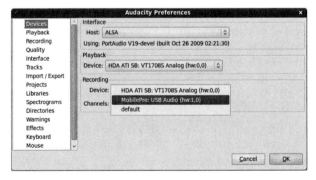

Figure 15-2: This is how it looks for Linux users: On my system, the default recording device chooser shows an onboard ATI chipset, the MobilePre USB, and the ALSA default.

The number of recording channels depends on what your recording interface supports. If you have a multichannel interface with 10 channels, for example, you could select 10 even if you weren't using that many. Audacity will then open 10 tracks, so if you record on 6 of them, you will have 4 empty tracks.

Playback

The Playback dialog (Figure 15-3) controls some special playback features that are helpful when you're editing your tracks.

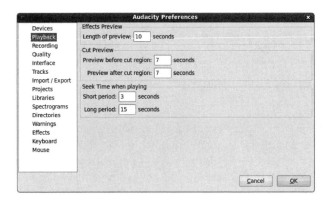

Figure 15-3: The Playback dialog

Many of Audacity's special effects (in the Generate and Effect menus) have Preview buttons so you can hear your changes before actually applying them to your tracks. Length of preview controls the duration of that preview.

Cut Preview is a slick tool for previewing what your track will sound like when you cut out a section of the track. The default is one second, but you can set it to whatever you like. Select a portion of a track that you think you want to cut, but don't cut it; just select it. Then press the C key on the keyboard, and you'll hear a preview of the audio before and after your selection, just as though you had already made the cut. To play the selection, press the spacebar.

Remember how to change the size of a selected area? Make sure you have the Selection tool active. Position the cursor near the edge of your selection; it should change to a little I-beam. Hold down the SHIFT key, and then click and drag. SHIFT-right arrow or SHIFT-left arrow expands the selection, and SHIFT-CTRL-right arrow or SHIFT-CTRL-left arrow shrinks it.

Seek Time when playing controls the length of Audacity's *jump ahead* feature. When you're playing a track, press the left- or right-arrow key to jump backward or forward by the number of seconds in the Short period setting. Press the SHIFT key plus the left- or right-arrow key to jump the length of the Long period setting.

Recording

The Recording dialog (Figure 15-4) controls some key recording features.

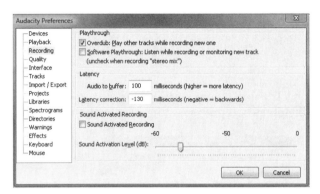

Figure 15-4: The Recording window

Check "Overdub: Play other tracks while recording new one" to record a new track while listening to an existing track or tracks. For example, you could first record a nice fiddle track. Then with overdubbing enabled, the fiddle track will play while you record a vocal track, a second fiddle, or whatever you want.

"Software Playthrough: Listen while recording or monitoring new track" enables monitoring of your recording session through your playback device. Software Playthrough works only when the recording input and playback are on the same sound card. (Linux users: If they are separate devices, you can create a connection with JACK.) This isn't the best way to monitor a recording session, because there will likely be noticeable lag and it may add enough CPU load to cause skips. A dedicated monitoring port on your recording interface is better. If you don't have one, give Software Playthrough a try. (Note that it says to "uncheck when recording stereo mix." In other words, it works only with mono tracks.) You can also enable and disable Overdub and Software Playthrough from the Transport menu.

You may find yourself spending some time in the Latency section, trying to find the best balance between performance and reducing latency. Audio to buffer controls how much audio is buffered in memory. When this buffer is larger, performance is smoother, but latency increases. When it is smaller, latency decreases, but if the audio buffer is too small, your CPU won't be able to keep up and there will be skips and stutters. Higher latency is noticeable when you are overdubbing or using Software Playthrough.

Latency correction compensates for the inevitable latency present in overdubbing. There is always some latency present in playback, so when you overdub, the new track always lags behind the playback track. (See "Overdubbing" on page 182 to learn more.)

Sound Activated Recording can be enabled here, and you can set the decibel level for triggering recording. You can also do this from the Transport menu.

Quality

The Quality dialog (Figure 15-5) sets the default audio quality values for both playback and recording.

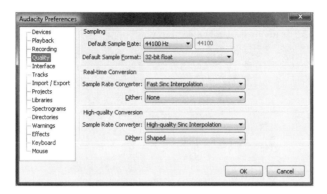

Figure 15-5: The Quality dialog

The Sampling section sets the default sampling rate and bit depth, which in this menu are called Sample Rate and Sample Format, respectively. These settings can be overridden on the individual Track menus and with the Selection toolbar. Mind the terminology confusion here—*sample format* and *bit depth* are the same thing, but bit depth is the correct term. Only in Audacity is bit depth called sample format.

The Real-time Conversion settings choose the types of sampling rate and bit depth conversions that are applied to audio files for playback in Audacity. Resampling happens when your audio files have a different sampling rate than your project rate. If the bit depth of an audio file is different from the project bit depth, it will be converted to the project value. This doesn't change the files because the conversion is done on the fly for playback only. Best Sinc Interpolater performs the highest-quality conversion. But it is CPU-intensive, so if playback bogs down, try Medium Sinc Interpolater. Fast Interpolator, Zero order hold (ZOH) interpolator, and Linear interpolation are very fast but not very good, and they introduce audible distortion.

Dither is deliberately adding a bit of noise to smooth out the waveform when a 32- or 24-bit audio file is converted to 16 bits. *Shaped* dither is supposed to give the best results, and it is the most CPU-intensive. *Triangular* is a compromise between quality and CPU cycles, and *rectangular* is lightweight and makes the smallest alterations. You don't have to apply dithering; your own ears will tell you if it makes any improvements or not.

The High-quality Conversion settings are just like the Real-time Conversion settings, except they are applied to tracks during mixing and export, so unlike the Real-time Conversion settings, your project files are changed.

Interface

The Interface dialog (Figure 15-6) controls some of the elements of the Audacity interface:

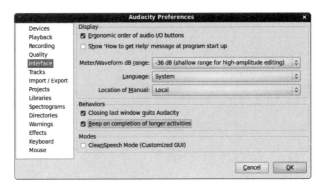

Figure 15-6: The Interface dialog

Ergonomic order of audio I/O buttons   Check this to put the buttons in the Control toolbar in this order: Pause, Play, Stop, Skip to Start, Skip to End, and Record. Unchecked, they go Skip to Start, Play, Record, Pause, Stop, and Skip to End.

Show 'How to get Help' message at program start up   Check this to see a message box full of links to Audacity help resources, such as the manual and wiki. You may need to install the Audacity manual separately if you want a local copy. The most current version will be online.

Meter/Waveform dB range   This is where you adjust the display scale in the Meter toolbar and Waveform dB view (Track menu), from −36 dB to −145 dB.

Language   This is a nice convenience if you want your Audacity session to be in a different language than your operating system default. You also need the language fonts installed on your system.

Location of Manual   Use this to program **Help** > **Manual** to either look for a local copy of the Audacity manual, or to go directly to the online version.

Closing last window quits Audacity   If you uncheck this box, closing the last open project will leave Audacity open, and you'll have to select **File** > **Exit** (or press CTRL-Q) to close completely. This is useful when you're doing a lot of projects, such as transferring a batch of vinyl records to CD, because you can close each project as you finish without closing Audacity.

Beep on completion of longer activities   Check this to make Audacity beep when tasks that take longer than a minute are finished.

CleanSpeech Mode   CleanSpeech Mode creates a customized, simplified Audacity interface for quick cleanups and quick MP3 exports. One extra button is added to the Control toolbar, and the menus are simplified (Figure 15-7). The Generate and Analyze menus are removed, and some of the remaining menus have simplified sets of commands and options. When you click the pretty orange CleanSpeech button, you see something like Figure 15-8. There are two prefab batches, or *chain* operations as they are called in Audacity: a fast MP3 converter and the CleanSpeech batch job for cleaning up plain-speech recordings such as podcasts.

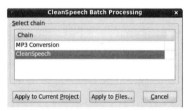

Figure 15-7: CleanSpeech Mode button

Figure 15-8: CleanSpeech Mode has two prefab operations: Clean-Speech and MP3 Conversion.

The MP3 conversion contains only two operations: normalization and export to 128Kbps MP3. If you apply CleanSpeech or MP3 conversion to an open project by clicking the Apply to Current Project button, the exported files go into a directory named *cleaned* in the project directory. You may also start with an empty project, click Apply to Files, and select files to convert from a file picker. The converted files will be exported into the same directories as the source audio files. With the second method, no new Audacity project is created.

The default CleanSpeech settings are rather harsh because they apply Noise Removal and the Leveller Effect. Noise Removal needs a custom noise profile to be effective, and there is no way to build a custom profile here. The Leveller Effect introduces a significant amount of distortion. It applies the Normalize effect twice, which can increase noise. You can modify either of these two chains or create new ones, though at the time this was written, the Audacity chains feature was still rather immature and not very well documented.

Select **File** > **Edit Chains** to see exactly what the prefab CleanSpeech and MP3 conversions do (Figure 15-9).

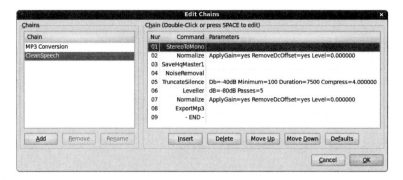

Figure 15-9: MP3 conversion and CleanSpeech options

But even in its current unfinished state, the Audacity developers have the right idea by making these custom batch jobs customizable through a graphical interface. To create a new chain, open the **File** > **Edit Chains** dialog (Figure 15-10) and click the **Add** button in the left pane. A little message window pops up and asks you to name your new chain. In this example, I created the new "test" chain.

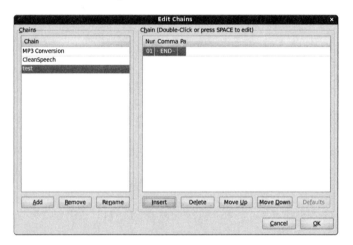

Figure 15-10: Creating a new custom chain

Now I can add a command to the test chain by clicking the **Insert** button (Figure 15-11). This opens the Select Command dialog. This has more commands in normal mode than in CleanSpeech mode.

To find out whether you can customize command parameters, first select a command, and then click the **Edit Parameters** button. In Figure 15-12, we do this with the Amplify effect. This opens its normal dialog, so we can set the Amplify parameters in the usual way.

This doesn't work for all the commands, but you may find you can create some useful chains to automate routine tasks.

 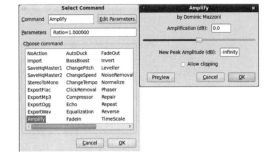

Figure 15-11: The Select Command dialog

Figure 15-12: Setting the Amplify effect parameters

Tracks

The Track dialog (Figure 15-13) controls how your Audacity tracks behave during recording, editing, and playback:

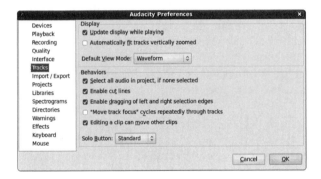

Figure 15-13: Setting the defaults for your track behaviors

Update display while playing   This autoscrolls during playback. If it bogs down your computer too much, you can disable it. Though if it does, you really need to think about upgrading your computer.

Automatically fit tracks vertically zoomed   This could be a convenient option: Your tracks are resized vertically to fit the screen. But if your project has too many tracks, they will get squished very small. Too few tracks and they will be expanded very large to fill the screen.

Default View Mode   Choose your default waveform display, which has the same selections as in the Track menu: Waveform, which is Audacity's default; Waveform dB; Spectrum; Spectrum log(f); or Pitch EAC. (See "Track Panel" on page 19 to learn more about these.)

Select all audio in project, if none selected   If this is not checked, all menu items requiring a selection will be grayed out until you select something. When it is checked, all of your tracks are selected by default when you make no selection.

Enable cut lines   This is a nice little feature that helps you keep track of recent cuts. When you make a cut, a light blue line marks the location. When you move the cursor elsewhere, the blue line turns red.

Enable dragging of left and right selection edges   This allows you to expand or reduce selections using the mouse. When this is not checked, you must use the keyboard or the selection bar.

"Move track focus" cycles repeatedly through tracks   When you have multiple tracks, you can change focus with the up- and down-arrow keys, and when the cursor comes to the top or bottom track, it automatically continues to cycle through the tracks as long as you hold the key down.

Editing a clip can move other clips   When this is checked, you can paste between clips, and Audacity will automatically create space for the new paste. When it is not checked, if there is not enough room, you will not be able to paste there.

Solo Button   This has a drop-down menu with three options that controls the behavior of the Solo buttons on the Track panels and Mixer Board: Standard, Simple, None. In Standard mode, clicking the Solo button on multiple tracks is equivalent to selecting them, and you can select multiple tracks this way. In Simple mode, clicking the Solo button on one track mutes all the others. None removes all the Solo buttons, leaving only Mute buttons.

Import/Export

Here you can set some useful defaults for importing and exporting audio files (Figure 15-14):

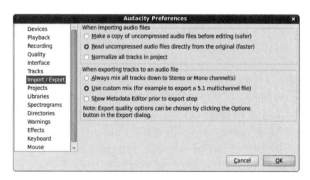

Figure 15-14: Setting default importing and exporting behaviors: Import/Export

When importing audio files   You must choose one of the first two options: "Make a copy of uncompressed audio files before editing (safer)" or "Read uncompressed audio files directly from the original (faster)."

The first option adds redundancy, and it allows you to manipulate or delete your source audio files without damaging your Audacity project. The second is faster and more frugal of disk space. If you aren't going to change the source files, then use this option. For example, suppose you have a long live recording of your band, and you're going to edit it and make some CDs and downloads from it. If you're like me, you preserve your originals intact, warts and all, and make backup copies, so you don't need Audacity to make additional copies of the originals.

Normalize all tracks in a project   This setting will normalize all audio files on import into your project according to the current settings of **Effect** > **Normalize**. I prefer to apply normalization as one of the final steps on most projects, especially when I'm mixing multiple tracks down to stereo, because mixing tracks together makes them louder. But this could be a useful option when you are doing a project that doesn't require a lot of editing, such as assembling a compilation from audio files that are already edited and mixed.

When exporting tracks to an audio file   "Always mix all tracks down to Stereo or Mono channel(s)" is the logical choice when you mainly create stereo or mono mixes. "Use custom mix" opens a channel mapper at export (Audacity calls it a *mixer*), which you need for multichannel surround exports and when you want a little more control of stereo exports.

Show Metadata Editor prior to export step   Checking this means the metadata editor will open for every individual song track or file at export so you can verify or edit the metadata for each one individually. This can be a big job if you are exporting a lot of individual songs or tracks. You should first enter information common to all tracks in **File** > **Open Metadata Editor**, and then Audacity will automatically enter this for every song and automatically enter each track number.

Projects

The Projects dialog controls autosave intervals and how to manage projects that are spun off from other projects (Figure 15-15):

When saving a project that depends on other audio files   I don't believe it is a good idea for Audacity projects to depend on other Audacity projects. They should be self-contained. If you need to be frugal of disk space, then you might want your Audacity projects to share dependencies, but I think this is asking for trouble, because if anything changes, it will affect multiple projects. The safe choice is "Always copy all audio into project (safest)." "Ask user" is all right if you want to decide for each project individually. You can check whether any project has dependencies by clicking **File** > **Check Dependencies**.

Auto save   Click this if you want Audacity to automatically save a copy of your project at whatever interval you select. The copy goes into

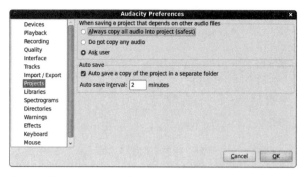

Figure 15-15: Setting default importing and exporting
behaviors: Projects

a separate directory, which Audacity uses for autorecovery of damaged
projects. It doesn't save the data files, which are the ones with the *.au*
extension, but rather the project metadata, which is kept in an XML file.
Linux users can see these autosave files in */.audacity-data/AutoSave/*;
they're just like the project *.aup* files. On Windows XP and Vista, look
in *Documents and Settings\<user name>\Application Data\Audacity*, and on
Windows 7, refer to *Users\<user name>\AppData\Roaming\Audacity*.

You can't save your project while Audacity is running, so it is a good
idea to take advantage of every opportunity to stop recording and save
your project by pressing CTRL-C or clicking **File > Save Project** as often
as you can.

Libraries

The Libraries dialog confirms if you have LAME and FFMpeg installed, gives
their locations, and gives their versions (Figure 15-16).

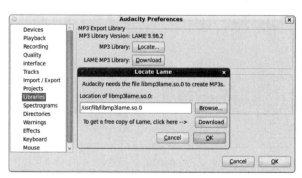

Figure 15-16: The Libraries dialog shows the version
number, 3.98.2, and the full file path. If LAME were not
installed, it would not show these.

If any of these is missing, just click the Download button to find and install them.

Spectrograms

This dialog controls the level of detail in the track display when you select the Spectrum or Pitch EAC views of your tracks. These are useful for in-depth frequency analysis. (Chapter 11 has a nice introduction to frequency analysis.) There is whole lot of math going on here that I do not understand, but I am grateful to the brainiacs who do understand the math and refine the algorithms that make digital audio engineering possible. The first setting, FFT (Fast Fourier Transform) Window, controls how much frequency detail is shown. Larger FFT sizes show more bass frequencies and less detailed time resolution.

Window type lists things like Rectangular, Hanning, Bartlett, Hamming, Welch, and Gaussian. In the plainest terms I can think of, without digging into the math, these are graphical views of digital signals intended to aid detailed analysis. According to the Wikipedia article "Window Function" (*http://en.wikipedia.org/wiki/Window_function/*), Blackman-Harris is a lower-resolution, high-dynamic range window, while all the others are high- and moderate-resolution windows.

The Minimum/Maximum Frequency settings are useful for trimming the display when you're working in limited frequency range, such as with a voice or a single instrument.

Directories

Tell Audacity what temporary directory you want it to use in the Directories dialog (Figure 15-17). The normal operating system temp file is best and should be already selected by Audacity.

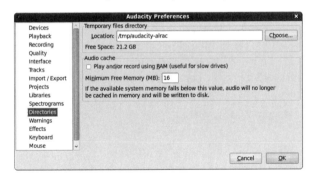

Figure 15-17: Temporary file location

The Audio Cache setting is a rather desperate option if you are stuck with a very slow computer. Checking this option keeps all recording in memory until you stop recording, and then it is written to disk. It will certainly speed up performance on a computer with a very slow hard drive. But one little power blip or running out of RAM means your recording session is lost. There isn't as much risk on a laptop since it has a battery, and you can set a minimum memory threshold to trigger writing to disk. Audacity has a hard-coded minimum of 16MB RAM, so you can't use a lower setting than that.

Warnings

This one is so easy you can do it in your sleep—decide which warnings you want Audacity to display for different operations (Figure 15-18).

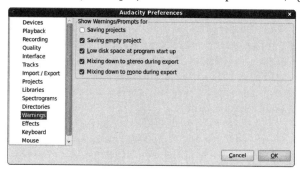

Figure 15-18: Turning warnings on or off

Effects

This dialog gives you the option to enable or disable Nyquist, VAMP, LADSPA, or VST effects. (Linux users will not see VST effects because they do not work on Linux.) I don't know why you would want to disable any of these, but you can if you want.

Keyboard and Mouse

In these two dialogs, you can set custom key bindings and see what the mouse shortcuts are. You can't change the mouse shortcuts, but you can customize keyboard shortcuts all you want. Click the function you want to create a keyboard shortcut for; let's say it's Open Metadata Editor. Click the box next to the Set button and press the keys you want for your shortcut. In Figure 15-19, I entered CTRL-S and clicked the Set button. Then Audacity kindly informed me that CTRL-S was already in use. Because Audacity finds any conflicts for you, it goes fast.

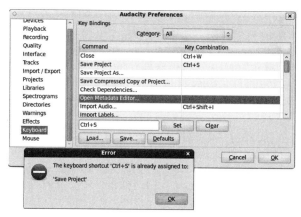

Figure 15-19: Changing keyboard shortcuts

A

AUDIO HARDWARE

The world of audio recording and processing hardware is large and bewildering, and it uncomfortably straddles both the analog and digital worlds. It's not always clear if a particular device will work with a computer, or what devices are necessary for digital audio recording.

This appendix contains a sampling of sound cards, mixers, analog-to-digital/digital-to-analog converters, microphones, and portable digital recorders in various price ranges to give you an idea of what is available. This is far from a comprehensive catalog, but hopefully it will give you a good start in understanding audio gear.

The simplest Audacity recording setup needs three things: a computer running Audacity, an analog-to-digital/digital-to-analog converter, and some kind of interface to connect microphones or musical instruments to your ADC/DAC. This could be as simple as a laptop and a microphone. You can start out cheap and simple and build up over time as you want.

Prices, models, features, and operating system support are all moving targets. My favorite online shopping site is zZounds (*http://www.zzounds.com/*). They carry a huge inventory, have great prices, and provide the best customer service. B&H Photo Video are also first-rate (*http://www.bhphotovideo.com/*).

Both sites are great for learning about products and pricing, and they generate a lot of useful customer reviews.

PCI, PCI-e, PCMCIA Sound Cards

I like PCI and PCI-e for very fast, trouble-free multichannel recording. PCI-e is faster than PCI, because each PCI-e slot has its down dedicated bus while PCI devices share bandwidth. Both are excellent and least-hassle.

PCMCIA interfaces are for laptops. PCI, PCI-e, and PCMCIA often require separate breakout boxes for connecting mics, mixers, preamps, and other devices. Some of them, in place of breakout boxes, use breakout cable bundles.

PCI

Digigram VX222HR   24-bit/192 kHz ADC/DAC, 2/2 stereo balanced analog and digital I/O, includes breakout cables. $550. Windows and Linux.

M-Audio Delta 44   24-bit/96 kHz ADC/DAC, 4-in/4-out balanced and unbalanced 1/4″ TRS, includes breakout box. $149. Windows, Linux, and Mac.

M-Audio Delta 1010LT   8 × 8 analog I/O, S/PDIF, 24/96 kHz ADC/DAC, word clock for accurate device synchronization, 2 mic/line preamps. Includes breakout cable bundle. If you want to connect more than two mics you'll need an external preamp. $199. Windows, Linux, and Mac.

M-Audio Delta 1010   24/96 ADC/DAC, 10-in/10-out rackmount breakout box, 7.1 surround playback, S/PDIF in and out, word clock for accurate device synchronization. Includes breakout box and cables. $799. Windows, Linux, and Mac.

PCI-e

AudioScience ASI5641   Professional digital-only sound card with four stereo/eight mono AES/EBU inputs and outputs, 24/96 kHz ADC/DAC. Requires a breakout box. Price is about $1,295, plus $295 for a breakout box. Windows and Linux.

RME Hammerfall Multiface II   The RME Hammerfall Multiface II audio interface is a high-end multichannel recording interface with multiple computer interface options: their own HDSP PCI, PCI-e, and PCMCIA cards. See the PCMCIA section for more information on the Multiface II. The HDSP PCI/PCI-e cards cost around $300.

PCMCIA

Digigram VXPocket 440   PCMCIA, S/PDIF stereo input and output, 24/48 kHz ADC/DAC, two balanced mic/line inputs, includes breakout cables. $650. Windows and Linux.

RME Hammerfall DSP Cardbus + Multiface II   The RME HDSP PCMCIA Cardbus Type II is the laptop interface card for the Multiface II audio interface. It delivers extremely low latency, high bandwidth, and low CPU load. $400. Windows, Linux, and Mac.

The Multiface II has 24/96 kHz ADC/DAC, 8 analog I/O, 1 ADAT, 1 S/PDIF, word clock, 1 stereo analog output for headphones or stereo mix out, 16-channel MIDI. It goes for around $800, and you can often find it bundled with the RME HDSP for around $1100. You'll need a separate preamp to connect microphones.

There are also PCI and PCI-e interfaces for the Multiface II.

USB Recording Interfaces

USB interfaces are portable and easy to connect. Class-compliant USB interfaces don't need any special drivers, but a lot of USB interfaces do. Many come with a driver CD even when they don't need them.

Behringer UCA222   This little portable 16/48 USB ADC/DAC is yours for $35. Carry it in your laptop bag; connects a pair of RCA inputs or a pair of RCA outputs. Use it to connect a turntable, tape deck, instrument, or analog mixer.

Behringer Xenyx X1204 USB Mixer   The Xenyx line of USB mixers comes in various sizes and gives you a nice combination analog mixer; 24-bit ADC/DACs; mic preamps; and extra goodies such as special effects, equalizer, compressors, monitoring ports, faders, and auxilary sends. Plug in all of your performers, adjust the mix, and these little mixers will output a ready-for-CD stereo recording. The Xenyx line ranges from $270 for the X1204 to $500 for the X1832. Windows, Linux, and Mac.

M-Audio Fast Track Ultra 8R   Rackmount USB 2.0 24-bit/96 kHz, 8 preamps, 8 XLR/TRS combo jacks, 2 headphone outputs. $499. Includes drivers for Windows and Mac, reported to work on Linux with stock ALSA drivers.

M-Audio MobilePre   My own little two-channel workhorse. Accepts up to four devices, such as two mics and two instruments. 16/48 ADC/DAC, nice knobs for gain control, headphone monitoring port, two mic preamps, phantom power, bus-powered, stereo input and output, line ins and outs. $179. Windows, Linux, and Mac.

PreSonus AudioBox 2x2   PreSonus makes nice audio hardware, and this little box is a nice value. You get a two-channel bus-powered preamp ADC/DAC with phantom power; it is very portable because it is small and doesn't need an external power supply. It has two combination TRS/TLR plug-ins for dynamic mics, condenser mics, or instruments; nice knobs for controlling gain; two MIDI ports; and a headphone monitoring port. $149. Windows, Linux, and Mac.

Pro-Ject Phono Box II USB Phono Preamp   16/48 kHz ADC for connecting a standard turntable to your computer, for both recording and playback. $199. Windows, Linux, and Mac.

Shure X2U XLR-to-USB Signal Adapter   Slick little XLR-to-USB microphone adapter with phantom power, 16/48 ADC, and mic preamp for both dynamic and condenser mics. Plug your favorite mic directly into your computer. $150. Windows, Linux, and Mac.

FireWire Recording Interfaces

FireWire is wonderful for high-end multichannel recording, though getting FireWire devices to work correctly can be a bit finicky. The new FireWire 800 standard creates the widest possible data path, which is a great boon for multichannel recording, allowing you to record more channels at full 24/192 resolution than with any other type of computer interface.

Echo AudioFire 2   Bus-powered portable 4×6, 24/96 ADC/DAC, S/PDIF in and out, MIDI, headphone port, $2 \times 1/4''$ TRS in, $2 \times 1/4''$ TRS out. You'll need a mic preamp to connect microphones. Windows, Linux, and Mac.

Edirol FA-101   Bus-powered, two XLR/TRS combo jacks, S/PDIF, 24/192 ADC/DAC, 2 phantom-powered mic preamps, 8×8 balanced analog I/O, MIDI. Nice little high-end portable for around $400. Windows, Linux, and Mac.

Focusrite Saffire Pro 26 I/O   8 XLR mic preamps, 8 TRS line/instrument inputs, 8 TRS outputs, $2 \times$ ADAT, 24/192 ADC/DAC, 1 S/PDIF in and out, word clock, two headphone ports, and 10 gain control knobs. Plug in your mics and instruments and start recording. Around $500. Windows, Linux, and Mac.

RME Fireface 800   24/192 ADC/DAC, 8 $1/4''$ TRS analog inputs, 8 $1/4''$ TRS digital outputs, $2 \times$ ADAT, $2 \times$ S/PDIF, phantom power, mic preamps . . . up to 35 signal sources can be connected to the Fireface 800 and recorded onto 28 separate tracks. This is a serious device for heavy-duty recording. FireWire 800 is the latest FireWire spec. It delivers double the throughput of the old FireWire 400 spec at 800Mbps. It is backwards-compatible to FireWire 400. You won't see lower latency but double the bandwidth for multichannel recording. This fine piece of gear sells for about $1,700. Windows and Mac, someday Linux support.

Stand Alone ADC/DACs

A key component in digital audio recording is a good ADC/DAC. As with all electronics, they come in many forms, from nice combination devices to as many separate specialized components as you can cram into your studio.

Behringer ADA8000   When you have a lot of mics to connect, you need something like this. Rackmount 8-channel 24/48 ADC/DAC, 8 microphone preamps, phantom power. All eight channels can be routed to the ADAT output for connecting to mixers or other devices, and each channel has individual line outs. $299. To connect this to your computer, you need an audio interface with ADAT ports like the Multiface II or the Focusrite Saffire Pro or an ADAT interface card in your computer. These come in all the usual interfaces: PCI, PCI-e, and FireWire. These range from a couple of hundred of dollars to several hundred dollars. Windows, Linux, and Mac.

Apogee DA16X   There are many stand alone ADC/DACs for the professional recording studio that do nothing but analog/digital conversion, like this one. 16 Channel 24/192 ADC/DAC, 2 × D-sub 25 pin analog outputs, 1 × D-sub 25 pin inputs, ADAT and word clock for synchronizing multiple devices. One way you might use this converter is to connect your performers to an analog mixer with mic preamps or perhaps a separate mic preamp, connect the mixer to the Apogee, and then connect the Apogee to your computer with a FireWire or PCI interface card. This unit will set you back about $3,000. Windows and Mac.

B

GLOSSARY

A–E

ADC/DAC

Analog-to-digital converter, digital-to-analog converter. Analog sounds such as a singer or an instrument are converted to digital form for recording and editing, then converted back to analog for playback. A CD player is a DAC. Your computer sound card is an ADC/DAC. An ADC is a crucial piece of equipment. A good one performs a good clean accurate conversion without introducing noise. Bad ones sound strange and add noise. Some are designed to add some color, for example to sound like a certain classic tube amp or recording style from the old days.

Amplitude

Amplitude, as it relates to sounds, can be thought of as *pressure*; the greater the pressure, the louder the sound. It is also described as *intensity* or *energy*. You can see amplitude in a waveform, as in Figure B-1. Higher peaks mean greater amplitude. Both tracks are 1,000 Hz sine waves created with the **Generate > Tone** dialog. The top track has an amplitude of 1.0, and the bottom track has an ampli-tude of 0.2. These two tones are identical except for their amplitudes.

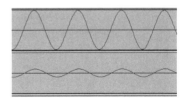

Figure B-1: Two identical sine waves with different amplitudes

This is physical pressure, which you can experience under certain conditions. For example, you can see the cone of a subwoofer pulsate when it is cranked up loud enough and feel the air movement when you place your hand in front of it. (And people miles away can "enjoy" listening to it.) Bill Nye the Science Guy has a cool stunt where he extinguishes a candle with a homemade sonic cannon. A loud blast of sound will ripple water.

Sonic cannons have been tested in a number of creative ways, such as being used as nonlethal police weapons for dispersing crowds. Theoretically, a powerful enough sound blast at the right frequency will burst eardrums. At less powerful levels, and at the right frequencies, it will create nausea and feelings of discomfort and nervousness.

Ambience, Ambient Sounds

Any sounds from your surrounding environment. Ambient sounds add color and energy, such as crowd noises, the sounds of birds and wind in the trees, or the special sound qualities from recording in a special location such as an open ampitheater or an old cathedral. Ambient sounds can also be unpleasant, like traffic noise and barking dogs.

Analog Hole

A scary bogeyman invented by the entertainment industry that demonstrates a fundamental misunderstanding of both technology and customer service. Digital media players must convert audio and video to an analog form so we can hear and see it; this is what comes out of your speakers and is what you see on your television. If we can see it, it can be photographed, and if we can hear it, so can a microphone. Of course, making copies in these ways results in lower-quality copies, but it shows there is no way to prevent copying by technological means. The industry's efforts to "close the analog hole" have resulted in crippled home entertainment receivers that send a purposely degraded signal to the analog outputs or that have disabled the analog outputs. This sort of crippling does not differentiate between media that you have the right use however you want, such as your home movies on DVD and homemade music CDs, and the mass-produced gluck they are trying to "protect."

It's all futile anyway, since all forms of copy protection are cracked sooner or later, and then you can easily make perfect digital copies.

Bit Depth

Controls dynamic range, signal-to-noise ratio, and overall fidelity and accuracy. A wider dynamic range results in a higher signal-to-noise ratio, which is also called a lower *noise floor*. In other words, you get more of the sound you want and less noise introduced by your equipment. In the olden days of recording on tape, there was always tape hiss and a certain amount of noise from the tape machines. On vinyl LPs, there is noise from defects in the vinyl and turntable hum. In digital audio, noise comes from your electronics; good electronics are described as delivering a clean sound without any introduced noise.

The common bit depths for audio production are 16 bits, 24 bits, 32 bits, and 32-bit floating point. A larger bit depth results in a more accurate, more faithful conversion from analog.

Bit depth goes hand in hand with *sampling rate.* Your analog-to-digital converter "samples" the audio signal so many times per second. For example, CD-quality is 16 bits at a sampling rate of 44,100 times per second. Each individual sample is given a binary 16-bit value. Converted to decimal, each sample is equal to or less than 65,535 (0–65,535).

24-bit depth has a range of 0–16,777,216 possible values, and 32-bit has 0–4,294,967,295. Note that these are unsigned integer values. For example, 32-bit floating point is a 24-bit mantissa plus an 8-bit exponent. Audacity and many other audio recording applications and DAWs use 32-bit float internally because the floating decimal point allows for a very high level of precision and creates all kinds of extra headroom so you can manipulate your audio files in all kinds of ways without degrading them.

A bit depth of 16 has a potential dynamic range of 96 dB; 24 bits, 144 dB; and 32 bits, 192 dB. Audio hardware has a hard limit of about 115 dB. The potential dynamic range of 32-bit float is about 1,500 dB, which means a super low noise floor and far less potential for clipping.

In some of Audacity's configuration dialogs bit depth is called *sample format.* Bit depth is the correct term.

Channel

A single path for any signal. For example, a mono microphone plugged into a mono input is one input channel. A stereo signal routed to two speakers has two playback channels. A music system with discrete 5.1 surround sound has six playback channels. If you plug 10 performers into a mixer and then plug that mixer into a single mono channel, that is still one input channel even though your entire band is recording into it.

Many surround-sound receivers can emulate multichannel surround from a stereo recording. This is not discrete multichannel surround but plain old two-channel stereo.

Clipping

When a digital audio signal goes over zero dBFS, it is truncated to the maximum value of the bit depth you are recording in. This can sound pretty awful, so avoiding clipping is very important in digital audio.

Cross-fade

This is a nice and common effect: A fade-out overlaps a fade-in. Audacity does not have a cross-fade effect, but it is easy to create a cross-fade using the Envelope and Time Shift tools. You need two tracks: Manually create a fade-out on one, a fade-in on the other, and then adjust the degree of overlap with the Time Shift tool.

DAW

Digital audio workstation, which is a combination recorder-mixer. This can be a stand alone hardware device or a software application or suite on a computer.

dBFS

Decibels relative to full scale; see Decibel.

Decibel

Decibels measure amplitude, or how loud sounds are. One decibel is one tenth of a bel, which was named for Alexander Graham Bell. Decibels are also used to measure voltage and signal strength.

In audio, a decibel is not an absolute measurement but a ratio between the sound we are measuring and an arbitrary reference level. About the smallest change we can perceive is 1 dB. A gain of 3 dB is about twice as loud, and a reduction of 3 dB is about half as loud. The intensity, or amplitude, of a sound is not proportional to how we perceive its loudness. Loudness is a psychoacoustic response, and it takes about a 10 times increase in the intensity of a sound to make it sound twice as loud.

In digital audio, we use the *decibels relative to full scale*, abbreviated as dBFS. Zero is the loudest we can go without clipping, and digital audio dB values are expressed as negative numbers.

You might see tables that show the decibel levels of various sounds from the quietest whisper a person can hear, which is zero, to the threshold of pain, which is usually stated as 120 dB. These are not like the dBFS scale we use in digital audio but the dBA scale, which is commonly used to measure environmental and industrial noise.

Discrete

This is discrete as in separate, not *discreet* as in able to keep one's mouth shut. Most stereo systems have two discrete playback channels, and discrete 5.1 surround sound means six separate playback channels. Sometimes 5.1 surround is emulated from a stereo track, so this is not discrete 5.1 surround.

Downmix

Combine multiple audio tracks into fewer tracks, as in downmixing six tracks to two-channel stereo.

Downsample

Convert to a lower sampling rate. For example, CD audio must be 16 bits/ 44,100 Hz sample rate, so a 48 kHz audio file must be downsampled to 44.1 kHz. Resampling can harm audio quality, so the less often you resample an audio file the better. Resampling once from a master file for export to different audio file formats is all right; if you resample the resampled file, chances are you will hear the difference.

DRM

Digital rights management, or digital restrictions management, depending on your point of view. DRM is various copy-protection technologies designed to prevent illegal copying of copyrighted media.

Frequency

Sound frequencies are measured in *hertz*, which are cycles per second, or how long it takes one complete sound wave to pass by a given point in one second. Higher frequencies create higher-pitched tones. Hertz is abbreviated as Hz. Kilohertz is kHz, megahertz is MHz, and gigahertz is GHz. The highest note on an 88-key piano is C8 at 4,186 Hz, or 4.186 kHz. The Guinness World Records holder for the lowest note produced by a human voice, Roger Menees, sang an F-sharp at 0.393 Hz. That's right, less than 1 hertz and far beyond the lowest key on an 88-key piano keyboard, which is A0 at 27.5 Hz.

Figure B-2 shows two sine waves of the same amplitude but different frequencies. The top waveform is 100 Hz, and the bottom is 1,000 Hz.

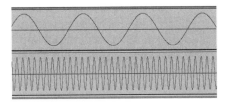

Figure B-2: Two sine waves of the same amplitude and different frequencies.

NOTE *The official recording that Mr. Menees made to win his Guinness World Record is the "property" of the Guinness company, so he cannot use this recording of his own voice.*

Fundamental Frequency

Nearly all sounds are complex and have multiple frequencies. When you play a trombone or strum a guitar, every note has multiple harmonic frequencies, so which one is the note? It is the lowest frequency; that is what we call the *pitch*, and that is what we tune our instruments to. Pitch is subjective rather than objective; pitch is what we perceive the note to be. Usually it's pretty easy to say, "That note is middle C," or A below C or F-sharp or what-have-you.

But with some instruments it is not so easy to detect the pitch. For example, when you beat a gong or a cymbal, can you pick out a distinct note? With most gongs and cymbals, the overtones and harmonics are so complex you can't.

Harmonic Frequencies

A harmonic frequency is a multiple of the fundamental frequency. For example, when the fundamental frequency is 100 Hz, the first harmonic frequency is 200 Hz, the second is 300 Hz, and so on.

Hertz

See Frequency.

High-Z, Low-Z

See Impedance.

Hotplug

Plug or unplug an electronic device while the power is on. Usually this is a bad idea because it can make a loud popping noise or even cause damage, so a good habit to form is to always power your equipment off before connecting or disconnecting anything.

Impedance

Impedance is electrical resistance. The short story is to always match your impedances for whatever audio hardware you are connecting.

You'll want to pay some extra attention to microphone impedance. Lower impedance is better: 600 ohms or less. Medium impedance is 600 to 10,000 ohms, and high impedance is more than 10,000. Some higher-end mics support multiple impedance ratings and have switches to select the one you want to use. When you see High-Z and Low-Z, that is shorthand for high impedance and low impedance. But these are imprecise, so it's better to know your exact ratings.

High-impedance mics are usually lower-quality mics, and they lose signal strength over longer cable runs. If you can't match impedances exactly, connect your mic to an input with the same or higher impedance. If you go the other way, you'll lose signal strength. Nothing seriously bad will happen with mismatched mic and input impedances, though you might experience loss of signal strength and lesser audio quality.

A *line matching transformer* is a useful gadget for connecting devices with mismatched impendances and converting them to match.

Intellectual Property

An imprecise, misused, meaningless propaganda term. The relevant legal terms are *trademark, copyright*, and *patent*.

K–O

Latency

Lag, delay. Low latency is important for overdubbing and for monitoring a recording session. Many things affect latency: the speed of your computer's CPU, how lean and clean your operating system is, sound card drivers, computer busses (USB, PCI, FireWire), special effects processors, and other outboard audio devices.

Metadata

Data about data; a means of storing information about a computer file inside the file headers. Audacity has a metadata editor for recording session information such as artist, title, date, and genre.

Mixdown

Same as *downmix*.

Overdubbing

Making a multitrack recording a few tracks at a time. It's how one person can record an entire symphony by themselves, one track at a time. Many commercial recordings are recorded in bits and pieces, and the performers may never be present at the same recording session or even use the same studio. In Audacity, you can record an instrument track and then play it back while you record a second track. There is always a bit of latency in overdubbing this way, so Audacity has a customizable latency correction.

P–T

Peak Level

Highest volume level in your recording. Usually peaks are transient events and are higher and more abrupt than your RMS levels. Peak and RMS levels are represented by two different shades of blue in Audacity waveforms.

Phase

Phase is about timing, the location in time of a waveform relative to its beginning. When the phase of a waveform is nonzero, it has been moved forward or backward in time. We do this in Audacity with the Time Shift tool. Sound waves interact with each other in all kinds of complex and interesting ways, and *phase shifting* is often used to create audio special effects. For example, you can create a pleasing echo by copying an audio track, shifting the phase of the copy a little bit, and mixing the copy and original back together.

Two waveforms that are exactly in phase combine their amplitudes and sound louder. Sounds that mix randomly may create totally new sounds. Two waveforms that are phase-shifted 180 degrees relative to each other cancel each other out. Noise-cancellation devices do this, though with varying degrees of effectiveness because sounds are complex and don't match up exactly. When loudspeakers are not placed correctly, you might hear part of the song disappear, like the lead singer sounds muted, because of phase shifting.

When you are placing microphones, you must take phase into account, especially if you are using multiple mics. For example, it is a common practice to use multiple mics on a drum kit, with some on the floor and some overhead. If they are not spaced correctly, they will be out of sync and create some lag or phase shift to cause some partial cancellation so the drums sound thin and weak.

Pitch

Pitch and frequency are often thought of as being the same thing, but they're not. Frequencies can be measured objectively, while pitch is usually subjective. The ear can be fooled, as demonstrated by the French composer Jean Claude Risset. Mr. Risset is known for creating auditory illusions such as the Risset rhythm, which sounds as though it is forever increasing in tempo when in fact it is maintaining the same tempo. The human ear perceives that a high pitch gets higher as it grows louder, while a low tone sounds as though its pitch is dropping as it gets louder. You can easily try this yourself by generating some sine tones at different frequencies in Audacity and gradually increasing and decreasing the volume.

In music, we think of pitch as being the musical notes, so we tune our instruments to a pitch of middle C, or G below C, or whatever the notes/pitches are.

Psychoacoustics

The study of how humans perceive sounds. Much of our perception is relative; for example, going out into traffic noise isn't as dramatic an event after a day of working in a noisy store as when leaving a quiet library. Some sounds mask other sounds, and so we might use white noise to mask other noise.

Audio is very subjective, and recordings can be tailored to take advantage of psychoacoustics. Modern high-tech hearing aids use psychoacoustic models to make noises sound more natural. Psychoacoustic models are used to make lossy audio formats such as MP3 and Ogg Vorbis sound better.

RMS

Root mean square, or the average volume of your recording over time. Contrast with the Peak Level, which is the highest volume level. Audacity represents RMS and peak levels with two different shades of blue in waveforms.

Sample Format

See Bit Depth.

Sampling Rate

The number of times per second the analog-to-digital converter "samples" the analog signal. The sampling rate determines the frequency range of your recording. Theoretically, a perfect digital representation of an analog audio signal is possible when the sampling rate is at least twice as high as the highest frequency in the signal. The best human hearing can hear up to 20–24 kHz, so a sampling rate of 40–48 kHz can (theoretically) reproduce the entire range of human hearing.

Tempo

The speed of the music in beats per minute. You might have noticed that tempo and energy don't always correlate with each other—that some songs with slow tempos have great energy, while some faster songs feel draggy. Try listening more closely when you notice this—is it some quality projected by the performers? The rhythm section? Is it because the song is in a minor key, or a major key?

Threshold of Pain

The sound pressure level (amplitude) at which we feel pain. This varies a little among individual people, and it varies only slightly at different frequencies.

Timbre

Timbre, pronounced TAM-ber, is a catch-all term for describing the quality of a sound, such as warm, cold, soft, brittle, reedy, full, rich, thin, breathy, stout, and so on. Timbre describes the qualities that differentiate different instruments even when they play the same notes, like cellos, violas, and violins; bassoons and bass clarinets; or very similar instruments such as two acoustic guitars.

Try listening to any older Allman Brothers Band recording and see if you can tell the difference between the two lead guitar players, Duane Allman and Dickey Betts. The Tiptons Sax Quartet is four saxophone players and a drummer, so their recordings are splendid for honing your listening skills. When you listen to the B-52s, can you tell Cindy Wilson and Kate Pierson apart?

Track

A track, like a channel, is any single audio path or unit. A mono track in Audacity is a single track. A stereo track in Audacity is also a single track, even though it has two discrete channels, because Audacity sees it as a single unit and anything you do to it is applied equally to both channels. When you burn an audio CD, you can choose TAO (track at once), which means the laser burns your entire track without pauses. This single CD track can have multiple songs, and a single song is also a track.

Transient Response

An abrupt high-energy peak in a waveform caused by a sudden event like a drumbeat, a hard-strummed string, or a bumped microphone.

U–Z

Upsample

Convert to a higher sampling rate; for example, resampling a 44.1 kHz audio file to 48 kHz. Upsampling is pointless because it does not improve audio quality and, in fact, may introduce some defects. You should upsample only when you have to meet specific requirements for certain tasks, such as upsampling a 22,050 Hz file for CD audio, which must be 44.1 kHz.

VU Meter

VU stands for *volume unit*. You might recall VU meters from the olden days of analog tape recording, which we used to monitor recording volume levels. VU meters typically had a scale of 20 to +3, a moving needle, and a little red clipping or peak light. VU meters had a rather slow response time, though avoiding clipping was not as crucial for analog recording as it is for digital recording.

C

SEVEN MYTHS OF DIGITAL AUDIO

 There are a number of persistent, silly audio myths that refuse to die. The funny part is that a few blind listening tests would disprove them, or as the old geek saying goes, "One experiment is worth a thousand arguments." Here are my favorites.

The Myth of the Golden Ear

Some audiophiles love to obsess over specs and are convinced that, yes, they too can hear super-high frequencies just like bats, and the super-low frequencies just like whatever animal hears super-low frequencies, and they need every last possible hertz, and it must be filtered through special organic electricity or their listening experience is ruined. Their equipment must be elite and overpriced, and the Sacred Listening Room must be specially engineered. They are more sensitive than ordinary mortals, and we just don't appreciate what they go through.

Salespeople and equipment reviewers exploit this attitude mercilessly. It's a proven way to sell overpriced gear. These salespeople and reviewers don't have any special hearing abilities, just acute sensitivities to the smell of money.

Of course, it is true that hearing acuity and perception vary among individual people, but in any random assortment of humans with good, undamaged hearing, the differentiator is how *educated* their ears are. This is true of all of our senses—when you know what to look for, you become an ace birdwatcher. When you learn to differentiate different flavors, aromas, and characteristics in wine, it becomes a multifaceted pleasure instead of just an easy, pleasant buzz. Experienced riders learn how to interpret all the signals a horse gives—mood, intent, what's ahead—and how to communicate back to the horse. Just like everything else we do, listening is a learning process. You might start out unable to tell the difference between a viola and a violin, but with experience you learn to identify the individual musicians in a band or orchestra. Even when it's the Billy Tipton Memorial Saxophone Quartet. That's right, four saxophone players and nothing else; two alto, one tenor, and one baritone sax. To the inexperienced ear, it's just a blur of saxophones, but with a bit of listening, you can tell right away who is playing what.

Back in the olden analog days, they didn't have super-duper hi-fi recording studios, and they sure as heck didn't have super-duper hi-fi playback devices. The best recordings from the olden days feature talented, skilled musicians and talented, skilled engineers who knew how to get the most out of their equipment. If specs are all that matter, we might as listen to pure sine waves. There are no shortcuts to spending time listening, comparing, experimenting, and learning to *listen*.

The Myth of Burn-In

This is another one that deserves a wooden stake through its vitals. Audio electronics and speakers sound the same when they're brand-new as they do after decades of use, barring damage and component failure. Giving them a period of "burn-in," which is simply switching them on and then leaving them on for whatever magic burn-in interval is required, is silly and does nothing to change how they sound.

Tube amp-o-philes are particularly prone to burn-in fits and will insist that a new amp sounds "cold" and, after 24 hours or whatever, sounds "warm." 'Taint so; it's all the same. There are many things that affect how we perceive sounds: temperature, humidity, mood, whether we are rested or tired, whether we have been in a quiet or noisy environment all day. Audio electronics are pretty much always the same.

The Myth of Tube Superiority

Tube amps are obsolete. Solid-state does everything they can do, cheaper and better and with less distortion. Tube amps need more service over their lifetimes because tubes burn out and lose power, and you might even need to re-tension their sockets. You've probably heard lyrical odes to the "tube sound." Tube amps are perfectly good for those who prefer them. If there is a "tube sound" that you like, it is most likely distortion created by the amp. If you want your amps to be neutral and reproduce your audio as accurately as possible, you want solid-state.

The Myth of Uber Cables

You're welcome to spend significant wads of money on cables if you really want to. You'll probably get more enjoyment out of papering your walls with dollar bills, lighting cigars with twenties, or making stylish garments out of Ben Franklins, because spending gobs of money on audio cables does not make them better than sensibly priced cables. You'll want to avoid weird, cruddy, no-name brands, but otherwise any cable that is manufactured to the appropriate specifications is equal to any other. Look for good construction, strong connectors, good insulation, and specs and identifying information printed on the sheaths. Sometimes there are useful options like right-angle plugs or swivel plugs. If you want to waste your money, do please pick something more worthy than overpriced audio cables.

Gold-plated connectors add shininess, higher price tags, and some corrosion resistance. They don't make the sound better.

The Myth of Analog Superiority

Analog audio cannot compete with digital audio for fidelity; signal-to-noise ratio; lack of distortion; and ease of editing, manipulation, and reproduction. Some folks like analog artifacts such as the "fat" sound of pushing analog circuits to their limits, distortion, feedback, and so on. No worries, everyone is entitled to their preferences. Though it's worth noting these can be reproduced in digital audio.

The Myth That You Don't Need Tone Controls

This one really gets my goat. You enter the high-end snooty audio store to try out some high-quality equipment. Hey, why not, you won't know until you listen to it, right? You are escorted to The Room of Acoustic Perfection. There you are seated in the precisely positioned Listening Chair, in front of banks of speakers, amps, preamps, no receivers because those are not snooty enough, and high-end CD players. These are all connected to a switching system so that you can easily try out different combinations. Very nice so far. Your salesperson will be into something above the common herd; perhaps jazz, maybe some classical, maybe some off-the-wall independent labels. Certainly no Top 40 or teenybop pop.

So on goes the music, and you sink back into pleasant bliss. But as you listen, you notice it's not quite right. You want a little less treble, perhaps, and a little more bass. Maybe the midrange is a touch wimpy and you want to kick it up a tick or two. Tough luck, buster, because those fine amps only control volume and balance. You don't get tone controls. Why? Because, as the salesperson explains, real audiophiles listen to the music as it is "meant to be listened to." So no tone controls for you, and if you want any, then you are defective. Though not too defective to drop a few thousand dollars on a hi-fi system with no tone controls; fortunately, the salesperson is magnanimous and will permit you to do that.

Unfortunately, this is a complete myth. Most recordings are not "perfectly engineered"; all of them are compromises. Because even the best-engineered recordings are not proof against the environments they are played in or the individual characteristics of your hi-fi components. They will sound different depending what they are played on, the rooms they are played in, temperature and humidity, your moods—every day it's a little different, and God gave us tone controls so we could hear recordings the way we want to. Maybe you have some big bad feelings to work off and need some aggressive subwoofering. Maybe you want it light and soothing. Maybe you just like to twiddle knobs. That is your right, and you must not allow pretentious salespersons to take it away from you.

The Myth That Someone Else Knows Better Than You

For the most part, fussy audiophiles are fussy about all the wrong things. There are two categories of people who can teach you actual useful knowledge, and those are musicians and recording engineers. I mean real musicians and real recording engineers, not wannabes who think that when the knob goes to 11 it means the amp is louder than amps that go to 10. Recording engineers are just as much artists as engineers, and even mediocre ones can teach you a lot about the nuts and bolts of making recordings.

It takes practice, experimentation, and a lot of listening, and the ultimate decision about what is good is entirely yours. You have to learn to train your own ear and taste and not depend on what other people tell you because they don't experience audio the same way you do. Especially if they're trying to sell you something.

REFERENCES AND RESOURCES

Books

Aldrich, Nika. *Digital Audio Explained: For the Audio Engineer.* 2nd ed. Fort Wayne, IN: Sweetwater Sound, 2004.

Everest, F. Alton and Ken C. Pohlmann. *Master Handbook of Acoustics.* 5th ed. New York: McGraw-Hill, 2009.

Grant, Rickford (with Phil Bull). *Ubuntu for Non-Geeks: A Pain-Free, Get-Things-Done Guide.* 4th ed. San Francisco: No Starch Press, 2010.

Pohlmann, Ken C. *Principles of Digital Audio.* 5th ed. New York: McGraw-Hill, 2005.

Online Resources

"Audacity Forum." *http://forum.audacityteam.org/*

"Audacity User's Manual." *http://manual.audacityteam.org/*

Linuxaudio.org *http://www.linuxaudio.org/*

Image Credits

A very big and grateful thank-you to Wikimedia Commons (*http://commons.wikimedia.org/wiki/Main_Page/*) and its contributors for freely sharing thousands of beautiful and useful photos and drawings and for allowing me to use some of them in this book.

The following images are released under the GNU Free Documentation License:

- Chapter 2, Figure 2-11
- Chapter 11, Figure 11-30

The following image is licensed under the Creative Commons Attribution ShareAlike 3.0, Attribution ShareAlike 2.5, Attribution ShareAlike 2.0 and Attribution ShareAlike 1.0 License:

- Chapter 11, Figure 11-6
- Chapter 11, Figure 11-11

GNU Free Documentation License

Version 1.3, 3 November 2008

0. PREAMBLE

The purpose of this License is to make a manual, textbook, or other functional and useful document "free" in the sense of freedom: to assure everyone the effective freedom to copy and redistribute it, with or without modifying it, either commercially or noncommercially. Secondarily, this License preserves for the author and publisher a way to get credit for their work, while not being considered responsible for modifications made by others.

This License is a kind of "copyleft", which means that derivative works of the document must themselves be free in the same sense. It complements the GNU General Public License, which is a copyleft license designed for free software.

We have designed this License in order to use it for manuals for free software, because free software needs free documentation: a free program should come with manuals providing the same freedoms that the software does. But this License is not limited to software manuals; it can be used for any textual work, regardless of subject matter or whether it is published as a printed book. We recommend this License principally for works whose purpose is instruction or reference.

1. APPLICABILITY AND DEFINITIONS

This License applies to any manual or other work, in any medium, that contains a notice placed by the copyright holder saying it can be distributed under the terms of this License. Such a notice grants a world-wide, royalty-free license, unlimited in duration, to use that work under the conditions stated herein. The "Document", below, refers to any such manual or work. Any member of the public is a licensee, and is addressed as "you". You accept the license if you copy, modify or distribute the work in a way requiring permission under copyright law.

A "Modified Version" of the Document means any work containing the Document or a portion of it, either copied verbatim, or with modifications and/or translated into another language.

A "Secondary Section" is a named appendix or a front-matter section of the Document that deals exclusively with the relationship of the publishers or authors of the Document to the Document's overall subject (or to related matters) and contains nothing that could fall directly within that overall subject. (Thus, if the Document is in part a textbook of mathematics, a Secondary Section may not explain any mathematics.) The relationship could be a matter of historical connection with the subject or with related matters, or of legal, commercial, philosophical, ethical or political position regarding them.

The "Invariant Sections" are certain Secondary Sections whose titles are designated, as being those of Invariant Sections, in the notice that says that the Document is released under this License. If a section does not fit the above definition of Secondary then it is not allowed to be designated as Invariant. The Document may contain zero Invariant Sections. If the Document does not identify any Invariant Sections then there are none.

The "Cover Texts" are certain short passages of text that are listed, as Front-Cover Texts or Back-Cover Texts, in the notice that says that the Document is released under this License. A Front-Cover Text may be at most 5 words, and a Back-Cover Text may be at most 25 words.

A "Transparent" copy of the Document means a machine-readable copy, represented in a format whose specification is available to the general public, that is suitable for revising the document straightforwardly with generic text editors or (for images composed of pixels) generic paint programs or (for drawings) some widely available drawing editor, and that is suitable for input to text formatters or for automatic translation to a variety of formats suitable for input to text formatters. A copy made in an otherwise Transparent file format whose markup, or absence of markup, has been arranged to thwart or discourage subsequent modification by readers is not Transparent. An image format is not Transparent if used for any substantial amount of text. A copy that is not "Transparent" is called "Opaque".

Examples of suitable formats for Transparent copies include plain ASCII without markup, Texinfo input format, LaTeX input format, SGML or XML using a publicly available DTD, and standard-conforming simple HTML, PostScript or PDF designed for human modification. Examples of transparent image formats include PNG, XCF and JPG. Opaque formats include proprietary formats that can be read and edited only by proprietary word processors, SGML or XML for which the DTD and/or processing tools are not generally available, and the machine-generated HTML, PostScript or PDF produced by some word processors for output purposes only.

The "Title Page" means, for a printed book, the title page itself, plus such following pages as are needed to hold, legibly, the material this License requires to appear in the title page. For works in formats which do not have any title page as such, "Title Page" means the text near the most prominent appearance of the work's title, preceding the beginning of the body of the text.

The "publisher" means any person or entity that distributes copies of the Document to the public.

A section "Entitled XYZ" means a named subunit of the Document whose title either is precisely XYZ or contains XYZ in parentheses following text that translates XYZ in another language. (Here XYZ stands for a specific section name mentioned below, such as "Acknowledgements", "Dedications", "Endorsements", or "History".) To "Preserve the Title" of such a section when you modify the Document means that it remains a section "Entitled XYZ" according to this definition.

The Document may include Warranty Disclaimers next to the notice which states that this License applies to the Document. These Warranty Disclaimers are considered to be included by reference in this License, but only as regards disclaiming warranties: any other implication that these Warranty Disclaimers may have is void and has no effect on the meaning of this License.

2. VERBATIM COPYING

You may copy and distribute the Document in any medium, either commercially or noncommercially, provided that this License, the copyright notices, and the license notice saying this License applies to the Document are reproduced in all copies, and that you add no other conditions whatsoever to those of this License. You may not use technical measures to obstruct or control the reading or further copying of the copies you make or distribute. However, you may accept compensation in exchange for copies. If you distribute a large enough number of copies you must also follow the conditions in section 3.

You may also lend copies, under the same conditions stated above, and you may publicly display copies.

3. COPYING IN QUANTITY

If you publish printed copies (or copies in media that commonly have printed covers) of the Document, numbering more than 100, and the Document's license notice requires Cover Texts, you must enclose the copies in covers that carry, clearly and legibly, all these Cover Texts: Front-Cover Texts on the front cover, and Back-Cover Texts on the back cover. Both covers must also clearly and legibly identify you as the publisher of these copies. The front cover must present the full title with all words of the title equally prominent and visible. You may add other material on the covers in addition. Copying with changes limited to the covers, as long as they preserve the title of the Document and satisfy these conditions, can be treated as verbatim copying in other respects.

If the required texts for either cover are too voluminous to fit legibly, you should put the first ones listed (as many as fit reasonably) on the actual cover, and continue the rest onto adjacent pages.

If you publish or distribute Opaque copies of the Document numbering more than 100, you must either include a machine-readable Transparent copy along with each Opaque copy, or state in or with each Opaque copy a computer-network location from which the general network-using public has access to download using public-standard network protocols a complete Transparent copy of the Document, free of added material. If you use the latter option, you must take reasonably prudent steps, when you begin distribution of Opaque copies in quantity, to ensure that this Transparent copy will remain thus accessible at the stated location until at least one year after the last time you distribute an Opaque copy (directly or through your agents or retailers) of that edition to the public.

It is requested, but not required, that you contact the authors of the Document well before redistributing any large number of copies, to give them a chance to provide you with an updated version of the Document.

4. MODIFICATIONS

You may copy and distribute a Modified Version of the Document under the conditions of sections 2 and 3 above, provided that you release the Modified Version under precisely this License, with the Modified Version filling the role of the Document, thus licensing distribution and modification of the Modified Version to whoever possesses a copy of it. In addition, you must do these things in the Modified Version:

- A. Use in the Title Page (and on the covers, if any) a title distinct from that of the Document, and from those of previous versions (which should, if there were any, be listed in the History section of the Document). You may use the same title as a previous version if the original publisher of that version gives permission.
- B. List on the Title Page, as authors, one or more persons or entities responsible for authorship of the modifications in the Modified Version, together with at least five of the principal authors of the Document (all of its principal authors, if it has fewer than five), unless they release you from this requirement.
- C. State on the Title page the name of the publisher of the Modified Version, as the publisher.
- D. Preserve all the copyright notices of the Document.
- E. Add an appropriate copyright notice for your modifications adjacent to the other copyright notices.
- F. Include, immediately after the copyright notices, a license notice giving the public permission to use the Modified Version under the terms of this License, in the form shown in the Addendum below.
- G. Preserve in that license notice the full lists of Invariant Sections and required Cover Texts given in the Document's license notice.
- H. Include an unaltered copy of this License.

- I. Preserve the section Entitled "History", Preserve its Title, and add to it an item stating at least the title, year, new authors, and publisher of the Modified Version as given on the Title Page. If there is no section Entitled "History" in the Document, create one stating the title, year, authors, and publisher of the Document as given on its Title Page, then add an item describing the Modified Version as stated in the previous sentence.

- J. Preserve the network location, if any, given in the Document for public access to a Transparent copy of the Document, and likewise the network locations given in the Document for previous versions it was based on. These may be placed in the "History" section. You may omit a network location for a work that was published at least four years before the Document itself, or if the original publisher of the version it refers to gives permission.

- K. For any section Entitled "Acknowledgements" or "Dedications", Preserve the Title of the section, and preserve in the section all the substance and tone of each of the contributor acknowledgements and/or dedications given therein.

- L. Preserve all the Invariant Sections of the Document, unaltered in their text and in their titles. Section numbers or the equivalent are not considered part of the section titles.

- M. Delete any section Entitled "Endorsements". Such a section may not be included in the Modified version.

- N. Do not retitle any existing section to be Entitled "Endorsements" or to conflict in title with any Invariant Section.

- O. Preserve any Warranty Disclaimers.

If the Modified Version includes new front-matter sections or appendices that qualify as Secondary Sections and contain no material copied from the Document, you may at your option designate some or all of these sections as invariant. To do this, add their titles to the list of Invariant Sections in the Modified Version's license notice. These titles must be distinct from any other section titles.

You may add a section Entitled "Endorsements", provided it contains nothing but endorsements of your Modified Version by various parties—for example, statements of peer review or that the text has been approved by an organization as the authoritative definition of a standard.

You may add a passage of up to five words as a Front-Cover Text, and a passage of up to 25 words as a Back-Cover Text, to the end of the list of Cover Texts in the Modified Version. Only one passage of Front-Cover Text and one of Back-Cover Text may be added by (or through arrangements made by) any one entity. If the Document already includes a cover text for the same cover, previously added by you or by arrangement made by the same entity you are acting on behalf of, you may not add another; but you may replace the old one, on explicit permission from the previous publisher that added the old one.

The author(s) and publisher(s) of the Document do not by this License give permission to use their names for publicity for or to assert or imply endorsement of any Modified Version.

5. COMBINING DOCUMENTS

You may combine the Document with other documents released under this License, under the terms defined in section 4 above for modified versions, provided that you include in the combination all of the Invariant Sections of all of the original documents, unmodified, and list them all as Invariant Sections of your combined work in its license notice, and that you preserve all their Warranty Disclaimers.

The combined work need only contain one copy of this License, and multiple identical Invariant Sections may be replaced with a single copy. If there are multiple Invariant Sections with the same name but different contents, make the title of each such section unique by adding at the end of it, in parentheses, the name of the original author or publisher of that section if known, or else a unique number. Make the same adjustment to the section titles in the list of Invariant Sections in the license notice of the combined work.

In the combination, you must combine any sections Entitled "History" in the various original documents, forming one section Entitled "History"; likewise combine any sections Entitled "Acknowledgements", and any sections Entitled "Dedications". You must delete all sections Entitled "Endorsements".

6. COLLECTIONS OF DOCUMENTS

You may make a collection consisting of the Document and other documents released under this License, and replace the individual copies of this License in the various documents with a single copy that is included in the collection, provided that you follow the rules of this License for verbatim copying of each of the documents in all other respects.

You may extract a single document from such a collection, and distribute it individually under this License, provided you insert a copy of this License into the extracted document, and follow this License in all other respects regarding verbatim copying of that document.

7. AGGREGATION WITH INDEPENDENT WORKS

A compilation of the Document or its derivatives with other separate and independent documents or works, in or on a volume of a storage or distribution medium, is called an "aggregate" if the copyright resulting from the compilation is not used to limit the legal rights of the compilation's users beyond what the individual works permit. When the Document is included in an aggregate, this License does not apply to the other works in the aggregate which are not themselves derivative works of the Document.

If the Cover Text requirement of section 3 is applicable to these copies of the Document, then if the Document is less than one half of the entire aggregate, the Document's Cover Texts may be placed on covers that bracket the Document within the aggregate, or the electronic equivalent of covers if the Document is in electronic form. Otherwise they must appear on printed covers that bracket the whole aggregate.

8. TRANSLATION

Translation is considered a kind of modification, so you may distribute translations of the Document under the terms of section 4. Replacing Invariant Sections with translations requires special permission from their copyright holders, but you may include translations of some or all Invariant Sections in addition to the original versions of these Invariant Sections. You may include a translation of this License, and all the license notices in the Document, and any Warranty Disclaimers, provided that you also include the original English version of this License and the original versions of those notices and disclaimers. In case of a disagreement between the translation and the original version of this License or a notice or disclaimer, the original version will prevail.

If a section in the Document is Entitled "Acknowledgements", "Dedications", or "History", the requirement (section 4) to Preserve its Title (section 1) will typically require changing the actual title.

9. TERMINATION

You may not copy, modify, sublicense, or distribute the Document except as expressly provided under this License. Any attempt otherwise to copy, modify, sublicense, or distribute it is void, and will automatically terminate your rights under this License.

However, if you cease all violation of this License, then your license from a particular copyright holder is reinstated (a) provisionally, unless and until the copyright holder explicitly and finally terminates your license, and (b) permanently, if the copyright holder fails to notify you of the violation by some reasonable means prior to 60 days after the cessation.

Moreover, your license from a particular copyright holder is reinstated permanently if the copyright holder notifies you of the violation by some reasonable means, this is the first time you have received notice of violation of this License (for any work) from that copyright holder, and you cure the violation prior to 30 days after your receipt of the notice.

Termination of your rights under this section does not terminate the licenses of parties who have received copies or rights from you under this License. If your rights have been terminated and not permanently reinstated, receipt of a copy of some or all of the same material does not give you any rights to use it.

10. FUTURE REVISIONS OF THIS LICENSE

The Free Software Foundation may publish new, revised versions of the GNU Free Documentation License from time to time. Such new versions will be similar in spirit to the present version, but may differ in detail to address new problems or concerns. See *http://www.gnu.org/copyleft/*.

Each version of the License is given a distinguishing version number. If the Document specifies that a particular numbered version of this License "or any later version" applies to it, you have the option of following the terms and conditions either of that specified version or of any later version that has been published (not as a draft) by the Free Software Foundation. If the Document does not specify a version number of this License, you may choose any version ever published (not as a draft) by the Free Software Foundation. If the Document specifies that a proxy can decide which future versions of this License can be used, that proxy's public statement of acceptance of a version permanently authorizes you to choose that version for the Document.

11. RELICENSING

"Massive Multiauthor Collaboration Site" (or "MMC Site") means any World Wide Web server that publishes copyrightable works and also provides prominent facilities for anybody to edit those works. A public wiki that anybody can edit is an example of such a server. A "Massive Multiauthor Collaboration" (or "MMC") contained in the site means any set of copyrightable works thus published on the MMC site.

"CC-BY-SA" means the Creative Commons Attribution-Share Alike 3.0 license published by Creative Commons Corporation, a not-for-profit corporation with a principal place of business in San Francisco, California, as well as future copyleft versions of that license published by that same organization.

"Incorporate" means to publish or republish a Document, in whole or in part, as part of another Document.

An MMC is "eligible for relicensing" if it is licensed under this License, and if all works that were first published under this License somewhere other than this MMC, and subsequently incorporated in whole or in part into the MMC, (1) had no cover texts or invariant sections, and (2) were thus incorporated prior to November 1, 2008.

The operator of an MMC Site may republish an MMC contained in the site under CC-BY-SA on the same site at any time before August 1, 2009, provided the MMC is eligible for relicensing.

How to use this License for your documents

To use this License in a document you have written, include a copy of the License in the document and put the following copyright and license notices just after the title page:

Copyright (c) YEAR YOUR NAME.
Permission is granted to copy, distribute and/or modify this document
under the terms of the GNU Free Documentation License, Version 1.3
or any later version published by the Free Software Foundation;
with no Invariant Sections, no Front-Cover Texts, and no Back-Cover Texts.
A copy of the license is included in the section entitled "GNU
Free Documentation License".

If you have Invariant Sections, Front-Cover Texts and Back-Cover Texts, replace the "with...Texts." line with this:

with the Invariant Sections being LIST THEIR TITLES, with the
Front-Cover Texts being LIST, and with the Back-Cover Texts being LIST.

If you have Invariant Sections without Cover Texts, or some other combination of the three, merge those two alternatives to suit the situation.

If your document contains nontrivial examples of program code, we recommend releasing these examples in parallel under your choice of free software license, such as the GNU General Public License, to permit their use in free software.

INDEX

C

G

H

I

M

The Electronic Frontier Foundation (EFF) is the leading organization defending civil liberties in the digital world. We defend free speech on the Internet, fight illegal surveillance, promote the rights of innovators to develop new digital technologies, and work to ensure that the rights and freedoms we enjoy are enhanced — rather than eroded — as our use of technology grows.

PRIVACY EFF has sued telecom giant AT&T for giving the NSA unfettered access to the private communications of millions of their customers. eff.org/nsa

FREE SPEECH EFF's Coders' Rights Project is defending the rights of programmers and security researchers to publish their findings without fear of legal challenges. eff.org/freespeech

INNOVATION EFF's Patent Busting Project challenges overbroad patents that threaten technological innovation. eff.org/patent

FAIR USE EFF is fighting prohibitive standards that would take away your right to receive and use over-the-air television broadcasts any way you choose. eff.org/IP/fairuse

TRANSPARENCY EFF has developed the Switzerland Network Testing Tool to give individuals the tools to test for covert traffic filtering. eff.org/transparency

INTERNATIONAL EFF is working to ensure that international treaties do not restrict our free speech, privacy or digital consumer rights. eff.org/global

EFF.ORG

ELECTRONIC FRONTIER FOUNDATION

Protecting Rights and Promoting Freedom on the Electronic Frontier

EFF is a member-supported organization. Join Now! www.eff.org/support

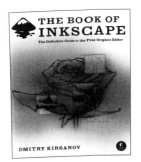

UPDATES

Visit *http://nostarch.com/audacity.htm* for errata, updates, and other information.

COLOPHON

The fonts used in *The Book of Audacity* are New Baskerville, Futura, The Sans Mono Condensed and Dogma. The book was typeset with LATEX 2_ε package nostarch by Boris Veytsman *(2008/06/06 v1.3 Typesetting books for No Starch Press)*.

This book was printed and bound by Transcontinental, Inc. at Transcontinental Gagné in Louiseville, Quebec, Canada. The paper is Domtar Husky 60# Smooth, which is certified by the Forest Stewardship Council (FSC). The book has an Otabind binding, which allows it to lie flat when open.